THE SCHOLAR'S PERSONAL COMPUTING HANDBOOK

The Little, Brown Microcomputer Bookshelf

THE SCHOLAR'S PERSONAL COMPUTING HANDBOOK

A Practical Guide

BRYAN PFAFFENBERGER

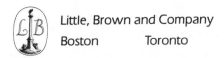

Little, Brown and Company

Boston   Toronto

Library of Congress Cataloging-in-Publication Data

Pfaffenberger, Bryan, 1949-
    The scholar's personal computing handbook.

    (The Little, Brown microcomputer bookshelf)
    Includes index.
    1. Microcomputers.   2. Learning and scholarship—
Data processing.   3. Word processing.   I. Title.
II. Series.
QA76.5.P399   1986   004   85-19838
ISBN 0-316-70401-6

Library of Congress Catalog Card Number 85-19838

ISBN 0-316-70401-6

9   8   7   6   5   4   3   2   1
ALP

Published simultaneously in Canada, by Little, Brown & Company (Canada) Limited

Printed in the United States of America

For Suzie, Julia, and Michael

PREFACE

The pages to follow introduce the personal computer as a tool for scholars, defined in the broadest possible sense as anyone who researches a literature, forms conclusions about it, and teaches or writes about those conclusions. It's just as relevant to the interests of a biologist who keeps up with a literature as it is to a humanist. And it's just as germane to the needs of amateur and corporate researchers as it is to college faculty or graduate students. If you'd like to know how a personal computer can help you write, manage bibliographies, do library research, organize research notes, and many other scholarly tasks, this book is for you.

Most scholars begin their involvement with scholarly computing with *word processing*, the computer-based creating, editing, printing, and storage of text. And word processing is this book's first concern. You'll find extensive treatment of word processing here, with special coverage of topics scholars want covered, such as how to set up a personal computer system to handle footnotes, foreign language characters, and equations.

Yet there's a world of scholarly computing beyond word processing, and this book explores it fully. Using readily available, off-the-shelf programs, scholars can automate the storage and retrieval of research notes, the compilation of personal bibliographies, literature searches, research network communication, data analysis, grade-crunching, and more. This book shows you how to make these powerful techniques part of your day-to-day routine, even if you've had no previous experience with computers.

No matter what kind of computer you have (or even if you don't yet own or have access to one), you'll find material of interest in the pages to follow. Where particular computers or programs are mentioned, they're discussed for illustrative purposes only. The book isn't, therefore, an introduction to scholarly computing with a specific set of equipment. On the contrary, it seeks to illustrate what can be done with four broad categories of software: word processing, data base management, telecommunications, and spreadsheet/graphics programs. To help you understand what these programs can do and how to choose one that meets your needs, you'll find useful typologies of the programs in each category and detailed examples of how they work.

Throughout, emphasis is placed on showing you not how to operate particular programs or computers (you've manuals and plenty of published handbooks to help you with that learning task), but rather something unique: how to apply these programs and computers to specific scholarly tasks, such as managing a personal bibliography or printing a paper with foreign language characters.

The programs and computers mentioned in this book were chosen for illustrative purposes only, not because they are the best or the only programs available for their purposes. This book doesn't seek, therefore, to mention every program of interest available to scholars at this writing—a task that would have been chimerical, anyway, since new and better ones doubtless will appear after this book's publication. Rather, it seeks to equip you with the background and perspective you'll need to know why a particular program—including new ones appearing after this book's printing—suits your needs (or doesn't). For up-to-date information on software for academic computing, two excellent sources are *The Research in Word Processing Newsletter* (South Dakota School of Mines and Technology, Rapid City, SD 57701) and Judith Axler Turner's computer column in *The Chronicle of Higher Education*.

This book was written, in case you're curious, on a Zenith Z-150 Personal Computer (an 8088-based IBM PC compatible) using the fine word processing program Microsoft Word (version 2.0). Research for the book was undertaken using the Zenith and a public-domain telecommunications program to contact a variety of online data base research services, including DIALOG Information Services, Knowledge Index, and BRS/After Dark. Research notes were stored and analyzed using Notebook II, and spelling was checked using The Word Plus.

I'd like to thank Mark Walsh at Little, Brown for his enthusiasm and helpful suggestions. The anonymous reviewers deserve special thanks for their spirited, constructive criticism and many specific contributions. Thanks, too, to everyone at Editing, Design, and Production, Inc. who contributed to the production of this book.

CONTENTS

THE SCHOLAR'S PERSONAL COMPUTING HANDBOOK

PART
ONE

INTRODUCTION

TOWARD ELECTRONIC SCHOLARSHIP

> Civilization advances by extending the number of important operations we can perform without thinking about them.
>
> **A. N. Whitehead**

Leroy Searle, associate chairman of the English Department at the University of Washington, bought a personal computer in 1982. "I did it," Searle recalls, "partly because computers made me incredibly nervous. Here's something on the order of the invention of print, and I didn't know anything about it. Fourteen-year-olds knew more about it."[1] But the computer's main attraction for Searle was word processing, or the computer-based creation, revision, and printing of text.

Searle and several of his colleagues installed their computers in their campus office, and Searle soon swore he'd never write with a typewriter again if he didn't have to. That kind of conviction speaks volumes to scholars who have long suffered the banes of white-out fumes, cut-and-paste sessions, and laborious retyping. Within a year, personal computer–based word processing had spread like wildfire through the social sciences and humanities divisions of the university.

Colleges throughout North America are witnessing their own versions of Washington's computer boom as scholarly writers look to electronics. At this writing, for instance, half of the United States's annual yield of 30,000 Ph.D. dissertations were being prepared on computers, as was half of the huge volume of scientific and technical works.[2] And it's no surprise: most writers love word

[1] Cited in Schuyler Ingle, "Who Needs a Mainframe?," *Pro/Files* (November/December 1983), p. 38.

[2] Kurt Supplee, "The PC Tapping at the Chamber Door," *PC: The Independent Guide to IBM Personal Computers* (May 29, 1984), p. 249.

3

processing. "The word processor," says the writing guru William Zinsser, "is God's gift, or at least science's gift, to the tinkerers and the refiners and the neatness freaks. For me it was obviously the perfect new toy . . . [I've] been on a writing high ever since."[3] Thousands of scholars agree, and word processing now occupies more campus computers than any other application.

Yet, for every scholar who takes the plunge into word processing, many more are waiting in the wings, confused by a plethora of programs, the unparalleled hyperbole of the personal computer marketplace, and—most of all— a lack of reliable information regarding the best equipment for their needs. Epitomizing these users, in Klaus Burmeister's words, is the professor who

> loves to write and is fascinated by word processing and all the possibilities it holds, but despairs when . . . [told] that what is on the screen is 'not necessarily' what the printer will churn out; that the program allowing for footnotes is considered inferior overall to the one that doesn't have any; that the 'Mac' is easiest to use but has no adequate word processing program; that . . . accent marks are as rare in good programs as hen's teeth; etc.—ad infinitum.[4]

Calls to computer salespeople and vendors aren't likely to cure the problem. You can stump almost any computer salesperson by asking whether a given computer/software configuration can handle diacritical marks or MLA-style footnotes. But you can't really blame them. The big money is in the business market, and that's where their expertise lies. They don't understand scholars' computer needs. And with a few refreshing exceptions, they don't care to. It's no surprise that many scholars have, as Burmeister puts it, been "panicked into buying computers and programs they can't fully use, that require expensive add-ons, or that are inappropriate to their requirements."

Even so, a judicious shopper can assemble a superb word processing system for scholarly work using currently available products. What's needed is the kind of guidance that shows you what this technology can do and provides you with the background you'll need to make a rational choice of equipment. And that's precisely what you'll find in the chapters to follow. *The Scholar's Personal Computing Handbook* explores the world of personal computer–based word processing from the scholar's viewpoint. Its primary aim is to help you make a start in personal computing the right way: with hardware and software that meet your needs.

BEYOND WORD PROCESSING

Word processing holds enormous appeal for scholars, yet it's only one of a variety of personal computer applications in scholarship. This handbook's second aim is to introduce the world of computing that lies beyond word

[3] *Writing with a Word Processor* (New York: Harper Colophon, 1980), p. 98.

[4] Personal communication, March 8, 1985.

processing. It's a world in which many scholarly tasks—for instance, managing research notes and bibliographies, doing library research, calculating student grades, and more—are done with the same electronic speed and ease that has made word processing so popular.

The key to the personal computer's wider application in scholarship lies in recognizing what you have on your desk. A personal computer isn't just a word processor, or a machine that's capable only of word processing duties. On the contrary, it's a *computer*—and that means, above all, that it's versatile. A computer is programmable. What it does—what kind of machine it becomes—depends on which kind of program you've loaded into its electronic memory. Running a word processing program, a personal computer becomes a splendid (although far-from-perfect) tool for writing. Running other programs, it becomes a tool for different tasks, such as alphabetizing a huge collection of bibliographic citations, analyzing a text's readability, or generating a diagram from a list of numbers you supply. To use a personal computer only for word processing, in other words, is like buying a sophisticated stereo system and playing only one record on it. The record may be a good one, to be sure, but there are others—and sooner or later, you'll want to know about them.

That's where another challenge presents itself. Tens of thousands of ready-to-run programs for personal computers are already available for applications other than word processing. There are so many, in fact, that just listing them—let alone making sense out of them—has become a major task even for experts. But much of the confusion disappears once it's realized that personal computer programs, diverse as they are, can be sorted into neat categories. A high proportion of available programs are addressed to specific applications in such areas as business (for instance, accounting or inventory control programs), home computing (home utility programs and games), and educational computing. Leaving them aside, four kinds of general-purpose software emerge. Including word processing software, they are:

Data base management software Programs for storing, organizing, retrieving, and printing collected information, such as measurements of archaeological artifacts or bibliographic citations.

Telecommunication software Programs for linking a personal computer with other computers, such as those maintained by online data base vendors.

Spreadsheet/graphics software Programs for working with tables of numbers and generating charts from them.

By equipping a personal computer with all four kinds of general-purpose software (and some accessory programs designed to work with them), a scholar can take a major step toward electronic scholarship: a form of scholarship in which virtually every task, from library research to final drafts of documented papers, relies on the computer's help.

AN ILLUSTRATION: CAROLINE'S DAY

To illustrate just what electronic scholarship looks like on a practical, day-to-day level, let's look in on a hypothetical scholar's day in a campus office.

Caroline Robinson is a professor of biology at Greenfield State University. She's lecturing next week on the behavior of baleen whales, and—since it has been six months since she checked the literature on that subject—she decides to start her day with some library research. But she doesn't go to the library; she sits down at her computer instead.

Caroline's computer is equipped with accessories that permit it to communicate with other computers over telephone lines, and she's going to do just that. Caroline's department subscribes to BRKTHRU, an online data base service that's designed to meet the needs of searchers other than professional librarians. BRKTHRU is a service offered by a private firm, Bibliographic Retrieval Services (BRS), which maintains a gigantic, ultrasophisticated computer system expressly designed for remote access by telephone. The computer's memory contains millions of bibliographic citations and abstracts, organized by subject into distinct files or data bases.

Caroline inserts her telecommunication program disk into her computer and loads the program into her computer's memory. Under the telecommunication program's direction, her computer becomes a remote terminal suitable for two-way communication, using telephone links, with a distant computer. Caroline instructs the program to dial BRKTHRU's number, and when BRKTHRU responds, she types her password code and gains admission to the system. Even though she's still sitting in front of her computer in her office, she's now in control of BRKTHRU's computer, more than a thousand miles away.

Selecting an option from a menu displayed on her screen, Caroline chooses the data base BIOSIS PREVIEWS, a massive repository of more than 4 million bibliographic citations and abstracts in the life sciences. Already containing abstracts of articles from more than 9000 journals and monograph series, BIOSIS PREVIEWS grows by more than 14,000 citations every 2 weeks. Caroline types a simple command that instructs BRKTHRU's computer to search this massive data base, looking for just those records that discuss baleen whale behavior. And since she last performed this search 6 months ago, Caroline asks to see only those records that have appeared since then. She presses the key that sends the command more than a thousand miles to BRKTHRU's computer, the computer searches through millions of records, and reports—on Caroline's screen—that 16 documents meet the criteria she has specified. The time required? About 45 seconds.

Caroline instructs BRKTHRU's computer to display these 16 citations and abstracts and enters a command that captures the incoming data on a disk file in her computer's magnetic disk drive. When the last citation and abstract have been captured, Caroline severs her connection with BRKTHRU and uses her word processing program to examine the retrieved information. She is informed that the search cost $12.75. Of the 16 citations and abstracts, 11 are of interest. She uses her word processing program's DELETE command to erase the 5 in which she's not interested, and adds a few coding characters to the other ones. Then she inserts the disk containing her data base management program, and gives a command that adds the coded citations and abstracts to her personal computer-based bibliography on animal behavior. She prints out the citations she just retrieved and, on her way to class, asks her student assistant to photocopy the full text of the articles in the library. In just 15 minutes of work, Caroline has brought herself up to date on baleen whale behavior, a subject of central interest in her teaching and research.

Caroline comes back from class with a stack of quizzes, which her student assistant grades, writing the number of correctly answered questions on the top. Under Caroline's direction, the student assistant sits down at Caroline's computer and types the raw scores into a grade analysis worksheet that Caroline has created with her spreadsheet program. Then, again following Caroline's instructions, the student uses a command that sets in motion a *macro*, or a sequence of instructions that Caroline designed and stored in a special worksheet. Under the macro's guidance, the spreadsheet program analyzes the scores, transforms them into the standardized *t* scores widely recommended by educational experts, looks up their letter-grade counterparts, and displays the letter grades on the screen. The time required? About 2 minutes.

That afternoon, Caroline uses her word processing program to put the finishing touches on a conference paper she's writing. It's time to put together a reference list for the paper. By hand methods, that would be a big job: the paper refers to 128 sources. But Caroline's computer can handle the whole task automatically. Wherever she cited a published work in the body of the text, Caroline inserted a brief code word consisting of a special marking character followed by the author's last name and the date of the work's publication. Now that the body of the text is finished, she runs an accessory program called Bibliography (Pro/Tem Software) that "reads" her paper, detects the code words and removes them from the paper, searches her animal behavior data base for the relevant citations, and constructs an alphabetized bibliography from it. The automatically generated reference list is formatted precisely the way her discipline requires it. With a few quick keystrokes, she appends it to her paper and prints out a final draft. The time required? Ten minutes.

THE MEANING OF ELECTRONIC SCHOLARSHIP

Caroline's day illustrates the personal computer's real contribution to scholarship: it holds out the promise of rapidly and automatically performing many of the tedious jobs scholars waste time on, such as going to the library, thumbing through volume after volume of reference works, writing out citations and abstracts by hand or photocopying them, alphabetizing bibliographic citations, and typing the reference list. Caroline can spend that time instead on doing what counts: giving students individual attention, thinking about her research, and talking over scientific problems with her colleagues.

Yet there's more to electronic scholarship than higher productivity and saved time. Scholars today are faced with an unprecedented explosion of knowledge, and it's becoming increasingly clear that only by adopting the use of computers can they hope to continue their long tradition of informed inquiry.

Back in the halcyon days when knowledge didn't grow and change quickly, being a scholar meant being learned or erudite: possessing an enormous storehouse of knowledge in one's head. This kind of erudition, however, is no longer enough—knowledge today grows and changes too rapidly. In *Future Shock*, for instance, Alvin Toffler cites the Oxford vice-chancellor, a chemist who took his degree in 1931, who admitted that he couldn't answer the questions on contemporary Oxford chemistry exams. "Not only can I not do them," he said, but "I never *could* have done them, since at least two-thirds of the questions involve knowledge that simply did not exist when I graduated."[5]

Being a scholar today in any field requires more than knowing a great deal: it means knowing how to keep up with the explosive growth of knowledge in every field. To be sure, knowledge proliferates most quickly in the scientific and technical fields, in which the amount of knowledge doubles every 5.5 years (some 6 to 7 thousand scientific and technical articles are written every day).[6] Yet the social sciences, humanities, and other fields aren't far behind. Between 1960 and 1975, for instance, the number of journals in English and American literature increased 192 percent.[7]

The only real education today is the one that never stops, and the only real scholarship today is the one prepared to deal with a far broader bulk of books, book reviews, articles, manuscripts, conference papers, and institutional reports than ever before. And that kind of education and scholarship argues strongly for the use of computers.

The vision of computer–based electronic scholarship you've seen in Caroline's workday may appear futuristic and ultrasophisticated, but it isn't. You can do everything Caroline does right now, using currently available computers and software, and you don't have to be a computer genius or even know how to write programs. If you can learn how to use a professional-quality word processing program, you can learn how to use the telecommunications, data base

---

[5]Alvin Toffler, *Future Shock* (New York: Bantam Books, 1970), p. 157.

[6]John Naisbitt, *Megatrends: Ten New Directions Transforming Our Lives* (New York: Warner Books, 1984), p. 16.

[7]National Enquiry into Scholarly Communication, *Scholarly Communication: The Report of the National Enquiry* (Baltimore: The Johns Hopkins University Press, 1979), p. 40.

management, and spreadsheet software that Caroline has put to such good use.

Still, choosing the right telecommunication, data base management, and spreadsheet software poses the same challenge as shopping for a word processing program: only a small proportion of the programs now available will meet scholars' needs. That's why, in the chapters to follow, you'll find all the information you need to go beyond word processing and to identify the right data base management, telecommunication, and spreadsheet/graphics software for your needs.

THE THOTH FACTOR

The world of electronic scholarship beyond word processing is just as exciting and inviting as word processing itself. Scholars' enthusiasm for personal computing, therefore, is sure to grow. Scholars may well come out of this century, not as helpless relics unable to cope with burgeoning knowledge and increasing teaching loads, but rather as savvy masters of a computer-based approach to knowledge and instructional management.

This prospect is appealing indeed, and yet there are grounds for caution—grounds stated by Plato more than two thousand years ago. In the *Phaedrus* (274–275), Socrates recounts the tale of the god Thoth's gift of writing to Thamus, the king of Egypt. Pleased with his invention (and himself), Thoth urged Egyptians to adopt writing, claiming it would improve their memory and wisdom. But Thamus took a different view. Chiding Thoth's infatuation with the invention, Thamus called attention to the negative potential of writing: "Those who acquire [writing]," Thamus argued, "will cease to exercise their memory and become forgetful; they will rely on writing to bring things to their remembrance by external signs instead of on their own internal resources."[8]

Thamus was surely right. The mnemonic features of the literate pale beside the achievements of oral tradition specialists, such as the storytellers of West Africa or the preliterate Brahmans of the Vedic period. What are the potentially negative effects of personal computers on scholarship, effects that we might not notice owing to the Thoth factor—our blind enthusiasm for the new technology?

A modern Thamus, Professor Joseph Weizenbaum of MIT, has warned of unwelcome consequences as scholars fall in love with computers. "It's useful to be afraid of the computer tail wagging the scholarly dog," Weizenbaum warns;

> Let me tell you a cautionary tale. A friend of mine used to have on his wall a map of the earth, with all the major faults and geological planes. It had been generated by a computer, using all the available data in machine-readable form, but not older,

[8]Walter Hamilton, trans. (Harmondsworth, U.K.: Penguin Books, 1973), p. 96.

nonreadable data. Essentially, the computer had determined that knowledge acquired before a certain time was, literally, negligible. That's dangerous, because it lets the instrument determine what will be studied, and what evidence will be used.[9]

No one, including Weizenbaum, doubts that scholars *will* use computers in the future. There's no more stopping computers than there was stopping literacy, and for the same reason: both technologies provide ways to cope with burgeoning knowledge. In the past 25 years, that growth has accelerated so rapidly that it has all but incapacitated scholarly research in many disciplines.[10] We will use computers for the same reason we adopted writing: there won't be any alternative.

What remains to be seen is whether computers will be used *well*. BIOSIS PREVIEWS, the massive life science data base that Caroline used, supplies a case in point. Although BIOSIS PREVIEWS contains more than four million citations and abstracts, they go back only to 1969. Literature appearing before that time isn't in the data base. That doesn't mean this literature is unimportant, only that the economics of data base production make it difficult to index material published before the data base's inception. A researcher using BIOSIS PRE-VIEWS feels in touch with the literature—it's a heady sensation indeed. But many pertinent pre-1969 materials are excluded from the bibliographies BIOSIS PREVIEWS generates.

Word processing provides another example. Splendid as it is, word processing has its negative side, as many writers are now discovering. Personal computer word processing programs show only a third of a page at a time; since the software pages through your document slowly, you wind up looking at your manuscript with a computer version of tunnel vision. It's hard to attain a sense of your document's overall structure and organization. Journal and book editors everywhere are reporting that manuscripts created with computers tend, not surprisingly, to have organizational problems.

You can surmount these and other computer perils as long as you're warned about them and offered strategies to overcome them. And that's the third aim of *The Scholar's Personal Computing Handbook*. Online data bases, for example, are extremely useful tools—as long as it's remembered that their contents have little time depth and that the library, pre-electronic though it may be, is still the prime source for serendipitous discovery. Ways exist, too, to overcome the organizational challenges that word processing poses.

Electronic scholarship, in sum, entails more than using computers to automate day-to-day scholarly tasks for higher productivity. It also involves

[9]Judith Axler Turner, "A Leading Computer Scientist Bemoans Our Love Affair with the Computer," *Chronicle of Higher Education* 29:21 (Feb. 5, 1985), p. 5.

[10]See, e.g., Warren J. Haas, "Computing in Documentation and Scholarly Research," *Science* 215 (12 Feb. 1982), p. 857; Alvin Toffler, *Future Shock* (New York: Bantam Books, 1970), p. 157; John Naisbitt, *Megatrends: Ten New Directions Transforming Our Lives* (New York: Warner Books, 1984), pp. 16–18.

preserving basic scholarly standards and values in the new world the computer is making for us.

HOW TO USE THIS BOOK

This handbook is designed to help you choose the best system for word processing, to show you how to use additional software resources for scholarly computing, and to suggest strategies for overcoming the computer's inherent limitations. It does so in five parts:

Part One/Introduction   Chapter 2, "A Scholar's Guide to the Personal Computer," presents a basic foundation in computer literacy from the scholar's viewpoint. You'll find a simple, straightforward typology that reduces the plethora of brands and models to three basic categories of computers, a discussion of how computers cope with (or fail to cope with) foreign language and mathematical characters, and a strategy for choosing the computer that best suits your needs.

Part Two/Writing   Chapter 3, "Software for Writing," surveys the three basic types of word processing software and assesses their strengths and weaknesses for scholarly writing. Chapter 4, "Getting Started: Freewriting and Idea Processing," introduces programs that can help you develop a well-structured approach to a writing task. Chapter 5, "Electronic Writing Techniques," presents strategies for overcoming the word processor's inherent limitations while writing scholarly works. Chapter 6, "The Electronic Editor," discusses word choice checkers and readability analysis software. Software for checking punctuation, capitalization, and spelling, as well as programs for footnotes, bibliographies, and indexes, is discussed in Chapter 7. Chapter 8, "Printers and Printing Techniques," explores the world of computer printers.

Part Three/Managing Information   The next three chapters take you beyond word processing to the world of *text-oriented data base management*, or the computer–based storage and retrieval of written text. Chapter 9, "Software for Managing Information," presents a typology of text-oriented data base management programs, assessing their strengths and weaknesses for a variety of scholarly tasks. Chapter 10, "Retrieving Research Notes," offers a detailed example of how information management software can be used not only for the management but also for the analysis of research notes. Chapter 11, "Managing Bibliographies," shows how text-oriented file management programs can be used to set up a sophisticated personal bibliographic system.

Part Four/Communicating   These chapters address the world beyond your computer's confines, a world that's accessible through direct computer connections to the telephone system. Chapter 12, "Software for Telecommunication," surveys your software options. Chapter 13, "The Online Reference Library," introduces online data base services, computer-searchable repositories of tens of millions of bibliographic citations and abstracts. Chapter 14, "Networking," introduces scholarly applications of electronic mail, local area networks, computer conferencing, and computer bulletin boards.

Part Five/Crunching Numbers   This final section introduces the scholarly applications of spreadsheet and graphics software. Chapter 15, "Software for Number-Crunching," surveys your software options and illustrates academic applications of spreadsheet and graphics software. Chapter 16, "Crunching Grades," presents a complete spreadsheet-based approach to the calculation of student grades.

Appendices   Appendix I, "A Scholar's Guide to System Expansion," explains the mysteries of memory boards, modems, asynchronous communication boards, visual digitizers, and other potentially useful additions to your personal computer. Appendix II, "Choosing a Bibliographic Data Base Service," compares four online data base services by cost, ease of use, and data base availability. Appendix III, "A Scholar's Guide to Online Data Bases," surveys online bibliographic data bases likely to prove of special interest to scholars.

Just where you should begin depends on your experience and interests. If you're new to scholarly computing, begin with Chapters 2 and 3. If you've already chosen a computer and learned a word processing program, you can begin anywhere you please. Each chapter concludes with a survey of resources and readings, and a glossary at the end of the book defines the computer terms used in the text.

A SCHOLAR'S GUIDE TO THE PERSONAL COMPUTER

Dozens of personal computers compete for your money in today's marketplace, and each—if you believe the ads—has some remarkable feature that makes it superior to all the others. What the ads don't tell you is that a tiny part hidden in the machine's circuits—the *microprocessor*—determines, more than any other single factor, what a personal computer can and can't do. And although brands of personal computers abound, every one of them uses one of just a few basic microprocessor designs.

To grasp the differences among personal computers, then, it makes sense to start with a working level of personal computer literacy, especially concerning microprocessors. To be sure, you'll be told that you don't need to know how personal computers work or how they're made to use one effectively. You'll probably hear, too, the oft-repeated analogy that you don't have to know what's under the hood to drive a car. Think, though, of people who purchased subcompact cars in the 1970s with poorly designed aluminum or early rotary engines and had to pay big repair bills every time they broke down. Just as surely as a car's engine determines its overall reliability, power, and economy, so too does the personal computer's "engine"—the microprocessor—determine what it can do. In today's personal computer marketplace, a bit of computer literacy—especially microprocessor literacy—can help you avoid the costly error of buying a computer that won't suit your needs.

The pages that follow introduce the personal computer from the scholar's point of view. Their chief aim is to provide the background you need to select the right computer. You'll find a definition of computers in general (and the personal computer in particular); a survey of the microprocessors currently in use; a discussion of a topic sure to interest scholars—how personal computers handle (or fail to handle) foreign language and mathematical characters; an introduction

13

to disks and disk drives; a survey of personal computer operating systems; and a note on system expandability.

WHAT IS A PERSONAL COMPUTER?

Computers, personal or otherwise, are poorly named. The word "computer" suggests numerical calculation, but that's only one of the tasks computers do well. The name stuck not because of its accuracy, but rather because scientists used the earliest computers only for performing extensive calculations. Computers process textual and graphic information just as well. A better name for the computer, as the physicist Louis Ridenour suggested in 1952, is *information machine*, a name that truly indicates the computer's versatility.

WHAT COMPUTERS DO

Although the name "information machine" better communicates the computer's versatility, it's not entirely accurate to say that computers work with information. It's better to say that computers perform automatic processing operations on coded or represented information, information that has been expressed in the binary numbers the computer can manipulate. Working with a computer, in fact, amounts to a communication process between humans and the machine. We give the computer information and instructions in terms we understand, and it codes them into terms it can work with. After following our instructions to process the information, it then decodes the information back into terms meaningful to us.

Conventionally, these steps are described by the following terms:

Input   Information you give the computer that it codes into binary numbers, together with the instructions—the *program*—that tell the computer what to do.

Storage   The computer's *main memory* (also called *random access memory* and abbreviated RAM), where the information to be processed is kept. It's stored with the program.

Processing   Manipulations performed on the information, such as sorting, rearranging, moving information from one place to another, comparing, or calculating.

Output   The results of the processing operation, decoded so that you can understand them and displayed on the video display screen or the printer.

AN ILLUSTRATION: CHECKING SPELLING

Suppose you'd like to check the spelling of a 10,000 word essay you've just written with a word processing program. That's a tedious job by hand, but the computer can do it easily and quickly. Here's how the computer checks spelling:

Input   Since you've typed your essay directly into the computer using a word processing program, the text has already been coded. Personal computers use the ASCII (American Standard Code for Information Interchange) coding system, representing letters, digits, and punctuation marks with 8 binary symbols (the letter A, for example, is coded 01000001). All you need do is insert the disk containing the spelling checking program into the computer and give it a simple command telling it where to find the essay you want proofread. The details of this process are handled automatically.

Storage   The computer loads the coded text and the program into its memory, again handling the details of the process automatically. The program includes a 75,000 word dictionary of correctly spelled words.

Processing   The program checks the essay's spelling using the following steps: (1) It transforms the essay into a long list of single words, eliminates all the duplicates, and alphabetizes them. The result is a list of *unique words*. (2) These unique words are compared, one by one, with the program's built-in dictionary of correctly spelled words. (3) Words from the essay that cannot be squared with words from the dictionary are put into a list of suspicious words, words that may be misspelled.

Output   When the program finishes compiling its list of suspicious words, it displays them on the screen, one by one, showing you the context in which the error occurred and permitting you to type in a correction.

THE COMPUTER'S MAJOR LIMITATION

The following example illustrates the computer's major limitation: It can process only information that is explicitly coded. And for this reason, computers sometimes generate spurious results. Let's look more closely at the spelling checker program to see why.

One major shortcoming of today's spelling checking software is that, in a strict sense, it really doesn't check spelling. On the contrary, it compares the words in a text to its built-in dictionary, and reports the discrepancies. To put it another way, it's not really checking spelling, it's just finding words it can't square with its dictionary of correctly spelled words. And if there are correctly spelled words in the essay that aren't in its dictionary, it reports them as "suspicious words" along with the typos and genuine misspellings. If you've chosen a program that uses a dictionary with only 20,000 words, you'll be greeted with a huge list of "suspicious words"—most of which are correctly spelled—on output. For academic work, you'll need a dictionary of at least 50,000 words, and preferably 75,000 or 100,000.

Even when you've a huge dictionary, however, today's spelling checkers can't help you with three kinds of spelling errors:

Homonym errors   For instance, *there* instead of *their*.

Misspellings that are correct spellings of another word For instance, *he* instead of *the*.

Double words For instance, *the the*.

Spelling checkers are unable to detect these errors because, to do so, they would have to be able to discern a word's meaning. They can't do that, and here's why.

It's easy to code a word's spelling. Using the ASCII codes, you can spell CAT this way: 01000011 01000001 01010100. It's another matter entirely, however, to code a word's meaning. Research on the computer coding of meaning has run into formidable obstacles, not the least of which are limited knowledge of how the brain manages the job and major disagreements among competing semantic theories. Although artificial intelligence researchers have had some success coding limited domains of meaning with computers, everyone agrees that the problem is extremely complex—and solving it will be extremely expensive. In short, you're not likely to find a spelling checker soon that knows you meant *there* when you typed *their*.

This example suggests the basic elements of an intelligent, three-pronged approach to the computer:

Understand the computer's limitations The computer is merely a tool for rearranging, sorting, moving, comparing, and performing calculations on information that has been expressly and explicitly represented or coded. Don't attach more importance to its output than is warranted.

Find out what the machine is doing The best way to grasp the computer's limitations and to judge how much importance to attach to its output is to find out what's going on inside the computer. You don't need a sophisticated background in computer science to get a working grasp of what it's doing: the circuitry is complex, but what it does is often rather simple. For instance, if you understand that the spelling checker cannot understand the meaning of words, you're less likely to accept its results uncritically.

Develop strategies to overcome the computer's limitations Once you grasp your system's limitations and develop a working idea of what it's doing, you're much better equipped to use it fruitfully and intelligently. In the terms of our example, you'll know that a final, hand proofreading is required to catch homonym errors, doubled words, and misused (but correctly spelled) words.

All three elements of this approach to the computer figure in the chapters to follow. In the chapters on word processing, for example, you'll find a critical analysis of word processing's limitations, together with an explanation of how word processing programs work and strategies for overcoming the problems they pose for writers.

SPEED AND ACCURACY

The computer's limitations are more than outweighed by its great speed and accuracy.

Sophisticated supercomputers operate so quickly now that events within them must be measured in billionths of a second. Even the smallest computers are capable of performing thousands of processing operations each second. That means, in practice, that people can work with much larger units of data than was practicable using hand methods. You can determine in minutes, for instance, the vocabulary richness of a 50-page paper. You don't have to confine your analysis to the short passages amenable to hand processing.

Another benefit of the computer's high speed lies in communications. One type of processing operation involves moving information from one place to another (from the disk drive, for instance, to the memory), and computers do this job at amazing speeds. Information moves from the disk drive to the memory, for instance, at the rate of about 30,000 to 150,000 characters per second. This information-handling prowess can also be used to move information between computers at rates of 500,000 characters per second and more. In fact, one of the computer's most fruitful uses lies in its role as an ultra–high-speed communication device.

Computers aren't just fast; they're also accurate. Of course, you've heard about "computer errors," such as being charged for someone else's long distance calls and the like. Behind almost all such errors is a human, not a computer mistake—errors in data input or programming. Computers have built-in error-checking mechanisms that make them highly accurate. Some computer components have been shown to make only one mistake in 100 billion operations. The quality of computer output, however, is only as good as the quality of the data and the programs the computer works with.

INTERACTIVE PROCESSING

The four terms—input, storage, processing, and output—well describe what computers do, but their arrangement in a rigid sequence is out of date. The sequence stems from the days of *batch processing,* when you had to perform every step in precise sequence. You gave the computer punched cards containing the program and the data to be processed; it stored the program and data, did the processing, and spat out the results on a teletype printer. More than likely, you discovered a mistake in the program or data input that required running the whole job over again.

To be sure, some of the tasks you'll do with your personal computer are best done in batch processing sequence. The spelling checker program provides an excellent example. But most of the software you'll use is *interactive.* What that means, in essence, is that once you've loaded the program into the computer's memory, it interacts with you: it accepts commands from you and displays messages when it encounters a problem or needs further input. You can use the commands to jump around just as you please in the formerly rigid sequence of input-storage-processing-output.

Here's an example. Once you've loaded the word processing program WordStar into your computer's memory, it gives you a flexible set of commands you can use to control computer operations. You can load an existing manuscript from disk (input), change the whole manuscript's line spacing from single to double space (processing), insert a quotation stored on disk in the middle of the text (input), format it so it matches the rest of the document (processing), and print a copy (output). If the program encounters a problem—for instance, if it can't find the manuscript on disk—it displays an *error message*.

Working with an interactive computer, in sum, only remotely resembles the tedium of working with an old batch-processing computer. If there's a problem, you're given an opportunity to correct it without having to exit the program and start all over again.

MAINFRAMES, MINICOMPUTERS, AND PERSONAL COMPUTERS

What's been said so far applies to most modern computers, including modern *mainframes* (large computers designed to meet all the computing needs of an organization) and *minicomputers* (smaller versions of mainframes intended for smaller organizations). But our interest here lies with the *personal* computer or *microcomputer*. Just what distinguishes personal computers from mainframes and minicomputers?

That distinction used to be easy to draw: personal computers were small, cheap, easy to use, and employed microprocessors—computing units on a tiny chip of silicon—for their processing operations. They were slow, short on memory, and much more likely to appeal to hobbyists or home computer enthusiasts than to professionals. Recently, however, that distinction has collapsed. To be sure, plenty of personal computers still show signs of their historical origins. But the newer computers, such as the IBM PC AT, make the minicomputer/personal computer distinction seem all but meaningless.

It's still appropriate to say, however, that personal computers seek to satisfy an individual's (rather than an organization's) computing needs—in particular, the needs of individuals who lack computer training or expertise. Mainframe and minicomputer designers still assume that their machines will be operated by trained personnel, and they're designed for use by several people at once.

It's no longer true, however, that personal computers are the only computers that use microprocessors. Several minicomputers do too, and attempts are underway—thus far unsuccessfully—to put a mainframe computer's central processing unit on a single chip of fabulous complexity. Even so, the personal computer's reliance on microprocessors provides a ready handle to characterize it.

UNDERSTANDING MICROPROCESSORS

Microprocessors stem from an unprecedented explosion of technology, one that saw 1948s bulky transistor shrink to a size expressed in terms of the wavelength of light, or millionths of a meter.

A transistor is an electronic device that, among other things, can function as a switch, making it a candidate for inclusion in a computer's central processing circuitry. (That circuitry amounts to a complex maze of switches that routes information first one way, then the other, following the program's dictates.) At first, transistors averaged about ⅛ inch in diameter, and hooking them up in electronic circuits was an expensive proposition: each one had to be soldered in by hand.

In the late 1950s, however, scientists realized that transistors didn't have to be so big to do their job, and the *integrated circuit* was born. An integrated circuit, or IC, starts out as a layered flake or chip of silicon. A process akin to photolithography etches a circuit diagram on it, creating the equivalent of many separate transistors. The first ICs packed dozens of transistors onto a single chip. Since then, a riot of technology has pushed the number of transistors successfully contained on one chip to ten thousand, a hundred thousand, a million, and more. The only barrier to the IC's complexity seems to be the ultimate, irreducible granularity of matter itself.

Not all ICs are microprocessors. A typical computer uses many ICs, each devoted to a specific function. One common use for ICs lies in computer memory. Each of the memory chips in many of today's personal computers store 64,000 bits, or units, of information; already available are chips that store 256,000 bits, and chips that store over a million bits each are on the way. These tiny memory chips and other ICs have helped shrink computers dramatically. A sophisticated minicomputer that would once have required the equivalent of several four-drawer filing cabinets of dense wiring now sits comfortably on a table top. A microprocessor containing the equivalent of 50,000 transistors packs into $\frac{1}{16}$ square inch circuitry three times more complex than that of the first electronic computer, ENIAC, which required 1600 square feet of floor space and weighed 60,000 pounds.

The IC not only made computers smaller, it also made them cheaper. Computer memories are a case in point. Computer memories used to be laboriously made of magnetic cores strung on wires, and they were expensive. In 1965, for example, core memory cost about 1¢ per bit, so that a memory capable of holding 256,000 characters of 8 bits each would cost well over $20,000. Today, you can buy the necessary memory chips for about $65. Were the aircraft industry to have made this kind of progress, according to Hoo-min Toong and Amar Gupta, today's Boeing 767 would cost only $500.[1]

A typical personal computer uses dozens of ICs, some devoted to memory and others to input/output. But the star of the show is the microprocessor. In a very real sense, the microprocessor *is* the computer: it's what counts (in both meanings of the word). Today's personal computer companies, the ones that market computers such as the Apple and Kaypro, really aren't computer manufacturers at all; they simply assemble and market existing IC components. And although there are many of these personal computer companies, there are only a few firms that produce microprocessors. The microprocessors currently in use boil down to three basic types: 8-, 16-, and 32-bit units.

8-, 16-, AND 32-BIT MICROPROCESSORS

Microprocessors vary considerably in their performance, at least on the test bench. For reasons that will be explained below, "real-world" conditions tend to mute these differences. But advertising hype makes much of them anyway. You'll hear, for instance, that 16-bit microprocessors are faster than 8-bit ones, and 32-bit microprocessors are faster still. What do these terms mean?

Computers process information represented in yes-no units called *bits*, which correspond nicely to the on-off states of electronic circuits. One bit, represented by the binary numbers 1 or 0, can't carry much information by itself, so it's necessary to string bits together into 8-bit strings called *bytes*. A byte (for example, 01000100) can represent a character: a letter, a punctuation mark, or a number from 0 to 9.

Computer circuits, like the lanes of a freeway, are laid out in parallel; information travels along these "lanes" in a precise synchrony laid down by the computer's built-in clock, which ticks away at several million strokes a minute. If there are 8 wires or lanes, as in 8-bit computers, all 8 bits of a character can travel through the wires and arrive at their destination at the same time. If, however, there are 16 "lanes," as in 16-bit computers, 2 characters can arrive at once.

Does that mean 16-bit microprocessors are twice as fast as their 8-bit counterparts? In practice, not necessarily. The Apple Macintosh, for example, uses a 32-bit microprocessor, a fact Apple's advertising makes much of. What you're not told, however, is that the microprocessor communicates with the rest of the computer using a data pathway (called a *data bus*) only 16 bits wide, which slows it down. Similarly, the IBM PC is described as a 16-bit computer. Yet the PC's data bus is only 8 bits wide.

In practice, the speed differences among microprocessors tend to be evened out by these and other real-world factors. The Mac's 32-bit microprocessor does have the edge over its 16- and 8-bit counterparts, at least on the test bench. But

[1]"Personal Computers," *Scientific American* (December 1982), p. 87.

the Mac's designers invested the chip's power not in speed but rather in an especially vivid video display, which demands so much of the chip's processing capability that it comes close to overwhelming it.

You'd be unwise, therefore, to base your choice of a personal computer merely on grounds of speed. But that doesn't mean that significant differences among microprocessors do not exist. They do, and they're most perceptible in the computer's memory size limitations.

MICROPROCESSORS AND MEMORY

Microprocessors need specific program instructions to do their work. You can't just tell a microprocessor, "alphabetize these words." You have to say, "take the word in memory location such-and-such, compare it to the word in memory location such-and-such," and so on. That means every single cell in the computer's memory must have its own, unique address, like post office boxes. What's more, the microprocessor must have a special circuit, called an *address bus*, to communicate the address number of the cell it wants opened.

The width of the address bus determines the maximum number of memory cells the computer can have. All the bits in the address have to travel down the bus in parallel, just like data in the data bus. If there are 8 wires or "lanes," the address number can be 8 bits long. Memory addresses, like everything else inside the computer, are expressed in binary numbers. So the maximum number of memory locations is 2^8 or 256—not very many.

By convention, the 8-bit microprocessors now available are built with 16-bit address busses, placing a 2^{16} (65,536) bit limit on the memory. For convenience, memory sizes are often expressed in *kilobytes* (K), or 1024 bytes. A 16-bit address bus, then, produces a maximum memory size of 64K.

Now, 64K sounds like a lot of memory locations, but it's important to remember that each location can hold only one character. Moreover, there must be room for the program along with the data. Figuring that a double-spaced typewritten page contains about 1500 characters, a memory of 64K can hold only about 44 pages of programs and data. That places sharp limits on program complexity and on the amount of data that you can work with at one time.

You may hear of computers built around 8-bit chips that can handle more than 64K of memory, thanks to a piece of engineering sleight-of-hand. The trick is called *bank switching*. The 8-bit microprocessor can't work with more than 64K of memory at a time, but it can switch between two banks of 64K memory chips. The effect (if handled correctly) generates the equivalent of a 128K memory.

A simpler way to get around 64K memory barrier, however, is to design the microprocessor with a wider address buss. That's exactly what the designers of 16- and 32-bit microprocessors did. Most 16-bit microprocessors use a 20-bit address bus, allowing a maximum memory size of over one million bytes (that is, a *megabyte*). The 32-bit chip in Apple's Macintosh uses a 24-bit address bus, permitting a maximum memory size of 16 megabites. (The Mac's designers, however, limited the Mac's memory to 512K, so all that room for memory expansion is wasted.) The current memory size champion is IBM's Personal Computer AT, which uses a 16-bit chip with a 22-bit address bus (maximum memory size: 4 megabytes).

These 16- and 32-bit microprocessors (and, by extension, the personal computers built around them) would seem on first glance to be clearly preferable to computers based on 8-bit microprocessors, especially for scholars. After all, scholars often work with manuscripts longer than 44 pages, the upper limit on the memory of most 8-bit machines. Nevertheless, a programming trick called *virtual memory* makes it possible for 8-bit computer users to work with documents whose size is limited in practice only by the capacity of the computer's disk drives.

Here's how virtual memory works. When you're working with a lengthy document, you don't really need the whole thing in the memory at once. After all, you work on only one page at a time. Of a 50-page manuscript, therefore, 49 can be stored on disk and paged in and out of the memory as needed. Virtual memory programming, therefore, makes the memory seem much larger. You can work with documents of 100 to 150 pages or more.

There's a big drawback to the virtual memory technique: it's slow. The computer's main memory transfers information more rapidly than the disk drives. The paging operations, therefore, slow down your work—indeed, they can freeze the whole computer for several seconds to a minute. The delay caused by paging becomes particularly noticeable when you're scrolling through the document page by page. With a long manuscript, it can take as much as 10 minutes to reach the end. To be sure, these delays seem inconsequential when measured against the computer's many benefits, but they're not to be lightly dismissed. I've known more than one scholar who, exasperated with paging and scrolling delays, traded up to a 16-bit computer—and took a big loss on the transaction.

Make no mistake about it: bank switching and virtual memory techniques have made 8-bit computers perfectly suitable for scholarly needs, and they're available at bargain-basement prices. Thousands of scholars are using 8-bit computers happily and productively. Yet the price of 16-bit computers is dropping rapidly, and their memories may be expanded quite easily and cheaply to 640K—ten times the 64K limit of most 8-bit computers. That means—at least potentially—you can put a big, complex word processing program and a manuscript of 150 pages or more in memory all at once, with an operating speed improvement of three to ten times.[2]

---

[2]Note, however, that relatively few word processing programs actually take advantage of the 16-bit computer's memory potential. An exception is Xywrite Plus (Xyquest).

SOFTWARE AVAILABILITY

Another characteristic of microprocessors shapes the personal computer world: their inability to run each other's software.

Microprocessors perform a set number of information-manipulation operations, such as moving characters from one place to another, comparing two characters to see which is larger, and the like. Most microprocessors perform several dozen such operations, and the program must refer to them by name. The list of named operations is called the *operation code,* or *opcode* for short.

The trouble is, each microprocessor has its own opcode; the code that means "store this character" to one microprocessor might mean "erase this character" to another. For this reason, software has to be written for a particular microprocessor, and a program designed to work with one microprocessor won't work with another one—at least, not without extensive modification.

"Pools" of software—some small, some big, some growing, some shrinking—have built up around particular microprocessors, and a large part of the computer literacy you'll need lies in understanding which of these pools is likely to contain the most programs of interest to you. To be sure, some programs have been issued in several versions so that they'll work with several different microprocessors; the spreadsheet program VisiCalc (Software Arts, Inc.) is a case in point. But issuing a program in several versions is expensive, and many of the small software houses that produce the programs scholars like best can't afford to do so.

Rockwell 6502

The 8-bit 6502 microprocessor, used in computers such as the Apple IIe, Apple IIc, Commodore 64, and Commodore 128, is something of an antique. On the market for 8 years at this writing, its design limitations place severe constraints on programmers: many of today's sophisticated, complex programs can't be made to run on the 6502. To be sure, there's a huge pool of software available for these machines, but little of it is of interest to scholars. Very few of the programs discussed in this book are available for 6502-based machines. A high proportion of scholars who use the Apple IIe, in fact, upgrade their systems (cost: $200 to $300) with a circuit board containing a Z80 microprocessor so they can run Z80-based software.

Zilog Z80

The 8-bit Z80 microprocessor, used in computers such as the Kaypro II and Morrow Micro Decision, uses a more sophisticated design than the older 6502, and its fertile programming environment attracted many outstanding contributions to its software pool (such as SuperFile, WordStar, and dBase II). Note, however, the use of the past tense. Even though Z80-based computers continue to sell briskly, software houses clearly believe that the future lies with 16-bit and 32-bit technology. It's rare indeed to see new software announced for Z80 computers. That's too bad, since Z80-based computers are adequate for many scholars, and they're cheap.

Intel 8088, 8086, 80186, 80286

These 16-bit Intel microprocessors provide the horsepower for IBM Personal Computers and their emulators, the "compatibles." The 8088, widely used in the IBM PC and PC-compatibles, uses an 8-bit data pathway and a 20-bit address bus; the 8086 (AT&T 6300), 80186 (Compaq Deskpro), and 80286 (IBM Personal Computer AT) use 16-bit data pathways and operate considerably faster.

Owing to the PC family's enormous success, a huge and growing pool of software has been created for it. In it scholars are almost sure to find the highest proportion of suitable programs. Be warned, however, that not all the programs written for the 8088 really take advantage of its benefits—namely, the larger memory. The IBM PC was designed so that Z80 software, written for such computers as the Kaypro, could be easily rewritten for the 8088 environment. And that's just what many software houses did. When you're using WordStar 3.3 on the PC, therefore, you're greeted with the same old paging technique used on the program's earlier, 8-bit versions—and that doesn't change no matter how much memory you put in the computer. WordStar simply doesn't know how to take advantage of it.

Motorola 68000

Just as the 8088 and related chips are inseparable from the IBM PC, so too is the Motorola 68000, a 32-bit chip, inseparable from Apple's Macintosh. The Mac's software pool took a long time to get going, but at this writing there were signs of rapid growth. It's likely that by the time you read this book, many programs of interest to scholars will be made available in the Macintosh environment.

MICROPROCESSOR HORIZONS

Snazzier microprocessors than the ones just mentioned already exist, but it's not certain they'll find their way into personal computers right away. There's no surer route to financial ruin than to introduce a new personal computer for which no software exists.

Future trends will doubtless see a steady evolution rather than radical innovations, and it's already clear where these trends are headed. Several of the nation's major universities are working with IBM at this writing on the ultimate scholar's computer. According to press descriptions, the machine will have at least 1 megabyte of main memory, a processing speed of a million instructions per second, and a graphics resolution of 1000 by 1000 dots or *pixels*. It will run IBM PC software, and communicate with larger computers at much higher speeds than today's crop of personal computers. It's not available yet, but you'll find me at the head of the line when it is.

THE CHARACTER SET

Another factor scholars will want to keep in mind when choosing a computer is the machine's built-in character set, or the repertoire of characters it can display on the screen. Some computers can display foreign language, Greek, Cyrillic, and other special characters on the screen, and if you're working in an area that requires frequent use of them, you'll surely find these computers especially attractive. Be forewarned, however: it's one thing to display the special characters on the screen, but it's quite another to print them. We're concerned here only with the display of special characters; the mysteries of printing them are disclosed in Chapter 8.

Here's a rough-and-ready typology of computers according to their character display capabilities. Many computers can display only the standard characters known as the *ASCII* character set (explained below). Sometimes, however, these computers can be modified to display additional characters. Others have a built-in set of additional characters, the extended character set, that may or may not include the characters you need. Still others operate in a graphics mode in which virtually anything can be displayed on the screen.

THE ASCII CHARACTER SET

Personal computers, as you've already seen, process information that has been coded by using an 8-digit binary number. That coding system is standardized, and the standards are those of the American Standard Code for Information Interchange (ASCII, pronounced "ASK-key").

The ASCII character set stems from an early effort to standardize telecommunications. It does well enough, except that its designers did not seem aware of the existence of other languages or mathematics. ASCII lets you work with the 26 characters of the upper- and lower-case English alphabets, the digits 0 through 9, and the punctuation symbols you'd likely find along the top row of a typewriter keyboard (see Figure 2-1). You'll find no accented vowels, no Greek characters, no European monetary symbols, no summation signs or integrals, and no umlauts. Most scholars find the ASCII character set unsuited to their needs, for obvious reasons.

Happily, ways can be found to get around ASCII's limitations. You can modify an 8-bit computer so that it displays more characters, or—and this route is

32	space	56	8	80	P	104	h
33	!	57	9	81	Q	105	i
34	"	58	:	82	R	106	j
35	#	59	;	83	S	107	k
36	$	60	<	84	T	108	l
37	%	61	=	85	U	109	m
38	&	62	>	86	V	110	n
39	'	63	>	87	W	111	o
40	(	64	@	88	X	112	p
41	)	65	A	89	Y	113	q
42	*	66	B	90	Z	114	r
43	+	67	C	91	[	115	s
44	,	68	D	92	\	116	t
45	-	69	E	93	]	117	u
46	.	70	F	94	^	118	v
47	/	71	G	95	_	119	w
48	0	72	H	96	`	120	x
49	1	73	I	97	a	121	y
50	2	74	J	98	b	122	z
51	3	75	K	99	c	123	{
52	4	76	L	100	d	124		
53	5	77	M	101	e	125	}
54	6	78	N	102	f	126	~
55	7	79	O	103	g		

FIGURE 2–1. ASCII Character Set (With Code Numbers)

to be preferred—you can buy a 16-bit or 32-bit computer that includes them in the built-in or resident character set.

MODIFYING 8-BIT COMPUTERS

In 8-bit computers such as the Apple IIe, Kaypro II, and Morrow Micro Decision, the computer's character set is built into the computer's *firmware*, or information permanently encoded into a special bank of *read-only memory* (ROM). Read-only memory, as the name suggests, contains permanent, unerasable information that can only be extracted (but not altered). Just because the character set does not contain foreign language or mathematical symbols, however, doesn't mean you can't print them. Some programs let you enter codes in the text that, when processed, print out foreign language and other symbols. But the inconvenience of this approach rules it out for all but occasional uses of non-ASCII characters.

The program CHARTECH (TechWare, P.O. Box 10545, Eugene, Oregon 97440) illustrates this approach's limitations. The program "patches" or modifies the popular word processing program WordStar so that it prints a set of technical and Greek characters—but you don't see them on the screen. To enter the symbols, you insert a control code into the text, or a command entered directly into the text (and visible on the screen) by holding down the computer's CONTROL key and pressing another key. The result is a character prefaced by a caret symbol (such as ^ E). Characters entered after the command, such as P or w, look as they normally do, but they print out as technical or Greek characters. Figure 2-2 shows CHARTECH's standard set of special characters, showing the

CODE	CHAR		CODE	CHAR		CODE	CHAR
!	′		A	↑		`	‖
"	ℓ		B	Γ		a	α
#	▽		C	∫		b	β
$	⟩		D	Δ		c	χ
%	∠		E	⌉		d	δ
&	ℱ		F	Φ		e	ε
'	′		G	Γ		f	φ
(	\		H	ℋ		g	γ
)	∫		I	⌠		h	η
*	½		J	⌡		i	ι
+	±		K	√		j	∂
,	¼		L	∧		k	κ
-	—		M	∫		l	λ
.	·		N	⟍		m	μ
/	≐		O	○		n	ν
0	◇		P	Π		o	ω
1	◆		Q	Θ		p	π
2	□		R	‡		q	θ
3	■		S	Σ		r	ρ
4	△		T	†		s	σ
5	▲		U	Υ		t	τ
6	◇		V	∇		u	υ
7	◆		W	Ω		v	ħ
8	»		X	Ξ		w	ω
9	«		Y	Ψ		x	ξ
:	≅		Z				y	ψ
;	≈		[	∟		z	ζ
<	≤		\	×		{	◁
=	≡		]	⌋		¦		
>	≥		^	→		}	↟
?	⅓		_	⊥		~	~
@	∝						

FIGURE 2-2. CHARTECH's Standard Set of Special Characters

key you press to produce the desired character on printout. To produce the Greek *pi*, for example, you'd enter ^ EP.

As this example shows, this approach is suitable for occasional use of foreign language or technical symbols, but it's all but useless when the non-ASCII characters are used frequently. The commands and codes clutter up the screen, making it all but unreadable.

One way around this problem is to modify the hardware itself. ROMs are usually supplied as integrated circuit chips, meaning that you can pry one off the circuit board and press another one on without doing any soldering. A few firms market replacement ROMs for 8-bit computers. Techware, for example, sells ROMS for the Apple IIe, Kaypro II, Osborne 1, and others. When used with CHARTECH, these computers can display Greek and technical symbols on the screen.

Although the ROM-swapping approach may help you if you already own an 8-bit computer, its limitations argue strongly against 8-bit computers in general if your work involves heavy use of non-ASCII characters. A Techware ROM chip and a CHARTECH-modified WordStar will recognize, display, and print the characters, but no other program will. If you wish to take advantage of the many scholarly uses of other programs, such as text-oriented data base programs (see Part Three) you'll have to do without non-ASCII characters when you use them.

THE IBM PC EXTENDED CHARACTER SET

A major advantage of the 16-bit IBM PC for scholarly work is that, besides the 94 ASCII characters, the machine is designed to display an additional set of 126 characters and graphics symbols called the extended character set (ECS). Among the available characters are a good assortment of Greek, mathematical, and foreign language characters (Figure 2–3).

Entering the special characters is simple enough. You hold down the keyboard's ALT key and type in the special character's code. ALT-168, for example, enters the upside-down Spanish question mark used at the beginning of interrogative sentences.

Because every IBM PC (and PC-compatible computer) contains this standard character set, software available for the IBM PC can (in principle) be designed to take advantage of it. And that means you can transfer foreign language text between applications. Ideally, for instance, you'd be able to write a bibliographic citation in French, store it in a bibliographic data base management program, and insert it into a word processing program file as you please. Sadly, only a fraction of PC programs take advantage of this capability. The ones that do, such as the integrated word processing and data base management program Nota Bene, make the IBM PC world attractive indeed for foreign language and scientific word processing.

128 – Ç	154 – Ü	180 – ┤	206 – ╬	232 – Φ
129 – ü	155 – ¢	181 – ╡	207 – ╧	233 – θ
130 – é	156 – £	182 – ╢	208 – ╨	234 – Ω
131 – â	157 – ¥	183 – ╖	209 – ╤	235 – δ
132 – ä	158 – ₧	184 – ╕	210 – ╥	236 – ∞
133 – à	159 – ƒ	185 – ╣	211 – ╙	237 – ø
134 – å	160 – á	186 – ║	212 – ╘	238 – ε
135 – ç	161 – í	187 – ╗	213 – ╒	239 – ∩
136 – ê	162 – ó	188 – ╜	214 – ╓	240 – ≡
137 – ë	163 – ú	189 – ╜	215 – ╫	241 – ±
138 – è	164 – ñ	190 – ╛	216 – ╪	242 – ≥
139 – ï	165 – Ñ	191 – ┐	217 – ┘	243 – ≤
140 – î	166 – ª	192 – └	218 – ┌	244 – ⌠
141 – ì	167 – º	193 – ┴	219 – █	245 – ⌡
142 – Ä	168 – ¿	194 – ┬	220 – ▄	246 – ÷
143 – Å	169 – ⌐	195 – ├	221 – ▌	247 – ≈
144 – É	170 – ¬	196 – ─	222 – ▐	248 – °
145 – æ	171 – ½	197 – ┼	223 – ▀	249 – ∙
146 – Æ	172 – ¼	198 – ╞	224 – α	250 – ·
147 – ô	173 – ¡	199 – ╟	225 – β	251 – √
148 – ö	174 – «	200 – ╚	226 – Γ	252 – ⁿ
149 – ò	175 – »	201 – ╔	227 – Π	253 – ²
150 – û	176 – ▒	202 – ╩	228 – Σ	254 – ▪
151 – ù	177 – ▒	203 – ╦	229 – σ	255 –
152 – ÿ	178 – ▓	204 – ╠	230 – µ	
153 – Ö	179 – │	205 – ═	231 – τ	

FIGURE 2-3. IBM Personal Computer Extended Character Set

PC Character Set Cautions

Even if your IBM PC software recognizes the extended character set, you may not be able to print the special characters. Chapter 8 returns to this subject in detail, but the pitfall is so treacherous that it deserves special mention here. Your printer must be specifically designed to print the extended character set. At this writing, few printers were available that had this capability. Those that did included the Citizen MSP-10, Diablo 360 ECS, IBM Graphics Printer, NEC Spinwriter 2050, Okidata Microline 92 Plug 'n' Play, Star Micronics Gemini 10X, Star Micronics Delta 15PC, and Star Micronics Radix 10PC. This list does not include the popular Epson printers RX-80, FX-80, and LQ-1500.

Note that many printers advertise "IBM compatibility," which means simply that they'll work with IBM computers. This claim does not necessarily mean the printers will print the full extended character set. If the salesperson will not say unequivocally, "Yes, this printer prints the extended character set" (and preferably demonstrate it before your own eyes!), it probably won't.

PC ROM Upgrades

If the extended character set doesn't have all the characters you need, or if you work extensively in foreign languages, you can play the same ROM-switching game just described for 8-bit computers.

An excellent source of replacement ROMS is Image Processing Systems (P.O. Box 5016, Madison, WI 53705). Image Processing Systems ROMs are designed to work with its scientific and foreign language word processing program ProofWriter. Available at this writing were ROMs for engineering, statistics, mathematics, Greek, Classical Greek, Slavic Cyrillic, Slavic Latin, Hebrew, Ugaritic, Egyptian, Arabic, and Sanskrit characters.

THE BIT-MAPPED GRAPHICS OPTION

The computers just discussed—8-bit machines such as the Kaypro and the standard IBM PC configuration—use characters built into the machines' firmware (ROM). You can achieve some impressive results by swapping ROMs, but there's another route: *bit-mapped graphics displays*. Bit-mapped graphics displays are available with the IBM PC (equipped with the color graphics card option) and the Apple Macintosh.

A bit-mapped graphics display turns the whole display screen into an electronic palette consisting of thousands of tiny dots or pixels, and every one of them can be lit up or switched off independently. (That's a very different matter from the nongraphics display in, for example, the standard IBM PC configuration, where you're limited to 254 configurations of dots—the characters stored in the PC's firmware—and nothing more.) A bit-mapped graphics display can display virtually anything (up to the limits of its resolution), including Japanese and Arabic characters.

Why, then, don't all computers have bit-mapped video displays? The answer is that the display delves deeply into the computer's reserves of processing power. Bit-mapped graphics displays require that a large portion of the computer's memory be reserved to serve as an electronic representation or map of what's on the screen. Every time you change something—such as erasing one word and typing another—the computer has to recalculate the representation. That's why bit-mapped graphics displays work best with the faster microprocessors, such as the 16-bit 8088 or the 32-bit 68000.

Just because a computer has a bit-mapped graphics display, however, doesn't mean that the computer's software knows how to take full advantage of it. In the IBM PC environment, the 256-character ROM chip is still there, and—knowing that many PC users wouldn't have the graphics card option—most programmers have opted to use the firmware character set rather than get involved in graphics-based character representation. Only a very few word processing programs for the IBM PC color graphics system make full use of the computer's bit-mapped capabilities. An example is ProofWriter Graphics (Image Processing Systems, P.O. Box 5016, Madison, WI 53705).

The Apple Macintosh presents a more unified picture. The Mac has a high-resolution bit-mapped graphics display built in, and it always operates in a bit-mapped graphics mode. What's more, no characters at all are built into the Mac's firmware. All the character sets are supplied on disk and read into the video circuitry's memory from disk at the start of an operating session. Changing Mac character sets, then, is as simple as buying a disk containing the new character set you want and using an accessory program called Font Mover to incorporate it into the system file. The new font will be available with almost all Mac software. For more information on disks containing a wide variety of foreign language, technical, and scientific characters for the Macintosh, see the Resources section at the end of this chapter.

The bit-mapped graphics display option is particularly attractive when it comes to printing the displayed characters. Many dot matrix printers (see Chapter 8) can operate in a graphics mode, which prints everything shown on the screen without special fussing. An excellent example is the Apple Macintosh/Apple Imagewriter Printer combination; the Imagewriter will print whatever is displayed on the Mac's brilliantly clear video display, even if it's written in Devanagari.

DISK DRIVES

Floppy disks and disk drives are part of a personal computer's *auxiliary memory system*. That system is necessary because the computer's main memory is *volatile*: that is, it loses the information stored in it when you switch off the current. Disks and disk drives give you a way, therefore, of loading programs and data into the memory at the start of a work session and of recording the session's results when it ends.

Made of flexible plastic and coated with a magnetically sensitive oxide, floppy disks spin in the disk drive at about 300 revolutions per minute. Poised over the disk's surface is a movable *read/write head*, an electromagnetic device akin to a tape recorder's record/play head. The head, as its name suggests, performs two functions: reading, or retrieving information from the disk, and writing, or recording information on it.

The standard personal computer configuration uses two floppy disk drives, one for the program disk (the disk containing applications programs) and one for the data disk (the one containing the work you're doing). Working with two disk drives vastly simplifies basic, day-to-day operations such as backing up the work you've done, a necessary precaution against accidental erasures and other disasters.

Disk drives vary considerably in their storage capacities. At one extreme is the Osborne 1 with 100K disk drives; at the other are advanced machines such as the IBM Personal Computer AT, whose drives store over 1200K. In general, drives with 350K to 400K or more storage will prove more convenient; drives of 100K to 150K fill up quickly, require you to swap disks in and out of the drive frequently, and increase user frustration. Remember that a 44-page, double-spaced manuscript will require about 64K of disk space. Since most word processing programs make an automatic backup file, for which room must be saved on the disk, using a 100K disk drive will limit the maximum size of your documents to well below 44 pages.

Increasing numbers of personal computer users are taking advantage of dramatic declines in the cost of *hard disks*. Hard disks work much like floppy disk drives, save that the disks spin in a dust-free, sealed environment (permitting closer contact between the read/write head and the disk) and at higher speed (about 3000 rpm). They offer dramatically larger storage capacities, too: 10 to 20 megabytes is the rule (see Appendix I for more information on hard disks).

THE DISK OPERATING SYSTEM (DOS)

A disk drive is something like a tape recorder in that it's designed to record and play back information from a magnetic storage device. But you doubtless will have noticed that the drive has no controls. You control the disk drive from the computer's keyboard; the details about how information is actually stored on the disk are all handled for you automatically. What makes this automatic operation possible is an essential program called the *disk operating system* (often abbreviated DOS).

WHAT DOS DOES

The first thing you'll do when you switch on the computer is insert the disk containing DOS, which the computer is poised to read automatically into its memory.

Among other functions, DOS takes care of storing and retrieving information on the disks. That information is stored in a complex patchwork of concentric tracks and radial sectors, but you don't have to worry about that. So far as you're concerned, you need only refer to a given unit of information (for instance, a program or manuscript) by referring to its *file name*. A program, for example, might be called WRITE.COM, while a manuscript might be called ESSAY1.TXT. The first part of the file name identifies the file's contents; the second part, the *extension*, tells you what kind of file it is (COM files are programs; TXT files are documents).

DOS also gives you a set of commands with which you can control the disk drives' operation. You can, for instance, ask to see a directory of files on a disk. You can erase files (or a whole disk, if you want to). You can move files from one disk to another. And you can load programs into the computer's main memory.

COMMAND-DRIVEN VERSUS MOUSE-ICON SYSTEMS

Two basic kinds of DOS are found in today's personal computer marketplace: *command-driven* disk operating systems and *mouse-icon* systems.

Command-Driven Systems

Command-driven disk operating systems require you to type commands (such as ERASE, DIR[ectory], or CHKDSK [check disk contents]) at the keyboard. Examples of command-driven operating systems are ProDOS (Apple IIe), CP/M-80 (Z80-based computers such as the Kaypro II), MS-DOS (IBM PC and compatibles), and UNIX (AT&T 7300).

Many beginners in personal computing find command-driven systems tough going. You'll have to memorize the five or six commands that you'll use often, and you'll have to develop some skill at writing command expressions (such as the MS-DOS expression COPY B:SAMPLE.DOC A:SAMPLE.BAK, which means "copy the file SAMPLE.DOC on Drive B to Drive A, and name it SAMPLE.BAK").

If you're new to computing, you'll almost certainly need some help to pass the command-driven DOS hurdle. Ask your dealer to give you two or three hours of instruction, or find someone who has successfully mastered the computer you're planning to buy.

Once you move past the hurdle, however, you'll find that the command-driven operating system becomes second nature. That's why I don't recommend DOS *shells*, or programs designed to make DOS easier to use (an example: GEM, a Macintosh-like shell for MS-DOS). Although these programs do make DOS easier to use, they take up valuable memory space and slow down the computer's operation. A little effort invested in learning the unshelled DOS will pay off handsomely in quick, efficient computer operation.

Mouse-Icon Systems

Mouse-icon disk operating systems were designed with the beginner and nonexpert in mind. Developed at Xerox's Palo Alto Research Center, their sole implementation (at this writing) in personal computers is the Apple Macintosh disk operating system, called the Finder.

The idea underlying mouse-icon systems is that computer objects and functions can be represented by graphic icons, or symbols that represent what they refer to. A file containing a word processing program, then, is represented on the Mac's screen by a file folder shape containing a hand writing with a pencil. Research demonstrates that people process graphic images of this kind faster than they process words.

The mouse's role in the Finder is to give you something to point with. Designed to fit the hand, the mouse rolls about on the table top as an arrow on the screen reflects its movements. To start a program, then, you need merely point at the program's icon and double-click the mouse button.

Without question, mouse-icon systems are considerably easier to learn than command-driven systems. Whether they're easier to use once you've become adept is another matter. Many experienced computer users find that the Mac's operating system isolates them from basic disk manipulation processes possible with command-driven systems. Others find the flashy graphics impressive at first, but soon tire of them when they realize how much computer time and processing power it's taking to display them on the screen.

EXPANDABILITY

Another personal computer feature to keep in mind is expandability, or the ease with which a personal computer can be equipped with add-on devices.

The Apple IIe and the IBM PC typify expandable systems, and they're worthy of praise. When you open the computer's case, you see several empty slots for add-on circuit boards. A host of third-party suppliers provides an amazing variety of accessories ready to fit into these slots. Expandable systems have another benefit: they're easy to upgrade. A novice user can add a 10-megabyte hard disk to an IBM PC, for instance, in about half an hour. (See Appendix I for more information on system upgrades.)

Nonexpandable systems have no slots for accessories, and it's more difficult and costly to upgrade them—if it's possible at all. The Apple Macintosh is a case in point. At this writing, adding a second disk drive to a Mac and upgrading the memory from 128K to 512K costs an outrageous $1500. An IBM PC user could carry out the same upgrade for about one-third the cost. An externally mounted 10-megabyte hard disk drive for an IBM PC, to cite another example, costs about $500, but the same unit for the Macintosh costs $1500.

SUMMARY: FOUR SYSTEMS

The material presented in this chapter should give you the tools you need to decide whether a particular computer will meet your needs. Only one additional caveat is needed: since scholars will spend most of their computer time processing words, you should begin your decision-making process by selecting a word processing program. Before you make any final decisions on choosing your system, be sure to read Part Two/Writing, carefully.

Even so, looking critically at hardware is an important part of the selection process, particularly for scholars who want to display foreign language and scientific characters. Other hardware-dependent considerations are software availability, system expandability, and disk drive capacity, which may matter a great deal to you if you plan to purchase many accessory programs, add hardware accessories, or maintain large disk-based data bases.

To illustrate the constraints imposed by choosing one particular computer over another, there follows an analysis of four popular machines. By the time you read this book, of course, one or more of the machines mentioned here may be history, and new ones will almost certainly have appeared. Still, the points raised in this chapter should apply to the new machines that are sure to come along. You'll want to ask: What microprocessor does this computer use? What limits does it impose on the computer's memory? How much software of interest to scholars is available for this machine? Are new programs of interest to scholars likely to appear for this machine? What's contained in its built-in character set? How much information do its disk drives hold? Is its operating system command-driven or menu-driven? Is system expandability easy or difficult? What will it cost you to add a hard disk?

Please bear in mind that the point of this analysis isn't to show that one of these machines is the best one for scholarly computing. For some scholars, an Apple II is the best system; others will prefer Kaypros or IBM PCs, and still others will swear by their Macs. All four are being used right now for scholarly computing applications. Rather, the point is to provide you with the information you need to make an informed choice among them (and to provide some criteria for evaluating the computers that will appear after this book's publication).

As you evaluate costs, bear in mind that some computers include in their purchase price accessories vital to day-to-day computing, such as a parallel port (for connecting printers), an RS-232 port or serial port (for connecting modems and other accessories [see Appendix I]), a second disk drive, a video display, and the disk operating system. Some even include software (which may or may not be of interest to you). Others do not. When you're comparing the price of two systems, therefore, take into consideration what the accessories will cost. A 128K Apple Macintosh, for example, may seem like a good deal at first, but when you add in what it will cost you to buy the additional disk drive (a necessity for scholarly computing), it turns out to be significantly more expensive than you thought. The IBM PC, too, doesn't include a serial port, a feature you'll have to add if you wish to try online data base research (Chapter 13), or the computer's disk operating system.

APPLE IIe

Note: No standard Apple IIe configuration exists. The system described was being widely promoted at this writing at a popular computer store chain.
Microprocessor: 6502 (8 bit, 8-bit data pathway, 16-bit address bus)
Memory: 64K (expandable by bank switching to 128K)
Accessories included: 64K additional memory (128K total), 80-column display card, two disk drives, monitor, DOS
Accessories not included: parallel port, serial port
Character set: ASCII character set only; ROM upgrades available at extra cost from third-party vendors

Disk drive capacity: 140K (low)

Operating system: Proprietary, command-driven (shell available as optional accessory program from third-party suppliers)

Software availability: The huge software pool is strong on games and programs for computer-assisted instruction; it's weak on programs of interest to scholars. Many scholars using Apple IIs will upgrade their systems with a circuit board containing a Z80 microprocessor so that they can run Z80-based software.

Expandable? Yes; wide variety of excellent options available from third-party suppliers. System expandability cheap and easy.

Comment: The Apple II has been around for a long time, and its microprocessor is slow and dated. Even so, a scholar who finds Apple II software suitable—and many do—may find this system perfectly acceptable. The system's expandability is a significant advantage. If you outgrow the slow 6502 processor, you can add a Z80 circuit board and run Z80-based programs such as dBase II or WordStar. But beware: buying an Apple II and then deciding you need a Z80 upgrade will probably cost you more than buying a good Z80 computer in the first place.

KAYPRO II

Microprocessor: Z80 (8 bit, 8-bit data pathway, 16-bit address bus)

Memory: 64K maximum

Accessories included: two disk drives, monitor, DOS, serial port, parallel port, DOS, software (WordStar, The Word Plus, dBase II, etc.)

Character set: ASCII character set only; ROM upgrades available at extra cost from third-party vendors

Disk drive capacity: 192K (Kaypro 4 model has 400K drives)

Operating system: CP/M-80, command-driven

Software availability: Within the Z80 software pool are many excellent programs of interest to scholars. Yet few new programs are appearing in Z80 formats.

Expandable? No circuit board slots; system expansion difficult and expensive

Comment: Includes several free programs, including WordStar and The Word Plus, an excellent spelling checker. If you're happy with the software currently available for the computer, the Kaypro might be an excellent choice, particularly because the price includes all necessary accessories (except a modem) and several programs of interest to scholars. If you like WordStar, for example, you may find this system of special interest since the program is included in the price. But don't count on exciting new programs appearing for this computer—the action's with the IBM PC and Apple Macintosh, and the programs being created are too big to fit in the Z80 computer's limited memory.

IBM PC

Note: No standard IBM PC configuration exists. The system described was being widely promoted at this writing at a popular computer store chain.

Microprocessor: 8088 (16 bit, 8-bit data pathway, 20-bit address bus)

Memory: 256K (expandable to the 640K maximum with optional memory expansion boards and chips)

Accessories included: monochrome monitor, monochrome monitor adapter card and parallel port, two disk drives

Accessories not included: serial port, DOS

Character set: ASCII character set plus IBM extended character set (some Greek, many useful foreign language characters, some mathematical symbols); ROM upgrades available at extra cost from third-party vendors. **Note:** Not all PC programs and printers take advantage of the extended character set.

Also available: color graphics card option for bit-mapped video display. **Note:** Only a very few PC programs (such as ProofWriter Graphics) know how to take advantage of the bit-mapped video display for foreign language or scientific characters.

Disk drive capacity: 360K

Operating system: MS-DOS, command-driven; shell available from third-party vendors

Software availability: Excellent. Almost every program of interest to scholars is available in the PC format.

Expandable? Yes; includes slots for add-on circuit boards. System expansion is easy and cheap.

Comment: Many scholarly writers do not like the nonstandard IBM PC keyboard layout; you may wind up purchasing a replacement keyboard ($200), but with that caveat in mind, it's clear that the PC is the most popular computer for scholarly applications. The software pool includes almost every program that scholars will find of special interest, and most new programs aimed at scholars are released first in the IBM PC format.

APPLE MACINTOSH

Microprocessor: 32 bit 68000 (16-bit data pathway, 24-bit address bus)

Memory: Theoretical limit of 16 megabytes; in practice limited to 512K due to the Mac's design. 128K standard.

Accessories included: monitor, DOS, 1 disk drive, serial printer port (no parallel port is available in the Macintosh system), serial modem port, DOS, software (MacWrite, MacPaint)

Accessories not included: second disk drive (warning: costs $400–$500)

Character set: Bit-mapped graphics display standard. Software supplied with system includes many foreign language and scientific characters; additional foreign language character sets available at low cost on disk from third-party suppliers.

Disk drive capacity: 400K

Operating system: Proprietary mouse-icon system

Software availability: Good, and improving

Expandable? No internal slots; external expansion units must use the computer's serial ports, which are suitable for some accessories (such as modems or optical character readers) but too slow for others (such as hard disks). Cost of system expansion is high—one might say outrageous.

Comment: It's hard not to like the Macintosh; it's a beguiling little machine. But the computer comes with only one disk drive, which is insufficient for serious applications, and the external disk drive costs a stiff $500 (a second disk drive for the IBM PC, in comparison, costs about $100 from mail-order firms). Those who purchased the 128K standard system in 1984 were informed that upgrading their systems to 512K would cost $995! If you can get a good deal on a 512K system that includes the external disk drive, the Mac might be worth a long, hard look (especially if your work involves foreign language or mathematical characters). Software availability is good; the Mac has a strong presence on college campuses and among faculty.

RESOURCES

For an excellent, brief introduction to the personal computer, see Hoo-Min D. Toong and Amar Gupta, "Personal Computers," *Scientific American* (December 1982), pp. 87–107. Newcomers to personal computing will find a comprehensible overview of hardware and software in Henry Horenstein and Eliot Tarlin, *ComputerWise: An Introduction to Understanding, Using, and Buying a Personal Computer* (New York: Random House, 1983). A readable, if hagiographic, account of the personal computer's history is Paul Freiberger and Michael Swaine, *Fire in the Valley: The Making of the Personal Computer* (Berkeley: Osborne/McGraw-Hill, 1984).

Several popular magazines can put you in touch with what's new in hardware. Recommended especially for beginners are *Popular Computing* and *Personal Computing*. More advanced is *Byte, MacWorld*, and *PC: The Independent Guide to IBM Personal Computers* chronicle events in the Macintosh and IBM Personal Computer worlds.

On microprocessors, readable introductions are C. D. Renmore, *Silicon Chips and You* (New York: Beaufort Books, 1980) and Christopher Evans, *The Micro Millennium* (New York: Washington Square Books, 1979). More technical, but still suited for a general audience, are several articles in *Scientific American:* Robert N. Noyce, "Microelectronics" (September 1977), pp. 62–69; Alan C. Kay, "Microelectronics and the Personal Computer" (September 1977); and Hoo-Min D. Toong, "Microprocessors" (September 1977), pp. 146–161. If you wish, you can develop a sophisticated grasp of the microcomputer's technical aspects (even if you lack a technical background) by reading Louis Frenzel's *Crash Course in Microcomputers* (Indianapolis: Howard W. Sams, Inc., 1980), a self-teaching workbook.

Several firms offer Macintosh character sets sure to interest scholars. A disk containing Russian, Czech, Polish, and Slovak character sets, as well as a full Greek alphabet, is available from Casady Co. (P.O. Box 223779, Carmel, CA 93922). Plugh, Inc. (595 Royal Springs, Springsboro, OH 45066) offers a disk containing more than 700 mathematical characters, including integrals and summation signs. GreekKeys (SMK, 5760 South Blackstone Ave., Chicago, IL 60637) lets you combine Greek and English text. Linguist's Software (P.O. Box 28, Mt. Hermon, CA 95041) produces several excellent disks of Greek, Hebrew, and Japanese characters. Many more character sets are available in the public domain.

If you're not happy with the commercially available or public domain Macintosh character sets, you can make your own with an Apple program called Font Editor. Font Editor isn't for sale; it's in circulation as if it were a public domain program, with the tacit consent of Apple Computer. To obtain a copy, join a Macintosh user's group.

On Font Editor for the Macintosh, see Dave Kliman, "Font Editor and RMover: Two Arcane Mac Utilities Could be Just Your Type," *The Club Mac News* (November 1984), pp. 37–42. Club Mac (735 Walnut, Boulder, CO 80302) is a for-profit Mac user's group; available on its online bulletin board are several character sets and other programs of interest to scholars. An excellent essay on Macintosh fonts is Gordon McComb, "Making the Most of the Mac's Fonts," *MacWorld* (January 1985), pp. 106–119.

PART
TWO

WRITING

SOFTWARE FOR WRITING

Finding one's way through the word processing jungle unaided requires the bravado of an Indiana Jones: each of the many word processing programs seem alluring, but each conceals some dark secret—and you might not find out about it until you've spent $350. It's by no means certain, moreover, that you'll find help from computer-using colleagues. Those who have adopted a word processing program tend to behave like new converts to an intolerant religion. Some become so immersed in computer jargon that, as Carolyn Heilbrun found, you feel as though you had asked a classicist about Antigone and received a reply in classical Greek.[1]

Yet there's a rational way through this jungle. As you've just seen for the world of personal computers, the apparent diversity of brands and products disappears once you realize that there are only four basic categories of word processing programs. To be sure, programs within these categories vary, but once you have a clear grasp of the options available you'll be far better poised to make an intelligent selection.

Before presenting these categories and explaining the variations, it's important to stress that no one word processing program is the best for scholarly writing. To be sure, you'll be told that Microsoft Word is the best—or WordStar, or any of dozens of others. Hence this caveat: the best word processing program is the one that meets *your* needs. Scholars' word processing needs vary. The program that's right for a prolific writer who submits book-length manuscripts on disk isn't necessarily right for the teacher who uses word processing to write and print course syllabi, tests, and class handouts.

---

[1]"Some Words for the Trepid," *A Grin on the Interface: Word Processing for the Academic Humanist* (New York: Modern Language Association, 1984), p. 2.

This chapter introduces word processing, therefore, as systematically as possible (and from the scholar's viewpoint). Beginning with an introduction to word processing, it surveys word processing program features and the four basic categories of word processing programs. Its aim is to show you how to identify the software that's most likely to meet your needs.

INTRODUCING WORD PROCESSING

Word processing refers to the creation, editing, formatting, printing, and storage of text with a computer's aid.

The computer need not be a personal computer; word processing software is generally available on large central computing systems, as well as on *dedicated word processors,* machines that are designed exclusively for word processing applications. Personal computers, however, provide the ideal vehicle for word processing: they're positioned just where you want them, they're small enough to fit on a desk, they're available just when you want them, and (as opposed to dedicated word processors) they can do a very great deal more than serve as a writing tool. A personal computer, unlike a dedicated word processor, lets you use other kinds of software, such as programs for analyzing the text, managing bibliographic information, and researching online data bases. With few exceptions, scholars will be better off buying a personal computer and a word processing program rather than a dedicated word processor.

WHAT PERSONAL COMPUTER
WORD PROCESSING PROGRAMS DO

Personal computer word processing programs transform the computer into a special-purpose machine designed for writing. More specifically, all word processing programs facilitate (to varying degrees) the following six tasks: writing, using commands, editing, formatting, printing, and storing.

Writing

After you've loaded the word processing program into your computer's memory, it displays a blank screen (perhaps with a *command menu,* a list of command options, or *status information,* such as the name of the disk file you're working with or the amount of disk space left; see Figure 3–1).

When you press a key on the keyboard, an electrical impulse courses into the computer, causing several things to happen. First, it's translated into the 8-bit binary code the computer uses (Q, for instance, is coded as 01010001). Next, this code is inserted into the first memory cubbyhole in a special part of the memory, called a *buffer,* that's reserved for the document you're writing. Finally, the video

```
    B:ESSAY.DOC              PAGE 1  LINE 1 COL 01      INSERT ON


                        < < < MAIN MENU > > >

    —Cursor Movement—    | —Delete— | -Miscellaneous-| -Other Menus-
^S char left ^D char right|^G char   |^I Tab .^B Reform| (from Main only)
^A word left ^F word right|DEL chr left|^V INSERT ON/OFF|^J Help  ^K Block
^E line up   ^X line down |^T word rt |^L FIND/REPLACE |^Q Quick ^P Print
    —Scrolling—          |^Y line    |RETURN end para |^O Onscreen
^Z line up   ^W line down |          |^N Insert RETURN|
^C screen up ^s screen dn |          |^U Stop         |

L——!——!——!——!——!——!——!——!——!——!——!————R

-
```

FIGURE 3-1. WordStar Screen Display

display lights up with a representation—in English, not binary code—of the letter you've typed.

All this may seem a bit technical, but it raises an important point: the text you enter isn't stored on disk right away. Instead, it is entered in the computer's main memory, which, as pointed out in Chapter 1, is volatile—its contents disappear when the power is switched off. This could happen by accident: someone could trip over the power cord or, more likely, the power could fail briefly. To avoid loss of work, you'll want to make frequent use of an output command, one that writes the buffer's contents to disk (about once every 15 minutes is a good rough-and-ready rule).

A quality word processing program and a personal computer equipped with a good keyboard place no physical or electronic limit on typing speed; the only limitation you'll experience is that imposed by the coordination of your fingers (and the irrationality of the QWERTY keyboard layout). Expert typists find they can type significantly faster on computers. If you don't know how to type, you can purchase typing tutorial programs that will speed you through the learning process.

Even though you're working with a typewriter-like keyboard, writing with a word processing program differs markedly from writing with a typewriter. You don't have to worry about the right margin, because a feature called *word wrapping* takes care of it automatically—it "wraps" words that would go over the margin down to the next line. You can type away, therefore, as if there were no right margin. The same holds for the bottom of the page. Indeed, no bottom of the page exists. It's as if, like Jack Kerouac, you were writing on a long scroll of shelf paper. The screen display shows you a *window* on the particular part of the scroll you're looking at (Figure 3-2).

One major drawback to the current generation of personal computers is the small size of the text window: you're shown only a third of the page at a time.

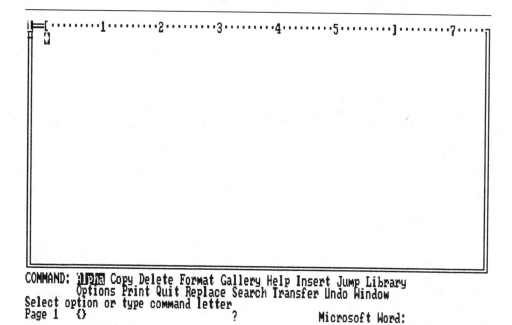

FIGURE 3-2. Command Menu of Microsoft Word (IBM PC Version)

That makes it difficult to get a sense of your document's overall structure, flow, and organization. One may look forward to a new generation of programs and video displays that, like many dedicated word processors, will show a whole page of text at a time; in the meantime, it's important to develop strategies to overcome this limitation (see Chapters 4 and 5).

A blinking marker or *cursor* shows you where the characters you're typing will appear. If you discover you've just made a mistake, you can use a *destructive backspace* key to rub out characters to the left of the cursor.

You can use the keyboard's *arrow keys* to move the cursor around on the screen, and they're useful for revising as you write. Suppose, for example, you realize you've left something out of the previous paragraph. To move the cursor up, press the up arrow key several times until you reach the line in which you'd like to add new text. Then use the left or right cursor keys to position the cursor precisely where the insertion will occur, and start typing. Here a major difference between older and newer word processing programs emerges. Older programs, such as WordStar 3.3, do not cope well with the insertion. As you add text, they simply push the existing text to the right beyond the right margin, out of sight. You have to use a special *reformatting* command to adjust the margins, and it's a bother. Newer programs offer *automatic reformatting*—a desirable feature.

Using Commands

Every word processing program provides a set of commands, usually entered at the keyboard, for carrying out the following actions:

Scrolling You can move or "scroll" up or down past the screen display (that is, the window on the text). To scroll up is to move toward the beginning of the text; to scroll down is to move toward the end. Most programs let you scroll a screenful at a time; the better ones also let you scroll one full page at a time and let you jump immediately to the beginning or the end of the document.

Text deletion Most programs give you commands for deleting a word and a full line at a time. Convenient additions in some programs are commands that delete an entire sentence or an entire paragraph.

Block commands Block commands let you mark a section or block of text (anywhere from a few characters to many pages in length). Once you've marked the block, you can copy or move the block's contents to another part of the manuscript (or to a different manuscript), delete the block, or write the block to a disk file of its own (useful when you've just written something that doesn't belong in the present manuscript but might be useful elsewhere).

Input/output commands These commands let you load a text file from disk, write or save the work you've done to disk, insert a separate disk file into the document you're working on, or print the document. The better programs provide commands for printing multiple copies of a document and for printing only specified pages. For more information on printing, see Chapter 9.

Search commands These let you specify a *search string* (usually at least 10 characters in length, and sometimes as many as 200) that the program will locate automatically (if it's in the manuscript). ("String," in computer parlance, means simply a series of characters.) Some word processing programs include *wild card* characters. A search-and-replace command lets you specify a search string and a replacement string, which will be substituted automatically. *Global* search and replace makes the substitutions throughout the entire document automatically; the best programs give you the option of confirming each replacement before it's made.

Full-featured word processing programs offer all these commands, but there are two different approaches to using them: keyboard commands and menu selection.

The keyboard command approach The personal computer keyboard has several extra keys, usually including a CONTROL and ESCAPE key. These keys, when pressed, redefine the signals sent by the alphabetical and numeric keys. They can be used, therefore, to send a large number of distinct messages to the computer, which can be programmed to recognize them as commands. WordStar, for instance, makes extensive use of keyboard commands. Most WordStar commands are given by holding down the CONTROL key and pressing one of the other keys on the keyboard. CONTROL-Y, for instance, deletes a line. To help you remember the commands, you can see a *menu* of them on the screen (see Figure 3–1). Still, there's no way around memorizing at least two or three dozen of them.

The menu selection approach   Programs using this approach show you a menu of command options on the display screen and let you set a command in motion by highlighting it in reverse video (see Figure 3–2). You may use the computer's arrow keys or, alternatively, a hand-held control device called a *mouse* to do the highlighting. The Macintosh uses a highly developed version of the command menu approach. Categories of commands are arrayed along the top of the screen. To see the command menu, you manipulate the mouse to point at the command, which "pulls down" the command menu (Figure 3–3).

The menu selection approach makes far fewer demands on beginners than the keyboard command approach. To learn WordStar, for example, you'll simply

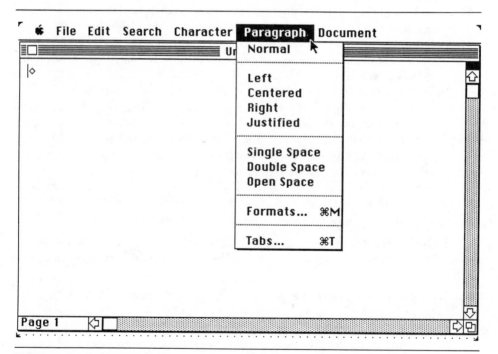

FIGURE 3–3. Pull-Down Command Menu: Macintosh Version of Microsoft Word

have to memorize at least two dozen keyboard commands—and to become truly proficient with the program, you'll have to memorize more than that. The menu selection approach, in contrast, shows you the commands and provides intuitively sensible ways to select them. Most users can gain proficiency with a program that uses the menu selection approach far more quickly.

In support of keyboard command-driven programs, however, it's sometimes argued that a good typist finds them much easier to use (once they've been memorized). Using menu-based commands, it's argued, slows down proficient users. Recent advances in the menu selection approach, however, have stripped this argument of weight. Beginning users of Microsoft Word, a menu-driven program for the IBM Personal Computer, may choose commands by looking at the command menu and highlighting the one they want using the space bar or backspace key. But an advanced user can issue the command more quickly by simply pressing the ESCAPE key and typing the command's first letter, a technique that's just as fast as the keyboard command approach.

One frequent objection to the menu selection approach still holds water, however: programs that use command menus often clutter up the screen to the point that you can't concentrate on your writing. Worse, the menu takes up space on the screen, letting you see even less of your work than the normal (and hardly satisfactory) one-third page. It should be possible to hide the menus once you've become proficient enough that you don't need to see them all the time. The early versions of Microsoft Word (1.0 through 1.15), for instance, saddled you with the menu and left you a 19-line window to write in. The newer versions (2.0 on) let you hide the menu while you're writing, producing a 23-line display; the menu pops up instantly when you press the ESCAPE key.

Editing

Depending on your preferences, the text may be edited as it is written, or it may be edited in a later session after the writing is completed. In either case, the chief benefit of word processing quickly becomes evident: the ease with which the entered text may be rearranged and revised.

All word processing programs facilitate editing, but not all of them do so to an equal degree. Some programs, for instance, scroll from page to page at a glacial pace. (This is particularly true of word processing programs that, to overcome the 8-bit computer's memory limitations, use the virtual memory technique [see Chapter 2] and page material to and from disk.) The delay worsens with longer manuscripts. It can become so dismaying, in fact, that you're discouraged from paging around in your manuscript to make needed revisions.

The one-third page view of the text, coupled with slow scrolling, can work insidiously to confine your revision efforts to the relatively unimportant level of words and sentences. Writing experts agree that the qualities most pertinent to good writing are good organization, coherence of argument, and unity, but many word processing programs seem to militate against them. A frequent result, especially for inexperienced writers, is bad writing.[2]

Even if the program you select scrolls quickly, you'll still need to keep this point in mind while you're writing. Chapters 4 and 5 discuss strategies you can use to overcome this inherent and serious drawback of personal computer word processing software.

Formatting

Formatting refers to the preparation of a document's text so that it will be printed in a pleasing and stylistically acceptable fashion.

Formatting is, in essence, a two-part process. First, the writer must use formatting commands to instruct the program how to format the text; subsequently, the program follows the instructions so that the document is prepared for printing. Programs vary widely in the ease with which their formatting utilities may be used. Some programs, known as *online formatting programs*, show the effect of the formatting commands on the screen (including, in some cases, page breaks). Others do not show the effect of these commands until the document is printed. We'll return to this important distinction and its meaning for scholarly writers below, when the four basic categories of word processing programs are surveyed.

Printing

Printing is a virtually automatic process in which the formatted document is routed through the computer's output ports to a printer. For more information on printing and printers, see Chapter 8.

Storage

Once written, the manuscript is stored on a magnetic disk. Should you decide to make a change in the work after printing it, it's a simple matter to reload the text into the computer's memory, make the necessary changes, and print out a new version.

WORD PROCESSING PROGRAM FEATURES

Almost every available word processing program offers the basic features just discussed for writing, using commands, editing, formatting, printing, and storing the text. Some offer more of these features, some less (see Table 3–1 for a list of word processing features).

[2]See Richard M. Collier, "The Word Processor and Revision Strategies," *College Composition and Communication* 34:2 (May 1983), pp. 149–155; and Kurt Supplee, "The PC Tapping at the Chamber Door," *PC: The Independent Guide to IBM Personal Computers* (May 29, 1984), pp. 249–255.

TABLE 3-1
BELLS AND WHISTLES: ADVANCED WORD PROCESSING FEATURES

arithmetic operators—Performs arithmetic operations (addition, subtraction, multiplication, division) on columns or lines of numbers. This feature, found in very few programs, will prove very attractive to scholars who often type tables and need a quick way to find sums of columns. (Example: WordStar 2000)

automatic cross-referencing—Automatically supplies the page number when a cross-reference is used (i.e., "see Chapter 4, p. 19"). A rarely found feature. (Example: WordStar 2000 Plus, with StarIndex.)

automatic equation numbering—Numbers equations automatically; renumbers them if any are deleted or inserted. A rare feature, but very desirable for mathematicians. (Example: ProofWriter.)

automatic footnote numbering—Numbers footnotes automatically; renumbers them automatically if any are deleted or inserted. (Example: ProofWriter.) **Warning:** Some programs that include footnoting capabilities do not number the footnotes. (Example: Wordix.)

automatic hyphenation—Automatically hyphenates words during word wrapping when the hyphenation will improve the distribution of words on the line. This feature is **not** desirable for writers of manuscripts to be submitted for publication; editors usually ask expressly that hyphenation not be used. Writers of manuscripts to be printed directly from program printouts (such as newsletters or proposals; see below) may find it useful. (Example: Microsoft Word 2.0.)

automatic pagination—Numbers pages automatically and inserts page number on each page of printed document (available with all full-featured programs).

automatic reformatting—Reformats the text automatically, preserving the right margin, when an insertion is made in the middle of a sentence or paragraph. This feature is found in the newer programs only. (Examples: Microsoft Word, WordStar 2000; but not WordStar 3.3.)

background printing—Permits the user to continue writing while another document is being printed. Offered with many programs. (Example: WordStar 3.3.)

chain printing—Links several documents for printing as if they were one document. Offered with many programs. (Example: Microsoft Word.)

context-sensitive online help—An "intelligent" online user assistance feature; allows the user to select a command and access information (displayed on the screen) about using it. This feature is desirable for learning the program and is offered only with the newer programs. (Example: Microsoft Word.)

endnotes—Positions footnotes at the end of the document. **Warning:** For scholarly applications, the program must be able to double-space the endnotes. (Example: Microsoft Word, but not Perfect Writer.)

equation mode—Special mode for entering equations; a rare and desirable feature for mathematicians. (Example: ProofWriter.)

extended character set—Allows screen display of extended character sets available with 16-bit IBM PC and PC-compatible computers. (Example: Microsoft Word but not WordStar 3.3.)

fail-safe features—Prevents work-destroying user errors, such as failing to save a document when exiting, by warning the user of impending loss of work. Available with most programs. (Example: WordStar 2000.)

floating footnotes—Footnotes carried over to next page if too long to fit at the bottom of a page. A rare feature, very desirable for writers of content footnotes. (Example: ProofWriter.)

footnotes—Positions notes at the bottom of the page (example: Microsoft Word). **Warning:** Some programs handle endnotes but not footnotes (example: WordStar 2000); others do not number footnotes automatically. (Example: Wordix).

forced page breaks—Allows user to override automatic pagination features and determine where a page break should be made (available with most programs).

glossary buffer—Permits storage (and easy insertion into the text) of often-used textual passages. Found only in the newer programs. (Example: Microsoft Word.)

graphics—Permits merging of graphics (charts, illustrations, etc.) and text in a single document. (Example: Microsoft Word, Macintosh version.)

graphics character display—Permits onscreen display of software-based (rather than firmware-based) characters in the computer's graphics mode; some programs let you construct your own characters and

TABLE 3-1 (continued)

BELLS AND WHISTLES: ADVANCED WORD PROCESSING FEATURES

store them for use. Requires bit-mapped graphics display (IBM PC and color graphics card or Macintosh) and dot-matrix printer. (Example: ProofWriter International.)

gutters—Automatically inserts extra space on the left margin of odd-numbered pages and the right margin of even-numbered pages for convenience when binding documents printed on both sides of a page. A desirable feature for writers of technical manuscripts to be reproduced directly from program printouts. (Example: WordStar 2000.)

headers and footers—Inserts text (such as a short version of a document's title) on every page (or only odd or even pages) in the top or bottom margin. Available with most programs. (Example: WordStar 3.3.)

horizontal scrolling—Permits use of extraordinarily wide paper and line lengths of up to 14 inches. (Example: Microsoft Word.)

index generation—Generates an index automatically from marked passages in the text. A desirable feature for writers of technical manuscripts to be reproduced directly from program printouts. (Example: Edix/Wordix with Indix option.)

justification—Evens the right margin. See also **microjustification** and **proportional spacing**, without which justification is unsightly and undesirable. (Example: WordStar 2000.)

keep lines together—Allows user to define a block of text that should always be printed on one page; if the whole block cannot be printed, the text is moved as a block to the next page. Can be used to avoid formatting errors such as splitting up tables or positioning a heading at the bottom of the page. A rare and very desirable feature for academic writing. (Example: Microsoft Word 2.0.)

macro—Stores a set of commands in a file and allows user to enter a single command to begin their execution. (Example: Edix/Wordix.)

microjustification—Evens out the gaps between words left by justification by inserting fractional spaces within words. See **justification.**

mouse—As cursor control device, permits rapid cursor repositioning for text insertion and block marking. (Example: Microsoft Word.)

multiple columns—Prints text using two, three, or more vertical columns on the page. A very desirable feature for writers of academic newsletters. (Example: Edix/Wordix, Microsoft Word.)

multiple windows—Displays two or more parts of the same document (or two or more different documents) on the screen. Virtually indispensable for accurate editing. (See Chapter 5; example: Microsoft Word.)

online spelling correction—Allows user to check the spelling of a word, paragraph, or entire document while writing. (Example: WordStar 2000.)

online thesaurus—Shows synonyms of a selected word while writing. (See Chapter 5; example: Perfect Writer.)

onscreen display of character formats—Shows italics, boldface, underlining, subscripts, and superscripts on the video display screen while writing. A desirable feature for text editing since you won't have to look at embedded commands. (Example: Microsoft Word.)

onscreen tutorial—Introduction to the program using the device of computer-assisted instruction (Example: Microsoft Word.)

operating system access—Allows access to DOS without leaving the word processing program; a valuable feature for making additional room on a disk for saving a document. (Example: Microsoft Word.)

orphan and widow suppression—Automatically suppresses single words (orphans) or single lines (widows) left alone at the top or bottom of pages. (Example: Microsoft Word.)

print merging—Generates personalized form letters from a mailing list. (Example: WordStar 3.3 or 2000 with optional MailMerge program.)

printer font selection—Allows full control over multiple type fonts available with many printers. A desirable feature available only with the newer programs. (Examples: Microsoft Word and WordStar 2000.)

programmable keyboard commands—Allows user to define customized keyboard commands for text

TABLE 3-1 (continued)
BELLS AND WHISTLES: ADVANCED WORD PROCESSING FEATURES

formatting. Very rare and highly desirable feature for complex formatting of academic manuscripts. (Example: Microsoft Word.)

proportional spacing—Assigns varying amounts of space to printed characters for elegant printing; drives printers capable of proportional spacing. (See Chapter 9; example: WordStar 2000, but not WordStar 3.3.)

reverse video display—Highlights marked blocks of text. This desirable feature makes much more intuitive sense for block operations than using embedded characters (the way WordStar 3.3 does). (Example: Microsoft Word.)

ruler—Measures the "page" displayed on the screen; shows current margin settings and tab stops (available with most programs).

style sheet—Allows user to define and save a complex list of formatting characteristics (margins, pagination, etc.); may be attached to documents as needed, making it unnecessary to do the formatting over again manually. A very desirable, time-saving feature well suited to academic writing. (Examples: Microsoft Word and WordStar 2000.)

superscripts/subscripts—Positions characters above or below the line; essential for most scholarly writing. Available with most but not all programs.

table-of-contents generation—Generates a table of contents from marked chapter titles, headings, and subheadings. An attractive feature for writers of technical manuscripts that will be directly reproduced from program printouts. (Example: Edix/Wordix.)

undo—Allows user to restore the system to the condition existing before the last command was given; a valuable fail-safe feature. Available only with the newer programs. (Example: WordStar 2000, but not WordStar 3.3.)

unlimited document length—Document length limited only by capacity of disk. Indispensable feature for scholarly writing. (Example: WordStar 3.3 but not early versions of MacWrite.)

variable margins—Allows user to change the default or preset margins (available with most word processing programs).

variable tabs—Allows user to change the default or preset tab stops (available with most programs).

Scholars will almost surely want to choose a full-featured program, one that includes many of the options listed in Table 3-1.

Indispensable features for scholarly writing are *automatic pagination, endnotes, fail-safe features, footnotes, forced page breaks, headers and footers, justification, superscripts/subscripts, variable margins* and *tabs,* and *unlimited document length.*

Desirable features include *automatic reformatting, background printing, chain printing, floating footnotes, graphics, keeping lines together, multiple columns, multiple windows, onscreen display of character formats, orphan and widow suppression, operating system access, print merging, printer font selection, proportional spacing, reverse video display, ruler, style sheet,* and *undo.*

For foreign language or technical word processing, desirable features include the *extended character set* and *graphics character display.*

For work in mathematics, desirable features are *automatic equation numbering* and *equation mode.*

For writing technical manuals, newsletters, or proposals to be directly reproduced from program printouts, select a program that offers *automatic cross-referencing, automatic hyphenation, index generation, gutters, multiple columns,* and *table-of-contents generation.*

A TYPOLOGY OF WORD PROCESSING PROGRAMS

Word processing programs vary in the features they offer. Some programs, for example, position footnotes at the bottom of the page but will not position them at the end of the document as endnotes. Others let you position footnotes anywhere you please, but will not number them. Still another numbers footnotes and endnotes but will not double-space them. Much of the detective work you'll have to do when you choose a program rightly focuses on finding one with the features you need.

A list of program features, however, does not tell the whole story about a word processing program. Equally important is the program's underlying architecture, or the programming design used to create it. The choice of a particular architecture or design approach lends a characteristic stamp to a word processing program, one that's shared by all the software using the same design. Features aside, you may find one design approach vastly preferable to another for the kind of writing you want to do.

There are just four basic types: *text editors/batch formatters, online formatters, advanced online formatters,* and *integrated word processing programs.*

TEXT EDITORS/BATCH FORMATTERS

Word processing software that fits into this category is immediately recognizable because two separate programs—a text editor and a text formatter—are necessary to complete the writing process. Sometimes the fact that two programs are needed is obvious from the program's name (for instance, Edix/Wordix [Emerging Technology]), but in other cases it's not (for instance, Perfect Writer [Thorn/EMI Software] or ProofWriter [Image Processing Systems]).

Text Editors

Text editors, the earliest type of word processing programs, were devised not for writers but for programmers. Programs are written and edited as text files, that is, as documents containing nothing but the standard characters available on the computer's keyboard. Once written, the program is translated and saved to disk in a form that the computer can read and execute as a program. The program is printed only to provide backup security; there is little concern for its appearance on the printed page.

Text editors, therefore, contain no provisions for the formatting and printing of documents; their job, rather, is to provide the user with the most efficient possible tool for entering and revising text on the display screen and saving it to disk. As the text is entered, it is displayed in a standard (and usually unalterable) format of single-spaced paragraphs aligned along the left margin. Few provisions (if any) are made for showing the user how the text will appear when it is printed. For writing purposes, text editors are obviously incomplete; that is why batch formatters (see below) have been devised to work with them.

ADVANTAGES OF TEXT EDITORS. Some writers prefer text editors because they permit the writer to concentrate on writing and editing, they present a visually uncluttered screen display, and they operate at high speed.

A text editor encourages the writer to concentrate on the text itself—that is, on writing and revising—to the exclusion of formatting considerations. It is possible, to be sure, to concern oneself with formatting while writing the text with text editors, but—for reasons that will be explored below when stand-alone formatting programs are discussed—this writing strategy is actively discouraged. Some writers prefer text editors for this reason: there is little temptation to be waylaid by formatting considerations during the writing and revising process.

A second advantage of text editing programs is that they present uncluttered screen displays. All that is seen (with the exception of a status line containing, perhaps, the name of the document and the location of the cursor) is the text, which is almost invariably placed into single-spaced paragraphs with flush left alignment.

Text editors operate rapidly. Because such programs lack formatting and printing functions, they are generally compact, leaving room in the main memory for the entire document.

DISADVANTAGES OF TEXT EDITORS. The chief disadvantages of text editors for scholarly purposes are entirely those of the batch formatting programs with which they must operate. See "Batch Formatting Programs" below for details.

EXAMPLE: EDIX. Edix (Emerging Technology Consultants, Inc., 2031 Broadway, Boulder, CO 80302, 303/447-9495, available for IBM PC and PC-compatible computers) is a text editing program of exceptional quality. It exemplifies the strengths of text editors for writing purposes.

Edix comes equipped with a full panoply of features appropriate for writing and revising the text, including a full set of block commands, search and replace, variable tabs and margins, and multiple windows. It does not include any features or commands for formatting or printing. (A companion formatting program, Wordix, provides these features.)

Text is entered directly into the computer's main memory up to the limits imposed by the computer's memory capacity. An IBM Personal Computer with

320K of main memory, for example, can accommodate an Edix document of approximately 50,000 words. Because the entire text is present in the main memory, scrolling and other commands execute at high speeds. Text saved to disk is stored in standard ASCII format, meaning that it can be easily used by many other programs.

Batch Formatting Programs

Batch formatting programs, separate programs that are designed exclusively for formatting the text of a document, are designed to equip text editors with the formatting and printing features necessary for writing (not just programming). They were created after it was realized that text editors were suitable for tasks other than writing programs.

The term "batch" provides an important clue to the way these programs work. Chapter 2 described the old, inconvenient method of batch processing, in which you fed the program and data into the computer, waited while it carried out the processing, and looked at the results when the printer spat them back at you. That's exactly how batch formatting programs work—and that's exactly what's wrong with them.

Batch formatting programs require the user to insert *embedded formatting commands* in the document's text using a special *marking character,* such as @ or %. One formatting program, for instance, requires the insertion of the following inserted or embedded command to justify the right margin of the text that follows the command:

.BW 65

The period is the marking character, which alerts the formatting program that a command is to follow. BW stands for "body width," or the length of lines in the body of the document, and 65 is an *argument,* or specification (in this case, 65 characters).

The embedded commands are placed in the text by using the text editor. After the text has been marked in this way, the formatting program reads the text and produces an *output file,* which may be viewed on the screen for a final check and then routed to the printer.

DISADVANTAGES OF BATCH FORMATTING PROGRAMS. Entering the embedded commands into the text is a tedious and difficult business. Worse, the outcome of the commands is not known for certain until the document is printed or displayed in its printed form on the computer's screen. Figure 3–4, for instance, shows a document prepared for formatting by Perfect Formatter (the companion program of the text editor Perfect Writer [Thorn-EMI Computer Software, Inc., 3187-C Airway Avenue, Costa Mesa, CA 92626, available for CP/M-80, IBM-PC, and PC-compatible computers]). These embedded commands produce the result shown in Figure 3–5—that is, they do if the commands are properly placed and punctuated.

```
@style(spacing 2 lines)

@Center(@Bold[Introduction])

    A pioneering work in the study of schizophrenia is Gregory Bateson's
1969 paper entitled "Double Bind."@footnote{Reprinted in his
@underline[Steps to an Ecology of Mind] (New York:  Ballantine Books,
1972), pp. 271-278).}
```

FIGURE 3-4. Document with Embedded Commands

As these two figures illustrate, using batch formatting programs can be tedious and difficult because of the high potential for erroneous use of the embedded commands. With Perfect Formatter, for instance, the text to be formatted must be enclosed in parentheses or brackets (with certain exceptions). Leaving one of the parentheses or brackets out will produce spurious results, but the user may not learn of the error until the document has been printed.

Using batch formatting programs almost always results in a tedious cycle of changing the document's embedded commands, saving the document to disk, running the formatting program, viewing the output file, finding new errors, reloading the document, making more changes, and so on.

The better batch formatting programs reduce the tedium of this process in two ways: by warning the user of inappropriate uses of formatting commands before the document is printed and by permitting the user to preview the output file on screen before it is printed. Even so, the efficiency and productivity gains made possible by text editors may be lost after spending hours formatting and reformatting the document so that it prints properly.

Another serious drawback of batch formatting programs is that the embedded commands vitiate the document's onscreen readability, making further editing difficult. As it is displayed on the screen, a document fully prepared for formatting and printing appears even to the practiced eye as a wilderness of special symbols, parentheses, and commands.

```
                          Introduction


A  pioneering    work  in   the study   of   schizophrenia   is

Gregory Bateson's 1969 paper entitled "Double Bind."¹


-------------


     ¹Steps  to   an Ecology  of Mind   (New York:    Ballantine
Books, 1972), pp. 271-278).
```

FIGURE 3-5. Printed Document

ADVANTAGES OF BATCH FORMATTING PROGRAMS. Batch formatting programs are so inconvenient that they can be recommended only to those who wish to take advantage of their merits (which, though few, do indeed exist).

One advantage of the text editor/batch formatter link is that it's possible to ignore formatting considerations (other than paragraphing) entirely while you're writing. For some writers, that's a big plus. Author David Stang started out with the page-oriented program WordStar, which simulates on the screen the text's appearance when printed—it's a "what you see is what you get" word processing program. But he found himself distracted by the "visual thrill on the screen." Stang found himself getting "caught up in the [onscreen] formatting and in fooling with margin width, page breaks, headers, and end-of-paragraph widows," wasting precious writing time. Finally, Stang switched to Edix/Wordix, and the problem ceased. "Since with these programs what you see is not what you get, the thrill was gone."[3] You can put the formatting off until later and concentrate on writing.

Even though formatting a document with a batch formatter isn't fun or thrilling, these programs offer a wide variety of formatting and printing options even when used on computers with limited memories. Generally included are all or almost all of the following formatting features: automatic footnote numbering, automatic pagination, chain printing, floating footnotes, headers and footers, gutters, microjustification, multiple columns, print merging, printer font selection, proportional spacing, and table-of-contents generation.

Moreover, because batch formatting programs concentrate on formatting and printing tasks, they are capable of an exceptional degree of control over the printing process. Some programs utilize the graphics mode of inexpensive dot matrix printers (see Chapter 8) to produce a printout that is close to typeset copy in quality. Others are available with optional hardware accessories that expand a computer's built-in character set to include foreign language, Greek, technical, mathematical, and engineering symbols.

EXAMPLE: WORDIX. Wordix (Emerging Technology Consultants, Inc., 1877 Broadway, Boulder, CO 80302, available for 8-bit, Z80-based computers and the IBM Personal Computer or compatibles), a formatting program designed to work with Edix and similar text editors, well illustrates the strengths and limitations of batch formatting programs. It is a comprehensive program, offering virtually every text formatting feature imaginable (with the unfortunate exception of automatic footnote numbering).

EXAMPLE: FANCY FONT. Fancy Font (SoftCraft, Inc., 222 State Street, Madison, WI 53703, available for most Z80-based computers and the IBM Personal Computer or compatibles) is a batch text formatting program with special printing capabilities.

[3]Cited in Kurt Supplee, "The PC Tapping at the Chamber Door," *PC: The Independent Guide to IBM Personal Computers* (May 29, 1984), p. 254.

The program, like Wordix, will work with standard text files created with virtually any text editor or word processing programs. Embedded commands must be added to the text file. Many formatting features are included, but Fancy Font does not offer as many of them as Wordix does. Missing, for example, are footnotes, index generation, multiple columns, and table-of-contents generation. What distinguishes Fancy Font from Wordix and other batch formatting programs, however, is what happens when the document is printed.

When used with popular and inexpensive dot matrix printers such as the Epson FX-80, Epson RX-80, IBM Graphics Printer, Star Gemini 10X, and C. Itoh Prowriter, Fancy Font produces a printout the quality of which approaches that of high-resolution laser printers and typesetting machines. Printing takes place, however, at very slow speeds.

Included with the program are several fonts (including Script and Old English) and a character data base from which it is possible to construct a very wide variety of fonts, including foreign language fonts (Figure 3–6).

A major disadvantage of Fancy Font for foreign language word processing, however, is that you don't see the foreign language characters on the screen. The characters in the fonts are "mapped" to the standard ASCII characters. When you're using one of the special fonts, for instance, the characters *dkgidhsi* might print out as a beautifully printed, correct word in classical Greek. Obviously, this technique is far from appropriate for foreign language word processing since it is difficult to proofread the foreign language words on screen. Far better are programs designed to work with the foreign language firmware (such as the IBM Personal Computer's built-in extended character set) or a bit-mapped graphics display (such as the IBM Personal Computer with the color graphics card option or the Apple Macintosh).

EXAMPLE: PROOFWRITER. ProofWriter and ProofWriter International (Image Processing Systems, 6409 Appalachian Way, P.O. Box 5016, Madison, WI 53705, available for IBM Personal Computer and compatibles or the Texas Instruments PC) offer a text editor and batch formatting program comparable to Edix and Wordix. What distinguishes this package is its exceptional cabilities for displaying and printing foreign language, technical, and scientific characters. ProofWriter International permits the user to redefine the IBM PC keyboard so that foreign language or mathematical characters are entered in place of the normal ones.

The program takes advantage of the foreign language and technical characters included in the IBM PC's built-in character set (see Chapter 2), which are encoded in a ROM chip on the computer's main circuit board. If these characters are not sufficient, Image Processing Systems offers a variety of optional ROM chips that may be installed simply by prying loose the standard IBM chip and pressing the replacement into the socket. Offered are ROM chips containing scientific symbols, the full Greek and Russian alphabets, and

ω a b c d e f g h i j k l m n o p q r s t u v w x y z ff fi fl ffi ffl ı ε θ φ ʒ ϼ ff fi fl ffi ffl ı

0 1 2 3 4 5 6 7 8 9 . , : ; ! ? ' " ° * / ( ) [ ] { } ⟨ ⟩ | ‖ – +

± ∓ × · ÷ = ≠ ≡ < > ≤ ≥ ∝ ∼ ^ ´ ` ˘ ' ‚ ' ' √ ⊂ ∪ ⊃ ∈ → ↑ ← ↓ ∂ ∇ √ ∫ ∮ ∞ % &

@ $ # § † ‡ ⨆ ⊙ ☿ ♀ ⊕ ♂ ♃ ♄ ♆ ♅ ☽ ☌ *

♈ ♉ ♈ ♈ ♊ ♋ ♌ ♍ ♎ ♏ ♐ ♑ ♒ ≈ ✳ · ‚ ′ ∘ ∘ •

♯ ♮ ♭ – – ‚ ' φ ☕ ⊞ · ‚ ′ ∘ ∘ • ♯ ♮ ♭ –

– ⌡ ′ φ ☹ ⊞ Π Σ ( ) | | } { \ /√ | A B

C D E F G H I J K L M N O P Q R S T U V

W X Y Z 𝒜 ℬ 𝒞 𝒟 ℰ ℱ 𝒢 ℋ ℐ 𝒥 𝒦 ℒ ℳ 𝒩 𝒪

𝒫 𝒬 ℛ 𝒮 𝒯 𝒰 𝒱 𝒲 𝒳 𝒴 𝒵 a b c d e f g h i j

k l m n o p q r s t u v w x y z a b c d

e f g h i j k l m n o p q r s t u v w x

y z   0 1 2 3 4 5 6 7 8 9 . , : ; !

? ' ' & $ / ( ) * – + = ' " °   0 1

2 3 4 5 6 7 8 9 . , : ; ! ? ' ' & $ / (

) * – + = ' " ° А Б В Г Д Е Ж З И Й К Л

М Н О П Р С Т У Ф Х Ц Ч Ш Щ Ъ Ы Ь Э Ю Я

FIGURE 3–6. A Portion of the Fancy Font Character Data Base

alphabetical subscripts. An additional advantage of ProofWriter and ProofWriter International is a special equation mode that facilitates the entry of multiline mathematical expressions (Figure 3-7).

EXAMPLE: PROOFWRITER GRAPHICS. ProofWriter Graphics (Image Processing Systems, 6409 Appalachian Way, P.O. Box 5016, Madison, WI 53705, available for IBM Personal Computer and compatibles) is a text editor/batch formatter identical to ProofWriter and ProofWriter International, except that the program is designed to work with the bit-mapped video display made possible by the PC's optional color graphics adapter (see Chapter 2). The program comes with a massive, disk-based data base of extended character sets corresponding to all the character sets available with the optional ROM chips just mentioned; these are listed in Table 3-2. Because the program drives the computer in its graphics mode, however, the ROM chips aren't necessary: the character sets can be read from disk. If the thousands of foreign language, scientific, technical, and Greek characters supplied don't suffice, you can construct your own characters and save them to disk.

$$w(\rho)=\frac{pa^4}{64D}\frac{5+\gamma}{1+\gamma}-\frac{2(3+\gamma)}{1+\gamma}\rho^4+\frac{32\rho^4}{3+\gamma}\sum_{m=3,6,9}\left\{\left[\frac{2}{m(m-1)(m+1)}+\frac{2(3+\gamma)}{m(m-1)(1-\gamma)}\right]-\rho^m\cos m\theta\left[\frac{1}{m(m-1)}+\frac{2(1+\gamma)}{(1-\gamma)m^2(m-1)}-\frac{\rho^2}{m(m+1)}\right]\right\}$$

$$\Xi = R_L\frac{\frac{e}{hc}\int_0^\infty \eta(\lambda)\Phi_{s,\lambda}(\lambda)\lambda d\lambda}{\int_0^\infty \Phi_{s,\lambda}(\lambda)d\lambda}$$

$$-\frac{\hbar^2}{2m}\frac{\partial^2\Psi}{\partial x^2}+V(\vec{r})\Psi = E\Psi$$

$$\sigma^2_{b_i} = \left\{\frac{1}{\sum_{u=1}^{n_i} x^2_{iu}} + \frac{\frac{\left[\sum_{u=1}^{n_i} x_{iu}\right]^2}{\left[\sum_{u=1}^{n_i} x^2_{iu}\right]^2}}{\sum_{i=1}^{m} n_i\left[1-\frac{n_i\bar{x}_i^2}{\sum_{u=1}^{n_i} x^2_{iu}}\right]}\right\}\sigma^2$$

FIGURE 3-7. ProofWriter Equation Mode

ONLINE FORMATTERS

Online formatters such as WordStar offer *interactive* or *online formatting*—that is, a formatting process in which formatting commands, entered by menus or keyboard commands, are directly reflected in the appearance of the text on the video display. These programs are often referred to as "what you see is what you get" word processors. You may run into the ugly acronym WYSIWYG when they're discussed.

Online formatters have their origins in the late 1970s in direct response to the batch formatter's limitations. They make it possible to work interactively with a representation of the page visible on the video display. If the writer wishes to see the effect of narrowing the margins, for example, a simple command makes the change and the screen shows the results, just the way the document will be printed on paper.

Advantages of Online Formatters

True online formatters do away with embedded commands entirely, and for this reason they are much easier to use than batch formatting programs. The formatting process is more intuitively sensible and much more easily managed: in

TABLE 3-2
ALTERNATE CHARACTER SETS: PROOFWRITER GRAPHICS

Character Set	Contents
IBM extended	Foreign language, some Greek, some technical, and some graphics characters
X2 Scientific	Standard-size scientific characters, including numeric subscripts and superscripts
X3 Scientific	Scientific characters including large sigma and pi
X4 Scientific/logic	Scientific and logic characters
A3 Scientific/Greek	Scientific characters with Greek characters and alphanumeric subscripts and superscripts
S1 Statistics	Characters for work in statistics, including alphanumeric subscripts
M1 Mathematics	Characters for work in mathematics, including alphanumeric subscripts and superscripts
C2 European/Greek	Western European characters, graphics characters, some Greek
C3 European/Greek	Same as C2, except more Greek and fewer graphics characters
GE General European	Full set of Western European characters and some Greek
R1 Russian (Slavic Cyrillic)	Full character set and some Greek
R3 Slavic scholars' set	All necessary characters for work in Slavic languages
G1 Classical Greek	All necessary characters for work in Classical Greek
AR Romanized Arabic	Characters for transliterating Arabic
SC Semitic	Characters for Hebrew, Ugaritic, and Egyptian

the place of embedded commands are keyboard or menu commands that directly and visibly affect the formatting of the text. In one program, for example, holding down the CONTROL key and pressing C centers the selected text on the screen, and that is precisely the way it will be printed.

You'll probably write and print more rapidly with an online formatter than you would with a text editor/batch formatting team. There's no mystery about the formatting command's effect; it's immediately visible. And if the effect is unsatisfactory, it's immediately repairable, without repeating the time-consuming operation of saving the document to disk, running the formatting program, and viewing the results.

Because there are no extraneous embedded commands to interfere with the document's readability, the documents produced by online formatters are easier to proofread on the screen. Moreover, line and page breaks are shown just the way they will appear when printed, making it possible to pay attention to design considerations such as balance and proportion.

Disadvantages of Online Formatters

A major drawback to early online formatters such as WordStar is that their design imposes limits on the number of features that can be included. The program must constantly reformat the document so that page breaks, line breaks, and page numbers are correctly displayed, and the complexities involved usually rule out such advanced features as automatic cross-referencing, footnotes, index generation, multiple columns, and table-of-contents generation. Later refinement cured this problem, but only by increasing program complexity and decreasing speed (see "Advanced Online Formatters," below).

An additional drawback of online formatters is that they use nonstandard (that is, non-ASCII) file formats. This fact can have serious consequences. For instance, many desirable accessory programs, such as spelling and readability checkers, will not work with non-ASCII text files unless they're specifically designed to do so. If you plan to choose any word processing program that does not use the ASCII file format, make sure that the accessory programs you want (see Chapters 6 through 8) are available for it.

Example: MacWrite

MacWrite (Apple Computer, 20525 Mariani Ave., Cupertino, CA 95014, available only for the Apple Macintosh) is a true online formatter in the most genuine sense of the term; the video display shows precisely what will appear on the printed page, right down to the size and style of the several character fonts which the program makes available. Active page breaks, which are adjusted when insertions or deletions are made, are displayed by a dotted line across the screen.

Because it was written for the limited memory of the 128K Macintosh, MacWrite is limited in its features. No provisions are made for such features as footnotes, automatic index generation, printing with multiple columns, automatic section numbering, and the like. Nevertheless, the program offers some attractive features, including onscreen display of the Mac's standard set of foreign language and mathematical characters, the ability to blend graphic images with text, printer font selection (and onscreen display of the selected font), and a printer control system that (with the Apple Imagewriter printer) produces a high-quality printout that corresponds precisely to the video display.

Example: WordStar

WordStar (MicroPro International Corporation, 33 San Pablo Avenue, San Rafael, CA 94903, available for most Z80- and 8088-based computers) is not a true online formatter; character formats (such as boldface, italics, and underlining) and printing characteristics (such as line height and running heads) are handled by the insertion of embedded commands. Nevertheless, WordStar displays most paragraph formats (such as line spacing, line width, centering, and right margin justification) precisely the way they will appear when printed. The program displays active page breaks, which are adjusted as insertions and deletions are made.

Like MacWrite, WordStar was written for small memories (64K or 128K) and it lacks, therefore, many features found in batch formatters, such as footnotes, index generation, multiple columns, print merging, printer font selection, proportional spacing, section numbering, table-of-contents generation, and windows. Accessory programs are available that equip WordStar with some of these features, but at the cost of turning the program into a batch formatter. For more information, see the section on WordStar accessories under Resources at the end of this chapter.

ADVANCED ONLINE FORMATTERS

Advanced online formatters combine the chief advantage of batch formatting programs (a wide variety of formatting features) with the early online formatter's interactive, visual representation of the page. The result: sophisticated formatting features such as footnoting are available online, without exacting the price of embedded commands or batch processing.

These programs were made possible by the dramatic expansion of personal computer memories that took place between 1982 and 1984. Before 1982, a memory of 64K was the practical maximum, so batch formatters and online formatters alike were written with 64K memories in mind. But the arrival of 16- and 32-bit personal computers, coupled with the decline in cost of 64K memory chips to less than $1 each, soon established 256K as a common memory size. (Growing numbers of Macintoshes and IBM PCs are running 512K or more.) Larger memories gave programmers more "headroom" to create bigger, more complex programs, and by 1984 several advanced online formatters appeared.

Whether the results are praiseworthy is questionable. Inevitably, advanced online formatters are big, sluggish, and complex programs. They tax processing hardware and beginners' patience, sometimes to their limits. To be sure, these programs give you all the formatting power you'll ever need, and that power is joined by a precise, onscreen representation of the page that often includes character formats (such as italics and boldface) as well as foreign language or technical characters. But there's more to creating good software than including every conceivable feature. Program speed and ease of use are important too, but in the rush to create these programs such considerations were too often put aside.

Advantages of Advanced Online Formatters

The best advanced online formatters combine the advantages of batch formatting programs (a full panoply of formatting features) with the page-oriented program's interactive, visual representation of the page. The result is appealing indeed: a program that makes sophisticated word processing features such as automatic index generation or complex patterns of running heads available without exacting the price of embedded commands.

Disadvantages of Advanced Online Formatters

SLUGGISH PERFORMANCE. Advanced online formatters tend to be memory-hungry, a fact that is not surprising when it is remembered that they combine the characteristics of batch formatting programs and page-oriented programs. For that reason, they are not available for 8-bit computers: as a rough guideline, these programs require a minimum of 128K or 192K of main memory. Even with a 16-bit computer with its larger memory capacity, however, it is rarely possible to fit the whole program into the memory at one time, meaning that portions of the program have to be read from disk when needed. And that means slow operation and tedious waits with systems lacking a hard disk.

Maximum performance from these programs is obtained with systems which are, at this writing, state-of-the-art (such as the IBM Personal Computer AT, with its ultrafast 80286 microprocessor, 640K main memory, and 20-megabyte hard disk). Performance on IBM Personal Computers equipped with the standard 8088 chip, 256K of main memory, and dual floppy disk drives is acceptable but sluggish in comparison to fast programs such as Edix.

NON-ASCII FILE FORMAT. Like early online formatters, advanced online formatters do not use the ASCII file format. Non-ASCII file formats can cause problems when you want to use the program with accessory software (see

Chapters 6 through 8). Before buying an advanced online formatter, make sure the accessory programs you want can work with its file format.

Example: Microsoft Word

Microsoft Word (Microsoft Corporation, 10700 Northrup Way, Box 97200, Bellevue, WA 98009, available for IBM PC, PC-compatible, and Apple Macintosh computers) is an advanced word processing program of exceptional power and flexibility.

The IBM PC and PC-compatible version of the program offers almost every advanced word processing feature listed in Table 3–1, including automatic reformatting, background printing, footnotes, glossaries, hyphenation, multiple columns, online spelling correction, onscreen display of character formats, onscreen display of paragraph formats, print merging, programmable keyboard commands, proportional spacing, style sheets, and windows. (Not offered are index generation, section numbering, and table-of-contents generation; the Apple Macintosh version also does not include online spelling correction or style sheets.) The footnote feature is of exceptional quality and flexibility. All this complexity, however, makes Word difficult to learn.

The program's many features are combined with a video display that approaches a true page orientation. Character formats, such as italics, boldface, and underlining, are displayed precisely the way they will print, as are paragraph formats such as line width, line spacing, and centering. No embedded commands are used. Page breaks are not, however, displayed while you're waiting. Page break markers are inserted in the text only when it is printed or deliberately paginated using a special pagination command. The markers may then be observed, but insertions and deletions will render the markers inaccurate until the document is paginated once again.

Like some batch formatting programs, Microsoft Word offers an exceptionally high degree of control over printing and printers. Its accuracy compares favorably with expensive typesetting machinery, and when coupled with highly accurate printers such as the Hewlett-Packard Laser Printer, the program can produce a printout which is virtually indistinguishable from set type. The combination of Microsoft Word and a laser printer (see Chapter 9) will bring phototypesetting capabilities to many organizations that could not previously afford them.

Microsoft Word, like MacWrite, can be used with a mouse control device, but unlike MacWrite there are keyboard equivalents of mouse control and editing techniques.

Microsoft Word's performance on the IBM PC and Apple Macintosh is acceptable, but working with the program makes it more than clear that it taxes these computer's processing capabilities to their limits. Opening additional windows on the display screen, for instance, leads to noticeable degradations in speed.

Example: WordStar 2000

WordStar 2000 (MicroPro International Corporation, 33 San Pablo Avenue, San Rafael, CA 94903, for IBM PC and PC-compatible computers), like Microsoft Word, is an advanced online formatter that blends the formatting capabilities of batch formatting programs with a page orientation. In its optional WordStar 2000 Plus configuration, the program offers virtually every word processing feature ever conceived, including all those offered by Microsoft Word (except programmable keyboard commands) with the addition of index generation, section numbering, table-of-contents generation, and telecommunications. All this is combined with a page orientation that rivals Microsoft Word's (and indeed surpasses it in that page breaks are shown while you're writing). The result is a program of fabulous versatility, but a hard disk is recommended to cure its sluggish performance.

INTEGRATED WORD PROCESSING PROGRAMS

With the 1984 arrival of the 512K Macintosh and IBM PCs running 512K or more of main memory, the stage was set for some fresh thinking about word processing software. All that additional memory opened the possibility of adding new kinds of program functions to the old standard ones.

Happily, a few programmers thought beyond the traditional confines of word processing programs, and the result is a new genre of *integrated word processing programs:* word processing programs that include one or more word processing accessories not usually included with word processing software, such as word choice checkers or idea processors. (Note that integrated word processing programs should be distinguished from the kind of integrated programs which, like Symphony, attempt to put all five basic software functions [word processing, data base management, spreadsheet, graphics, and communications] together into a single package. We are speaking here of programs that integrate several formerly separate *word processing* programs and accessories.)

A word processing program, after all, is only one of several programs useful for writing. Other programs, such as idea processing programs and word choice checkers, can work with word processing software to help you do a better job organizing and proofreading your text.

But using these accessory programs forces you back into the old batch processing mold. You write your document, save it to disk, leave the word processing program, and run the accessory program on it. Now here's the bright idea: why not have these tools available online, or active in the computer's memory and within the reach of your word processing program's commands, so that you can use them while you're writing?

WordStar 2000 exemplifies this idea's potential in a limited way. Its spelling correction program, CorrectStar, is available online while you're writing;

you can check, for instance, the spelling of a particular word or paragraph and then go on writing. But this is hardly a radical innovation. A program conventionally sold with word processing software was simply moved into the program so that it was available online. A truly integrated word processing program would make a variety of word processing accessories available online.

The idea of integrated word processing software is so new that one can speak only provisionally of its inherent advantages and disadvantages. The advantage of such software is that you would have several word processing accessories available online while writing, but just how useful this feature would be depends almost entirely on which accessories were provided. A poet, for instance, would have little use for an automatic index generation program, but would surely find helpful a program that scans an 80,000 word dictionary for all the words that rhyme with the one on which the cursor is positioned.

As for disadvantages, one may look for instruction at the efforts to blend all five software functions (word processing, data base management, spreadsheet, graphics, and communication) in such programs as Symphony. Often, one function is highly developed—Symphony's spreadsheet, for instance, is the state-of-the-art—but the others may have been pared down or deprived of features so that they would fit.

Example: Framework

Framework (Ashton-Tate, 10150 West Jefferson Blvd., Culver City, CA 90230, for the IBM PC and PC-compatibles) isn't an integrated word processing program in the sense used here, but it points the way towards one direction such software may take. It includes (among other things) a sophisticated *idea processor* or outlining program linked to a word processor (an online formatter with limited features).

Idea processing programs such as ThinkTank let you create and restructure an outline. By linking an idea processor with its word processor, Framework goes a step further: each heading in the outline contains a hidden block of text. You can look at your document, then, either in terms of its overall structure (the outline view, in which the text is hidden) or the text itself (the text view, in which the outline is hidden). What is more, making changes in the idea processor's outline actually restructures the text of the document.

The combination of an idea processor and word processor makes for a powerful and elegant solution to a major drawback of word processing: the limited view of your document provided by that 24-line display and slow scrolling pace. Unfortunately, the current version of Framework's word processor does not include features necessary for scholarly writing, such as unlimited document length and superscripts.

Example: Nota Bene

The promise of things to come is evident in Nota Bene (Dragonfly Software, 409 Fulton Street, Suite 202, Brooklyn, NY 11201, for the IBM PC and PC-compatibles), a complex, difficult program that combines an advanced, full-featured online formatter with a text-oriented, free-format data base management program. Among other things, this combination permits a writer to pause while writing a document, search a large file of notes (using logical or Boolean operators) for needed material, and paste the material directly into the document.

WORD PROCESSING SOFTWARE AND ACADEMIC WRITING

Making an intelligent selection of a word processing program for scholarly purposes requires an assessment of the tasks that will be demanded of it. For instance, a simple, easy-to-use online formatter such as MacWrite may prove adequate for writing course syllabi, but technical reports may require the formatting prowess of a batch formatter or advanced online formatter.

Academic and scholarly writers generally prepare four kinds of documents:

Complex documents for direct reproduction   Included in this category are technical manuals, newsletters, research reports, grant proposals, and other complex documents that will be directly reproduced from the program's printouts.

Short, well-designed documents   Course syllabi, resumes, class handouts, and examinations are examples of documents for which the balance, proportion, and arrangement of elements on the printed page is of crucial importance.

Manuscripts to be submitted for publication   With material for publication, what matters above all else is that the document meet the publisher's style guidelines. Features related to the cosmetic appearance of the document, such as justification, headers/footers, or proportional spacing, are of little or no consequence. Programs employed for this purpose must be able to produce a document in the format required by the publisher, which generally means that all material, including quotations and footnotes, must be double-spaced.

Manuscripts submitted on disk   Increasingly, academic authors are requested to submit their manuscripts on disk. Publishers can save money in the production process by sending the disk (once the editor's revisions have been made) to a typesetting service, which can produce set type from the disk files. No rekeying is necessary. This kind of manuscript submission requires a word processor capable of producing a straight ASCII file—one consisting only of the 128 characters recognized in the

American Standard Code for Information Interchange—with no formatting whatsoever.

COMPLEX DOCUMENTS FOR DIRECT REPRODUCTION

Batch formatting programs and advanced online formatters are excellent choices for writers who create complex documents for direct reproduction.

Full-featured programs such as Wordix or WordStar 2000 Plus, with their features for index generation, automatic section numbering, and table-of-contents generation, are especially good choices for the production of technical manuals and research reports.

Programs that offer exceptional degrees of printer control, such as Fancy Font and Microsoft Word, are especially good choices for the production of documents that require high print quality.

SHORT, WELL-DESIGNED DOCUMENTS

Writers who produce short documents in which balance and proportion are important elements will do well to choose a page-oriented program such as MacWrite or an advanced online formatter that shows page breaks, such as WordStar 2000.

MacWrite, with its strong page orientation and its ability to produce printouts of high quality, is exceptionally well suited to the production of course syllabi, course handouts, resumes, and similar documents. Many academic writers who use more complex word processing programs for other tasks prefer to use MacWrite for these purposes.

Advanced online formatters with the ability to produce high quality printouts are also appropriate choices for producing short, well-designed documents, although the lack of active page break displays in a program such as Microsoft Word can create doubt about where page breaks will occur in the printed document.

DOCUMENTS PREPARED FOR PUBLICATION

The primary concern of a writer submitting a hard-copy manuscript for publication should be meeting the publisher's style guidelines. Formatting niceties such as proportional spacing and multiple columns are superfluous.

Batch formatting programs and advanced online formatters are appropriate choices for this kind of writing, so long as they include usable footnoting features. The programs must permit the footnotes to be double-spaced and placed at the end of the document. Online formatting programs such as MacWrite or WordStar 3.3 are not well suited to the production of documented academic manuscripts for publication.

MANUSCRIPTS SUBMITTED ON DISK

An increasingly common practice is the submission of a manuscript in disk form. This practice may eventually lead to revolutionary changes in the very nature of publishing as more and more material becomes available in computer-based media, such as on-demand publishing. Academic authors who believe they may wish to submit a manuscript in this way would do well to consider the following:

Choose an IBM PC or IBM PC-compatible printer   Although publishers can handle material submitted on disks with non-IBM PC formats, the evidence strongly indicates that the IBM PC disk format is becoming a de facto standard.

Choose a word processing program capable of producing a straight ASCII file   Some word processing programs, such as WordStar 3.3 and Microsoft Word, use a nonstandard file format. These programs can still be used for submitting disks provided they are capable of producing a straight ASCII file. WordStar 3.3 (in its document mode) isn't, but most publishers have translation programs. Microsoft Word can print a file to disk in ASCII format.

Choose a program that offers automatic stripping of formatting commands   The best program for submitting manuscripts on disk is one that lets you produce two versions of your manuscript: (1) a printed version that shows your editor your ideas for formatting (such as underlining, boldface, position of headings, etc.) and (2) a disk version with no formatting at all. A very desirable feature, therefore, is one that lets you write up your document with formatting, print a formatted version, and then strip all formatting from the text automatically for the disk version. If the program lacks this automatic formatting stripping capability, you'll have to go through the entire document by hand, removing the formatting from the text—a tedious prospect at best. Microsoft Word is one program that provides this capability.

CHOOSING A PROGRAM

The world of word processing software is truly a jungle, but its complexity and diversity has a bright side. Somewhere among the hundreds of available programs is the right one for you.

To identify it, throw out all dogma. There's no such thing as the "best" program for scholarly writing. To be sure, "what you see is what you get" word processing programs are very appealing, but you shouldn't omit text editors/ batch formatters from your consideration—especially if you're interested in foreign language word processing. ProofWriter Graphics, for example, has all the disadvantages of batch formatters, but its fluency with foreign language characters may well give it an edge.

Above all, the program should have the features you want. If you often write scholarly articles for journals that require the notes to be positioned on a separate page at the end of the manuscript and double-spaced, you'd better make sure the program can do just that. If you're the kind of writer who does heavy editing by moving blocks of text around, you'll find multiple windows to be close to indispensable (see Chapter 5). Consider, too, whether the program will work with word processing accessory programs such as spelling checkers or word choice checkers (see Chapters 6 and 7).

You'll also want to devote some thought to what kind of documents you'll be using the program to create. A scholar who mainly produces short, well-designed documents such as course syllabi, handouts, and short committee reports may find MacWrite perfectly suitable, while a scholar who produces 60-page scholarly articles for academic journals will prefer a full-featured program with footnoting (such as WordStar 2000). What counts is what's important for you.

An excellent way to choose a word processing program, therefore, is to begin with a "wish list." Try to put the features you want in rank order. A classicist's list might look like this:

1. Onscreen display of full Greek character set
2. Footnotes at bottom of page, double-spaced
3. Unlimited document length
4. "What you see is what you get" orientation
5. Multiple windows on the text
6. Glossary buffers for insertion of frequently used terms

A mathematician's might include:

1. Equation mode for handling equations
2. Onscreen display of equations as they'll print out
3. Ability to number equations automatically
4. Notes positioned at end and numbered automatically
5. Unlimited document length
6. ASCII file format for telecommunications
7. High quality spelling checker (see Chapter 6) available

And a technical writer's:

1. Automatic table-of-contents and index generation
2. Advanced page formatting with gutters, headers, etc.

3. Ability to handle documents 100–200 pages long
4. High quality spelling checker available
5. Proportional spacing
6. Multiple columns
7. Gutters

The classicist would doubtless be pleased with the Macintosh version of Microsoft Word, equipped with an optional Greek font; the mathematician would be equally pleased with ProofWriter. The technical writer might find Edix/Wordix attractive. Make your list and don't settle for anything less than a program that will give you everything you want.

RESOURCES

A good introduction to word processing is Andrew Fluegelman and Jeremy Joan Hewes, *Writing in the Computer Age: Word Processing Skills and Style for Every Writer* (Garden City, NY: Anchor Press/Doubleday, 1983). William Zinsser, the author of *On Writing Well*, provides a delightful account of one writer's introduction to word processing in his *Writing with a Word Processor* (New York: Harper and Row, 1983).

Works on word processing from the scholar's viewpoint include Alan T. McKenzie (ed.), *A Grin on the Interface: Word Processing for the Academic Humanist* (New York: The Modern Language Association of America, 1984) and Judith Axler Turner, "Scholars Who Use Word Processing Programs Agree They Never Want to Be Without Them," *Chronicle of Higher Education* (April 10, 1985), pp. 25–27 (includes a list of recommended programs).

Accessory programs for WordStar 3.3 include Footnote (Pro/Tem Software, 814 Tolman Drive, Stanford, CA 94305), MagicIndex (Computer Editype Systems, 509 Cathedral Parkway, New York, New York 10025), StarPolish (TDI Hungerford Drive, Suite 33, Rockville, MD 20850). Writing Consultants (11 Creek Bend Drive, Fairport, NY 14450) reveal the secret of WordStar proportional spacing in their book *Proportional Spacing on WordStar*.

Reviews of word processing programs from the scholar's viewpoint appear in *Research in Word Processing Newsletter* (South Dakota School of Mines and Technology, 500 East St. Joseph, Rapid City, SD 57701).

Critical works on word processing are Kurt Supplee, "The PC Tapping at the Chamber Door," *PC: The Independent Guide to IBM Personal Computers* (May 29, 1984), pp. 249–255; Robert Boice and Ferdinand Jones, "Why Academicians Don't Write," *Journal of Higher Education* 55:5 (Sept./Oct. 1984), pp. 567–582; J. D. Gould, "Composing Letters with Computer-Based Text Editors," *Human Factors* 23 (October 1981), pp. 593–606; and Richard M. Collier, "The Word Processor and Revision Strategies," *College Composition and Communication* 34:2 (May 1983), pp. 149–155.

On typesetting directly from word processor files, see Ed Joyce, "Making Book with Word Processing," *PC: The Independent Guide to IBM Personal Computers* (May 28, 1985), pp. 355–356; Sandra K. Paul, "Roadblocks in Typesetting from the Word Processor," *Scholarly Publishing* (July 1981), pp. 323–327; Paul Starr, "The Electronic Reader," *Daedalus* 112:1 (Winter 1983), pp. 143–156; and Terry Ulick, "Typesetting for Writers," *PC: The Independent Guide to IBM Personal Computers* (March 19, 1985), pp. 329–330.

GETTING STARTED: FREEWRITING AND IDEA PROCESSING

Researchers and teachers who specialize in composition now agree that composition is a complex process, one that includes far more than the actual process of setting hand to paper (or keyboard). The great importance of prewriting, the stage of the writing process that precedes writing, is now widely recognized. A new emphasis has emerged on the quality of that process, rather than merely on the quality of the end product.

This chapter introduces two personal computer strategies for prewriting: *freewriting,* or writer-based private writing that can help you overcome writer's block, and *idea processing,* or using outlining programs to generate ideas and develop a plan for writing.

FREEWRITING

Some psychologists object to the vague terms in which writer's block is defined (in one author's words, "an obstacle to the free expression of ideas on paper"[1]). But no one who has experienced writer's block views it as a vague phenomenon. A dark paralysis, writer's block stops writers dead in their tracks—sometimes for hours, sometimes for days, sometimes permanently.

Among the several causes of writer's block is the "internal editor," the nagging, internalized voice of vicious editorial criticism. Its origins may be as diverse as a high school English teacher or an aggressive, anonymous reviewer. But wherever it comes from, it has the same effect: an incapacitating anxiety and an unwillingness to put anything on paper owing to fear of receiving harsh criticism or losing self-esteem.

[1]M.H. Bornstein, cited in Robert Boice and Ferdinand Jones, "Why Academicians Don't Write," *Journal of Higher Education* 55:5 (Sept./Oct. 1984), p. 659.

One way to silence the internal editor and break through the block is a kind of prewriting called freewriting, or writing that you will never show to anyone or even bother revising. It's private writing: writing that you do only for yourself, and for a single purpose: to get the juices flowing, to establish writing momentum, and to lubricate the connection between ideas and the page. In freewriting you simply write anything that comes to mind about the subject, without worrying about putting all the ideas in logical order or making all the sentences neat and clean. Freewriting techniques can lead to dramatic break-throughs for blocked writers.

You can freewrite on paper, of course, but freewriting with a computer has additional benefits. Because you don't have to worry about the right margin or the bottom of the page, you needn't concern yourself with the niceties of page formatting. Moreover, you can turn off the video display by simply twisting the brightness control all the way counterclockwise, thus obscuring the visual feedback on your test that might lead you to become involved with revision (and your internal editor).

Freewriting provides fertile soil for generating ideas about a manuscript. Indeed, it's so useful that you may want to try it even if you're not suffering from writer's block. As the writing guru Peter Elbow says, our editorial instinct is often much better developed than our producing instinct.[2] Any device that can aid in the generation of ideas is likely to play a positive role in your writing.

IDEA PROCESSING

Prewriting has a wider role to play than just generating ideas. Ideally, it should help you generate a strategy for writing your document: a plan for what you want to say and how to say it best.

THE NEED FOR PLANNING

Planning is particularly important in the word processing environment. Since the video display shows you only a third of a page at a time, it's difficult to achieve a sense of your document's overall structure. Paying attention to your document's organization, particularly through planning in the prewriting stage, may contribute markedly to writing quality.

You were probably taught one such planning device in high school: the outline. Most good writers do at least some outlining on paper before plunging into composition. Yet outlining on paper, although of some value, seems to defeat its own purpose. Outlining should involve a process of discovery, in which preparing the outline makes you more aware of what you're trying to say, and it

[2]*Writing Without Teachers* (New York: Oxford University Press, 1973), p. 25.

should suggest fruitful ways to change the outline. Yet the difficulty and mess involved in altering a paper outline inhibits the reorganizing and restructuring that ideally ought to characterize the process.

A word processing program provides the tools needed to overcome the paper-based outline's rigidity. Block move and copy commands can be used to move parts of the outline around, and text deletion or insertion features make revision easy. Still, when you're outlining a lengthy document, the kind scholars are most likely to write, a major limitation of word processing programs for outlining emerges: the limited, one-third page view of the document you're given. An outline's usefulness declines rapidly when you can't see its overall structure.

INTRODUCING IDEA PROCESSING SOFTWARE

Idea processing programs such as ThinkTank (Living VideoText, Inc., 2432 Charleston Rd., Mountain View, CA 94043, for the IBM Personal Computer, PC compatibles, Apple IIe, and Apple Macintosh) or MaxThink (MaxThink, Inc., 230 Crocker Ave., Piedmont, CA 94610, for IBM Personal Computer) were designed to overcome the word processor's limitation as an outlining tool. Like a word processing program, an idea processor includes commands that let you restructure your outline and add (or delete) material as you please. But what distinguishes the idea processor is its ability to collapse, or hide from view, all the subheadings under a heading. With all the subheadings of a lengthy outline collapsed, you can see all or almost all of the outline's overall structure on the single screen display.

When you've loaded an idea processing program into your computer's memory, you're presented with a screen display that looks much like a word processor's: there's a big, blank screen, and a command menu at the bottom. But that's where the resemblance ends. You're going to write outline headings, not text, so you're restricted to one line of text for each heading. Each line is treated as a single, undifferentiated unit of text for such matters as copying, moving, or deleting headings. The first line you'll type will be the outline's subject (Figure 4–1).

As you type, you'll note that the idea processor includes a rudimentary word processor, allowing you to correct errors with the destructive backspace key (see Chapter 3).

Since this heading is the outline's title, the next line you'll type will be automatically indented one level to the right, indicating that it's subsumed under

---

- Trio sonatas of Georg Philipp Telemann (1681–1767)

FIGURE 4-1. First Line of Outline

+ Trio sonatas of Georg Philipp Telemann (1681-1767)
   - Influence of Arcangelo Corelli

FIGURE 4-2. First- and Second-Level Headings

the title. To put it another way, the outline's title is a first-level heading, and the next line is a second-level heading (Figure 4-2).

Note that the minus sign in front of the first-level heading has changed to a plus sign. The plus sign indicates that there's a subheading under the heading—a point that's obvious now, but won't be obvious later (as you'll see).

Brainstorming

An excellent idea generation technique akin to freewriting becomes possible at this point. Because it's so easy to restructure the outline, as you'll see below, you don't have to worry about putting everything down in the right order. Just "brainstorm" everything you can think of that might be relevant to the topic (Figure 4-3).

The outline can be fleshed out by adding third-level headings (Figure 4-4). Note the plus sign that now appears before the "instrumentation" heading.

Collapsing the Headings

Even though this outline still doesn't fill up a whole screen, it's already complex enough to daunt the eye. So it makes good sense to use the collapse command, which when used on the "instrumentation" heading conceals the subheadings under it (Figure 4-5).

Now the function of all those pluses and minuses becomes clear. The plus sign in front of the "instrumentation" heading warns you that there are subheadings tucked away in there; the headings prefaced by minus signs have none.

Expanding the Headings

Using the "expand" command on the "instrumentation" heading reveals the subheadings again (Figure 4-6).

+ Trio sonatas of Georg Philipp Telemann (1681-1767)
   - Influence of Arcangelo Corelli
   - Telemann's esteem for the sonata form
   - Quantz's praise of Telemann's trio sonatas
   - Sonatas' approachability for musical amateurs
   - Instrumentation: popular instruments predominate
   - Flexibility of instrumentation possible
   - Great technical demands avoided
   - Telemann revival in 20th century

FIGURE 4-3. "Brainstorming" Under a Heading

```
+ Trio sonatas of Georg Philipp Telemann (1681-1767)
  - Influence of Arcangelo Corelli
  - Telemann's esteem for the sonata form
  - Quantz's praise of Telemann's trio sonatas
  - Sonatas' approachability for musical amateurs
  + Instrumentation:  popular instruments predominate
    - Court compositions feature unusual instruments
    - But most violin, flute, viola de gamba, etc.
    - These instruments widely used by amateurs
  - Flexibility of instrumentation possible
  - Great technical demands avoided
  - Telemann revival in 20th century
```

FIGURE 4-4. Adding Third-Level Headings

You can collapse and expand the headings as you please, and at any level. Collapse them to see the overall structure; expand them to work on details.

Restructuring the Outline

Idea processors provide tools for restructuring the outline, which come in handy indeed. Consider the headings "flexibility of instrumentation possible" and "great technical demands avoided." These two headings, together with "instrumentation: popular instruments predominate" really belong under the "sonata's approachability for musical amateurs" heading. Commands that move headings and change their level in the outline produce the following result (Figure 4-7).

Collapsing the "sonata's approachability for musical amateurs" heading reduces the outline's complexity considerably and reveals its overall structure (Figure 4-8).

This outline still needs some work before it will provide an effective writing guide, but what's been shown should demonstrate the idea processor's value for creating an outline. The problem emerges once you've finished it, as we will see in the next section.

```
+ Trio sonatas of Georg Philipp Telemann (1681-1767)
  - Influence of Arcangelo Corelli
  - Telemann's esteem for the sonata form
  - Quantz's praise of Telemann's trio sonatas
  - Sonatas' approachability for musical amateurs
  + Instrumentation:  popular instruments predominate
  - Flexibility of instrumentation possible
  - Great technical demands avoided
  - Telemann revival in 20th century
```

FIGURE 4-5. Third-Level Headings: Collapsed

```
+ Trio sonatas of Georg Philipp Telemann (1681-1767)
  - Influence of Arcangelo Corelli
  - Telemann's esteem for the sonata form
  - Quantz's praise of Telemann's trio sonatas
  - Sonatas' approachability for musical amateurs
  + Instrumentation: popular instruments predominate
    - Court compositions feature unusual instruments
    - But most violin, flute, viola de gamba, etc.
    - These instruments widely used by amateurs
  - Flexibility of instrumentation possible
  - Great technical demands avoided
  - Telemann revival in 20th century
```

FIGURE 4-6. Expanding the Collapsed Heading

THE FROZEN OUTLINE

Few outlines survive the ultimate test—lending their structure to a written document—without undergoing change, sometimes radical change. After all, the discovery process doesn't end with prewriting. Sometimes, in fact, the best way to find out what you want to write is trying to write it. And if the discovery involves major restructuring, the outline you created so carefully with the idea processor suddenly becomes all but worthless. Rigid, inflexible plans of any sort endanger writing fluency.[3]

To be sure, you could quit the word processing program, switch disks, load your idea processor, make the necessary changes to the outline, save the outline, quit the idea processor, reload the word processor, and resume writing. But you're fighting a rearguard action against the outline's frozen form. It's no longer providing you with a discovery device: the discovery's going on in the document you're writing. Keeping the discoveries updated on the outline has become a chore, not a tool for further discovery.

Most writers simply abandon the frozen outline at this point; it's nothing more than an artifact of the document's early stages, like a first draft. One could say it has served its purpose and is no longer needed. But that's to forget the word processing program's major drawback: the limited view it gives you of your document. You still need a guide to its overall structure—and the frozen outline doesn't provide it.

All these factors conspire to make you try to adhere to the outline, even if you find as you write that it's not fully satisfactory. Updating the outline is a big chore. Abandoning it throws you into the vast expanses of your document with only the tunnel vision the screen display gives you. And so the outline that was so flexible and fertile in the prewriting stage suddenly becomes rigid and prohibitive when you write.

[3]Mike Rose, "Rigid Rules, Inflexible Plans, and the Stifling of Language: A Cognitive Analysis of Writer's Block," *College Composition and Communication* 31 (Dec. 1980), pp. 389–399.

```
+ Trio sonatas of Georg Philipp Telemann (1681-1767)
  - Influence of Arcangelo Corelli
  - Telemann's esteem for the sonata form
  - Quantz's praise of Telemann's trio sonatas
  + Sonatas' approachability for musical amateurs
    + Instrumentation: popular instruments predominate
      - Court compositions feature unusual instruments
      - But most violin, flute, viola de gamba, etc.
      - These instruments widely used by amateurs
    - Flexibility of instrumentation possible
    - Great technical demands avoided
  - Telemann revival in 20th century
```

FIGURE 4-7. Changing Heading Levels

RECURSIVE WRITING: A NEW DIRECTION IN WORD PROCESSING

What's wrong with idea processing, in essence, is that it doesn't recognize that writing is recursive: writers move back and forth between the planning and writing stage. You start out with a plan, you try writing with it, it doesn't quite work, you update your plan, and you try again. Programs that build a wall between planning and writing, as idea processing programs do, frustrate the recursive, back-and-forth process that appears to play a major role in the creative process of accomplished writers.

This diagnosis suggests a ready solution: put an idea processor and a good word processor together in a single, integrated program. With both the idea processor and the word processor online at the same time, you can switch back and forth between them without exiting the program. That's a major improvement, but it's possible to go even further. The outline's headings can subsume portions of the text under them, so that restructuring the outline actually restructures the text. Ideally, you'd work with two modes or ways of viewing your document: a text mode, in which you see your document just the way you would if you were writing with an ordinary word processor, and an outline mode, in which what's visible is the overall structure of the text expressed as an idea processor–like outline.

```
+ Trio sonatas of Georg Philipp Telemann (1681-1767)
  - Influence of Arcangelo Corelli
  - Telemann's esteem for the sonata form
  - Quantz's praise of Telemann's trio sonatas
  + Sonatas' approachability for musical amateurs
  - Telemann revival in 20th century
```

FIGURE 4-8. Revealing the Outline's Structure

Precisely this vision of the integrated idea processor/word processor has already been implemented in Framework (Ashton-Tate, 10150 W. Jefferson Blvd., Culver City, CA 90230, available for the IBM Personal Computer and compatibles), and it is to be hoped that more will be developed. Framework offers far more than an integrated idea processor/word processor; included also are spreadsheet, graphics, data base management, and telecommunications modules.

Framework's word processor, to be sure, does not offer all the features one would expect in a sophisticated, state-of-the-art word processing program; it does not include, for instance, footnoting, online spelling checking, or glossaries. Experienced word processors will find annoying the lack of certain formatting features, such as superscripted or subscripted numbers. Yet the word processor, in sharp contrast to the nearly unusable word processing modules included with most integrated packages, is of basically excellent quality: it reminds one forcefully of Microsoft Word.

A typical Framework writing session begins with the construction of an idea processor–like outline (Figure 4-9).

An important feature that distinguishes Framework from ThinkTank is the "frame" that is automatically attached to each outline heading as it is created. This frame is nothing more than an expandable box into which text (or other kinds of information, such as spreadsheets or charts) can be inserted. To write the section on "Literature Before 1970," for example, the user presses a function key that opens the frame and expands it to fill the screen. To work on the next section, the user gives additional commands that close the current frame and open the next one. A Framework document, then, is made up of a linked series of frames, the overall structure of which is indicated on the outline.

You can switch back and forth between the outline and the text modes with ease. In Framework's outline mode, the document is shown as an outline. In its

---

```
Introduction
The Problem
   Statement of the Problem
Survey of Relevant Literature
   Literature Before 1970
   Literature 1970-1980
   Recent Literature

[ . . . ]

Research Results
   Summary of Results
   Analysis of Results
   Graphic Presentation of Results
Conclusions
Appendices
```

FIGURE 4-9. Framework Outline

text or frames mode, however, the user sees a full-screen display of the text, which looks just like a document prepared with any word processing program, save that the frame boundaries are visible at the beginning and end of the frame (Figure 4–10). A single keystroke permits you to jump from writing to viewing the outline of the document, helping to keep the overall organization clearly in mind. When the writing is finished, the entire document may be printed as if the outline did not exist; neither the frame boundaries nor the headings appear on the printout.

Writing a document in this way—putting each section and subsection of the document into its own text frame—gives a writer precisely the control over the document's structure that is missing in conventional word processing programs. When major restructuring of the document is necessary, it is edited not by working with the text but rather by working with the outline. Subsections and whole sections of the document can be instantly and conveniently rearranged in a few keystrokes by restructuring the outline. The overall plan and organization of the document is visible in the outline all the while. The outline is automatically renumbered (if the user chooses) to reflect the changes.

Working with Framework in this way provides fertile soil for precisely those recursive processes that are believed to be major elements in the creative writing process. Invariably, writers find good reasons to depart from the outlines they create, however well conceived they might appear. As the document is restructured with a conventional word processor, the outline becomes increasingly inaccurate and finally useless. With Framework, the outline always shows with precision a view of the document's current structure.

Integrated idea processor/word processor software is, however, only a promising avenue of future software development at this writing. Framework has many other jobs to do besides providing tools for writing, and most scholarly

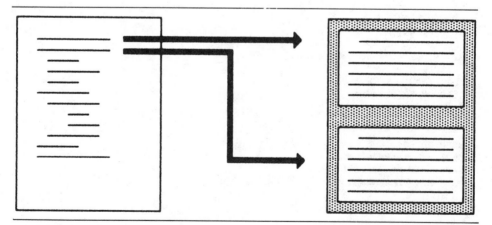

FIGURE 4–10. Framework: Outline Mode and Text Mode

writers will doubtless find its features too limited. By the time you read this book, a word processor of the quality of Microsoft Word or WordStar 2000 will perhaps be available with a recursive idea processing function included.

For now, writers will want to develop strategies for overcoming the current deficiencies of word processing programs. That topic and others are covered in the chapter to follow, "Electronic Writing Techniques."

RESOURCES

On writer's block and freewriting, see J. Minninger, "Reteachering: Unlearning Writing Blocks," *Transactional Analysis* 7 (Jan. 1977), pp. 71–72; P. Elbow, *Writing with Power* (New York: Oxford University Press, 1981); Mike Rose, "Rigid Rules, Inflexible Plans, and the Stifling of Language: A Cognitive Analysis of Writer's Block," *College Composition and Communication* 31 (Dec. 1980), pp. 389–399; and Robert Boice and Ferdinand Jones, "Why Academicians Don't Write," *Journal of Higher Education,* 55:5 (Sept./Oct. 1984).

On the process model and recursion in writing, see the brief and useful overview in Dan Watt, "Tools for Writing," *Personal Computing* (Jan. 1984), pp. 75–78. See also D. Gordon Rohman, "Pre-Writing: The Stage of Discovery in the Writing Process," *College Composition and Communication* 16 (May 1965); Donald Murray, "Write Before Writing," *College Composition and Communication* 29 (Dec. 1978), pp. 375–381; and Linda Flower and John R. Hayes, "A Cognitive Process Theory of Writing," *College Composition and Communication* 32 (Dec. 1981), pp. 365–387.

On idea processors, see Jonathan Kamin, *The ThinkTank Book* (Berkeley: Sybex Computer Books, 1984); Jared Taylor, "Get Smart with MaxThink," *PC: The Independent Guide to IBM Personal Computers* (May 14, 1985), pp. 163–175.

Many programs for prewriting have been developed by writing teachers; some may interest blocked scholarly writers. See, for instance, Hugh L. Burns and George H. Culp, "Stimulating Invention in English Composition Through Computer-Assisted Instruction," *Educational Technology* (Aug. 1980), pp. 5–10 (describes interactive programs for prewriting that utilize Aristotelian and other strategies for invention); William Wresch, "Computer Essay Generation," *The Computing Teacher* 10 (March 1983), pp. 63–65, and his "Computers in English Class: Finally Beyond Grammar and Spelling Drills," *College English* 44:5 (Sept. 1982), pp. 483–490. Good sources for recent information in this area are the periodicals *The Computing Teacher, Educational Technology,* and *Pipeline.*

ELECTRONIC WRITING TECHNIQUES

All too often, writers using word processing computers treat them as if they were glorified typewriters, failing to take advantage of electronic writing techniques that could save them time (and even improve their writing). A survey revealed recently, for example, that two-thirds of a full-featured word processing program's users were unaware of its advanced features and what the features could do. To be sure, many of these writers have little incentive to go beyond the program's surface features; they're just writing letters and memos. But scholars write long, complex documents. You'll want to go beyond the surface to realize the full promise of electronic writing.

Illustrated in the pages to follow are strategies for making full and intelligent use of this new writing medium. It begins with an overview of how experienced writers have learned to adapt to writing and revising with word processing software. It continues with a survey of electronic writing tools, such as glossary buffers, macros, programmable keyboard commands, style sheets, multiple windows, and an online thesaurus.

WRITING STRATEGIES

You'll have taken a major step toward word processing proficiency when you decide which of several word processing strategies works best for you. Among the strategies writers use are:

Writing a draft out in longhand, typing it into the computer, and revising it there Novelist Dick Francis uses this technique, chiefly because he likes to write while lounging around on the sofa or taking walks by the sea. So do John Updike, Erica Jong, and Isaac Asimov, established writers who have long-established writing routines.[1] The curious marriage of pen and word processor isn't ideal, but it makes sense for experienced writers. For some, the sensory stimulus of writing in longhand—for instance, the scratch of a fountain pen on a yellow legal pad—stimulates old habits of invention and concentration. Once written, the text can be typed into the computer, where it can easily be revised.

Entering text directly into the computer, but perfecting each sentence and paragraph before moving on This "bricklayer" approach, as William Zinsser calls it,[2] is ideally suited to word processing, which militates against a broader scope of revision anyway. (Note that most paragraphs in Zinsser's *Writing with a Word Processor* are short enough to fit comfortably within the screen's confines.) Scrutinizing a printout of the manuscript can help you make sure all the bricks are headed in the same direction.

Writing the text rapidly without doing any revision until it's completed This technique, variously called "zipping," "sprinting," or even "flaming," seems appealing at first. After all, you can always revise later. But it's risky. On the screen, the text looks wonderful even when it isn't. And "zipped out" manuscripts are likely to have precisely the kind of large-scale structural problems that can't be seen on the screen. Zipping may be fine for freewriting (see Chapter 4), but it should be used only with caution for writing drafts. Zip only when you feel certain that you have a good handle on your overall plan.

Experiment with these different approaches to find the one that best suits you. And don't be afraid to alternate them. Some writers, for example, find that they can get themselves started on a writing project by beginning with the old pen-and-paper approach and typing it into the computer. Once they've laid the foundation, they can continue writing new material with the computer using the bricklaying or, in lucid moments, the zipping approach.

REVISING FROM PRINTED COPY

Wonderful as the computer may be, the printed page still has its merits. Detecting errors on printed copy is easier by far than finding them on the screen. Subject/verb disagreements, dangling modifiers, and other horrors that can't be electronically detected (see Chapter 6) seem to scream out from the printed page, even though they hid modestly and quietly on the video display. Moreover, for all the benefits of electronic writing, the paper-based manuscript can't be beat for

[1]The writing and word processing styles of these and other writers are described in Kurt Supplee, "The PC Tapping at the Chamber Door," *PC: The Independent Guide to IBM Personal Computers* (May 29, 1984), pp. 249-255.

[2]*Writing with a Word Processor* (New York: Harper Colophon Books, 1983), p. 97.

accessibility. You can thumb through pages and find a passage far more quickly, in fact, than the computer can scroll you to its location in the disk file.

For both these reasons, it makes good sense to revise your document with a printed copy at hand. This isn't to say that you need to make the actual revisions on the printed copy, although some writers will prefer to do just that. Rather, use the printed copy as a guide to the disk file's contents. You'll find that your sense of your document's overall organization, a sense of vital importance to writing quality, will improve measurably.

As you find errors on the printed copy, you'll want to scroll through your manuscript on screen to correct them. If you're moving more than a few screenfuls, you'll want to take advantage of two commands—the jump page and search commands—that can move you there more quickly. And some corrections can be made throughout a manuscript automatically using the search and replace command.

THE JUMP PAGE COMMAND

Not all word processors offer a jump page command, but it's a desirable feature indeed—particularly if you're working with lengthy manuscripts.

The jump page command lets you specify the number of a page in your manuscript that you'd like to scroll to directly. Obviously, this technique is quicker and less tedious by far than scrolling laboriously, a third of a page at a time, through 20 or 30 pages of text.

THE SEARCH COMMAND

If your word processor lacks a jump page command, you can achieve the same accuracy in locating a portion of your manuscript by using the search command.

Suppose, for example, you want to work on a paragraph that begins "Among the Tupinambi, hammock construction. . . ." It doesn't make good sense to search for "among the" since those two words are likely to occur elsewhere in the manuscript. For locating specific passages (rather than every instance of a phrase), it's more productive to lengthen the search string (if possible). Most full-featured word processors allow search strings of at least 25 or 30 characters. Searching for "Among the Tupinambi, hammock" would almost surely take you to exactly the passage you're interested in fixing, unless you've inadvertently repeated yourself by using this construction elsewhere (and that's worth knowing about).

Be careful with your spelling when you enter the search string. If you enter, for instance, "Among the Tunipambi, hammock" you'd be told—after a long wait—that the program could not locate the search string in the manuscript.

Some word processing programs include search options that can help you target your search more accurately. For instance, some programs let you choose a *case-sensitive search*, one that would find "Strong" but not "strong," and a *whole-word search*, one that finds "book" but not the same four letters in "bookbinding." Often included is an option to search up (toward the beginning of the manuscript) as well as down (toward the end).

THE SEARCH AND REPLACE COMMAND

The search and replace command can substitute one word or phrase for another throughout a manuscript, but use it with caution. It's tempting to use the option (if available) of having all the replacements done automatically, without checking each one, but this choice will almost certainly produce errors.

Consider this example. Suppose, in a manuscript on the Civil War, you had used "antebellum" liberally, but decide to change the word—which might be unfamiliar to young readers—to "pre-Civil War." The search and replace feature will make all the substitutions quite literally, even in a title, changing the heading "The Structure of Antebellum Society" to "The Structure of pre-Civil War Society."

Some programs (Microsoft Word, for example) are designed intelligently enough to avoid capitalization and other mistakes when searching and replacing. Even so, you should use the search and replace command with the okaying or confirmation option left on.

If your word processing program lacks a glossary buffer feature (see next section), you can achieve much the same results using the search and replace command. Suppose you're writing a paper on flower morphology and, in its course, you'll refer to *Asclepias syriaca, Taraxacum officinale,* and *Sium ciutaefolium* repeatedly (that is, milkweed, dandelion, and water parsnip). Instead of writing out each name each time it's used, you could, instead, type ASC (for *Asclepias syriaca*), TAR (for *Taraxacum officinale*), and SIU (for *Sium ciutaefolium*). These combinations of letters are unlikely to occur (at least as whole words) elsewhere in your manuscript. Then, once you've finished, you can use the search and replace command to make the substitutions (for instance, "replace SIU with *Sium ciutaefolium*").

USING GLOSSARY BUFFERS

Glossary buffers are areas of memory set aside for storing frequently used text. The buffer's contents can be inserted by typing a short reference (such as SIU) and using the glossary insert command, which retrieves the full text (*Sium ciutaefolium*) and substitutes it for the short reference. And that example well illustrates one use of glossary buffers: entering terms (hence "glossary") that are tedious to type over and over.

A notorious use of glossary buffers is the insertion of *boilerplate*, or standard passages of text that are routinely used to deal with a situation: ("You're the only customer we've ever heard from who had problems with the Snazzy Tomato Chopper! Frankly, we're puzzled, but to show we care, a new one's on its way to you right now!") In legal writing, boilerplate serves to ensure that standard passages whose exact wording is crucial are entered the right way, time after time. A scholar's version of such niceties of wording might include an acknowledgment of a funding agency's support ("This research was supported by grant number such-and-such from such-and-such agency, but responsibility for the views and opinions expressed here lies with the author and not with the agency").

MACROS, PROGRAMMABLE KEYBOARD COMMANDS, AND STYLE SHEETS

If you write often, formatting the same kind of document over and over again becomes a tedious chore. Suppose, for example, you're unhappy with WordStar's default formatting settings (and most people are). Every time you start a new document, then, you'll have to enter the commands for right margin justification, double spacing, line length, and the like.

With WordStar there's no way out. But more advanced word processing programs offer three ways to create and save complex lists of formatting instructions: *macros* (stored collections of commands), *programmable keyboard commands*, and *style sheets* (stored formatting specifications). Please note that these terms aren't always used as consistently as they're presented here, but the distinctions on which they're based help make sense of a rather muddy area of terminology.

MACROS

Macros are similar to glossaries (stored passages of text that can be inserted by typing a few characters). Instead of text, however, the macro stores a series of commands that can be set in motion by using just one command. With a program that offers macros, for example, you can get around the WordStar problem very easily. Instead of manually entering a half-dozen commands, you'd enter the "get macro" command, type the name of the macro (say: MSS, for "manuscript format"), and the program would read the commands in the macro file as if you were entering them from the keyboard. It's very much like having a robot enter all those commands for you.

Just what macros do depends on which kind of word processing program you're using. In a text editor/batch formatter, for instance, the macro would probably contain a list of embedded commands, whose effects would not be discernible until the document was printed. Edix/Wordix, for example, offers a sophisticated macro capability that, once you've mastered it, lets you set up complicated macros that can handle a wide variety of complex formatting tasks (such as printing labels, printing with multiple columns, and printing dramatic scripts). Because writing the macros is rather complicated, the documentation provides fully worked-out examples, both for your edification and for use. Be warned, however: writing macro files for a batch formatter, although not to be confused with programming in a strict sense, is quite close to it, and learning to use macros may require a greater investment of your time than you're willing to make. Just as if you were writing a program, you don't see the results until you "run" it (that is, print the file), and you'll probably find mistakes.

In an online formatter, the macro file would contain a series of keyboard commands which, when read, would produce effects immediately discernible on the screen. For instance, a macro containing commands for right-margin justification and double-spacing would produce precisely that effect on the displayed material, letting you see instantly whether you've made some mistake. Obviously, using macros with an online formatter is much easier than using them with batch formatters.

PROGRAMMABLE KEYBOARD COMMANDS

Another approach to storing detailed and customized formatting information is to permit the user to define or program a set of keyboard commands. For scholarly writers who must produce precisely formatted manuscripts to suit the often quirky formatting specifications of academic journals, this feature can be very attractive indeed.

Microsoft Word (IBM Personal Computer version only) offers a well-developed menu-driven approach to programmable keyboard commands. Suppose, for example, you tire of using the commands and keystrokes needed to center a heading, boldface it, leave three blank lines above it, and two blank lines below. By using a series of menus, you can select formatting characteristics—for instance, boldface character formatting, three blank lines above, and so on—to be attached to the command, which you can name by using any combination of two letters or numbers (for example, H1, for first-level heading). You can even program the command to prevent the heading from being printed alone at the bottom of the page. Once you've created the command, you can enter it by pressing the keyboard's ALT key and then typing H1. The cursor jumps down three lines, and the text you enter appears in the center of the display screen, boldface. After you press the return key, the cursor jumps down two lines, and you're ready to type the body of the section under the heading.

Keyboard command programmability is a very desirable feature for academic writing. Scholars often write for journals with precise formatting specifications, such as leaving three blank lines after every second-level heading. Some journals refuse to accept submissions that do not observe these specifications. Defining your own formatting commands for these specifications can help you format with precision and speed.

STYLE SHEETS

As used by professional typists, a style sheet is a checklist of page design specifications, such as margin settings, lines per page, header or footer position, page number position, line length, and other characteristics. The typist interviews the author and fills in the style characteristics to use as a guide during the manuscript's production.

A computer-based style sheet works the same way. A word processing program that includes one gives you a special style sheet command which, when used, brings up a style sheet menu, or a list of options to which you can respond (such as "text justified or ragged right?"). As you make the responses, the program saves them to a special format file, which is given a distinct name (for instance, MLA STYLE) and stored on disk. It can be attached to any document you wish to write. Table 5–1 lists the formatting characteristics that WordStar 2000 lets you control in this way.

To illustrate the style sheet's great value for academic writing, consider the case of an engineering researcher who contributes papers to a variety of journals. The American Mathematical Society, for example, requires 1.25-inch left and right margins for such journals as *The Mathematics of Computation,* but the American Society for Testing and Materials requires a 1.5-inch left margin and a 1.0-inch right margin. The researcher could define one style sheet called AMS for the American Mathematical Society style, and another called ASTM for the other one.

A FELICITOUS COMBINATION

Microsoft Word (IBM Personal Computer version only) offers an appealing combination of programmable keyboard commands and style sheets. Just as you can with WordStar 2000, Word lets you set up a style sheet to control page formatting specifications. But you can also attach to that style sheet a list of customized keyboard commands, which vastly increase the style sheet's usefulness.

Take the example just mentioned. For the American Mathematical Society format, the heading that begins a paper's reference section should be centered and typed with upper-case letters. For the American Society of Testing and Materials format, however, the heading should be typed flush left, with both

TABLE 5-1

FORMATTING CHARACTERISTICS CONTROLLED BY
STYLE SHEETS WITH WORDSTAR 2000

Characteristic	Range	Default
Line spacing	1 or 2	1
Lines in top margin	0 to 500	6
Lines in bottom margin	0 to 500	6
Column of right margin	10 to 240	65
Column of left margin (even pages)	0 to 132	10
Column of left margin (odd pages)	0 to 132	10
Spaces between tab stops	1 to 240	5
Lines per page	3 to 500	66
Right margin justification	yes or no	yes
Automatic hyphenation	on or off	on
Underlining between words	yes or no	yes

Other Formatting Information Stored in Style Sheets

Type font for document (options vary with printers)
Location of page numbers (center of page, at left margin, at
right margin, alternating between left (even-numbered pages)
and right (odd-numbered pages), or none)

Source: *WordStar 2000 Reference Guide* (San Rafael, CA:
MicroPro International Corporation, 1984).

upper- and lower-case letters, and boldface. The writer could define a keyboard
command ALT-RH ("reference heading") for the AMS style sheet containing the
AMS formatting specifications, and another keyboard command with the same
name for the ASTM style sheet containing the ASTM formatting specifications.
When writing a paper for the ASM, the engineer would use the ASM style sheet;
when the ALT-RH command is entered, the ASM format appears. But when she
or he is writing for the ASTM, the ASTM style sheet is used. This time when
the ALT-RH command is entered, the ASTM format appears. Note that the
writer has had to memorize only one command, ALT-RH. Its formatting effect,
however, depends on which style sheet has been attached to the document.

USING MULTIPLE WINDOWS

The video display screen can be thought of as a window or picture frame
positioned over part of a long scroll of text. Some programs permit more than one
window to appear on the screen at once, so that you can look at two (or more)
parts of the same document or two (or more) different documents.

MULTIPLE WINDOWS ON A SINGLE FILE

It's a little disconcerting to work with two windows on one file. After you get used to the idea of the document as a scroll (see Chapter 3), it seems reasonable that even though you're looking at two different sections of the manuscript they'd both scroll when you enter a scrolling command in one window. But they don't. If you use a scrolling command in one window, the other part of the manuscript stays put.

Opening two windows on a single document can help you achieve a better sense of its organization and speed your work. Try these techniques:

Displaying a signpost paragraph   A signpost paragraph is an introductory passage that tells your reader where you're going and what's going to be covered. (For instance, "this section defines the current direction in theory, describes the evidence that cannot be explained, and suggests a direction for theoretical development.") Displaying the signpost paragraph in the top window while you're writing in the bottom helps remind you of the structure you're using.

"Anchoring" while scrolling   Suppose in a lengthy manuscript you're writing on page 32 and decide you need to look briefly at something on page 6. Without multiple windows, you'd have to scroll all the way back to page 6 and then all the way ahead to page 32, a tedious prospect at best. But here's an easier technique. Split the screen so that two windows appear. Scroll the top window to page 6 and read the text you want to check, then close the top window. Since the bottom window never moved, you're still on page 32.

Split-screen editing   Multiple windows provide a fertile context for moving text around in a document. You can display a passage of text in the top window, for example, and a place in which you think it might work better in the bottom window. Using block move commands, you can cut the text out of the top window and insert it in the bottom one, and see the change in both places. If the change doesn't work, you can use the undo command to restore the text to its original appearance.

Typing a table   If you are typing a lengthy table, try opening a narrow top window for the headings column. Enter the data in the bottom window. The bottom window will scroll but the top one won't, so the headings are always in view.

MULTIPLE WINDOWS ON TWO OR MORE DOCUMENTS

A word processing program that lacks multiple windows puts you in a fix when you want to read or copy material in another document file. You have to save the document you're currently working on, close it, and load the other file.

Far more convenient is the multiple window technique, which lets you create two windows and load a second one without closing the document you're working on.

Multiple document viewing has several desirable uses, including:

Moving text between documents   Having both documents on the screen vastly simplifies and speeds copying or moving text from one document to the other.

Working with an outline   If you're using an idea processor such as Think-Tank or MaxThink (see Chapter 4), you can write the outline it creates to a standard text file and display it in a top window while you're working in the bottom window. This technique gets around part of the recursion problem described in Chapter 4, but it must be remembered that the outline has been transformed into a text file: the chief benefits of the idea processor (such as collapsing, expanding, and restructuring headings) are lost.

Working with research notes   Research notes written and saved with a word processor (see Chapter 12) can be displayed in the top window while you're writing in the bottom one.

THE ONLINE THESAURUS

At the dawn of the nineteenth century, Peter Roget, a British physician and physiologist, completed a "classed catalog of words" that he found "of much use to me in literary composition."[3] First published in 1852, *Roget's Thesaurus* has guided four generations of writers to more vivid words. But they need thumb through the book no longer: the computer can do it automatically. Roget, who tinkered for years trying to perfect a calculating machine, would have been pleased—or perhaps not, since the extant computer-based thesauruses are based on *The Random House Thesaurus: A Dictionary of Synonyms and Antonyms*[4] and other similar works, rather than on one of the volumes that claims direct descent from Roget's work itself.

ONLINE THESAURUS ACCESS

What makes the computer-based thesaurus appealing to writers is that it works *online*, that is, within a word processing program. Here's an illustration.

Suppose you had just written, "The Brahman picked his way through the crowd of pilgrims, carefully avoiding the contact that would have polluted him,"

[3]Preface to the First Edition of *Roget's Thesaurus* (1852), reprinted in *Roget's International Thesaurus* (New York: Thomas Y. Crowell Co., 1962), p. xii.

[4]Ed. Laurence Urdang (New York: Random House, 1960).

---

crowd   throng, host, mob, squeeze, cramp, shove, push

The Brahman picked his way through the crowd of pilgrims, carefully avoiding the contact that would have polluted him.

FIGURE 5-1. Looking up a Word in the Electronic Thesaurus

and you're not sure about "crowd." The word suggests a close gathering, particularly one in which individuality and moral purpose become submerged (hence "crowd mentality," "the madding crowd's ignoble strife," etc.). It works poorly with "pilgrims," who may well have submerged their individuality, but for a high purpose. Highlighting "crowd" and using the thesaurus search command produces the results shown in Figure 5-1. Note that the screen has divided into two parts; the text is shown at the bottom, with the search term highlighted, and the synonyms appear at the top.

The space bar or backspace keys can be used to highlight one of the synonyms, as in Figure 5-2. Pressing the ESCAPE key inserts the highlighted word in the text.

"Mob" clearly isn't the right choice; it connotes a crowd bent on destruction. "Host" works better (Figure 5-3), with its connotation of a multitude sharing a single purpose.

Don't expect an online thesaurus to show you synonyms for obscure or little-used words. Currently available electronic thesauruses use an old text compression technique that takes up huge amounts of disk space, so there's rarely room for more than 50,000 synonyms of 5000 or so words.

A CASE FOR THE ONLINE THESAURUS—AND A CAVEAT

More than a few writers who use computers believe online thesauruses to be fanciful frills, arguing that one can keep a thesaurus next to the computer. Yet

---

crowd   throng, host. mob, squeeze, cramp, shove, push

The Brahman picked his way through the mob of pilgrims, carefully avoiding the contact that would have polluted him.

FIGURE 5-2. Substituting a Synonym

```
crowd      throng, host, mob, squeeze, cramp, shove, push
```

```
The Brahman picked his way through the host of pilgrims, carefully avoiding
the contact that would have polluted him.
```

FIGURE 5-3. Substituting Another Synonym

this example makes a case for using the thesaurus online. You can cycle the various options into and out of your sentence quickly and easily; all that's required is a few keystrokes. You can see the effect of word substitutions and experiment with them, and that's sure to refine your sensitivity to the language.

Even so, finding a program that works with an online thesaurus shouldn't rank among your top considerations in choosing word processing software. Sadly, only a few word processing programs work with online thesauruses, and they're not the best ones available. Perfect Writer 2.0, a quirky text editor/batch formatter, includes Perfect Thesaurus (Thorne/EMI Computer Software, Inc., P.O. Box 10425, Costa Mesa, CA 92627), and WordStar 3.3 (a page-oriented program of some antiquity) works with The Random House Electronic Thesaurus, an accessory program (Wang Electronic Publishing Co., P.O. Box 367, Tijeras, NM 87059).

You can do without an electronic thesaurus if you must. But other accessory programs do exist that you're sure to find close to indispensable, such as word choice checkers and programs for documenting the text. The chapters to follow, "The Electronic Editor," and "Documenting and Proofreading the Text," examine them in detail.

RESOURCES

On advanced word processing techniques, see John Stratton with Dorothy Stratton, *Magic Writing: A Writer's Guide to Word Processing* (New York: New American Library); the occasional "Writing" column in *PC: The Independent Guide to IBM Personal Computers;* and *Research in Word Processing Newsletter* (South Dakota School of Mines and Technology, 500 E. St. Joseph St., Rapid City, SD 57701).

If the word processing program you're currently using lacks macro capabilities, you may be able to add them by using programs such as ProKey (RoseSoft, 4710 University Way, N.E., Seattle, WA 98105) or SuperKey (Borland International, 4585 Scotts Valley Drive, Scotts Valley, CA 95066). The ultimate guide to using programs such as ProKey is David F. Noble and Virginia Noble, *Improve Your Writing with Word Processing* (Indianapolis: Que, 1984).

THE ELECTRONIC EDITOR

6

"Objective consideration of contemporary phenomena," George Orwell wrote, "compels the conclusion that success or failure in competitive activities exhibits no tendency to be commensurate with innate capacity, but that a considerable element of the unpredictable must inevitably be taken into account."[1] With those words Orwell lampooned what bureaucrats might have done with the beautiful language of Ecclesiastes (King James version):

> I returned, and saw under the sun, that the race is not to the swift, nor the battle to the strong, neither yet bread to the wise, nor yet riches to men of understanding, nor yet favor to men of skill; but time and chance happeneth to them all.

What's wrong with the bureaucrat's version (and what's right with Ecclesiastes) can be stated with some precision. The bureaucrat's version overuses:

Abstract nouns   (phenomena, success, failure, activities, capacity) instead of definite, concrete, and specific ones (sun, race, swift, battle, bread);

Nominalizations   (consideration, conclusion), which add to the passage's murkiness;

Vague modifiers   (considerable element of unpredictability) instead of unequivocal, forthright statements (time and chance happeneth to them all); and

Passive voice   (be taken into account) instead of active verbs (I returned, and . . .).

To be sure, using these flawed forms isn't always inappropriate. Sometimes, for instance, there's no way around an abstract noun such as "justice." The

---

[1]Cited in William Strunk and E.B. White, *The Elements of Style,* 3rd Ed. (New York: Macmillan, 1979), p. 23.

danger lies, rather, in the overuse of such words. With that caveat aside, writing experts show surprising consensus on the undesirability of these usages (and certain others, such as overly long sentences and expletives).[2]

That's enough to prick up the ears of any good programmer. A major limitation of computers, remember, is that they can process only that information we can explicitly represent (Chapter 2). This limitation makes computers next to useless for meaning-sensitive tasks, since we're not sure—not yet, anyway—how to represent meaning.[3] But meaning aside, if the writing experts agree that usages a, b, c, and d are bad, then programmers can put together a program that detects and marks them. And that's just what they have done. The result: a host of personal computer programs for text analysis. Included are programs that check for the kind of word choice problems Welles lampooned and others, such as overuse of the passive voice, unreadability, and impoverished vocabulary. Such programs include word choice checkers, passive voice detectors, and readability checkers.

WORD CHOICE CHECKERS

Computer-based spelling checkers have been around for some time. They provided programmers with a ready model with which to put together a word choice checker, a program that would look for—and mark—questionable words and phrases such as "considerable" or "center around." A spelling checker works with a large dictionary of correct words, words that are correctly spelled; as it reads a text file, it marks only those words that it can't find in its dictionary. The word choice checker works in the opposite way. It works with a dictionary of questionable words or phrases; as it reads a text file, it marks only the words it *can* find in its "dictionary." Simple enough.

Word choice checkers had their origins in the research labs of the giants AT&T and IBM. AT&T's Writer's Workbench was widely distributed during the early 1980s because, owing to the government's prohibition (since lifted) on AT&T's entry into the computer market, it couldn't sell the software it developed (such as the UNIX operating system). AT&T therefore donated UNIX (often with Writer's Workbench) to many colleges and universities, and a generation of programmers and computer freaks grew up with it. Writer's Workbench, therefore, has supplied the main inspiration to programmers who have developed personal computer versions of it.

---

[2]Compare, for instance, Richard Lanham, *Revising Prose* (New York: Charles Scribner's Sons, 1979); William Zinsser, *On Writing Well: An Informal Guide to Writing Nonfiction,* 2nd ed. (New York: Harper and Row, 1980); Raymond Lesikar, *Basic Business Communication* (Homewood, IL: Richard D. Irwin, 1985); and Strunk and White, *Elements of Style,* 3rd ed. (New York: Macmillan, 1979).

[3]A superb essay on this subject is Terry Winograd, "Computer Software for Working with Language," *Scientific American* (Sept. 1984), pp. 130–145.

Writer's Workbench isn't readily available for personal computers at this writing owing to its huge size (it requires a megabyte of main memory) and its dependence on the UNIX operating system, which is only slowly becoming available for personal computers. Far more than a word choice checker, Writer's Workbench actually contains 30 programs for textual analysis (see Table 6-1 for an overview of their functions). The program also analyzes the style of a textual passage, presenting a screen display summarizing its conclusions (for instance, "This text contains a much higher percentage of passive verbs [44%] than is common in good documents of this type [22%]," or "You have appropriately limited your nominalizations").

PERSONAL COMPUTER WORD CHOICE PROGRAMS

Several microcomputer programs are available that perform some (but not all) of the Writer's Workbench functions. These programs include Punctuation & Style (Oasis Systems, 2765 Reynard Way, San Diego, CA 92103) and Grammatik (Digital Marketing, 2363 Boulevard Circle, Walnut Creek, CA 94595), two widely used and readily available programs sold directly to computer users.

At best, Grammatik and Punctuation & Style are only subsets of Writer's Workbench; they include most of the bigger package's proofreading functions (Table 6-1) but, sadly, none of the style analysis features.

THE WORD AND PHRASE DICTIONARY

Punctuation & Style and Grammatik include word and phrase dictionaries derived from such sources as Strunk and White's *The Elements of Style*. The dictionary itself is an ASCII text file, and it contains the questionable phrase followed by a suggested revision (Figure 6-1).

TABLE 6-1
WRITER'S WORKBENCH WRITING AIDS

Programs for proofreading check for (1) spelling errors, (2) doubled words ("the the"), (3) punctuation errors (such as commas and periods incorrectly positioned outside quotation marks or unbalanced quotation marks or brackets), (4) capitalization errors (such as first letter of sentence not capitalized), (5) diction errors (such as wordy, archaic, or vague words or phrases), (6) split infinitives, and (7) sexist usage (chairman, man and wife).

Programs for analysis of style compute or identify (1) percentage of verbs in the passive voice, (2) percentage of sentence types (simple, complex, compound, and compound-complex), (3) percentage of short sentences (fewer than 17 words) and long sentences (more than 32 words), (4) readability grade level (using the Kincaid and other formulas), (5) level of nominalization usage (e.g., "distribution" instead of "distribute"), (6) level of abstract noun usage (e.g., truth, beauty, justice), and (7) level of use of long words.

A program for improving organization prints to the screen the first and last sentence of each paragraph (providing a view of the text's organization).

```
ALONG THE LINE OF+LIKE
ALONG THE LINES OF+LIKE
ALONG THE SAME LINE+LIKE
ALONG THIS LINE+SIMILARLY
ALRIGHT+ALL RIGHT
ALTERNATIVE CHOICE+CHOICE
ALTERNATIVE CHOICES+CHOICES
AN ADDITIONAL+ANOTHER
```

FIGURE 6-1. Part of Punctuation & Style's Word and Phrase Dictionary

Punctuation & Style's word and phrase dictionary contains the following kinds of entries:

Awkward phrases   Examples: as a consequence of, includes the necessity of

Cliches   Examples: any and all, intents and purposes

Erroneous phrases   Examples: cannot help but, irregardless, must of, reoccurrence

Folksy phrases   Examples: all the farther, more or less, sort of

Muddy phrases   Examples: a number of, fairly, relatively, seems to

Pompous phrases   Examples: a preference for, accentuated, exhibit a tendency, of the order of, take cognizance of

Redundant phrases   Examples: absolutely complete, collaborate together, generally as a rule

Wordy phrases   Examples: call your attention to, due to the fact that, in a number of cases, the question as to whether

TEXT CRITIQUING

The program "reads" the document file and, if it finds matches for the words or phrases in its dictionary, the matches are presented on the video display, together with a suggestion for revision (Figure 6-2). If you wish, you may mark the word or phrase for editing later with your word processing program.

Occasionally, the program wrongly criticizes a correct usage. For example, it's set up to catch the error "media is," an apparent subject–verb agreement error so it will flag "Each investigative journalist in the radio and television **media is**

```
ACCORDINGLY:  SO
AGGREGATE:  TOTAL
INCONTROVERTIBLE:  PROVEN

[Accordingly], the [aggregate] was determined, and it appears
[incontrovertible] that the theory is wrong.
```

FIGURE 6-2. Punctuation & Style's Screen Display During Text Critiquing

aware of the risks involved." Punctuation & Style's manual warns that only you can decide whether its suggestions are germane.

THE BROHAUGH OBJECTION

For some, however, the problems of Grammatik and Punctuation & Style run deeper. In a *Popular Computing* essay (April 1984), William Brohaugh, the editor of *Writer's Digest*, argues persuasively that such programs cannot contribute much to the revision process—and may even hamper it.

Here's a paraphrase of Brohaugh's argument, which is made through the use of three examples. The first shows a passage of text before checking with Punctuation & Style:

> After the third crash, the Ministry of Railways decided, finally, to initiate the investigation. A spokesman for the Railway Worker's Union said that the investigation could not operate within the constraints of the Ministry's estimate of the problem. This estimate, as he put it with evident sarcasm, was not "of a high order of accuracy."

Accepting Punctuation & Style's suggestions for revision produces the following mishmash:

> After the third crash, the Ministry of Railways decided, lastly, to start a study. A spokesman for the Railway Worker's Union said that the study could not operate because of the Ministry's estimate of the problem. This estimate, as he put it with evident sarcasm, was "inaccurate."

One improvement, to be sure, is made: "start" is more direct than "initiate." But "lastly" does not work in place of "finally," and—as anyone who has ever worked within a bureaucratic context knows fully well, working "within constraints" refers to a specific and lamentable reality not described by "because of." And the sarcasm in the phrase "not of a high order of accuracy" is lost by the substitution of the feeble "inaccurate," which also introduces a misquote.

The truth is that this paragraph needs an entirely different kind of revision than the one it's receiving from Punctuation & Style. The original passage is telegraphed: the information needed for the reader's understanding is expressed in, at best, abbreviated form. Here's a genuine revision:

> After the third crash, the Ministry of Railways decided, finally, to investigate the tracks in the Northern Division. Yet a spokesman for the Railway Worker's Union voiced his suspicion that the investigation would be, at best, perfunctory. Unless the Ministry was willing to concede the magnitude of the problem, he said, the investigation would operate under crippling constraints. The Ministry's current assessment of the tracks' condition, the spokesman stressed with evident sarcasm, was not "of a high order of accuracy."

Diction checks, in short, cannot be viewed as a substitute for revision and rewriting. At best, they can provide a specific brand of textual criticism which, when used with a clear conception of its limits, may prove of some value for writers who have problems with diction.

THE ELECTRONIC CRITIC

What's the value, then, of word choice checkers? They're best viewed, not as ready-made tools for textual analysis, but rather as springboards for adventures in dictionary writing. The dictionary is, after all, an ASCII file. You can use your word processing program to revise it. And doing just that will give you a powerful way of improving your writing.

Start by using your word processor to edit the word choice checker's dictionary. Remove lines containing words or phrases you're not likely to misuse, such as awfully or ain't. Then read or reread an excellent work on writing, such as Richard Lanham's *Revising Prose,* and take a good hard look at your manuscript. Add to the dictionary words and phrases that *you* tend to misuse.

An academic writer who tries this technique might discover such questionable usages as these: are constituted by, causes a loss of, factors of, it was hypothesized, on balance, ongoing, seeks to reveal, and the practice of. Sure to be netted in the catch, too, are a host of nominalizations such as adumbration, consideration, or sanctification, which tend to be overused in academic writing. Abstract nouns, doubtless, will abound (system, truth).

Don't try to come up with specific suggestions for revision. The real value of these programs doesn't lie in automating the revision task, but rather in their potential to stimulate a critical approach to your writing. You can realize this potential by coding the dictionary with criticisms instead of specific substitutions (Figure 6–3). Figure 6–4 shows what a modified dictionary of this sort might have to say about Welles's passage.

What counts here isn't that the program has found some errors. Rather, it has exposed a tendency toward pompous, abstract, and vague writing. And the solution doesn't lie in changing a few words. It lies in rethinking your attitude to the communication—or lack of it!—that's taking place.

PASSIVE VOICE DETECTION

In his *Revising Prose,* Richard Lanham recommends a revision approach called the Paramedic Method. This approach encourages cutting out useless prepositional phrases, which grow like Hydra when a writer uses the passive voice ("A

```
CAUSES A LOSS OF+WORDY
CONSIDERABLY+VAGUE MODIFIER [BE MORE PRECISE OR TAKE STAND]
CONSIDERATION+NOMINALIZATION [USE ACTIVE VERB FORM]
SYSTEM+ABSTRACT NOUN [FIND A MORE CONCRETE, SPECIFIC NOUN]
```

FIGURE 6-3. Word and Phrase Dictionary with Criticisms Instead of Specific Substitutions

---

CONSIDERATION: NOMINALIZATION [USE ACTIVE VERB FORM]
PHENOMENA: ABSTRACT NOUN [FIND A MORE CONCRETE, SPECIFIC NOUN]
CONCLUSION: NOMINALIZATION [USE ACTIVE VERB FORM]
ACTIVITIES: ABSTRACT NOUN [FIND A MORE CONCRETE, SPECIFIC NOUN]
EXHIBITS: POMPOUS, WORDY VERB [USE FAMILIAR LANGUAGE]
COMMENSURATE: POMPOUS USAGE [USE FAMILIAR LANGUAGE]
CAPACITY: ABSTRACT NOUN [FIND A MORE CONCRETE, SPECIFIC NOUN]
CONSIDERABLE: VAGUE MODIFIER [BE MORE SPECIFIC OR TAKE A STAND]

Objective [consideration] of contemporary [phenomena] compels the
[conclusion] that success or failure in competitive [activities]
[exhibits] no tendency to be [commensurate] with innate
[capacity], but that a [considerable] element of the
unpredictable must be taken into account.

FIGURE 6-4. Sample Output for Modified Word Choice Checker

---

cold was caught by Joan on Wednesday" instead of "Joan caught a cold
Wednesday"). Here's the technique:

1. Mark the prepositions.
2. Mark instances of the verb "to be."
3. Ask "who is kicking whom?"
4. Put this "kicking" action in a simple (not compound) active verb.

Punctuation & Style will automatically mark passive voice sentences this
way. Here's a marked sentence:

Shown **[in]** the preliminary analysis **[of]** the findings **[of]** the study **[were]** major
disagreements **[between]** the hypotheses expressed **[in]** the proposal and the survey
data.

Note that this sentence uses 26 words and five prepositions. And here's its
revision:

The preliminary study revealed major discrepancies **between** the proposal's hypotheses and the survey findings.

This sentence uses only one preposition and ten fewer words to say exactly
the same thing. Note that there's nothing informal about it; this sentence would
pass muster in even the stuffiest academic journal.

Be forewarned, however, that using Punctuation & Style's passive voice
detector can be a tedious business. It isn't looking, really, for the passive voice. It's
looking for the verb to be,[4] which has some legitimate uses in nonpassive
sentences. A case in point is the progressive tense ("The horses are trotting").

[4]Detected terms include: is, are, was, were, shall be, will be, have been, has been, had
been, shall have been, and will have been.

The program will show you all the sentences in which "to be" occurs, even if you're using the verb in a nonpassive construction.

SOFTWARE FOR ASSESSING READABILITY

Subscribers to a Florida telephone service are admonished:

Any person who shall willfully refuse to immediately relinquish a party line when informed that such line is needed for an emergency call, and in fact such line is needed for any emergency call, to a fire department or police department or for medical aid or ambulance service, or any person who shall secure the use of a party line by falsely stating that such line is needed for any emergency call, shall be guilty of a misdemeanor and be punished by law. Emergency as used in this section means a situation in which property or human life is in jeopardy and the prompt summoning of aid is essential.

Clear as a bell, right? Now here's a translation:

1. You must instantly hang up when a party line member asks to make an emergency phone call. To refuse is illegal.
2. You must not pretend there is an emergency to get use of the party line. This is illegal.
3. An emergency exists when human life or property is in danger. Instant help is needed. You must call the fire department, the police, a doctor, or an ambulance.[5]

According to a readability analysis, or a quantitative analysis of these two passages, you'd need at least one year of college to grasp the first passage. A seventh grader, in contrast, would have little difficulty with the second one: it's more readable.

Few would argue with that assertion, but accepting the theoretical premises of readability analysis is another matter. Readability clearly stems from many qualities of a text, such as coherence. But readability analysis tries to reduce all the complexity down to a pat formula, such as the one used in the Flesch Reading Ease Formula:

$$205.835 - (\text{sentence length} \times 1.015) -$$
$$(\text{number of syllables per 100 words} \times 0.846)$$

Despite this reductionism, it's clear that readability analysis measures *something*. The Flesch formula, for instance, produces a readability index on a scale of 0 (unreadable) to 100 (very easy), with academic and scholarly writing falling in the 30 to 50 (difficult) range. One can sit down with a collection of texts, some

---

[5]The examples are from Glenda M. McClure, "Computerized Writeability Analysis," *Conference Record: The Many Facets of Computer Communications,* IEEE Professional Communication Society, Atlanta, Georgia (Oct. 19–21, 1983), pp. 31–33.

more readable than others, and obtain surprisingly consistent results. A passage from Veblen's wordy *The Theory of the Leisure Class,* for instance, scores 48, while one from William James' more readable *Psychology* scores 60. A passage from Emerson's eminently readable *The American Scholar* scores 66.

Just what to do with readability analysis has been a hot issue ever since its invention. Its proponents, such as Flesch, have pointed to the evidence that it really does give a rough-and-ready index of readability, while others have jeered and pointed instead to the host of readability factors it ignores.

Until recently, the tedium of performing readability analysis by hand kept a lid on use; most writers ignored it, save for school textbook writers (who, as will be seen below, were as likely to abuse it as to use it fruitfully). But now you can perform readability analysis on a computer. It's a cinch to write a simple program that measures sentence length and the number of syllables in a manuscript, performs the necessary calculations, and cranks out a score. Many such programs are in the public domain (see the Resources section at the end of this chapter).

Should you give readability analysis a try? Used with care and caution, a readability analysis can provide a useful and even illuminating way of looking critically at your writing. But the "care and caution" caveat is a big one. A closer look at readability analysis will reveal why.

WHICH FORMULA TO USE?

The Flesch Reading Ease Formula just described seems as exact as Newton's gravitational equations, but more than 50 competing readability formulas have been proposed. No one formula is universally accepted.

Since a computer can handle the computations speedily and effortlessly, however, there is no obstacle to using several of them at once. This strategy promises—at least in principle—to yield a range of findings for a particular passage of text. One could, perhaps, develop an overall picture from the several findings about the grade level for which the text is appropriate.

That is precisely the strategy employed by the program Readability (Micro Power and Light Co., 12820 Hillscrest Road, Suite 219, Dallas, TX 75230), which uses nine formulas. Readability's screen output, shown in Figure 6–5, shows the results of a test run on a 307-word software review column. The results, as the figure shows, range all the way from the seventh grade to the second year of postgraduate study.

Do these scores have any meaning? One could argue that the mean of the eight grade-level scores (11.7) or their median (12.14) suggests something meaningful, but their standard deviation is a hefty 3.21 grades. One could say (but with little confidence!) that few eighth graders (but most college seniors) would grasp it. Some of the variation can be cut down by omitting the Powers results (always too low) and the Fog Index (always too high), but the remaining

```
***********************************************************
*                                                         *
*        CURRENT PASSAGE "b:example.txt"                  *
*                                                         *
*  307 Words                    488.00 Syllables          *
*    46 3-Syllable Words        158.96 Syllables per 100 wds*
*    12 Sentences                 3.91 Sentences per 100 wds*
*                                                         *
*                      16.23    Fog Reading Level         *
*                      46.39    Flesch Reading Ease Score *
*                      11-12    Flesch Grade Level        *
*                       7.02    Powers Reading Ease       *
*                       7.39    Holmquist                 *
*                      14.67    ARI                       *
*                      13.14    Flesch-Kincaid            *
*                      12.14    Coleman                   *
*                      11-12    Dale-Chall                *
*                                                         *
***********************************************************
```

FIGURE 6-5. Readability Indexes for a 307-Word Passage

variability makes it clear that the overall picture these scores present cannot be taken seriously.

One solution to this dilemma is to prefer one formula over the others for certain kinds of writing. The Flesch-Kincaid formula, for instance, was devised by testing adults reading technical material, and it could be argued that the formula is therefore more appropriate for scholarly and academic writing than most of the other indexes (which were devised by testing children).

USING READABILITY ANALYSIS AS A GUIDE FOR REVISION

If we accept the Flesch-Kincaid analysis, the passage measured above requires more than a year of college to grasp. It's in the same ballpark, therefore, with the Florida phone book and Thornstein Veblen—not exactly exalted company. Naturally, one desires strongly to reduce the score.

That's exactly where a major problem arises. When you're working with a readability program, you learn quickly that shortening the sentences and using fewer three-syllable words lowers the score. In the passage tested above, for instance, revising the text for shorter sentences—say, 20 words instead of 25— would raise its Flesch Reading Ease score to about 60, well within the standard range.

Would that make the text more readable? Probably, but not necessarily. According to Colin Harrison,

> Readability formula scores tend to be determined by word length and sentence length, and if these are reduced the readability score will be [better], but this will not

necessarily make the text more comprehensible. It tends to be the case that long words and long sentences are found in difficult prose, but it is not the word length and sentence length as such which are *causing* the difficulties; they are associated with it in a more complex and subtle way. . . . It is . . . naive to assume in advance that reading difficulty can be determined simply by manipulating sentence length and word length.[6]

A British writing laboratory's experience demonstrated this point recently. School textbook authors, in an experiment, received readability analyses of their work. At first, the analyses stimulated productive revisions. As time went on, the authors (perhaps unconsciously) strove to write prose that produced improved readability scores. But the prose became less readable and was, at its worst, "disjointed and incomprehensible."[7]

Readability measurement can be profitable, but only when it is used with the same caution as word choice checkers: the results must not provide the sole consideration for revision. Coherence, not a good readability score, should always stand supreme among a writer's revision criteria. For the above results, one can say that shortening sentences where appropriate would likely contribute to the text's readability. Many reading experts believe, for example, that an average sentence length of 17 to 20 words is optimal, as is an average word length of about 5 characters or 1.5 syllables. Sometimes, however, a sentence will have to be longer to express a complex thought; sometimes, too, three-syllable words are the only ones that will do.

If readability scores are determined by little more than average sentence length and average word length, it makes good sense to use software that shows you these measurements directly. Readability scores are computed by using these figures, of course, but most readability programs show you only the score (and not the figures used to determine it). Seeing those figures gives you immediate feedback on what's wrong. For instance, if the average sentence length is 27 words, a remedy might be to break up sentences where doing so doesn't obscure meaning. If the average word length is 7.5 characters, hunt for unnecessary three-syllable words (and add them to your word choice checker's dictionary). Several public domain programs are available that provide precisely these measurements (see Resources below).

LEXICOGRAPHIC ANALYSIS

Word frequency analysis and similar programs can be used to detect over-used vocabulary and provide tools for literary analysis.

---

[6]*Readability in the Classroom* (Cambridge: Cambridge University Press, 1980), pp. 134–137.

[7]*Readability in the Classroom*, p. 135.

DETECTING OVERUSED VOCABULARY

Often a writer becomes so enamored of a freshly discovered word or a particularly germane term that it becomes horribly overused. A word frequency analysis program can detect this potential abuse.

An excellent program for this application is WORDFREQ, a utility program supplied with The Word Plus, a spelling checker (Oasis Systems, 2765 Reynard Way, San Diego, CA 92103). WORDFREQ "reads" a text file and reports the number of types and tokens it finds (see Chapter 2 for an explanation of these terms). It also automatically creates a file containing a word frequency list, which lists words according to how often they were used. The most frequently used words top the list (Figure 6-6).

"System" and "development" may be overused in this manuscript. To be sure, it's possible that no acceptable substitute can be found for these two words in certain instances. It's more likely, however, that the writer grew lazy and used these vague words instead of more specific, concrete language. A sentence in the original might have read, for instance, "The planning board and the investment committee should cooperate on the development of a coordination system." A revision might read, "The planning board and investment committee should figure out a way to work together."

Here's a multiple window technique for a quick revision of overused vocabulary (see Chapter 5 for a discussion of multiple windows):

Use WORDFREQ to analyze the document's vocabulary.

Load your word processing program and split the screen into two windows.

Load the document into the top window and WORDFREQ's word frequency list into the bottom window.

253	THE
154	OF
141	A
122	AND
94	TO
68	IN
63	FOR
51	THAT
45	WITH
45	IS
42	AS
42	SYSTEM
40	IT
37	DEVELOPMENT
33	BE
30	OR

FIGURE 6-6. Part of a WORDFREQ Word Frequency Analysis

Scroll down the word frequency list for an overused word—especially a vague word that occurs as frequently as articles or prepositions.

Use your word processor's search command to locate the first instance of the word. Try to express the sentence using more concrete, specific, and vivid language. Do not change the sentence, however, if no other word or words will do.

Continue through the manuscript, locating each instance of the overused word and changing the sentence if possible.

LITERARY ANALYSIS

Students of literature have made increasing use of computers in recent years, but computer-based literary analysis has been hampered by the expense of mainframe computer time. The personal computer's arrival has made computer-based literary analysis cheaper by far, and as more literary analysis software becomes available, personal computers are likely to play a major role in computer-based literary research. One program already mentioned, WORDFREQ, can be used to generate an alphabetized word frequency list of a text keyed in with a word processing program. A word processing program with a good search command can be used for sequential searches to find all occurrences of a word or phrase.

Personal computer programs of great interest to literary researchers will be found in John R. Abercrombie, *Computer Programs for Literary Analysis* (Philadelphia: University of Pennsylvania Press, 1984). The text includes program listings (in Microsoft BASIC and Pascal) of many programs of interest, including programs for preparing an index of a text, constructing a concordance with text location and frequency information, searching a text, and parsing Spanish texts.

ELECTRONIC EDITING AND REVISION STRATEGY

Used cautiously, computer-based text editing with word choice checkers, passive voice detectors, and readability analyzers can help you improve your writing. But remember that writing quality arises from such characteristics as paragraph coherence, sentence unity, and good organization, more than from any factor directly measured by these programs. Revision that ignores these characteristics will produce, at best, only superficial results.

RESOURCES

On Writer's Workbench, see Lorinda L. Cherry, Mary L. Fox, Lawrence T. Frase, Patricia S. Gingrich, Stacy A. Keenan, and Nina H. Macdonald, "Computer Aids for Text Analysis," *Bell Laboratories Record* (May/June 1983), pp. 10–16, and Charles R. Smith,

Kathleen E. Kiefer, and Patricia S. Gingrich, "Computers Come of Age in Writing Instruction," *Computers in the Humanities* 18 (1984), pp. 215–224. Field tests of Writer's Workbench as a teaching tool are reported in Kathleen E. Kiefer and Charles R. Smith, "Textual Analysis with Computers: Tests of Bell Laboratories' Computer Software," *Research in the Teaching of English* 17 (1983), pp. 201–214, and, by the same authors, "Improving Students' Revising and Editing: The Writer's Workbench System," in *The Computer in Composition Instruction*, William Wresch, Ed. (Urbana, IL: National Council of Teachers of English, 1984), pp. 65–82.

Other text-critiquing systems, some of which are now finding their way to microcomputers, are described in Malcolm G. Scully, "The 'Literacy Panic' Revisited: Writing Begins to Mature as an Academic Field," *The Chronicle of Higher Education* (June 22, 1981), pp. 3–4; Michael E. Cohen and Richard A. Lanhan, "HOMER: Teaching Style with a Microcomputer," in *The Computer in Composition Instruction: A Writer's Tool*, William Wresch, Ed. (Urbana, IL: National Council of Teachers of English, 1984), pp. 83–90; Ruth Von Blum and Michael E. Cohen, "WANDAH: Writing Aid and Author's Helper," in *The Computer in Composition Instruction* (to be marketed as HBJ Writer by Harcourt, Brace, Jovanovich in late 1985); Lance A. Miller et al., "Text Critiquing with the EPISTLE System: An Author's Aid to Better Syntax," *Proceedings of the National Computer Conference, May 4–7, 1981* (Arlington, VA: AFIPS Press, 1981), pp. 649–655; George E. Heidorn, et al., "The EPISTLE Text-Critiquing System," *IBM Systems Journal* 21 (1982), pp. 305–326.

On the analysis of readability, see Rudolf F. Flesch, *How to Test Readability* (New York: Harper & Brothers, 1951); George R. Klare, *The Measurement of Readability* (Ames: Iowa State University Press, 1963); and Colin Harrison, *Readability in the Classroom* (Cambridge: Cambridge University Press, 1980).

Personal computer magazines occasionally publish BASIC program listings for readability programs. See, for instance, Steve Irving and William Arnold, "Measuring Readability of Text," *Personal Computing* (Sept. 1979), pp. 34–36 (Dale-Chall formula), and George Stewart, "The Text Scanner," *Popular Computing* (July 1984), pp. 199–203.

A public domain BASIC program is described in Michael Schuyler, "A Readability Formula Program for Use on Microcomputers," *Journal of Reading* (March 1982), pp. 560–591. A public domain readability checker for the IBM Personal Computer is FOGFIN (based on the Gunning Fog Index of readability, which is appropriate for adult reading material). You can obtain it by sending a blank formatted disk (IBM PC-DOS 2.0 or above, double-sided 360K format), $2.00, and a self-addressed, stamped return envelope big enough for the disk to Nelson Ford, Houston Area League of PC Users Public Library, P.O. Box 61565, Houston, TX 77208. When you receive the program, send $15.00 to Joey Robichaux, Wash 'n' Ware, 1036 Brookhollow Dr., Baton Rouge, LA 70810 to receive free updates. A readability checker called Readability Analysis is available from Random House School Division (2970 Brandywine Rd., Atlanta, GA 30341, for the TRS-80 and Apple II).

Programs that produce average sentence length and average word length statistics are available from several sources. Available from the Houston Area League of PC User's Public Library (address above) is a disk containing several text analysis utilities for the IBM Personal Computer, including TALLY (a program that counts the number of words in a text file) and WORDFREQ (a program that determines the average length of words and prints a snazzy onscreen column chart showing the number of words with 1 to 20 characters). FOGFIN, the public domain utility program mentioned above, lists the number of sentences and words read in the sample passage, but stops at 50 sentences. Grammatik, one of the two word choice checkers discussed in this chapter, reports the number of sentences, average sentence length, average word length, length of the shortest sentence, length of the longest sentence, the number of short sentences (less than 14 words), the number of long sentences (more than 30 words), the number of constructions using *"to be,"* and the number of prepositions used. The Word Plus (Oasis Systems, 2765 Reynard Way, San Diego, CA 92103), a spelling checker includes WC, a word count program that tells you how many words are in the file (useful for manuscripts destined for publication).

On computer-based literary analysis, see Susan Hockey, *A Guide to Computer Applications in the Humanities* (Baltimore: Johns Hopkins University Press, 1980); see also P. C. Patton and R. A. Holoien, Eds., *Computing in the Humanities* (Lexington, MA: Heath, 1981). A major journal in this area, available in most research libraries, is *Computers and the Humanities* (Joseph Raben, Ed., City University of New York). The Association for Computers and the Humanities (membership $15.00) publishes a newsletter; a $25.00 subscription brings *Computers and the Humanities* too. Contact Donald Ross, Jr., Secretary, Association for Computers and the Humanities, Dept. of English, 216 Lind Hall, University of Minnesota, Minneapolis, MN 55455. *Computing the Humanities* is a newsletter published by the Center for Computer Applications in the Humanities at the University of Nevada (contact Scott Locicero and Gary Palmer, Codirectors, Center for Computer Applications in the Humanities, University of Nevada, Las Vegas, NV 89154). *Humanities Communication Newsletter* (Dr. Mary Katzen, Office for Humanities Communication, University of Leicester, Leicester, U.K. LE1 7RH) includes some material on computer-based literary research. Dr. John R. Abercrombie, the author of *Computer Programs for Literary Research* (discussed in this chapter), plans to make available diskettes for the IBM Personal Computer and other personal computers (including DEC Rainbow, HP 150, and Apple Macintosh). To receive the programs and a subscription to his newsletter, send $75.00 to Dr. John Abercrombie, University of Pennsylvania, Box 36, College Hall, Philadelphia, PA 19104.

DOCUMENTING
AND
PROOFREADING
THE TEXT

Much of scholarship's drudgery involves documenting and proofreading the text: inserting and numbering footnotes, making an alphabetized list of cited works, preparing an index, and proofreading for errors. Worse, documentation and proofreading tend to paralyze your writing. Once you've numbered 50 footnotes, prepared a lengthy citation list, and made sure no spelling errors exist in the document, you've created a powerful disincentive to further revision. If you add material here and there, you'll probably wind up doing these jobs all over again.

Software for documenting and proofreading text helps with both of these tasks. First, these programs automate the drudgery: footnotes are automatically numbered, and reference lists and indexes are automatically alphabetized. The text of a 10,000-word essay can be automatically checked against the correct spellings in an 80,000-word dictionary. Second, such programs let you make substantial changes to your work even after you've numbered footnotes, created a reference list, compiled an index, and checked the spelling. In most cases, simply running the documentation or proofreading program over again will bring the numbering and alphabetizing up to date.

This chapter discusses in detail software for documenting and proofreading the text. It begins with a survey of the footnoting features included in some word processing programs (as well as accessory programs that add footnoting capabilities to programs that lack them). Discussed also are Pro/Tem's Bibliography, which generates an alphabetized reference list from citations placed in a document, software for creating indexes, and software for proofreading for spelling, punctuation, and capitalization errors.

WORD PROCESSING SOFTWARE AND FOOTNOTE UTILITIES

Finding a happy marriage of footnoting utilities and word processing software isn't easy, as thousands of scholars have found to their dismay.

Here's an illustration. A colleague of mine purchased (on ostensibly reliable advice) the word processing program Perfect Writer, which includes a footnote utility. She found, however, that Perfect Writer writes footnotes only with single-line spacing, ruling the program out for producing manuscripts destined for scholarly journals. Moreover, Perfect Writer's footnote utility doesn't work well.[1] It can't handle footnotes that occur near the top or the bottom of the page. The only way you can print the manuscript is to stop the formatting, go into the file, insert a forced page break near the problem, and try again. After trying this a few times most writers give up for good on Perfect Writer footnotes.

Before you buy any word processing program because it offers footnoting, find out the answers to the following questions. Does the program permit you to:

Choose between single and double spacing of the footnotes?

Handle footnote calls that occur near the top or the bottom of the page?

Superscript the footnote reference mark?

"Float" the text of lengthy footnotes over to the next page to preserve overall page balance?

Position the notes at either the bottom of the page or the end of the document?

Permit footnotes to contain character formatting (italics, boldface, and so forth)?

Allow footnotes to be formatted the way your publisher or scholarly organization requires?

It may not be easy to find out the answers; computer salespeople probably won't know them. Your best bet is to call the software publisher and ask to speak to a technical assistant.

Many footnote utilities fall down when subjected to this scrutiny. The footnoting utility in Edix/Wordix (version 2.02 of Wordix), for example, works well enough. But the program won't number the footnotes automatically, and that's a major inconvenience.[2]

Just how footnoting utilities work depends on the word processing program's design. Here's a brief overview.

---

[1] This criticism applies equally to all versions 1 and to version 2.0. The program's inability to cope with footnotes seems incapable of correction, but check with the vendor (Thorne/EMI Computer Software, Inc., 3187C Airway Ave., Costa Mesa, CA 92626) about later versions.

[2] This shortcoming may have been eliminated by the time you read this book. Check with Emerging Technology Consultants, Inc., 1877 Broadway, Boulder, CO 80302.

TEXT EDITORS/BATCH FORMATTERS

Text editors/batch formatters such as ProofWriter handle footnotes the same way they handle other formatting tasks: by using embedded commands, with their attendant disabilities (see Chapter 3).

ProofWriter isn't being singled out here for abuse; on the contrary, it's worthy of praise. Its footnoting utility, even if it does require you to use embedded commands, works (a rare asset!). What's more, it meets all the criteria mentioned in the checklist above. The program numbers the footnotes automatically, "floats" excess text to the next page, permits you to double-space the notes, lets you choose between footnotes and endnotes, and so on.

ONLINE FORMATTERS

Footnoting utilities are one of those fancy formatting extras that early online formatters can't cope with (see Chapter 3). Even so, you can buy accessory footnoting utilities for WordStar 3.3, the premier online formatter; two examples are StarMate[3] (Solution Technology, Inc., 1499 Palmetto Park Road, Suite 218, Boca Raton, FL 33432, for Z80-based and IBM Personal Computers) and Footnote (Pro/Tem Software, 814 Tolman Drive, Stanford, CA 94305, also for Z80-based and IBM Personal Computers). But you'll be turning WordStar into a text editor/batch formatter.

Figure 7-1 shows how Footnote works. If you're not a WordStar user, this example may look bizarre; it includes certain WordStar commands (such as .pa) that WordStar users (but no others) will recognize.

After you've written the file this way, you run Footnote on it and then print it. Footnote, in other words, acts as a batch formatter for WordStar files.

This is the way the text appears on the WordStar screen as you type it in.@ Footnote calls are indicated by the "at" sign.@ At any time, you can insert the text of the footnotes in a special environment set off from the text by a CONTROL-PR command.@

^R

@This is the first footnote.

@This is the second footnote.

@This is the third footnote.

FIGURE 7-1. WordStar Display with Footnote Entries

[3]StarMate does much more than add footnoting capabilities to WordStar; it also generates a table of contents, section numbers, and an index.

The WordStar/Footnote combination may turn WordStar into a text editor/batch formatter, but the combination works well. It meets all the criteria listed for footnoting utilities at the beginning of this section.

ADVANCED ONLINE FORMATTERS

Batch formatting approaches such as the WordStar/Footnote combination can do a good job with footnotes, but they have one major liability: they make a mess of the screen display (as in Figure 7–1). Advanced online formatting programs such as Microsoft Word or WordStar 2000, in contrast, handle footnotes without making a mess of your text on the screen. These programs, as explained in Chapter 3, strive to provide a full complement of formatting features while still showing the effects of formatting commands on the display screen.

No program available at this writing has, however, managed to blend active page break displays (that is, page break markers that remain accurate as you enter and delete text) with true footnotes (notes printed at the bottom of the page). The complex calculations required to determine active page breaks with true footnotes would overwhelm the current generation of personal computer technology. The advanced online formatters available at this writing, therefore, do not include versatile footnoting utilities if they show active page breaks. Just what this may mean for you is well exemplified by comparing the footnoting utilities in Microsoft Word and WordStar 2000.

Microsoft Word does not show active page breaks, but its footnote utility is excellent. To insert a footnote, you use one of the commands arrayed at the bottom of the screen, and the program gives you an opportunity to provide a reference mark (such as an asterisk). If you make no response, the program assumes you want the notes numbered automatically. Next, you jump to the footnote window, a special area at the end of the file for footnotes. The reference mark you've entered (or, if you've made no response, the note's number) is displayed, and you may then type the note. Another command takes you back to the text, right where you left off.

If you wish, you may open the footnote window so that it's visible at the bottom of the screen, and there's much to be said for doing so. The footnote window is "smart": it automatically shows you any note that's cited in the text you're displaying in the main window. This agreeable feature encourages you to treat the footnotes as a running commentary on the text. The footnote relevant to the text you're editing is always right there. If no footnote reference mark appears in the displayed text, the footnote window is blank.

Word will print footnotes at the bottom of the page or, if you wish, at the end of the document. The footnotes can be formatted just as you please. A sophisticated document sectioning capability lets you divide a document into distinct chapters, each with its own footnote numbering series. The footnotes for a document's Chapter 4, for example, can be numbered beginning with 1 and printed at the end of the chapter.

Although few programs give you a more detailed simulation of the text's actual appearance on the screen, page breaks are not shown until you've done a special formatting pass (using the program's repaginate command), which you can set in motion without leaving the program. The repaginate command takes footnotes into account as it operates, and when it has finished its pass, you'll see where the page breaks will appear in the text. You won't, however, see the footnotes as they'll be printed; they're always shown onscreen in the footnote window.

WordStar 2000, with a different approach to the onscreen display of footnotes, offers less footnoting flexibility. When you wish to enter a footnote, you use a special command (CONTROL-O CONTROL-N, for "option: note") and a special footnote text area opens just below the line the cursor was on when you gave the command. You type the footnote text in that area, and when you're finished, you use a second command (CONTROL-O CONTROL-D, for "option: display") to turn off the footnote display. The footnote text area disappears, and in its place the footnote number appears. You may see the footnote again by use of the CONTROL-O CONTROL-D command (a "toggle," which switches a feature on or off).

As noted in Chapter 3, WordStar 2000 shows page breaks actively as you're writing, but there's a price to be paid for this attractive feature: the program cannot position footnotes at the bottom of the page. They're printed, instead, at the end of the document.

PRO/TEM'S BIBLIOGRAPHY

Bibliography, an accessory program created by Pro/Tem Software, constructs an alphabetized reference list from citations inserted in the text. You begin by using your word processing program to create a library file, containing the full citations of the works you're likely to cite in the papers you write. Then you write a paper. As you do, you insert *keynames* that refer to items in the library file. Finally, you run Bibliography on your manuscript. Bibliography detects the keynames, looks in the library file for the full citation, and constructs an alphabetized list of them.

You may create the library file with a word processing program if you wish, although it's far more desirable—for reasons explained in Chapter 11—to use Pro/Tem's Notebook, a text-oriented data base management program. Since data base management programs have yet to be introduced, however, our discussion here will be limited to the library as created with a word processing program.

Each entry in the library file contains special symbols and a special arrangement of information (Figure 7-2).

```
%Key:Cohen and Cohen 1980
%Author:  Cohen, J.M. and M.J. Cohen
%Title:  The Penguin Dictionary of Modern Quotations, Rev. Ed.
%Publisher: Harmondsworth, England:  Penguin Books, 1980.
%:
```

FIGURE 7-2. Library File Entry (Bibliography)

Note that each entry begins with %Key:, and ends with %:. The %Key: entry is the keyname that you'll insert in the text as you write. As you're writing, you'll insert keynames whenever you've just cited a work. Suppose, for example, you've just written a footnote referring to Cohen and Cohen 1980, and you want that work to appear in the reference list. You'd add, therefore, the keyname prefaced by a percent sign (%Cohen and Cohen 1980) somewhere in the document. When you've finished writing your document and saved it to disk, you run Bibliography on it, giving the program the name of the library file and the name of the document file. Bibliography "reads" the document, compiles a list of the keynames, removes the keynames from the document,[4] retrieves the bibliographic information corresponding to these keynames from the library file, and constructs a file containing an alphabetized list of the works cited.

Bibliography includes several operating options that enhance its flexibility. You can choose to:

Arrange the bibliography in alphabetical order or by number, in order of citations.

Print the author's last name in upper-case letters.

Include nonprinting annotations in the library file.

Leave the keynames in the text, remove the percent sign from the keyname, replace the keyname with a reference number, or replace the keyname with the full bibliographic citation.

Print exactly the information you want printed from the library entry (for instance, you can exclude the annotation but print everything else).

Bibliography's obvious virtues make it all but indispensable. To be sure, creating the library file requires some work, and if your working bibliography is extensive, much rekeying may be required to enter all the necessary citations. If you're planning to go to the trouble, be sure to read Chapter 11 first: you might as well create a Notebook bibliographic data base (which Bibliography can read).

---

[4]This feature can be switched on or off, and it's good practice to leave it off until you're sure that your manuscript is finished. Leaving it off leaves the keynames in the document. Should you revise your text and add more citations, you can easily construct a new, more up-to-date bibliography simply by running Bibliography again.

INDEXING SOFTWARE

Indexing utilities—accessory programs such as StarIndex that create indexes and alphabetize them automatically—seem attractive at first. They can automatically construct an alphabetized index, with correct page references, from index entries linked to specific locations within a disk-based manuscript. But it's important to realize that most scholars do not index their work on disks. They index page proofs, a printout of the document after it has been typeset. Indexing utilities such as StarIndex can provide some limited help with this job, but they can't automate it.

If you're interested in software for indexing, therefore, you'll want to pay some attention to just what kind of writing you'll be doing (see Chapter 3). On the one hand, if you're planning to create documents for direct reproduction, such as a proposal or a research report, an indexing utility designed to work with a disk-based document may prove useful to you. On the other hand, if you're planning to write documents that will be submitted to publishers, typeset, and indexed from page proofs, you'll be best off with software that's suited to that purpose.

INDEXING A DOCUMENT FOR DIRECT REPRODUCTION

If you're planning to use your personal computer to write documents destined for direct reproduction from the computer's printouts, an indexing utility may be of strong interest to you. After the document has been written and paginated, these programs can construct an alphabetized index showing the page location of each item in the text.

StarIndex

StarIndex (Micropro International, 33 San Pablo Ave., San Rafael, CA 94903) is an optional accessory for Micropro International's WordStar word processing programs. StarIndex for WordStar 2000 (included in the Plus version of that program) well exemplifies the capabilities (and limitations) of indexing software generally.

Suppose you're writing a technical report on groundwater pollution with WordStar 2000 and you've just typed a paragraph about groundwater radioactivity. It occurs to you that this subject should appear in the index. To index the term, you leave the cursor right in the middle of the relevant passage and use the command COMMAND-OII ("Option Insert Index"). When the special indexing window appears, you see a prompt that says "index entry," and you respond with "groundwater." Next, you see a prompt that says "subentry," and you respond with "radioactivity." Pressing the return key returns you to the writing mode with no visible evidence of the entry left in the text.

Groundwater. 19, 21, 24
    Agricultural pollutants, 19, 27
    Declining levels in Wilson aquifer, 20
    Radioactivity, 25

FIGURE 7-3. Index Created by Starindex

To construct your index, you save your work to disk and run StarIndex (a separate utility program) on the disk file. StarIndex finds each place where you used COMMAND-OII and creates an index from the entries and subentries you made (Figure 7-3).

If you wish, you can create the index after you've finished writing the document. To do so you would page through it screen by screen, using COMMAND-OII to create entries and subentries as you find material to be placed in the index. After running StarIndex, you may find that some important material is missing from the index. That's no problem. Just use WordStar 2000 again to add more index entries with COMMAND-OII and run StarIndex again.

Indix

Indix (Emerging Technology Consultants, 1877 Broadway, Boulder, CO 80302) is an indexing utility designed to work with Edix/Wordix and other word processing programs that use a standard ASCII file format. Like StarIndex, Indix lets you write your own index entries and link them to specific locations in the text. The problem with this indexing technique, however, is that you may inadvertently omit terms that belong in the index. Indix includes an additional feature that makes sure little of importance will be omitted from the index list.

Indix's special feature automatically indexes every word in the document, save those listed in a special exclude list (common words such as articles or prepositions) and those you specifically ask it to omit. The drawback to this technique is that many more words are indexed than would be desirable in even the most complete index. But you can go through the overly comprehensive index and delete the lines containing undesirable entries.

INDEXING FROM PAGE PROOFS

If you'll be doing most of your indexing from page proof, indexing programs such as StarIndex or Indix will prove of limited value. To be sure, you'll be writing your material with your computer before you submit it for publication, so you could use StarIndex or Indix to create a draft of the index. Later, when you receive the page proof, you can plug in the correct page numbers. But there's a drawback to this technique. The publisher's editorial staff will have made changes to the document after they receive it, and these changes may not be reflected in your disk files. It's best to begin the index only after receiving the final version of the manuscript in the form of page proof.

You could use a text-oriented data base management program (such as Pro/Tem's Notebook) (see Chapter 11) to enter index entries. When used for indexing, these programs allow you to make entries (such as "groundwater, 26") in any order. After you've finished, you can instruct the program to alphabetize the entries. But this software has an inherent drawback for indexing applications: if a term appears on more than one page, duplicate entries will result when you print out the index (Figure 7-4).

One way to solve this problem is to print the program's output to a disk file, which you may then edit with your word processor—a tedious job.

Happily, software is available that gets around this problem. Even better, it's available through users' groups for free. The program is Book Indexer (available for the IBM PC and compatibles), created by Peter Norton. To obtain the program, send $2.00, together with a blank, double-sided, and formatted (PC-DOS 2.0 or higher format) disk and a self-addressed, stamped mailer, to Nelson Ford, Houston Area League of PC Users Public Library, P.O. Box 61565, Houston, TX 77208, and ask for a copy of Book Indexer.

Book Indexer is a set of simple programs that facilitate indexing from page proof. To use the program, you type in the entries (such as "groundwater, 26" and "groundwater, 31") in any order you wish. When you're finished, the program alphabetizes the entries and concatenates duplicates (producing, for instance, "groundwater, 26, 31").

SPELLING CHECKERS

Spelling checkers vary considerably in quality. At one extreme are programs that simply mark the errors they find, requiring you to go through the text with a word processing program and repair them. At the other extreme are programs that identify close to 100% of the errors, display them in their context, look up the correct spelling, and insert the correct spelling in the text file.

HOW SPELLING CHECKERS WORK

Spelling checkers generally follow these steps to proofread a document:

Reading the document The checker "reads" the document and compiles an

---

```
groundwater, 26
groundwater, 28
groundwater, 35
```

FIGURE 7-4. Index with Duplicate Entries

alphabetized list of the unique words it contains (that is, the list of words compiled after eliminating all duplicates).

Comparing the unique words to the dictionary Next, the checker compares the list of unique words to the words contained in its main dictionary. When one of the unique words cannot be matched with the items in the dictionary, it is put into a list of questionable words.

Displaying the questionable words Finally, the spelling checker shows you the list of questionable words. Quality programs show you the questionable word in its context (the line or paragraph in which it occurs) and permit you to type a correction, which is inserted into the document in place of the error.

LIMITATIONS OF SPELLING CHECKERS

Spelling checkers are likely to list as questionable many words that are correctly spelled. Further, there are some kinds of spelling errors that they cannot detect at all.

Correctly Spelled Words in the Questionable Word List

Programs with small dictionaries (for instance, 20,000 words) are likely to report an unacceptably long list of questionable words after checking a scholarly manuscript. For that reason, such programs cannot be recommended for scholarly work. Even a large dictionary (for instance, 75,000 words) does not, however, guarantee that correctly spelled words will be absent from the list. One of the best spelling checkers available, Microsoft Spell (Microsoft Corporation, 10700 Northrup Way, Box 97200, Bellevue, WA 98009), is likely to list the following types of words as questionable:

Plural forms of many words that are present in the dictionary only in their singular form (dissertations, drawbacks, encodes).

Names and unfamiliar geographical terms (Williamson, Timbuktu, Tirukit-tesvaram) (note, however, that "Cucamonga" is in the main dictionary).

Technical terms peculiar to a field (pathogenesis, paraplate, stochastic).

Infrequently used words with the prefixes or suffices un-, non-, pre-, -able, -tion, -arity, and the like (nonterminal, nontutorial, preindustrial, non-algorithmic).

Spelling Errors That Cannot Be Detected

Spelling checkers cannot detect erroneous use of homonyms, incorrect spacing between parts of compound words, and truncations in which the truncated part forms a different but correctly spelled word. See Chapter 2 for a discussion of these limitations.

FEATURES OF SPELLING CHECKERS

A spelling checker's quality is largely dependent on the features it offers. Among the features to inspect in a prospective program are dictionary size, dictionary structure, update dictionary, user dictionary, document dictionary, in-context viewing, and automatic lookup.

Dictionary Size

An important measure of a spelling checker's quality, but by no means the only one, is the size of the checker's main dictionary, the dictionary that is automatically and routinely consulted every time the checker is used.

At one extreme are programs that offer dictionaries of only 20,000 words. Small dictionaries present long lists of questionable words, many of which are spelled correctly. (The story is told of a writer who bought a program with a 20,000-word dictionary and used it on a journal article, after which he was presented with a list of 111 questionable words—97 of which were correct.) At the other extreme are programs with dictionaries containing 75,000 to 100,000 words, including many geographical terms and abbreviations. These programs will present as questionable only a few correctly spelled words.

Dictionary Structure

The structure of a dictionary is just as important as its size. Some programs include only word roots (without prefixes and suffixes, such as *spell* but not *speller, spelling, spells*), using a system of rules to check the spelling of words formed from the root. This system is unacceptable for scholarly purposes because it virtually guarantees that some incorrectly spelled words will not be detected. One program that uses this technique misses approximately 2.2 errors for every 1000 it is capable of detecting; it cannot detect at all such misspellings as "flys" or "mysterys."

A better system maintains complete words (spell, spells, spelling, speller, etc.) in its dictionary. Although the dictionary is perforce larger and processing times are longer, this system has the advantage of great accuracy.

Update Dictionary

Every spelling checker will display some words as questionable even though they are correctly spelled. So that these words will not reappear on the questionable list the next time you use the program, quality spelling checking programs give you the option of adding them to a special update dictionary.

To ensure that you do not accidentally add a misspelling to the main dictionary, the main dictionary is usually off-limits to additions, but the update dictionary is checked automatically as if it were part of the main dictionary. If you discover that you have inadvertently added a misspelling to the update dictionary, it can be edited with a word processing program.

User Dictionaries

User dictionaries are special dictionaries that you can create yourself using a word processing program. Unlike the update dictionary, user dictionaries are not consulted routinely and automatically every time spelling is checked; you must tell the program explicitly that you want the user dictionary used.

To explain the advantages of user dictionaries, it is first necessary to explain that the update and user dictionaries operate much more slowly than the main dictionary does, so adding numerous words to them noticeably degrades the program's performance. The update dictionary is automatically consulted (along with the main dictionary) every time the checker runs, so you should think twice about adding words to it. Since user dictionaries are consulted only when you expressly tell the program to do so, they're an ideal repository for terms that need be considered only for certain kinds of documents.

A scholar who often writes in two distantly related fields—say, philosophy and art history—might create two user dictionaries, one for each field. That way, when a philosophy essay is being checked, the program won't get bogged down checking the word list against art history terms.

Document Dictionaries

Document dictionaries are dictionaries that are attached to one particular document (and no other). Like user dictionaries, they provide you with a way of isolating a dictionary so that it will not be routinely and automatically considered. A document dictionary would be useful, for example, to store words used only in a highly technical research report.

In-Context Viewing

A valuable feature in spelling correction programs is in-context viewing, or the automatic presentation of the context in which the word appears (generally, four or five words on either side of the questionable word). In-context viewing is close to invaluable. In some cases, it's not at all obvious from the misspelling alone what word is being presented for correction (consider "advire," which could be "advice" or "admire"). Being able to view the context clarifies any doubts ("The council was asked for *advire,* not criticism").

Automatic Lookup

Automatic lookup features make use of a set of rules to determine, in a high proportion of cases, the correct spelling of a questionable word. Advanced spelling checking programs such as Microsoft Spell and CorrectStar propose what they believe to be the correct spelling to you, and if you accept it, it's automatically inserted into the text.

Automatic lookup features are based on the fact, discovered through research, that most misspellings are of four types:

Extra letter (assetts)
Missing letter (occurence)
One letter wrong (apparant)
Letters transposed (nieghbor)

The automatic lookup feature uses a trial-and-error technique to discover the correct spelling of the word. Beginning with the misspelling, it applies rules based on the above four kinds of spelling mistakes to create versions of the words that might be correct. In most cases—about 90% of the time—it finds one or more words that match.

Automatic lookup features are highly desirable. After all, many misspellings (typographical errors aside) arise because the writer does not know how to spell the word correctly, meaning that—even with a spelling checker's help—the dictionary or a pocket spelling guide will still have to be consulted. An automatic lookup feature shows you the correct spelling within, at most, a few seconds, saving quite a bit of time.

CHECKING PUNCTUATION AND CAPITALIZATION

Included in Writer's Workbench, the mainframe style analysis program developed by Bell Laboratories (see Chapter 6), are programs that check for punctuation and capitalization errors. Personal computer word choice checkers such as Punctuation & Style and Grammatik also include punctuation and capitalization checkers. Unlike spelling checkers, however, they're so limited in scope that few writers find them of much value.

PUNCTUATION

Punctuation & Style and Grammatik both check for punctuation errors, including:

Misplaced punctuation   Any punctuation mark found in an unexpected location (The Hill Country of. southwestern Texas abounds in wildlife.)
Punctuation outside quotation marks   Example: "Buy 1000 shares", he said.
Missing spaces at end of sentence   Example: Two spaces should occur after a period.   If not, the program marks the error.
Extraneous punctuation   Example: "What does it matter?," he asked.

Isolated punctuation Punctuation marks surrounded by white space (Before February , the orders were brisk.)

Spaces missing in ellipses Example: Acres and acres...were cleared without the tribe's permission.

Odd number of quotation marks, parentheses, braces, or brackets Example: "Just a minute," Garrison said. 'You forgot this."

Unbalanced embedded WordStar commands Example: The term <B> macrolateral was introduced by Freewheeler.

Incorrect use of dash Dashes should not be followed by commas or periods or preceded by white space.

The two programs differ somewhat in the comprehensiveness of their punctuation checkers (Table 7-1), but both are marked by an inability to detect punctuation errors linked to the nuances of meaning in a sentence—nuances to which the computer is completely insensitive. Consider, for instance, the following errors, all of which would escape detection:

```
The Womens' Club is holding a meeting.
Henry Jacobs who drives a Porsche is considered a good
worker.
Albermarle County the home district of the sales
division, is experiencing rapid growth.
```

TABLE 7-1
PUNCTUATION PROBLEMS DETECTED BY GRAMMATIK AND PUNCTUATION & STYLE

Punctuation Problem	Program	
	Grammatik	Punctuation & Style
Misplaced punctuation	No	Yes
Punctuation outside quotation marks	Yes	Yes
Missing punctuation	No	Yes
Extraneous punctuation	Yes	Yes
Isolated punctuation	No	Yes
Spaces missing in ellipses	No	Yes
Odd number of quotation marks, parentheses, braces, or brackets	Yes	Yes
Unbalanced embedded commands	No	Yes
Missing spaces	Yes	Yes
Incorrect use of dash	No	Yes

CAPITALIZATION

The following capitalization errors can be detected by word choice checkers.

> **Mixed upper and lower case letters**   Example: ANd.
> **Missing capital letter**   Example: One sentence ends. another begins.

Capitalization errors dependent on meaning, however, will escape detection. Consider these examples, which would escape detection:

```
Charles chose the Southern route, the one that gets to
the barn by going through the bushes.
Take a walk on vine Street.
The most beautiful season is Fall.
```

Punctuation and capitalization checkers, as you've just seen, can detect only a fraction of the punctuation and capitalization errors likely to occur in a manuscript; indeed, the ones they're most likely to catch are simple typographical errors, such as doubled punctuation, unmatched quotation marks, missing capitalization at the beginning of a sentence, and so on. Those are precisely the kind of errors a scholar is most likely to make, which argues for the use of these checkers. Even so, they're of markedly less use, sophistication, and practical value than word choice or spelling checkers, and shouldn't rank high on your list of priorities.

RESOURCES

Several programs are available to equip WordStar 3.3 with documentation capabilities (in addition to Micropro's own StarIndex). Among them are StarMate (Solution Technology, Inc., 1499 Palmetto Park Rd., Suite 218, Boca Raton, FL 33432) and MagicIndex (Computer EdiType Systems, 509 Cathedral Pkwy., New York, NY 10025). StarMate adds footnoting, bibliographic, and indexing capabilities to WordStar 3.3, as does MagicIndex, which also provides WordStar 3.3 with true proportional spacing (see Chapter 8). Note, however, that although StarMate's footnoting utility is good and versatile, its bibliographic reference feature lacks Bibliography's flexibility. MagicIndex does not let you position footnotes at the end of the file, nor does it number them automatically.

PRINTERS AND PRINTING TECHNIQUES

Printers for personal computers vary widely in speed, flexibility, and the quality of the printed output. Indeed, the world of printers is a jungle whose complexity and pitfalls rival that of word processing software. This chapter begins, therefore, with a typology of printers, and goes on to address a matter of special concern to scholars: the mysteries of printing foreign languages and mathematical symbols. It closes with a note on printing techniques, including *print merging,* or the automatic production of form letters from a mailing list.

A TYPOLOGY OF PERSONAL COMPUTER PRINTERS

Printers vary in the way they form the printed character, and that determines the quality of their output more than any other factor. The three most common printing techniques are found in dot matrix printers, letter-quality printers, and laser printers.

DOT MATRIX PRINTERS

Dot matrix printers, as their name implies, form a printed image that looks (on close inspection) like a matrix or pattern of dots.

The mechanical heart of a dot matrix printer is a *print head,* an electromagnetic device that extrudes first one matrix of tiny pins and then another on signals from the printer's electronic controls. As the print head moves back and forth across the paper the extruded pins strike the ribbon and leave an impression (Figure 8–1).

124

CORPORATION   A legal entity that is distinct from the
individuals who own it and work for it.

PARTNERSHIP   A business in which two or more individuals
agree to pool their financial resources. their
expertise, and their labor to operate a business
jointly.

FIGURE 8-1. Dot Matrix Printer Output: Draft Mode.

Quality of Output

The output produced by dot matrix printers is often described in the following vague terms:

Near-letter quality   So many dots are used to form the character that they run together, producing an image that's almost as good as that formed by a good office typewriter.

Correspondence quality   The dots, although they don't quite run together, are still numerous enough to form an easily discernible, solid-looking image.

Draft quality   The dots are few in number and separated by discernible spaces, making the characters faint and harder to read.

Draft-quality printing is all but useless for scholarly writing. To be sure, it's fast, but you'll want to proofread your work carefully by hand, and you'll probably use the draft as a guide to revision (see Chapter 5). Correspondence or near-letter quality will ease eyestrain when you're working with drafts (Figure 8-2). A caveat: "near-letter quality" and "correspondence quality" reflect no

CORPORATION   A legal entity that is distinct from the
individuals who own it and work for it.

PARTNERSHIP   A business in which two or more individuals
agree to pool their financial resources, their
expertise, and their labor to operate a business
jointly.

FIGURE 8-2. Dot Matrix Printer Output: Near-Letter-Quality Mode.

universally accepted standard, and—like the similarly unregulated term "organically grown"—can be claimed by anyone for anything. Before choosing a printer, ask to see an actual printout.

Speed

Printer manufacturers often make exaggerated claims for their printers' speed. You'll hear of printers that can print 160 or even 200 characters per second. What's referred to here is the draft-quality speed, and it's of little interest to scholars. Of interest to scholars, rather, is how fast the printer operates in the correspondence or near-letter-quality modes. And the biggest determinant of speed in those modes is not the draft-quality speed; it's the number of pins the print head contains.

To form a correspondence-quality or near-letter-quality image, a printer must print two dozen dots or more per character. The cheapest dot matrix printers have only nine pins. These printers, therefore, must make several passes—as many as four or five—over the character to form the high-quality image. The better, more expensive dot matrix printers have as many as 24 pins. To form high-quality characters, therefore, they need make fewer passes—as few as two or even one. Now both the cheap and the more expensive printers may be rated in draft mode at 160 characters per second. But there's a major difference in their speed in the higher-quality modes. The 24-pin printer, for example, might be able to print in 15 minutes a high-quality, 40-page document that the cheaper printer would take an hour to complete.

Advantages and Disadvantages

Dot matrix printers have several advantages that make them the printer of first choice for most scholars:

Speed A $500 dot matrix printer will print far faster—perhaps 10 to 20 times faster—than a comparably priced letter-quality printer. That fact alone inclines most scholars to the purchase of a dot matrix printer. After all, a major advantage of word processing is that you can easily and rapidly produce multiple drafts of a document. Since your revision efforts may well come to employ (or even center on) printed copy, the speed with which you can print drafts will determine whether you can realize this advantage in practice. A $500 letter-quality printer could well take all day to print two or three chapters of a book.

Graphics Most (but not all) dot matrix printers have a graphics mode in which every dot in the matrix is directly addressable by the computer. This means the printer can print virtually anything, including charts, digitized images (see Appendix I), and other graphics.

Low price Fast, reliable dot matrix printers are available for less than $500.

The dot matrix printer's major disadvantage is the poor quality of the printout. Even the printers capable of producing near-letter-quality characters inevitably produce output that is noticeably coarser than that produced by letter-quality printers.

LETTER-QUALITY PRINTERS

Letter-quality printers produce printed output that is indistinguishable from that produced by a fine office typewriter. Indeed, their technology is rooted in the venerable IBM Selectric office typewriter, with its rapidly gyrating print ball. Instead of a print ball, however, letter-quality printers use a print wheel (often called a daisywheel because of its flower-like appearance) or a thimble. Most of these print elements contain 96 characters, corresponding to the standard ASCII keyboard (for exceptions, see "Printing Foreign Language and Mathematical Symbols" below). The print wheel strikes a ribbon, producing a fully formed image of high quality (Figure 8–3).

Speed

The letter-quality printer's major drawback is slow speed. The least expensive letter-quality printers print at only 12 or 15 characters per second, not much faster than a good typist. Getting a letter-quality printer that prints faster costs money. You'll have to pay over $1000, for instance, to get a letter-quality printer that can print over 60 characters per second. For that amount of money, however, you could buy two printers: an inexpensive (but fast) dot-matrix printer for drafts and an inexpensive letter-quality printer to be used only for final printouts.

CORPORATION   A legal entity that is distinct from the individuals who own it and work for it.

PARTNERSHIP   A business in which two or more individuals agree to pool their financial resources, their expertise, and their labor to operate a business jointly.

FIGURE 8-3. Letter-Quality Printer Output.

Advantages and Disadvantages

Letter-quality printers are desirable for scholarly work, in which the typewriter tradition is long and influential. Make no mistake about it: a perfectly typed scholarly essay, with perfectly positioned footnotes and letter-perfect spelling, looks impressive. But letter-quality printers have a major disadvantage (other than slow speed): the lack of graphics capabilities. Most letter-quality printers can only print alphanumeric characters; they can't print charts, graphs, illustrations, or the special characters that some word processing programs let you design on the screen.

LASER PRINTERS

Laser printers, the newest technology in personal computer printing, use the printing mechanism created by Canon for its Personal Copiers.

Laser printers work somewhat differently than the photocopying machines on which they are based. In a photocopying machine, a lens forms an optical image of the material being copied, and the image is transferred to a copier drum that is coated with photosensitive material. The image on the drum attracts toner, which is fused to the paper using a heat process. In a laser printer, there's no lens. Instead, the laser follows a complex, built-in set of programming instructions to simulate a lens-projected image of a page of text. The laser's resolution is about 9000 dots per square inch or more. The image produced is nearly comparable to set type.

It's a long way, however, from the signal the printer gets from the computer ("print character 55") and the precise gyrations of the laser that print ASCII character 55 (the number 7) on the page. Laser printers therefore require large memories to store all the necessary instructions. The more memory there is, the more character styles and fonts the printer can handle.

Speed

Laser printers are exceptionally fast. The Hewlett-Packard Laser Printer, for example, will print about 8 pages per minute.

Advantages and Disadvantages

Laser printers produce printed output of exceptional quality (Figure 8–4) and at high speed, but there's a price to be paid: at this writing, laser printers are still too expensive for individual scholars (save the independently wealthy) to purchase. Price reductions, however, seem inevitable. Networking, moreover, can reduce the cost. A major rationale for *local area networks* (see Chapter 12) is that several personal computer users can share a single laser printer.

```
Laser printers form characters using a
process akin to photocopying machines.
Most offer several font options,
including the Courier monospace
typewriter font (as in this example),
the Times Roman proportionally-spaced
font, and the Helvetica sanserif font.
```

FIGURE 8-4. *Laser Printer Output.*

HANDLING PAPER

Printers may also be distinguished in the way they handle paper. Most common are tractor feed printers, but you'll also encounter printers that handle single sheets using friction feed.

Tractor feed   Tractor feed printers use sprocketed gears to feed continuous or fan-fold paper, which has perforated margins, through the printer. It's hard to beat tractor feed for convenience, although you have to tear off the perforated margins. Some people object to the appearance of the pages after they've been separated; you can tell by the rough, fuzzy edges that they had their origins in continuous paper.

Friction feed   Friction feed printers advance the paper by the pressure exerted by the platen. They're suitable for printing one sheet at a time, but in most cases you have to start the sheet manually (a major inconvenience). The best friction-fed printers offer a cut-sheet feeder attachment that feeds in the single sheets automatically.

COMMUNICATING WITH THE COMPUTER

Two kinds of interfaces, or electronic connections, predominate in today's world of personal computers: *parallel* and *serial.*

Parallel printer interface   A printer with a parallel interface is designed to be connected to your computer's parallel printer port (sometimes called a *Centronics* port). Parallel connections are well standardized and it's usually not difficult to get a parallel printer working properly.

Serial printer interface   Printers with serial interfaces are designed, like modems (see Appendix I), to be connected to your computer's serial port (sometimes called an RS-232 or RS-232C port). There are standards for the serial port, but they leave much room for variation. What this means is that getting a serial printer to work with a specific computer often proves to be a long and frustrating process. Stay away from serial printers unless the dealer you buy one from can demonstrate to you that he or she knows how to hook it up to your computer!

THE PRINTER DRIVER

Take extraordinary care to select a printer for which your word processing program has a *printer driver.*

A printer driver is a disk file (usually provided with word processing programs on a separate utility disk) that contains information the program needs to operate (or drive) a particular brand of printer. This information is necessary because there is little standardization (apart from the 96 standard ASCII character codes) in the communication links between computers and printers.

Just because a word processing program has a printer driver for a particular computer does not mean it can take full advantage of the printer's capabilities. The NEC Spinwriter, for example, is included in one popular word processing program's list of supported printers, but the program cannot take advantage of two desirable Spinwriter features: microjustification and proportional spacing.

Microjustification and proportional spacing address a major flaw of computer-based word processing: the unsightly appearance of the text when right-margin justification is used. Often, right-margin justification leaves gaps between words. Lines of text that include fewer than the maximum number of characters must be filled in with blank spaces, sometimes three or more of them. The gaps become even more pronounced with short lines. Microjustification features address this problem by evening out the gaps left between words in a right-justified line of text, giving the text a smoother and more even appearance.

Further improvement is achieved with proportional spacing. Proportional spacing is a printing technique that assigns different amounts of space to printed characters. Thin letters, such as "i" or "l," are allotted less space, and wider letters such as "m" or "w," are given more. The space allotted each character, in other words, is proportional to its width.

Proportional spacing produces a typescript of high quality. Thus it is of interest to scholarly writers who produce material destined for direct reproduction from a program's printout, but of less value for writers who submit manuscripts to journals or book publishers.

Word processing programs usually include a "generic" printer driver, one that you can customize, in case the printer you have isn't on its list of supported printers (that is, printers for which a driver has been supplied). You can usually use this generic driver to get your printer working at least partially. With some experimentation, you might be able to take advantage of its more advanced features, such as boldfacing or italics. But customizing a printer driver is recommended only to those with extensive personal computer experience.

PRINTING FOREIGN LANGUAGE AND MATHEMATICAL SYMBOLS

If you're hoping to put together a personal computer system that can print foreign languages and mathematical symbols, you'll need to pay even more attention to the word processor–printer connection. Understanding a few basics about the technical aspects of printing will help immensely. We'll begin with more information on character coding.

LOWER-ORDER AND HIGHER-ORDER CHARACTER SETS

Computer printers are designed to reproduce the standard, 96-character ASCII character set that's used by all personal computers (see Chapter 2). These characters are named according to the order in which they appear in the ASCII character table. Codes 0 through 31 are reserved for a set of control codes, which cause the printer to do such things as start a new line, advance to a new page, and the like. Codes 32 through 126 contain the standard characters, and those codes will produce consistent results when sent to any printer. These highly standardized codes are sometimes called the *lower-order character set* to distinguish them from the nonstandardized *high-order* or extended character set, which uses locations 127 through 254. The standard character set, in other words, is surrounded on the low end by nonstandard control codes and on the high end by an equally nonstandard set of additional character codes.

Personal computer printers handle characters in several ways. Many letter-quality daisywheel and thimble printers respond only to the 96 standard character codes. Some letter-quality printers, however, offer 128-character daisywheels (one offers 192), with the extra characters located in the higher-order territory. Dot matrix printers almost always come equipped to print higher-order character sets of 96 alphanumeric symbols and 32 graphics symbols.

DAISYWHEEL PRINTERS WITH 96 CHARACTER ELEMENTS

Of the printers just discussed, daisywheel letter-quality printers that use 96-character print elements are the simplest and most straightforward to use. The 96 characters correspond to the 96 standard ASCII characters.

You may, to be sure, encounter some variation in the symbol sets included with some printwheels. Instead of the reverse slash (ASCII lower-order location 92), for example, one popular daisywheel produces a single-character fraction (½). This variation can be rather disconcerting, since what you type and what you see on the screen isn't necessarily what will print. If you purchase a printwheel, ask to see a complete printout of its character set to make sure it has the symbols you want.

Just because daisywheels respond only to the 96 standard ASCII character codes doesn't mean you can't use them for foreign language word processing. You can purchase European or international daisywheels that substitute a few diacritical marks (acute accents, etc.) for some of the little-used, lower-order ASCII symbols, such as curly brackets, reverse slash, and the like.

To make use of these diacritical marks, however, you'll have to choose a word processing program that can send a backspace command directly to the printer. An example of a word processing program with this capability is WordStar 2000. To print a vowel with an acute accent, for example, you'd enter COMMAND-P-O ("print overstrike") followed by the acute accent followed by the vowel. This command causes the printer to print the acute accent symbol and then to backspace and print the vowel under it. Not all word processing programs let you send a backspace command to the printer in this way. WordStar 3.3, Edix/Wordix, and ProofWriter do, for instance, but Microsoft Word doesn't.

A major drawback to this technique for printing foreign language and other special characters is the confusing screen display. WordStar 2000, for instance, displays

```
montan[o]~a
```

for the Spanish word "montaña," making proofreading difficult. The problem reaches its peak with technical/mathematical symbol printwheels, which print (for instance) an infinity sign instead of the displayed B or pi instead of the displayed quotation mark. To use the symbol print element, moreover, you'll have to switch printwheels in the midst of printing the document; it contains no alphanumeric symbols at all. Some word processing programs let you embed a "halt printing temporarily" command where you'll need to change the print element, but using this technique means that you'll have to stand by your printer while your document is being printed (a tedious task at best).

MULTIPLE FONTS WITH DOT MATRIX PRINTERS

Some dot matrix printers offer a limited version of the daisywheel-switching technique by offering alternative lower-order fonts. The fonts are selected by throwing a switch—to which access can usually be gained only by removing the printer's copy. Switching back and forth between these fonts rapidly or in the course of a single document's printing, therefore, is all but impossible.

The Epson RX-80, for instance, includes fonts called USA, France, Germany, England, Denmark I, Sweden, Italy, and Spain. The Spanish font, for example, prints Pt (the symbol for peseta, the national currency of Spain) instead of a dollar sign, an upside-down exclamation point instead of a left bracket, an upside-down question mark instead of a right bracket, and so on. It does not include accented vowels, which would have to be formed by using the backspacing technique just described for 96-character daisywheels.

EXTENDED CHARACTER SET PRINT ELEMENTS

NEC Spinwriter letter-quality printers use a print thimble with room for up to 128 characters, and the bilingual and multilingual print thimbles (offered for such languages as Spanish, German, and Russian) make full use of them. The Diablo ECS daisywheel includes 192 characters. Whether your word processing program can take advantage of these additional characters is another matter entirely.

In both the Spinwriter and Diablo ECS print elements the additional characters are located among the higher-order ASCII codes (that is, above ASCII code 127), which (except in the IBM Personal Computer environment) aren't standardized. Whether your word processing program can make use of them depends on its capabilities. To take advantage of these additional characters, your word processing program will need embedded printer control commands, manual character mapping, or automatic character mapping.

Embedded Printer Control Commands

To turn on a printer's extended character set, your word processing program must permit you to embed printer control commands within the text as you're writing. The NEC Spinwriter's extended characters, for example, are switched on by a printer control command called shift out (ASCII code 14) and switched off by another command called shift in (ASCII code 15). For instance, to print the Greek letter alpha, you'd need to embed the command ASCII 14 (shift out), a higher-order code number for the letter alpha, and the command ASCII 15 (shift in). The embedded command might look something like this on the display screen:

$$^{C/14/129^{C/15}}$$

Obviously, this embedded command vitiates onscreen readability and will prove unsatisfactory for those who often use foreign language or technical characters. It's far better to choose a word processing program that not only permits you to enter printer control commands but also provides manual or automatic character mapping.

Manual Character Mapping

Edix/Wordix provides a way to map or link existing keyboard characters to multicharacter sequences that can control the Spinwriter. Suppose, for example, you're using a Spinwriter thimble that includes Greek characters in the extended character set. Using a special accessory program supplied with Edix/Wordix, you can set up the program so that when you type "~omega," the Spinwriter shifts to the higher-order characters, prints the Greek letter, and shifts back to the normal mode. The link can be made using single characters; @, for example, could produce an omega. But writing out the character's name makes the document more comprehensible on the screen.

Automatic Character Mapping

By far the most attractive way to deal with the extended character set is to buy a word processing program that features automatic character mapping. Automatic character mapping, unique to programs such as ProofWriter or CharTech that can display extended character sets on the screen, automatically links the displayed characters with their printer counterparts without any special effort on your part.

CharTech (Techware, 474 Willamette St., Suite 201, Eugene, OR 97440, designed to work with WordStar and a wide variety of computers) provides a case in point. With the help of a ROM upgrade (see Chapter 2), CharTech displays up to 94 special characters (Greek, foreign language, mathematical symbols, etc.) on the screen. Best of all, it automatically handles the tedious job of telling the printer how to print them.

A special and congenial version of automatic character mapping is found in the IBM Personal Computer environment.

The PC includes in its character-generating ROM (see Chapter 2) a standardized extended character set including many foreign language, Greek, and mathematical characters. Some word processing programs (for example, Microsoft Word and WordStar 2000), but not all of them, let you display these special characters. A few printers are designed to print them automatically without any special effort on your part. Included in this brief list are the IBM Personal Computer Graphics Printer, the Diablo ECS, and a few others. *Note:* Just because a printer is described as IBM PC-compatible does NOT mean that it can print the PC's higher-order, extended character set.

THE GRAPHICS MODE

One way to circumvent the uncertainty of linking characters on the screen to printed output is to drive a dot matrix printer in its graphics mode, a mode in which every dot in the matrix can be controlled independently from the computer. But it's not guaranteed that you'll see on the screen what you get at the printer.

Example: Fancy Font

Fancy Font (SoftCraft, Inc., 222 State Street, Madison, WI 53705, available for a wide variety of Z80-based and 8088-based computers and compatibles), a batch formatter described in Chapter 3, drives certain popular dot matrix printers in their graphics modes to produce a wide variety of fonts and characters, including full Greek and Russian alphabets and many musical, electronic, mathematical, and technical symbols. However, you don't see these characters on the screen. Depending on which font you're using, the onscreen character "a" could be printed as an Old English character, a musical note, or a Greek character.

Example: ProofWriter Graphics

ProofWriter Graphics (Image Processing Systems, 6409 Appalachian Way, Madison, WI, 53705, available for the IBM Personal Computer with color graphics adapter and a dot matrix printer with a graphics mode) goes Fancy Font one better by letting you see on the screen the characters that will be printed out in the graphics mode on dot matrix printers. The program comes with 15 disk-based fonts, including scientific symbols, mathematical symbols, Western European language symbols, Russian, Classical Greek, Romanized Arabic, Semitic, Hebrew, Ugaritic, and Egyptian. You can even create your own symbols or characters, display them on the screen, and print them.

Example: Apple Macintosh/Apple Imagewriter

An even more comprehensive realization of foreign language and mathematical character printing is found with the Apple Macintosh/Apple Imagewriter combination. As noted in Chapter 2, the Mac is always in a graphics mode, and you can freely change fonts. If the fonts and characters the Mac provides aren't sufficient, you can buy additional ones or design your own. Getting the Imagewriter to print the special characters requires no effort at all: the printer simply prints anything and everything that's on the screen. Moreover, most Macintosh programs—not just one or two specially prepared word processing programs—take advantage of this extraordinary flexibility.

PRINTING TECHNIQUES

Once achieved, a good working connection between a word processing program and a printer can markedly improve your productivity in repetitive writing tasks such as creating resumes, course syllabuses, and correspondence.

USING GENERIC DOCUMENTS

A major advantage of personal computer technology and word processing software is the ease with which documents can be stored on disk. This capability can greatly speed the production of documents in which major amounts of text remain unchanged no matter how many times the document is used.

A scholar who often teaches a course, for example, can keep on disk a "generic" version of the syllabus, one that doesn't list specific dates for the lectures or assignments. This generic syllabus can be modified with the word processing program and printed without disturbing the original generic copy. Other applications for this technique include:

Examinations and quizzes For classroom security, it's often advantageous to print out several different versions of a test with the questions in different order.

Course handouts Generic versions of course handouts (for example, an essay question) can be called up from disk and modified as needed.

Resumes A generic curriculum vita can be expanded or reduced as needed for a particular job application.

PRINT MERGING

Print merging features are useful for the printing of form letters, or letters addressed to many correspondents using a single master letter. In a sense, print merging is an automated extension of the generic document technique just discussed. The print merge utility automatically inserts the necessary information (for instance, name, address, and salutation) from a mailing list into each copy of the generic document or form letter.

Print merging has obvious applications in business, but its usefulness for scholarly writing should not be overlooked. Many college teachers and researchers find themselves saddled with secretarial duties pertaining to small scholarly organizations or correspondence work pertaining to job searches. Print merging features can make light of these and other burdensome correspondence tasks.

To illustrate briefly what print merge features can do, consider the responsibilities of the chairperson of a search committee. She or he must compile a list of job applicants, acknowledge their applications, and keep them informed of the progress of the selection deliberations. Finally, the candidates who are selected for an interview are sent one letter, and the candidates who are not selected are sent another.

The entire process can be handled by a word processing program equipped with print merging features. The program can be used to create a data file containing the names and addresses of the applicants. As each application is received, the applicant's name and address can be added to the data file; with a simple command, a personalized acknowledgment letter can be generated. When decisions have been made about which candidates will be interviewed, two form letters can be created, one for the candidates still in the running and another for those who have been rejected. The print merge commands can be set so that the computer goes through the list of applicants, one by one, asking (on the video display) "Will this candidate be interviewed?" If the answer is "yes," the candidate is sent the interview letter. If the answer is "no," the candidate is sent the rejection letter.

RESOURCES

On getting printers with serial interfaces to work properly, see Joe Campbell, *The RS-232 Solution* (Berkeley: Sybex Computer Books, 1984).

A program that can give you more control over Epson printers is Printer Boss (Connecticut Software Systems Corporation, 30 Wilson Ave., Rowayton, CT 06853, for IBM PC and PC-compatible computers). If your computer has a BASIC interpreter, you may be able to send your own commands to the printer; see Alfred Poor, "Put a Better Face on Your Printer," *PC: The Independent Guide to IBM Personal Computers* (Nov. 27, 1984), pp. 400–410. A program akin to Fancy Font is LePrint (LeBaugh Software Corporation, 2720 Greene Ave., Omaha, NE 68147, for the IBM Personal Computer and PC-compatibles).

On print merging with MailMerge, WordStar's print merging accessory program, see Julie Anne Arca, *Practical WordStar Uses* (Berkeley: Sybex Computer Books, 1983).

PART
THREE

MANAGING INFORMATION

SOFTWARE FOR MANAGING INFORMATION

Vannevar Bush, a physicist who did pioneering work on computers during the Second World War, wrote in 1945 of the uses to which information processing technology might be put in peacetime. Scientists of the future, Bush predicted, would use an intelligent desk that he termed MEMEX. A MEMEX is a machine in which

> an individual stores all his books, records, and communications, and which is mechanized so that it may be consulted with exceeding speed and flexibility. *It is an enlarged intimate supplement to his memory.*[1]

More than a record keeper, MEMEX would be an aid to thought. People think, Bush noted, using association: "with one item in [the mind's] grasp, it snaps instantly to the next that is suggested by the association of thoughts." MEMEX's real value, therefore, would be to provide people with a device that traces an associative trail through a vast library of material, with near-instantaneous response. A MEMEX-using historian interested in the origins of the bow and arrow, for instance, might begin with an encyclopedia article, continue with relevant historical works, branch into the physics of elasticity, and end with inserting a page of her own notes into MEMEX. The MEMEX's point wouldn't be to replace human thought, but on the contrary, to provide it with a tool that "beats the mind decisively in regard to the permanence and clarity of the items resurrected from storage."[2]

[1] My italics. "As We May Think," originally published in 1945 (*Atlantic Monthly*), reprinted in *Perspectives on the Computer Revolution,* Zenon W. Pylyshyn, ed. (Englewood Cliffs, NJ: Prentice-Hall, 1970), p. 55.
[2] Ibid.

MEMEX doesn't yet exist in the way Bush foresaw; the job of digitizing a scholar's library of books is a big one by any measure, and by no means does every expert believe it worthwhile. Books may be bulky, but they have aesthetic qualities that MEMEX would presumably lack, and they're portable. And the computer power needed to process all that information, moreover, still wouldn't sit on a desk.

Yet the personal computer can indeed provide a MEMEX-like machine on your desk right now. The key to creating this "enlarged intimate supplement to memory" lies in the computer-based storage and retrieval of textual information.

Personal computers permit scholars to store and retrieve textual information in two ways:

Personal computer-based information storage and retrieval systems   Using information storage and retrieval software, personal computers can provide the staging ground for individual data bases of research notes, bibliographic citations and annotations, and other collections of information.

Mainframe computer–based information storage and retrieval systems   Using telecommunications software, personal computers can utilize the massive reference resources of *online data base* services, which maintain millions of bibliographic citations and abstracts in all areas of scholarship and science. The software used by these data base services closely resembles the software available for personal computer information management.

Part Three of this book, "Managing Information," introduces software for personal computer–based information management (this chapter), and explores its applications in the storage and retrieval of research notes (Chapter 10) and bibliographic information (Chapter 11). Part Four, "Communicating," introduces telecommunications software (Chapter 12) and online data base services (Chapter 13). These two parts of the book are closely linked. The software that online data bases used for searching their massive data bases, for example, is remarkably similar to the software described in this and the following chapters. Reading the three chapters in this part of the book is recommended, therefore, for those who wish to attempt online information retrieval (Part Four).

INTRODUCING TEXT-ORIENTED DATA BASE MANAGEMENT SOFTWARE

Software designed to aid the storage and retrieval of text is usually termed text-oriented data base management software. Here's a path through this jungle of terms.

THE DATA BASE CONCEPT

A *data base* is nothing more mysterious than a collection of information pertinent to a particular subject. This collection provides a base or foundation for drawing conclusions or making decisions. A *data base management* program, therefore, is a program for managing (that is, storing, organizing, and retrieving) the information in the data base.

To illustrate the basic concepts underlying data base management, consider a box of three-by-five index cards that contain bibliographic citations and notes.

The point of keeping these cards is to store and retrieve bibliographic information. The bibliography's usefulness, however, depends on whether you remember to write down all the necessary information on each card. If, for instance, you leave out the publisher's name, the citation will be next to useless when it comes to preparing the final draft of a journal article: you'll have to go to the library and look it up again. When you set up a card file of bibliographic citations, therefore, you devote some thought to how you want to arrange the information on the cards.

If you're especially careful, you'll probably include a set of headings (such as "author," "title," etc.) so you don't forget to write down the necessary information on every bibliographic card. The headings, however, may be implicit in the data base's design and not actually written on every card. That's fine, so long as you remember to include all the necessary information. A typical heading design is shown in Figure 9-1. A completed index card, containing responses to the headings (now implicit), is shown in Figure 9-2.

SOME BASIC TERMS

With the index card example in mind, it's now possible to define the three fundamental terms of data base management:

Data record   A single unit of related information in the data base (corresponding to a single index card in the above example).

```
Author
Title
Place of Publication
Publisher
Date of Publication
Abstract
Location
```

FIGURE 9-1. Design for a Bibliography Card

de Silva, Lynn
Buddhism: Beliefs and Practices in Ceylon
Colombo, Sri Lanka
Wesley Press
1984

Excellent overview of Theravada Buddhism in Sri Lanka by a
sympathetic and scholarly observer. Covered are not only the
doctrinal aspects of Buddhist belief and practice but also the so-
called "popular" aspects of everyday Buddhism, which have much in
common with neighboring Hindu customs and beliefs and rarely receive
treatment in works of this type.

In my personal collection

FIGURE 9-2. Completed Bibliography Card

Data field   A space for entering a particular kind of information in a data
record (corresponding, for instance, to the "author" or "abstract" fields
in the above example).

Data record format   The overall design of data fields is repeated in every
data record.

LIMITATIONS OF PRECOMPUTER DATA BASES

A card file is a true data base and can be described in the terms just defined.
But it has several limitations that you doubtless know only too well:

There's only one way you can file the cards. Suppose, for instance, you're a
geologist and you've created a file of rock specimens in your personal
collection. You could file them by type of rock (using three sections for
igneous, sedimentary, and metamorphic rocks) *or* by the location of their
discovery, but not both. What happens, then, if you want a list of all the
rocks in your collection from the Mammoth Caves? The only way you
can retrieve the information is to search through every single card
manually.

You have to alphabetize them and search through them by hand. This
problem isn't overwhelming when you've got only 25 or 50 cards, but
what about 200? 500? Unless you've an assistant to help you (rare, these
days, and growing rarer), alphabetizing all these cards could discourage
you from creating a filing system (or making any more additions to it).

There's only one way you can list facts from your card files: by going
through the cards manually, extracting the facts you want, and typing
them up, an unbelievably boring job at best (or expensive, if you hire a
typist). And when you've finished, you've a data base that's frozen in
time. Making any additions to it means retyping the whole thing, dou-
bling the tedium (or expense).

A card file stores information well—so well, in fact, that it's more than difficult to get it back out again. In a bibliography sorted by author, for example, how do you find that classic 1968 work on pesticides by an author whose name you've forgotten? A good fact-crunching system should permit you to retrieve information just as easily as you can store it.

ADVANTAGES OF COMPUTERIZED DATA BASE MANAGEMENT

Data base management programs dramatically cure the retrieval problem by performing the following tasks quickly and almost automatically: *sorting, searching*, creating a *view*, and printing.

Sorting

Most data base management programs include a sorting or ordering command that permits you to arrange the data records in any of the following ways:

Ascending numerical order (1, 2, 3 . . .)
Descending numerical order (. . . 3, 2, 1)
Ascending alphabetical order (a, b, c . . .)
Descending alphabetical order (. . . c, b, a)

Generally, you're given a choice about which data field you'd like to use as a *key* or basis for sorting the records, and that's a handy feature. A major limitation of precomputer data bases is that records could be sorted only on one key (for instance, "author" in the bibliography example used above) and the sorting is so tedious that one is discouraged from repeating it. Computer data base management programs, however, can be used to sort an extensive bibliography repeatedly and quickly. To look only at the most recent works, for instance, a bibliographic data base sorted by author could be resorted in descending numerical order using the "date" field as a key.

Some programs permit multiple key sorts, or sorts that employ sorting keys successively to organize the information in a data base. Suppose, for example, a bibliographic data base is to be sorted by author and then by date. First, the program would sort all the records alphabetically (Abrams, Anthony, Bardwell, etc.). Then, when it encounters more than one record by a single author, it would sort those records by date (Abrams 1981, Abrams 1982, Abrams 1984, etc.).

Searching

A data base management program's search command (sometimes called a *query* or *select* command) provides a way to find specific information within the data base.

TYPES OF SEARCHES. Most data base management programs provide the tools needed to do three kinds of searches:

SIMPLE SEARCHES. The simplest search involves the use of a single search phrase, such as "nineteenth century communes." To use just this one search phrase is to ask the computer, in effect, to find all the records that contain the words "nineteenth century communes." Simple searches may produce more records than you can conveniently read in one setting if the search phrase is a general one. They're useful, however, when you're trying to locate all instances of a term or you're trying to pinpoint records pertaining to a topic that you know to be mentioned in only a few records (such as "Frederick, Harriett").

SEARCHES USING A LOGICAL OPERATOR. More finely tuned search questions may be phrased using a *logical operator*, such as AND, OR, or NOT. Using these operators permits you to frame more precise (or more inclusive) search questions than you could using simple search techniques.

MULTIPLE-OPERATOR SEARCHES. Multiple operator searches use search questions written with two or more logical operators.

LOGICAL OPERATORS. Some programs provide search commands equivalent to those found in word processing programs, which let you specify a simple *search question* (a word or a phrase) and show you where it's located in the text. Most data base management programs, however, give you more advanced searching functions using logical operators (sometimes called *Boolean operators* after George Boole, the nineteenth-century mathematician who invented the logic on which these operators are based), which let you frame even more precise search questions.

Logical operators, which are expressed as the connectives AND, OR, or NOT, permit you to specify a set of criteria about the data records you'd like to see. You might ask, for example, for "all the records where the field Rock Type is equal to "Igneous" **AND** the field Site is equal to "Mammoth Caves."

Venn diagrams help to clarify the meaning and function of logical operators. Suppose, for instance, you have a data base of classical recordings that you've labeled by genre ("string quartet" or "piano trio") and period ("eighteenth century" or "nineteenth century"). Phrasing a search question using the AND operator produces a highly restrictive search (Figure 9–3): only the records that meet both criteria are retrieved.

The OR operator is as inclusive as the AND operator is exclusive (Figure 9–4): records that meet either criterion are retrieved.

The NOT operator permits the exclusion of a subset of the records that contain an undesirable element (Figure 9–5).

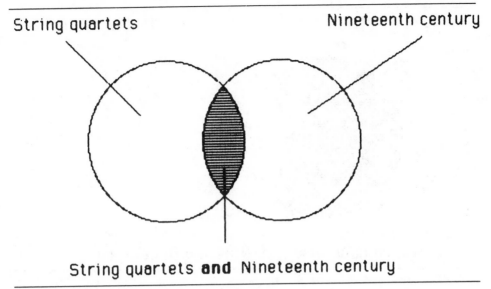

FIGURE 9–3. Restrictive Search using the AND Operator.

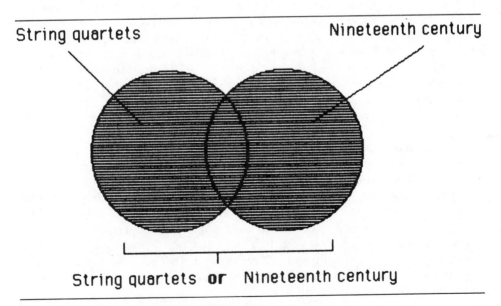

FIGURE 9–4. Inclusive Search using the OR Operator.

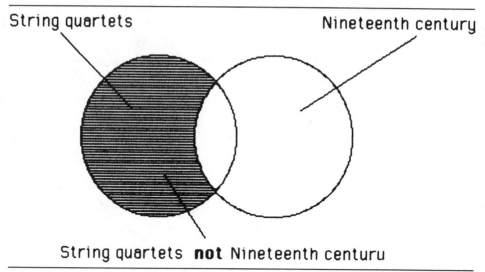

String quartets   Nineteenth century

String quartets **not** Nineteenth centuru

FIGURE 9–5. Exclusive Search using the NOT Operator.

ORDER OF EVALUATION. Just as it's important to understand the order of evaluation when you're using mathematical operators, so too is it important that you understand how a data base management program evaluates search terms. A common order of evaluation puts terms linked with OR first; AND expressions are evaluated second. Therefore, "dolphin AND whale OR porpoise" finds all the records that mention either "whale" or "porpoise" AND also mention "dolphin." That may or may not be desirable. "Dolphin OR porpoise AND whale" is a completely different expression; it finds those records that mention either "dolphin" or "porpoise" and also mention "whale." Understanding these logical operators and their use is basic to data base management proficiency, and you'll meet with several examples of their use in the chapters to follow. They play a key role, too, in the searching of online data bases, to be discussed in Chapter 13.

THE WITH OPERATOR. A desirable addition to a program's set of logical operators is the WITH/n operator, which lets you phrase a question of the form "find all instances of TERM A that occur within n words of TERM B." Consider, for example, searching for "economic stratification." One could simply enter the two words, but most programs would search for precise matches. Were *"stratification"* used where "economic" was implicitly understood, the passage would not be retrieved. Phrasing the search question "stratification WITH (20) economic" returns all instances of "stratification" that occur within 20 words of "economic," in either direction. The WITH operator, in other words, lets you put the context into the search question.

WILD CARD SEARCHING. Wild card searching (sometimes called truncation) is a valuable feature that lets you expand your search question's inclusiveness. Consider, for example, searching for "fiction." Without wild cards, the program would not retrieve records containing "fictions," "fictional," "fictitious," or "fictive." To avoid this exclusion of kindred terms, you could use AND operators ("Find fiction AND fictions AND fictional AND fictitious AND fictive"), but this procedure is tedious and error-prone; you might forget to enter one or more related forms. Wild card characters let you enter a root word such as "soc" (social, society, socialization, etc.) or "publici" (publicity, publicist, publicizes, etc.).

SINGLE-CHARACTER WILD CARD SYMBOLS placed at the end of a word retrieve only those words that contain the root plus one additional character. Often, the single-character wild card symbol is a question mark. The search term "education," for instance, retrieves "education" and "educations" but not "educational."

MULTICHARACTER WILD CARD SYMBOLS placed at the end of a word retrieve all the words that contain the root plus any additional characters, no matter how numerous. Often, the multicharacter wild card symbol is an asterisk. The search term "education*," for instance, retrieves "education," "educations," "educational," and "educationally." Be careful, however, not to truncate the root too much when you're using the multicharacter wild card symbol. Consider searching for terms related to the subject of sociology. The search term "soc*," for instance, returns not only the desirable sociological terms (socialization, society, etc.) but also soccer, socks, Socrates, and many more unrelated ones.

PARENTHETICAL EXPRESSIONS. Programs that permit you to enter parentheses in search expressions let you control the order in which operators are evaluated. As noted above, data base management programs follow a fixed order of precedence when evaluating search terms; if you're unaware of that order, you can obtain spurious results in your search. Parentheses let you tell the computer which expression to evaluate first. Just as it's good practice in mathematical calculation to use parentheses liberally, so too is it in writing search terms. The search question "(porpoise OR dolphin) AND whale" doesn't need the parentheses to work correctly, since the OR expression is evaluated first with most programs, but it helps immensely in clarifying the search term's logic. In some cases, adding the parentheses changes the search term's meaning. Consider, for instance, "porpoise OR (dolphin AND whale)." In this search question, the computer is instructed to look for those records that contain "dolphin" together with "whale" OR records that contain "porpoise."

QUANTITATIVE OPERATORS. Some data management programs let you include quantitative operators, such as LESS THAN, LESS THAN OR EQUAL TO, EQUAL TO, GREATER THAN OR EQUAL TO, and GREATER THAN in search questions. One could enter a search question such as "Find all the records which contain a date GREATER THAN OR EQUAL TO 1967." It's important to remember, however, that to the computer everything that's represented for processing is a number, even the letters A through Z. So long as you understand the order in which ASCII characters are represented (the *ASCII collating sequence*, Table 9-1), you can make use of these operators even when you're searching for nonnumerical material. The word "enormous," for example, is less than the word "minuscule," since it comes before "minuscule" in the collating sequence.

Creating a View

The result of a search operation is a subset of the data base—that is, a *view*—that contains only those records that meet the specified criteria. A view is a way of temporarily reducing the size of a data base so that it includes only those records in which you're interested at the moment (for instance, "string quartets AND piano trios but NOT those of the eighteenth century"). Creating the view does not harm or restructure the information contained in the data base.

Printing

Most programs permit you to print out the whole data base or a view of it, producing a *report* of its contents. The better programs let you specify which fields you want printed and give you a good degree of control over the appearance of the report.

A desirable feature for scholarly data base management is the ability to print the data base to an ASCII text file (using only the standard characters as defined

---

TABLE 9-1
THE ASCII COLLATING SEQUENCE

Control characters
Space
Punctuation characters !" # $ % & ' ( ) * + - . /
Numbers 0 through 9
Punctuation characters : ; < = > ? @
Upper-case letters A through Z
Lower-case letters a through z
Additional punctuation characters [\ ] _ ' { , }
Extended characters (foreign language, technical, graphics)

---

by the American Standard Code for Information Interchange). ASCII text files can be read by word processing programs, meaning that the information printed out from the data base can be utilized directly, without retyping, when you sit down to write about it.

DATA BASE MANAGEMENT SOFTWARE

A data base management program, in the broadest sense of the term, is any program that:

Facilitates the storage of massive amounts of information in a data base.
Provides commands for sorting, searching, creating views, and printing the contents of the data base.

TEXT-ORIENTED DATA BASE MANAGEMENT

Not all data base management programs are designed to handle extensive amounts of text. Data base management programs can store, organize, and retrieve three kinds of information, and most specialize in just one or two:

Quantitative data such as serial numbers, census data, sales figures, part numbers.
Graphic images such as maps, diagrams, illustrations of parts, X-rays, or computer-created images.
Text such as correspondence, bibliographic citations, research notes, or the full text of scientific or technical articles.

Most of the data base management programs on today's personal computer market are designed to deal with quantitative data (with limited amounts of text), and for good reason: that's where the market is. Businesses make many uses of quantitatively oriented data base management programs for such matters as maintaining inventories, updating mailing lists, and storing customer records. Although these programs are well suited to business applications, they tend to place restrictions on the amount of text that can be stored (a typical limit is about 1000 characters per electronic "index card"). They're of little use, therefore, for scholars. Graphics-oriented data base management programs may appeal greatly to those who wish to maintain data bases of illustrations, maps, or charts, but they're only now becoming available for personal computers (see Appendix I for more information). Our concern, therefore, is with text-oriented data base management programs: programs for the storage and retrieval of large amounts of textual information.

A TYPOLOGY OF TEXT-ORIENTED DATA BASE MANAGEMENT SOFTWARE

Text-oriented data base management programs, defined in the broadest possible sense, can be said to include word processing programs, free-format information storage and retrieval programs, text-oriented file management programs, and idea processors.

WORD PROCESSING PROGRAMS

It's possible to use a word processing program's search function for simple information management purposes, but it's not recommended if other alternatives are available. You can use the word processing program, for instance, to create a data file, and the search function will help you find portions of the file in which a specified word or two appears. You're given no tools, however, for more advanced searches using logical operators, for sorting the data base, or for printing a selection of records.

FREE-FORMAT INFORMATION STORAGE AND RETRIEVAL SYSTEMS

A free-format information storage and retrieval system (FFISR) lets you see a word processing program to set up your data base. Two kinds of FFISRs are now available for personal computers: *automatic indexing* and *controlled vocabulary* programs.

Automatic Indexing FFISRs

Automatic indexing FFISRs let you create a massive data base that includes as many as several thousand distinct text files, each created with a word processing program. The program automatically indexes every significant word in the whole data base, with the exception of unimportant "noise words" such as articles or prepositions. As they create the index, they note where the word is located.

Automatic indexing FFISRs represent the ultimate in free-format data base management. No restrictions are placed on how the material is written up; the software can put an article, a chapter from a book, a loosely organized file of research notes, and a set of bibliographic citations and abstracts into the same massive data base. Furthermore, no special preparation of the word processor-created manuscript file is necessary; you simply tell the program which files you want indexed, and away it goes.

How, then, does the program distinguish one data record from another? It doesn't: automatic indexing FFISRs treat the data record concept arbitrarily. One program (FYI 3000) considers a paragraph of text as a unit, and shows you retrieved paragraphs. Another (ZyIndex) takes a whole disk file as a unit, and shows you the beginning of the file in which the information you want is stored. Pressing a button takes you to all the screenfuls of text in that file in which the search terms you entered are mentioned.

ADVANTAGES. Automatic indexing FFISRs are exceptionally easy to use. Unlike controlled vocabulary FFISRs (see below), you don't have to worry about making up controlled vocabulary key words or putting symbols in to demarcate the records. They operate very rapidly, moreover, because they search an index (rather than the actual text). This feature makes these programs suitable for truly massive data bases containing up to 10,000 pages or more of material.

DISADVANTAGES. The chief disadvantage of the automatic indexing FFISR is the *full text search* technique it employs. You're not searching a carefully controlled and deliberately selected set of search terms, the way you do when you use a controlled vocabulary FFISR. On the contrary, you're searching through the entire text, and that means you're certain to retrieve a high proportion of irrelevant material. Here's an illustration.

Let's suppose you want to search for material on Type I supernovas in a data base of information on supernovas. The program will take you with supreme accuracy to all instances of the term "Type I." Among those instances will be several passages that are mainly about Type I supernovas. That's fine; that's the target. The problem is that you'll also see material that's about something else but mentions Type I supernovas peripherally. Notes on Type II supernovas, for example, will almost invariably mention Type I supernovas, but the term may be mentioned only in passing.

The major drawback of automatic indexing FFISRs, in sum, is that they can tell you with supreme accuracy what a passage contains, but they don't give you any way to indicate what it is *about*.

EXAMPLE: ZYINDEX PROFESSIONAL. (ZyLab Corporation, 233 East Erie St., Chicago, IL 60611, for the IBM Personal Computer and PC-compatibles), indexes files created with a wide variety of word processing programs.[3] You can create a single data base containing 5000 disk files, each 125,000 words (500K or more) in length. ZyIndex includes an unusually complete set of logical operators,

---

[3] As of this writing, EasyWriter II, Microsoft Word, Multimate, Palantir, Smart Word Processor, Volkswriter Deluxe II, Wang Word Processor, Word Perfect, WordPlus PC, WordStar, WordStar 2000, Xywrite II, and all ASCII-based text editors such as ProofWriter, Edix, and so on.

including OR, AND, NOT, and WITH/*n*. Available also are parenthetical expressions as well as single-character and multicharacter wild cards, extremely attractive features indeed.

The WITH/*n* operator is of particular value since ZyIndex considers an entire disk file to be equivalent to a single data record. A 10,000-word disk file, for instance, might contain the words "business" and "software" but have nothing to do with business software; indeed, the two words could be separated by a dozen pages. Searching for "business WITH/15 software," however, makes sure that the file won't be retrieved unless the two words are closely related somewhere in the text. What makes this feature so desirable is that it gives you a way to overcome (if only partially) a major drawback of automatic indexing FFISRs, namely, their inability to label what passages of text are about. Using the WITH/*n* operator gives you some assurance that when you search, you'll retrieve a document that's in some way about business software rather than a completely irrelevant one that happens to mention the two terms separated by vast gulfs of text.

ZyIndex's prowess was amply demonstrated during General William Westmoreland's libel suit against CBS in 1984 and 1985. Legal researchers used the program to index and search daily court transcripts, which totaled 10,000 pages at the end of the trial. The program indexed each day's court transcripts, 200 pages in length or more, in about 10 minutes, giving the lawyers by late afternoon a complete record, searchable in seconds, of everything that had transpired in the courtroom up to that point. In the legal setting, having rapid access to massive transcripts can prove invaluable in plotting courtroom strategy. If you need to know just who said what about malice in the trial, for instance, you can find out in seconds.

RECOMMENDED APPLICATIONS. Automatic indexing FFISRs are especially recommended for creating and searching massive textual data bases of unstructured or loosely structured material, such as court transcripts or chronologically organized field notes. Because these programs automatically construct an index to these data bases, they provide sophisticated access to the information the data bases contain without requiring tedious or costly modifications to the information. They're less useful for storing and retrieving material that can be separated into distinct data records, each of which is about something in particular (for example, a data base of notes on specific articles).

Writers can use an automatic indexing FFISR to create a data base of their manuscripts. Suppose, for example, you want to check what you've written and published previously on a particular subject. With your disk-based manuscripts indexed by a FFISR, you can load the program, type in the search terms, and in seconds find all the passages in everything you've written that pertain to the search terms.

Controlled Vocabulary FFISRs

Controlled vocabulary FFISRs let you set up a massive textual data base with distinct data records and give you a way to indicate what each data record is about. That's their principal advantage—and, as will be seen, their principal liability.

Each record is stored with a set of *key words*, or index terms that you deliberately type into the record. The program creates an index that contains only those words (and no others); the text of the record is not indexed. In other words, you control the index's vocabulary.

ADVANTAGES. Like automatic indexing FFISRs, controlled vocabulary FFISRs operate rapidly because they search the index (not the actual text). They are exceptionally well suited, therefore, for truly massive textual data bases.

A controlled vocabulary FFISR lets *you* control the vocabulary with which you'll be searching. The only information a controlled vocabulary FFISR will retrieve when searching is the information you have deliberately placed in the key word field. Controlled vocabulary searching is recommended when it's vital to reduce the retrieval of irrelevant information or to indicate what a data record is about.

Suppose you're setting up a data base of research notes on supernovas. Supernovas are divided into Type I and Type II, and a particular item in the literature is likely to report research on one or the other. But an article on Type I is likely to mention Type II peripherally. If you're controlling the search vocabulary and, after reading an article, you know it's on Type I supernovas, you can put Type I in the key word list (but not Type II). That way, when you're searching for articles on Type I supernovas, you'll retrieve essays that are mainly about Type I supernovas (and none that are mainly about Type II supernovas).

DISADVANTAGES. The chief disadvantage of controlled vocabulary FFISRs is that information in the rest of the data record is not indexed and cannot, therefore, be retrieved if the key word list does not include any reference to it. That can be an advantage. But it often happens that when you're indexing you're looking at an article from a certain angle, even though you may not be aware of it. Later, you might want to look at the same literature from another angle, but you may have neglected to index the article with that second angle in mind. It's always hard to predict in advance the different ways you might want to look at your notes or a bibliographic citation in the future.

Another major disadvantage of controlled vocabulary searching is that it's tedious to format the file with the necessary markers and write your own key words. Controlled vocabulary FFISRs can use files you've created with your word processing program, but you have to format the file first with special markers that tell the program where data records begin and end. Moreover, you have to think up key words for each record and type them in. For huge information management projects, formatting the file and sorting all the information into distinct data records could prove prohibitively tedious.

EXAMPLE: SUPERFILE. SuperFile (FYI, Inc.) well illustrates controlled vocabulary FFISRs. To create a data base with SuperFile, you use your word processing program to write up the material you want to store and retrieve (say, a set of bibliographic citations and abstracts). So that SuperFile will know how to demarcate the data records, you insert special signal characters, prefaced with an asterisk, to inform the program how to tell where one record ends and the next one begins. Figure 9-6 shows a typical SuperFile entry, the example being drawn from a bibliographic data base. The *C marker tells the program that a data record begins; the *E marker tells it that the record has ended.

The *K marker tells SuperFile that the words to follow are key words; that is, they're words that are especially pertinent to the content of the record. SuperFile searches only for the words you've listed in this special key word section. You may include up to 250 key words in each key word field.

This example points up the limitations of FFISRs in general. Suppose, for example, you wished to search for "nationalism," a term that's relevant to this data record. But SuperFile won't retrieve it. You weren't looking at this citation from that angle when you wrote the key words; you were concentrating on ethnicity and language conflict. SuperFile would tell you that no records existed

---

*C

Vijaya, Samaraweera, "The Evolution of a Plural Society," in K.M. de Silva (ed.), Sri Lanka: A Survey. Honolulu: Univ. Press of Hawaii, 1977.

Abstract: This short essay well summarizes the development of the classic, strife-torn "plural society"—a society marked by ethnic rivalry, nationalism, and conflict—after the rise of mass political participation in colonial Ceylon and, especially, after the island's independence. Particular attention is paid to the rise of nationalist political organizations (particularly S.W.R.D. Bandaranaike's Sri Lanka Freedom Party [SLFP]) among the island's dominant ethnic population, the Sinhalese, which led to the adoption of Sinhala as the country's "sole official language," much to the dismay of minority Tamil speakers.

*K

PLURAL SOCIETY / ETHNICITY / ETHNIC CONFLICT / COLONIAL PERIOD / INDEPENDENCE / TAMIL / SINHALA / SINHALESE / BANDARANAIKE /SRI LANKA FREEDOM PARTY / SLFP / 1958 RIOTS / LANGUAGE

*E

FIGURE 9-6. SuperFile Data Record

that contained information on this topic when in fact there is at least one (and perhaps many more).

Like automatic indexing FFISRs, controlled vocabulary FFISRs let you create truly massive textual data bases (even when you're using a floppy disk drive-based system). SuperFile, for example, lets you create a massive data base containing up to 20,000 separate disk files, each containing millions of characters. The data base can be distributed over a maximum of 255 floppy disks.

SuperFile gives you a powerful set of searching options. You can construct a complex, well-focused search question using logical operators, the connectors AND, OR, and NOT, to form search questions such as "show me all the data records that mention 'Sinhala' AND 'language conflict' but NOT the ones that mention '1958 Riots.'"

RECOMMENDED APPLICATIONS. Controlled vocabulary FFISRs are an excellent choice when you want to create a large textual data base and, at the same time, exercise conscious control over how the information in it is organized for retrieval purposes. These programs operate rapidly and can work with massive amounts of text. At the same time, they let you demarcate distinct data records and indicate precisely what the text in the records is about.

An astronomer whose research notes include entries that are about Type I supernovas (but contain references to Type II supernovas), for instance, will appreciate the ability to label a record as being about Type I supernovas. As will be seen in Chapter 10, moreover, controlled vocabulary searching can provide a way to bring about a working version of Vannevar Bush's MEMEX, with its permanently encoded trails of association that provide illuminating pathways through the material.

Bear in mind, however, the limitations of the controlled vocabulary FFISR: you have to format the file with markers and create your own key words. That's a lot of work. If you start with a massive amount of material (say, 3000 pages of field notes), you might find the job so tedious (or expensive) that you'll give up before finishing the project. In such cases, automatic indexing FFISRs are recommended. Controlled vocabulary FFISRs are excellent choices when you're starting a data base from scratch and plan to add small amounts of material to it steadily (for example, a page or two of reading notes per day).

TEXT-ORIENTED FILE MANAGEMENT PROGRAMS

Text-oriented file management software (FMS) represents the next step up in complexity and power from free-format information retrieval systems. The major advantage of a text-oriented FMS is that you can combine the virtues of controlled vocabulary and full text searching without suffering either one's liabilities.

Text-oriented file management programs do not require you to create a data base with your word processing program. Instead, they have their own word processing functions (which are rudimentary, but sufficient for their intended purposes) built in. The most important difference is that a file management program lets you design your own data record format, using a pattern of named data fields (such as, for instance, "author," "citation," and "annotation") that appears on each data record. You can sort the records on any of the fields you've defined (you can sort your bibliography, for example, by author, by date, or by call number). When you're printing, you don't have to print the whole record; you can print only the fields you want printed (leaving out, for instance, the abstracts in a bibliographic data base so that only the citations are printed). The information contained in the data records is, in short, highly structured, and that gives you the ability to manipulate it in many ways.

Advantages

To illustrate the advantages of text-oriented FMS, consider setting up a data base with a field for a record's full text and a second field for controlled vocabulary key words (Figure 9-7).

CITATION	Vijaya, Samaraweera, "The Evolution of a Plural Society," in K.M. de Silva (ed.), Sri Lanka: A Survey. Honolulu: Univ. Press of Hawaii, 1977.
ABSTRACT	This short essay well summarizes the development of the classic, strife-torn "plural society"—a society marked by ethnic rivalry, nationalism, and conflict—after the rise of mass political participation in colonial Ceylon and, especially, after the island's independence. Particular attention is paid to the rise of nationalist political organizations (particularly S.W.R.D. Bandaranaike's Sri Lanka Freedom Part [SLFP]) among the island's dominant ethnic population. the Sinhalese, which led to the adoption of Sinhala as the country's "sole official language," much to the dismay of minority Tamil speakers.
KEY WORDS	PLURAL SOCIETY, ETHNICITY, ETHNIC CONFLICT, COLONIAL PERIOD, INDEPENDENCE, TAMIL, SINHALA, SINHALESE, BANDARANAIKE, SRI LANKA FREEDOM PARTY, SLFP, 1958 RIOTS, LANGUAGE

FIGURE 9-7. FMS Data Record

Suppose you're interested in nationalism, but only as it pertains to Sri Lanka. To retrieve relevant records, you could search in the following way: "Find all the records in which the field ABSTRACT contains NATIONALISM and the field KEY WORDS contains SRI LANKA." Note that searching this way returns all the records that mention nationalism in the full text of the abstract, as long as they also mention Sri Lanka in the key word field. What you've done, in essence, is pointed the search with great accuracy toward precisely those records which are about Sri Lanka and mention nationalism in any way.

To illustrate the great virtues of this search flexibility with another example, let us return to Type I and Type II supernovas. A record that's *about* Type I supernovas will have that term in its key word list. You can pinpoint your search, then, to just those articles that are about Type I supernovas without worrying about retrieving irrelevant articles that mention Type I supernovas only peripherally (but are really about something else). At the same time, you can also search the full text of the abstracts for concepts or terms you may have neglected to index. You can search, for example, for all the records which are about Type I supernovas but which also mention the Magellanic Clouds in the abstract field. And if you want to see every record that mentions Type I supernovas, however peripherally, you can do a full text search of the abstract field.

Disadvantages

The major disadvantages of text-oriented file management programs are their slow speed and limited data base size.

Because most of these programs search the full text of each and every record, rather than an index, operation becomes increasingly sluggish in direct proportion to the number of records in the data base. A good FFISR can search 100 data records per second; a file management program may take from one to several minutes to do the same job.

These programs usually limit the size of the data base to disk capacity. If you're using a hard disk (see Appendix I), of course, you'll have enough disk space to create a large data base, but the slow operation of the FMS then becomes a problem.

Example: Notebook II

(Pro/Tem Software, 814 Tolman Drive, Stanford, CA 94305, available for the IBM PC and PC-compatible computers; Notebook I, an earlier version, is available for most computers.) Notebook II is a text-oriented information management system that's in a class by itself. Designed for scholars and scholarly applications, Notebook II is a sophisticated file management program that's specifically designed for the storage and retrieval of text.

In its IBM PC version, Notebook permits you to enter up to 30,000 characters in each of up to 50 data fields per record, and gives you the full panoply of FMS utilities (searching, logical operators, sorting, selection, and printing). The program is exceptionally easy to use. Scholars will appreciate Notebook II's ability to make full use of the IBM PC's extended character set, which includes many foreign language and scientific symbols. Notebook II is of special interest to scholars because it's designed to work with a particularly ingenious Pro/Tem product called Bibliography (Chapter 7).

Example: Microsoft File

(Microsoft Corporation, 10700 Northrup Way, Bellevue, WA 98004, for the Apple Macintosh) Microsoft File can be viewed as a text-oriented file management program. Up to 1023 data fields may be defined for each data record, and each data field may contain up to 32,767 characters. All the foreign language and scientific symbols available with Mac's Option key are available to Microsoft File. In addition to its excellent text-handling features, Microsoft File permits the user to establish numerical fields and provides tools for performing computations on them (however, no built-in statistical functions are provided).

Recommended Applications

Because of their slow speed and data base size limitations, text-oriented file management programs aren't well suited to storing and retrieving massive textual data bases containing thousands of pages of text (see Chapter 10). They're better suited to storing and retrieving information from smaller data bases, such as a scholar's annotated bibiography of several hundred citations and abstracts (see Chapter 11).

IDEA PROCESSING PROGRAMS

To include idea processing programs such as ThinkTank (see Chapter 4) under the rubric "data base management software" is to stretch that term's definition. Idea processing programs are, in essence, aids for creating an outline, and they were originally intended for writing applications. Nevertheless, for certain purposes such programs can indeed be viewed as tools that can facilitate the storage and retrieval of information, and they're considered here from that angle.

What makes certain idea processing programs suitable for data management purposes is their provision of a text storage feature. The programs that include this feature let you store, under the headings of an outline, free-format entries that can contain tens of thousands of characters. One could create, therefore, an idea processor–based data management system that organizes free-format textual entries under a complex set of headings and subheadings.

```
+ Outline for Research Monograph
   + Introduction
   + The Problem
   + The Method
   + The Data
   + Results
   + Interpretation
   + Conclusions
```

FIGURE 9-8. ThinkTank Outline

Example: ThinkTank

(Living Videotext, Inc.) is the first outline-oriented file management program, and it well exemplifies the strengths (and limitations) of this type of software for data base management. You can use ThinkTank to create a complex outline, which could, for instance, represent a plan for a research monograph (Figure 9–8).

The plus signs (+) in front of the headings indicate that they precede a subordinate heading (or headings) that may be visible or hidden from view. The hidden, or collapsed, headings may be made visible if you wish (Figure 9–9).

ThinkTank permits you to place up to 20,000 characters (or 900 lines) of free-format text under any subheading of the outline. The program, therefore, isn't merely an outlining program; it's also useful for storing massive amounts of text (up to the limits imposed by your computer's disk drive). In contrast to free-format or file management programs, however, this information is stored under hierarchically organized headings and subheadings (Figure 9–10). You may restructure the framework of headings and subheadings if you wish.

Advantages

Managing data with an idea processing program makes good sense when the information to be stored must be subsumed under a complex, hierarchically

```
+ Outline for Research Monograph
   + Introduction
   + The Problem
      + Survey of the Literature
      + Defining the Problem
      + Statement of Hypothesis
   + The Method
   + The Data
   + Results
   + Interpretation
   + Conclusions
```

FIGURE 9-9. Expanded Heading

```
+ Outline for Research Monograph
  +  Introduction
  +  The Problem
     + Survey of the Literature
        +  Jenkins 1956
        +  Rodale 1959
        +  Peterson and Roberts 1962
        +  Radkin 1968
        +  Chen 1975
```

Chen, Li, "Urban Development in the Third World," Urban Affairs and Redevelopment 3:5 (September, 197), pp. 23-28.

Chen directly addresses the theories of Peterson and Roberts (1962) and Radkin (1968) and presents new evidence that contradicts their predictions. Rates of internal migration and seasonal migration in Third World cities, Chen argues, cannot be squared with their theories. Chen introduces a new model which represents a more accurate and sensitive estimator of urban development processes considering several factors connected with migration.

```
     + Defining the Problem
     + Statement of Hypothesis
  +  The Method
  +  The Data
  +  Results
  +  Interpretation
  +  Conclusions
```

FIGURE 9-10. Free-Format Textual Entry

organized structure. An excellent example is a data base of lecture notes, handouts, and other material for a course. You're not stuck with the structure you've chosen because the program gives you tools for reorganizing it.

Disadvantages

Because idea processing programs such as ThinkTank do not include sophisticated search features such as logical operators, they make it difficult to search for information stored in the text areas, which are usually hidden from view. The best guide to the contents of the text areas is the headings themselves. When the information to be stored cannot be readily categorized by the framework of headings and subheadings, idea processors are likely to impede rather than assist data base management. For that reason, an idea processing program works well for storing and organizing research notes under the organizational framework of a planned writing project, as in the above example.

But it would be much less useful for creating a general data base of research notes in which the overall structure is of little prominence or concern. For that purpose, free-format information storage and retrieval systems excel, as you'll see in the chapter to follow.

Recommended Applications

Because the hierarchical organization of the stored material is so pronounced, idea processing programs are at their best for storing and retrieving data when the overall structure of the material is known in advance. This isn't to deny, of course, that the structure can be changed with the program's restructuring commands. Even so, the software's limited searching capabilities make other programs such as FFISRs or FMS more appealing when the overall structure to be imposed on the material is vague or temporary.

Where that structure is clear, however, idea processing programs can work beautifully as data base management programs. Consider, for example, a biologist who wishes to store her research notes under Linnaean classifications. A major heading for the order Cetacea, for example, could be expanded to reveal the suborders Mysticeti and Denticete; expanding Denticete could reveal further biological subclassifications or a series of articles listed in alphabetical order by author's last name.

INFORMATION MANAGEMENT HORIZONS

What you've just learned about personal computer data base management programs will pave the way for your exploration of online data base services in Chapter 13. These services let you connect your computer, via telephone lines, to huge mainframe computers whose auxiliary memories contain as many as 75 million bibliographic citations and abstracts. After you've made the connection, your computer becomes, in essence, a control terminal of the service's computer.

The software these services use is fully comprehensible in the terms established in this chapter. In essence, this software—the software you'll actually use after you connect with the service—is much like the text-oriented file management software discussed above and exemplified by the program Notebook. The bibliographic data records have distinct data fields, and you can search them by using controlled vocabulary techniques (there's a separate key word field) or full-text searching of the abstracts. The logical operators (OR, AND, NOT, and WITH), wild cards (single-character and multicharacter), and parenthetical expressions work just the same way. The only difference is that, unlike personal computer–based FMS, the mainframe software creates a FFISR-like index and searches it instead of the individual records. The result is extremely fast retrieval time even with data bases containing a million or more records.

Online data base services provide a significant part of the personal computer's MEMEX-like capabilities, and you'll surely want to explore them (see Part Four/Communicating). For now, learning how to use a personal computer–based data base managment program provides excellent training and preparation for going online. Remember that when you're doing online searching you're being charged for every second you're connected, so online searching isn't a good way to become familiar with the intricacies of searching with logical operators. It's far better to practice with a personal computer–based data base management program first.

RESOURCES

On creating a data base with a word processing program, see Dara Pearlman, "Managing Data with a Word Processor," *Popular Computing* (Feb. 1984), pp. 160–163, and her "Throw Out Your Index Cards," *PC: The Independent Guide to IBM Personal Computers* 4:4 (Feb. 19, 1985), pp. 331–332. For an extensive illustration, see Chapter 6 of my *Macintosh for College Students* (Berkeley: Sybex Computer Books, 1984).

For a readable overview of theoretical issues in the design of data base management systems, see Michael Lesk, "Computer Software for Information Management," *Scientific American* 251:3 (Sept. 1984), pp. 162–173. A standard technical work on data base software technology for mainframes and minicomputers is C. J. Date, *An Introduction to Data Base Systems: Vol. 1.* 3rd ed. (Reading, MA: Addison-Wesley, 1981), and *An Introduction to Data Base Systems: Vol. II* (Reading, MA: Addison-Wesley, 1983). Less technical is Date's lucid and readable work on data base management from the user's viewpoint, *Database: A Primer* (Reading, MA: Addison-Wesley, 1984).

For do-it-yourselfers, a fine introduction to data file programming (suitable for any computer which runs BASIC, not just the IBM PC) is Alan Simpson, *Data File Programming on Your IBM PC* (Berkeley: Sybex Computer Books, 1984).

An excellent automatic indexing FFISR is FYI 3000 (FYI, Inc., P.O. Box 26481, Austin, TX 78755, for the IBM Personal Computer and PC-compatibles). See Hunter McCleary, "FYI 3000: The Unconventional Database Management Program," *Database* 7:4 (Dec. 1984), pp. 49–53.

RETRIEVING
RESEARCH NOTES

Taking notes is an essential part of scholarly work. Whether you're an anthropologist in the field, a judicial scholar reviewing dozens of court battles, or a linguist carefully noting the patterns of speech used by children, you're sure to accumulate a voluminous sheaf of notes.

Under precomputer conditions, however, finding notes you've already taken is so tedious that, in practice, they're seldom fully utilized. Personal computer technology, happily, puts a sophisticated storage and retrieval system for research notes within the reach of every scholar. And, as you'll see below, you can do more than merely store notes and retrieve them rapidly and accurately. You can also work with your research notes data base the way Vannevar Bush foresaw in 1945 (see Chapter 9): as an aid to thought and discovery.

Free-format information storage and retrieval (FFISR) software (see Chapter 9) provide the ideal tool for retrieving information from massive data bases of research notes. Because these programs construct an index of search terms and search the index rather than the full text, they can search massive data bases rapidly. ZyIndex, for example, can search a 48,000-word document to locate 64 instances of a search term in about 10 seconds. Moreover, FFISRs let you create massive data bases even under the constraints of a floppy disk drive–based personal computer. SuperFile, for instance, can handle a single data base with the material distributed over 255 floppies. File management programs, by contrast, search far more slowly and limit data base size to the capacity of a single disk.

This chapter illustrates the application of FFISRs to the storage and retrieval of research notes. Discussed are both automatic indexing and controlled vocabulary FFISRs, continuing the discussion begun in Chapter 9 of their advantages and disadvantages.

THE AUTOMATIC INDEXING APPROACH

Automatic indexing FFISRs are best applied to voluminous data bases of research notes, such as the transcripts of a court trial or a scientist's field notes. In particular, they're well suited to large data bases in which it would be uneconomical, inconvenient, or otherwise unadvisable to segregate the material into short, distinct data records.

The transcripts of the Westmoreland-CBS libel case, for example, required about 10,000 double-spaced typewritten pages. To separate all this material into separate data records and add key words, as a controlled vocabulary FFISR (or FMS) requires, would require far too much work. Furthermore, it wouldn't serve any purpose. What's of interest is being able to find out what was said about a particular topic. Dividing up all the material into distinct data records (for example, a record containing testimony about Westmoreland's performance as a general in Vietnam) wouldn't improve the program's performance or the data base's usefulness. It would just take a lot of time and cost a lot of money. The point, rather, is to throw a huge mass of material into one, gigantic data base, so that you can find every instance of a given search term throughout the whole thing.

A case in point is a project under way in the University of Chicago's Department of Behavioral Science, where anthropologist Alan Fiske is using ZyIndex to retrieve information from a massive data base of anthropological field notes. The data base, which will ultimately occupy about 8 megabytes of disk space, stems from on-the-site tape recordings in the Indian state of Orissa. Translated into English by a team of Indian specialists, the material was keyed into an IBM Personal Computer. Using this single, massive data base, a researcher could, for instance, type in a search question, such as "Barber? WITH/25 pollution," and be shown every place in the data base where the Barber caste is mentioned within 25 words of the term "pollution."

Commenting on the data base's value, Fiske says, "It's something like collecting a lot of personal observations and then trying to remember specific ones a couple of years later. The computer provides us with a vast memory, and with ZyIndex, we retrieve precisely the information we want for a particular study or project." Fiske expects that the easily searched material will provide the basis for several scholarly articles and books.

Even if automatic indexing FFISRs save money by doing the indexing for you, there's still the expense of keying the material into the computer. But *optical character recognition* (OCR) technology can take care of that problem handily. Until recently, OCR readers, which translate typewritten or printed material into ASCII-coded disk files, cost several thousand dollars or more. Omni-Reader (Oberon International, 5525 MacArthur Blvd., Suite 630, Irving, TX, 75038), for example, provides OCR capabilities for any personal computer with an RS-232 serial interface (see Appendix I) for less than $500.

THE CONTROLLED VOCABULARY APPROACH

In some textual data base management applications, it makes good sense to label the records with a key word indicating what they're about or what they contain, especially when those key words are ones that aren't actually used in the stored text. Consider, for example, an astronomer's data base of reading notes that contains (among other things) some specific examples that might prove useful, say, in writing a paper or giving a lecture. If you're able to label a data record with key words that summarize its content and include the word "example," you could search (for instance) for "black hole AND example." Controlled vocabulary FFISRs provide precisely this record categorizing capability, and that's exactly why they're desirable for some applications.

The pages to follow explore a controlled vocabulary FFISR approach to a scholar's data base of reading notes, an application that's perfectly suited to the controlled vocabulary FFISR's capabilities.

CREATING DATA RECORDS

Controlled vocabulary FFISRs let you create a data base of reading notes with a word processing program and they place few restrictions on the way you organize the actual text of the data records. That's convenient when you're taking reading notes; there's no telling how you'll want to format the notes you take. But you must insert special symbols in the data file to demarcate individual data records, and you'll have to decide what key words you want the program to use in indexing the data record. SuperFile, for example, requires you to mark the beginning of a data record with *C, the beginning of the key words section with *K, and the end of the record with *E. Figure 10-1 shows a data record from a SuperFile data base. Note the key words after the *K marker.

SuperFile lets you create data records up to half a million characters in length, but there's every reason to suggest that you keep your records short. The point of an information storage and retrieval system is to give you quick and accurate access to the knowledge you've stored in it. Creating lengthy data records frustrates this goal. SuperFile can only take you to the beginning of the record; to find what you want within it, you have to search manually. Keeping your records short, therefore, gives you pinpoint control over your data base. Write several data records on a piece you're reading rather than just one.

Another reason for keeping your record short (preferably, no more than 20 lines of single-spaced text) is that it's very helpful to have the whole record in view on the screen when you're constructing a list of key words. The key words are of paramount importance since they're the terms by which SuperFile indexes (and finds) the data records. If there's a topic covered in the data record that's not reflected in the key word list, SuperFile won't be able to find the information. You

---

*C

Kanter (1972) defines communes as essentially egalitarian in
ethic and ethos. Communes that incorporate inequality in any
relationship, including sex role relationships or economic
inequality, are inherently unstable and "neither very communal
nor very cohesive"(305).

*K

COMMUNAL STUDIES / ROSABETH KANTER / DEFINITION / IDEOLOGY / SEXUAL
EQUALITY / ECONOMIC INEQUALITY / SEX ROLES /
SOCIAL DISORDER / COHESION

*E

FIGURE 10-1. Data Record from a SuperFile Data Base

may write up to 250 descriptors, each comprising a word or phase of up to 64
characters.

An excellent way to keep your data records short is to segregate them
according to the kind of information they contain. When you're taking notes on
an essay, for example, you can put a note about the essay's theoretical position in
one note, some interesting substantive information in a second one, a key
definition in a third one, and a particularly appealing quotation in a fourth. See
"Analytical Key Words" for more information on this approach and its value.

USING KEY WORDS

Whether a controlled vocabulary FFISR will do the job it's supposed to do
depends on how much thought you put into the key words you attached to each
data record.

Writing good key words requires more than merely summarizing the data
record's contents. You'll need to develop the ability to look at those contents from
several different angles, and to do so consistently. For a data base of research
notes, you may find it helpful to distinguish between:

Content key words   Key words that indicate what the data record is about.
Analytical key words   Key words that indicate what kind of information
the data record contains.

Content Key Words

Content key words are of two kinds, *descriptors* and *identifiers*.

Descriptors are key words that describe the overall subject (communal
studies), main concepts (sexual equality), or type of material discussed
(quotation, example).

Identifiers are key words that describe the particular topics that make this data record unique, such as geographical locaters (Kentucky, Heavenly Pastures), important works discussed (Kanter 1972), specific subtopics (communal economic systems), named persons (Harriett Frederick), or any other words or phrases that describe the specific contents of the record.

Descriptors let you classify a data record in terms of broad, overarching categories, while identifiers let you indicate the specific content of a particular record. In other words, you've two pathways to the information contained in the data base. You can search broadly for all the records that touch on the general subject or concept, as indicated by the descriptor (for instance, "Show me all the records that pertain to communal studies"), or you can search narrowly for only those records that pertain to a particular subject ("Show me the record or records that pertain to Heavenly Pastures").

So that you use your descriptors consistently, it makes good sense to jot them down in a notebook that you can keep near your computer. You may introduce new descriptors in the data base as need arises, of course, but try to be as consistent in your usage as possible. Remember, when you search broadly for all your notes on communal studies you want to retrieve all relevant data records. Those that are indexed under "utopian studies" or "commune studies" will not be retrieved.

Analytical Key Words

Analytical key words describe the kind of information contained in a data record. Data records written after reading a scholarly article, for example, could be differentiated by using the following analytical key words:

Argument   Epitomizes the theoretical position or argument the article makes.

Replication   Provides data in support of a position taken by another author.

Counterargument   Epitomizes the argument an article makes against a recognized position in the literature.

Reply   Epitomizes the reply an author is making to a counterargument.

Key data   Contains some significant substantive information, such as a table of data or extensive quotations from first-hand, original field research.

Definition   Definitions of key terms.

Quotations   Quotations of unusual eloquence, aptness, or importance that you think you might like to cite.

Example   Particularly telling or engaging examples.

Reflection   A data record containing your own thought on a subject.

Trail   A data record containing a list of search questions that you've used successfully to explore a particular topic in the data base.

Whether these analytical key words will prove useful to you depends on the kind of work you're doing. This particular set is designed for categorizing reading notes, and they're intended to let you encode the patterns of scholarly debate (argument, counterargument, reply) as well as label the nature of the data record's contents (key data, definition, quotation, example). The last two, reflection and trail, are designed to let you record for future reference your own conclusions and the precise avenue by which you reached them.

The Trial Run

Just how these key words can be used and what they'll do will become clearer in a moment. Note, however, this caveat: Write up about ten or 12 data records with key words and try searching your data base before writing any more. You'll almost certainly find that you could revise your key words to achieve better control over the information contained in your data records. If you've only written ten or 12 records, it's an easy matter to return to the data file and change the key words. You can then extend the new principles underlying your new key word decisions to the new records you add. If you've written a hundred records, you've a nasty job ahead of you.

Taking Notes

We now continue with our communal studies example to illustrate the MEMEX-like functions of the content and analytical key word types just introduced. We begin with adding a record to the data base, continue with an illustration of a hypothetical search, and conclude with a note on adding reflections and other notes to the data base once you've successfully completed a search.

The point of using these key words (particularly the analytical ones) is, as you'll see, not merely to facilitate the retrieval of information from the data base. What's more, it's intended to give you the data analysis capabilities that Vannevar Bush foresaw in his prediction of the MEMEX. The MEMEX, in Bush's view, would help the mind in its associative mode of thought in which, "with one item in its grasp, it snaps instantly to the next that is suggested by the association of thoughts," and so on down a complex pathway or trail of associations.[1]

Suppose you're reading an article that's just appeared. Here are a couple of paragraphs from an imaginary article in that field:

By twentieth-century standards of women's liberation, Harmonious Pastures (1871–1879, located in southwestern Kentucky) was remarkably advanced. Its founder and leader, Harriett Frederick, was a woman, itself a rare phenomenon even among the more advanced communal societies of the 19th century. The women of the commune were encouraged to hold offices, to play key roles in management, and

[1]Bush, "As We May Think," reprinted in *Perspectives on the Computer Revolution,* Zenon W. Pylyshyn, ed. (Englewood Cliffs, NJ: Prentice-Hall, 1970), p. 54.

to develop their full spiritual potential. More than one observer has seen Harmonious Pastures as a true harbinger of a social movement that would transform the fabric of American society a century later.

Yet there is one respect in which Harmonious Pastures seems, at least to modern eyes, to have failed to live up to its ideals. In their economic roles, women were almost wholly restricted to the domestic sphere: sewing, cooking, cleaning, and the like. This gap between ideal and reality, so characteristic of nineteenth century utopias, was rationalized by the commune's leaders as a lamentable but necessary compromise. To safeguard the members' commitment to celibacy, men and women were segregated during the workday. And to survive, the commune had to make best use of its members' skills, which were unevenly distributed: men, for instance, were skilled in farming and the trades, while women were skilled in sewing and canning. The commune desperately needed the skills of its good farmers, merchants, seamstresses, and canners, and it couldn't afford to put them in other jobs for ideological reasons. Notwithstanding its lofty ideals, therefore, Harmonious Pastures provides us with yet another example of the difficulties communal utopias encounter when they try to branch away from the social and cultural context in which they arise.

Figure 10-2 shows a SuperFile data record on this article, which would be directly entered into the computer (and saved in a floppy disk file) with the aid of a word processing program.

---

*C
Smith argues (1984) that communes may have difficulty isolating themselves from the surrounding society (and achieving utopian alterations in conventional work and sex roles) if economic circumstances force them to make use of the differentially distributed skills of incoming members. At Harmonious Pastures (led by Harriett Frederick, 1871-1879), for instance, sexual equality was emphasized. Yet the men who joined the commune were farmers, blacksmiths, potters, etc., while women were skilled in cooking, canning, weaving, etc., and those are the economic roles to which they were assigned. Despite the commune's commitment to sexual equality, therefore, economic realities tended to place men into traditionally masculine occupations and women into traditionally feminine ones. An additional factor at Harmonious Pastures, moreover, was the segregation of men and women during the work day, a move taken to safeguard celibacy. [Note excellent data in table of occupational roles, pp. 34-35]

*K
SMITH 1984 / KENTUCKY / 1871-1879 / HARRIETT FREDERICK / HARMONIOUS PASTURES /CELIBACY / COMMUNAL STUDIES / NINETEENTH CENTURY COMMUNES / WORK / SEX ROLES / ECONOMIC ORGANIZATION / OCCUPATIONAL ROLES / ARGUMENT / KEY DATA

FIGURE 10-2. Data Record

Note the use of:

> **Identifiers**   Examples: Smith 1984, Kentucky, 1871–1879, Harriett Frederick, Harmonious Pastures, celibacy.
>
> **Descriptors**   Examples: communal studies, 19th century communes, work, sex roles, economic organization, occupational roles.
>
> **Analytical key words**   Examples: argument, key data.

Note, too, that it's not necessary to take voluminous notes on everything in an article. That would defeat the purpose of the data base. This particular passage is a juicy one; it states the article's thesis, and naturally it receives a lot of space in the data base. But remember a major goal of this information retrieval system isn't to retype everything you read, but rather to provide pointers to the information that's contained in the article. A data record of key data, for example, could contain little more than the words "See Wren 1981:388–390 for an excellent list of communes active in Kentucky in the late 19th century."

RETRIEVING READING NOTES

Categorizing records in this way can help you follow what Vannevar Bush would call an associative trail, a "trail of interest through the maze of materials" available in the data base. Here's an illustration of how a SuperFile reading notes data base can play this role. You know from your research expertise that Rosabeth Kanter set down a major position in the field of communal studies in 1972, and you're writing a paper that summarizes the recent contributions to the debate on her position. You've read and taken notes on dozens of scholarly articles, and you've used the key word classification scheme suggested above.

To begin, you enter the search question "argument AND Kanter 1972," which returns the data record shown in Figure 10-3.

To see notes you've taken on studies that agree with or confirm Kanter's point of view, you next use the search question "replication AND Kanter 1972" (Figure 10-4).

Now you're interested in seeing whether you have any notes that expressly take issue with Kanter and Conover's thesis. You try the search question "counterargument AND (Kanter 1972 or Conover 1975)," producing the results shown in Figure 10-5.

By now it's clear that this debate hinges on a crucial concept, "commitment mechanism." To refresh your memory on just what Kanter means by that term, you try the search question "definition AND commitment mechanism," producing the results shown in Figure 10-6.

If Singer and Wagner are right, sexual inequality and sexual equality can both function as commitment mechanisms in communal utopias. Examples and quotations should provide illustrations of both. You first enter "example OR quotation AND sexual equality," obtaining the results shown in Figure 10-7.

---

*C
Kanter (1972) asserts that communes (both in the nineteenth and twentieth centuries) are, by necessity, egalitarian in ethos and practice. The communal ethic involves brotherhood, harmony, and equality. Communes that incorporate inequality in any relationship, including sex role relationships, are therefore inherently unstable and "neither very communal nor very cohesive" (305).

*K
KANTER 1972 / COMMUNAL STUDIES / NINETEENTH CENTURY COMMUNES / TWENTIETH CENTURY COMMUNES / SEX ROLES / SEXUAL EQUALITY / SEXUAL INEQUALITY / SOCIAL COHESION AND DISORDER / COMMUNE SUCCESS AND FAILURE / ARGUMENT
*E

FIGURE 10-3. Argument Data Record

Here's a particularly appalling taste of the other side of the story, found by the search question "example OR quotation AND sexual inequality" (Figure 10-8).

Adding Your Conclusions to the Data Base

Evidence exists, in sum, that—contrary to Kanter's and Conover's thesis—sexual inequality can function as a commitment mechanism in communal societies. Further searching reveals, moreover, that sexual inequality isn't merely a fluke exhibited by a few short-lasting communes; some of the longest-lasting and most successful communes, in both the 19th and 20th centuries, have used sexual inequality and harsh traditions of male dominance to break down the dyadic marital bond that threatens communal solidarity.

---

*C
According to Patrick Conover (1975, providing support for Kanter 1972), modern communes tend towards sexual equality. The basis of communal life, he suggests, is economic and sexual equality, and relationships that are inherently unequal (such as traditional sex roles) would bring intolerable and disruptive relations of antipathy into group life.

*K
KANTER 1972 / CONOVER 1975 / COMMUNAL STUDIES / TWENTIETH CENTURY COMMUNES / SEX ROLES / SEXUAL EQUALITY / SEXUAL INEQUALITY / SOCIAL COHESION AND DISORDER / ECONOMIC ORGANIZATION/ COMMUNE SUCCESS AND FAILURE / REPLICATION /
*E

FIGURE 10-4. Replication Data Record

Adding your conclusions to the data base will help you retrace your thought, if necessary, in the future. You could add, at this point, two data records:

Reflection   A record containing the conclusions just mentioned and the key words KANTER 1972 / SEXUAL EQUALITY / SEXUAL IN-EQUALITY / MALE DOMINANCE / COMMITMENT MECHANISM / COMMUNE SUCCESS AND FAILURE / REFLECTION

Trail   A record listing the successful search terms you used and the key words KANTER 1972 / SEXUAL EQUALITY / SEXUAL INEQUALITY / MALE DOMINANCE / COMMITMENT MECHANISM / COMMUNE SUCCESS AND FAILURE / TRAIL

---

*C

Kanter (1972) argues that communes which do not foster sex role equality are necessarily unstable, but the evidence from the 19th century suggests otherwise. By Kanter's own measurement of communal success, a longetivity of 25 years, a high proportion of the successful 19th century communes practiced male dominance (Wagner 1982:10). Kanter's argument (and Conover's [1975]) can be maintained only by branding as "exceptions" or "isolated cases" those communes that practiced male dominance. But communes practicing male dominance were, both during the 19th and 20th centuries, both numerous and successful; indeed, 20th century communes may be predominantly male dominant.

*K

KANTER 1982 / CONOVER 1975 / WAGNER 1982 / COMMUNAL STUDIES / MALE DOMINANCE / COMMUNE SUCCESS AND FAILURE / / SEXUAL EQUALITY / SEXUAL INEQUALITY / COUNTERARGUMENT

*E

*C

Merrill Singer has argued (1982) that male supremacy isn't necessarily a source of discord in a communal society; in fact, the evidence suggests that it's a commitment mechanism (in Kanter's [1972] sense of the term). In his study of the Black Hebrews, a successful commune (of American origins) in Israel, Singer found that male supremacy discourages "dyadic withdrawal" (by imposing a strong hierarchy in all male-female relations) and blocks pair bonding—it functions, in short, as a commitment mechanism.

*K

KANTER 1972 / WAGNER 1982 / BLACK HEBREWS / COMMUNAL STUDIES / ISRAEL / TWENTIETH CENTURY COMMUNES / MALE DOMINANCE / COMMUNE SUCCESS AND FAILURE / SEXUAL EQUALITY / SEXUAL INEQUALITY / DYADIC WITHDRAWAL / COMMITMENT MECHANISM / COUNTERARGUMENT
*E

FIGURE 10-5. Counterargument Data Records

*C
Successful communal societies, according to Kanter, attempt to
deemphasize the nuclear family, since family attachments tend to
interfere with commitment to the community. Kanter depicts
"familism" and "dyadic withdrawal" as enemies of communal
solidarity. Communes, therefore, try to break down nuclear
families by emphasizing such arrangements as celibacy (or free
love). A natural consequence of this commitment mechanism, she
argues, is that the status of women is enhanced; women have more
political power, and they're less likely to be restricted to
domestic chores. Furthering this tendency towards sexual
equality is the essentially egalitarian nature of the communal
society (Kanter 1972, pp.87-88, passim).

*K
KANTER 1972 / COMMITMENT MECHANISM / DEFINITION
*E

FIGURE 10-6. Definition Data Record

*C
The Shakers strongly emphasized sexual equality. They permitted
women to hold political offices within their own communities, and
they believed that someday women would hold political offices in
the "outer world" as well (Nordhoff 1875 [1965], pp. 165-166).

*K
SHAKERS / NORDHOFF 1875 / SEXUAL EQUALITY / POLITICAL EQUALITY /
EXAMPLE
*E

*C
A woman who resided at the nineteenth century commune Brook Farm
remembered fondly, "and now began my first delightful experience
of `Woman's Rights:' for in the meetings of the Association no
distinction was made on account of sex; and a proposition could
be put, discussed, and voted on, with entire freedom, by women
and men alike. This new sense of power and responsibility
widened my horizon, and included all the benefits I was prepared
to take advantage of." (Cited in Lauer and Lauer 1983, p. 24)
*K
BROOK FARM / LAUER AND LAUER 1983 / SEXUAL EQUALITY / POLITICAL
EQUALITY / QUOTATION
*E

FIGURE 10-7. Example and Quotation Data Records

*C
"It's really unbelievable what those chicks have learned to do
over a fire that's nothing more than a hole in the ground. I
think we're really lucky and I've been in a lot of communes
before this, three of them before we got together. If the chicks
aren't making it, if the chicks don't have any energy and don't
want to do anything, like be chicks, you know, wash dishes, cook,
then you're in for trouble because there's nothing worse than not
getting your food, having all the dishes stacked up." (Cited in
Wagner 1982, p. 36)

*K

WAGNER 1982 / SEXUAL INEQUALITY / EXAMPLE / QUOTATION
*E

FIGURE 10-8. Another Quotation Data Record

The reflection data record will become part of the corpus of records retrieved by future subject searches on the indexed topics, and the trial data record provides a record of the search strategy you used successfully.

Limitations of the PC MEMEX

A personal computer data base will exhibit these MEMEX-like properties only if you've put the necessary material in it (and done a good job of labelling the records with useful key words). And that takes planning and work. Unlike an automatic indexing FFISR, achieving these kinds of results with a controlled vocabulary program requires some experience and expertise at writing key words, and there's some drudgery thrown in. Writing key words can be illuminating—it helps to sharpen your own sense of what the literature is about—but there's no pretending it's great fun.

These drawbacks may discourage you from trying this system, but consider its potential benefits. Imagine that some years from now, you have a massive textual data base containing well over 3000 data records on material you've read in your field, each indexed with a system of key words that's grown more precise as you've become more accustomed to using them. Embedded in the data base are your own reflections on the material, together with records recording successful trails through it that you've already used. You'll find that the data base becomes more responsive and more useful as you progressively refine it; you'll become more adept at writing key words that epitomize your interests and the way you think, for instance, and the reflections you add to it will provide a counterpoint to the exploration of the literature it contains. In the end, you'll have something

```
+  Kanter's thesis (1972)
```

Kanter (1972) asserts that communes (both in the nineteenth and
twentieth centuries) are, by necessity, egalitarian in ethos
and practice. The communal ethic involves brotherhood, harmony,
and equality. Communes that incorporate inequality in any
relationship, including sex role relationships, are therefore
inherently unstable and "neither very communal nor very
cohesive" (305).

```
+  Conover's replication (1975)
+  Wagner's counterargument (1982)
+  Singer's counterargument (1982)
+  Kanter's definition of commitment mechanism
+  Example and quotes about communes practicing sexual equality
+  Example and quotes about communes practicing sexual inequality
+  My reflections on sexual equality & inequality in communes
```

FIGURE 10-9. ThinkTank Outline Containing Ported Data Records

deeply personal: a supple and responsive record of your confrontation with the
literature and your intellectual response to it.

PORTING SEARCH RESULTS

The records that SuperFile finds may be ported, or directed, to your printer
or to a disk file. All the records you retrieve while tracing an associative trail
through the data base, for instance, could be written to do a disk file in ASCII
format, which is readable by your word processing program.

You've doubtless guessed already why that's so useful. Everything captured
in the search just described, for example, could be placed into a disk file that would
form the nucleus of a paper. There would be no need to retype quotations; and
some of the material you've retrieved—your reflections on the subject, for

```
+  My reflections on sexual equality & inequality in communes
+  Kanter's thesis (1972)
    +  Kanter's definition of commitment mechanisms
+  Conover's replication (1975)
+  Example and quotes about communes practicing sexual equality
+  Example and quotes about communes practicing sexual inequality
−  Conclusions
```

FIGURE 10-10. Reorganization of the Outline for Rhetorical Purposes

instance, or particularly telling examples—could be used verbatim.

An even more fruitful strategy is to port the results to an idea processing program such as ThinkTank (see Chapter 4). These programs let you subsume units of text under an outline, which you can easily restructure until you have the information ordered just the way you want it. In ThinkTank, the data records can be stored as free text paragraphs under headings. In Figure 10-9, for instance, the first heading is shown with the paragraph (a data record from the data base) expanded. The other headings contain paragraphs, too, but they're hidden or collapsed so that you can see the outline's overall structure. The plus signs in front of the headings show that there's material hidden under them.

This structure reflects what happened in the search, but it isn't necessarily the right one for rhetorical purposes. Figure 10-10 shows a rearrangement of the material in rhetorical form, providing the basic structure for an essay on the subject. Note that the reflections have been moved to the top, providing a thesis statement for the paper, and Kanter's definition of commitment mechanism has been made a subheading under her 1972 thesis.

RESOURCES

On writing useful key words, see Brenda Gerrie, *Online Information Systems: Use and Operating Characteristics, Limitations, and Design Alternatives* (Arlington, VA: Information Resources Press, 1983) and ERIC (Educational Resources Information Center) indexing rules reprinted in Judith Yarborough, "A Novice's Guide to ERIC—The Database of Education," *Online* 1:3 (July 1977), pp. 24-29. On the technical aspects of indexing techniques used by business data base software, see C. J. Date, *Database: A Primer* (Reading, MA: Addison-Wesley, 1984), pp. 165-175.

MANAGING BIBLIOGRAPHIES

Useful as they are for creating massive textual data bases, free-format information storage and retrieval programs require you to choose between automatic indexing and controlled vocabulary approaches. Each has its advantages and disadvantages, but working with either leads one to appreciate the merits of programs that combine these two approaches. And such software indeed exists. Text-oriented file management programs such as Notebook II let you create records with distinct data fields, some of which can be used for full-text searching and others used for controlled vocabulary key words.

Were these programs not so slow, they'd be recommended for all text-oriented data base applications. But they run like molasses next to a FFISR's quicksilver. SuperFile, for instance, can search 100 records in a second, but it will take Notebook II at least a minute to do the same job. Moreover, file management programs usually limit data base size to disk capacity. If you're using a floppy disk drive–based IBM Personal Computer system, Notebook II limits you to a data base of under 360K (a far cry from SuperFile's 96 megabytes).

If you're creating a data base that's limited in size, however, text-oriented file management software is strongly recommended. An excellent example, and one that's treated in detail in this chapter, is a scholar's personal bibliography. The point of creating a personal bibliography isn't to rival the Library of Congress card catalog. On the contrary, it's to create a highly specialized guide to useful literature in areas of interest to you. At any one time, a scholar's working personal bibliography in this sense would include, perhaps, about 200 to 500 (but rarely more than 1000) citations and abstracts. A file management program can easily take a data base of this size in stride. And if the bibliography threatens to grow beyond bounds, you can divide the material by subject matter into two or more separate data bases.

THE FMS ADVANTAGE

Text-oriented file management software (FMS) takes you to the next step up in complexity and sophistication from the software discussed in Chapter 9. And you'll put the more sophisticated features to good use. Here's a sampling of what such programs will support:

Multiple data fields   Unlike free-format information storage and retrieval programs, which permit you to distinguish (at most) only two fields, file management programs let you define as many as you want. The data base can, moreover, be searched on any one field or any combination of them, vastly increasing the variety of ways you can retrieve the information contained in the data records.

Sorts   File management programs give you tools for sorting your bibliography (even if it contains several hundred citations) in a variety of ways. You can sort it by author's last name, the usual strategy. If you wish, however, you can sort the bibliography in other ways (for instance, by date of publication, library call number, or the first key word). Besides keeping your bibliography organized, sorting techniques make the information in it available. Before going to the library, for instance, you could make a list of the books you want to check out, sorted by Library of Congress call number, thus simplifying their retrieval from the stacks.

Printing views   File management programs offer the same search features discussed in the last chapter, but the fact that they permit you to set up distinct data fields gives you much more control over the information in the data base. With a file management program, for instance, you can instruct the computer (in effect) to "Find all the records in which the field DESCRIPTORS contains the key word MEDICAL PRAC-TICES—ETHICS and the field LIBRARY HOLDINGS contains YES." You'd be given a list (a special "view" of the data base's contents) containing only those works on the ethics of medical practices that are available in your library. You can then elect to print that view, specifying exactly which portions of the data record you want printed.

Most text-oriented file management programs will prove useful for bibliographic management but you'll have to make a decision about whether you'll use a general-purpose FMS—one that can be used for other purposes besides bibliographic work—or a dedicated FMS—one that's designed to serve bibliographic purposes only.

If you choose a general-purpose file management program, you'll be able to use it for applications other than bibliographic management. A researcher could use Notebook II, for example, to store and retrieve research notes when the data base is sure to be of modest size. A teacher could use the program to store examination questions and generate tests from them. An archaeologist could use it to catalog artifacts from a specific excavation. Like all general-purpose software tools, Notebook II's main attraction lies in its flexibility. It can do an excellent job with bibliographic management, as you'll see in the pages to follow. And it can do many other tasks just as well.

But dedicated programs have their advantages, too. A case in point is Personal Bibliographic Software's Professional Bibliographic System (PBS) (Ann Arbor, MI 48106, available for the IBM Personal Computer and PC-compatibles and for the Apple Macintosh). PBS is a dedicated file management program designed to serve one and only one purpose: bibliographic work.

PBS, unlike general-purpose programs such as Notebook II, is ready to go: you don't have to do much to set it up. The data fields are already set up for you (with 20 options, including fully developed data record formats for everything from monographs to sound recordings and even art works). Already developed, too, are printing definitions for printing the bibliography in a wide variety of formats (and you may, if you wish, define your own format for printing).

PBS provides the usual file management software tools for managing and organizing your data base, such as searching using logical operators (AND or OR) and truncation or wild card searching. Up to 30,000 citations and abstracts can be stored and searched on a system equipped with a hard disk.

BIBLIOGRAPHIC DATA MANAGEMENT WITH AN FMS

Appealing as dedicated programs are, it isn't difficult to customize a good file management program for bibliographic work. And the program's available for other uses, too. The pages to follow show how to set up a bibliographic data base management system with Notebook II; the approach is generally applicable to other text-oriented data base management programs.

DEFINING THE DATA FIELDS

File management programs, unlike free-format information retrieval systems such as SuperFile, require you to define data fields, or areas for a specific kind of information (such as "author" or "abstract").

You can't simply enter information anywhere you want or in any format that suits you the way you can with free-format programs. But this constraint, you'll find, is more than balanced by the other major advantages that file management programs have over their free-format counterparts: they permit you to design your own data record format, with an arrangement of headings and data fields that suits your needs, and you can include useful information that you wouldn't want to print (such as a bibliographic abstract). File management programs, as you'll see, give you much more control over the information they store and retrieve.

The first step in creating a bibliographic data base is to consider what data fields you'd like to include and how you'd like them arranged. Those aren't easy questions to answer if you're new to computing and especially to data base management techniques. They require you to have a good idea in advance of how you'll use the data base once you've created it.

Beginning users will almost certainly underestimate the variety of ways the stored information can be used. Ways to modify the data base will become apparent later, but by then dozens or even hundreds of citations have been entered. And because most file management programs don't let you change the data record format significantly after you've established it and entered data, you'll have to create an entirely new data base and enter the data all over again. Good planning, in other words, is essential.

One approach to this planning problem is to make up a wish list of all the things you'd like your electronic bibliography to do besides the obvious function of storing and retrieving bibliographic citations and abstracts. Here's mine:

> The bibliographic data base should work with Pro/Tem's program Bibliography (see Chapter 7), which "reads" a manuscript, compiles a list of the works cited in it from key words embedded in the manuscript, "reads" the bibliographic data base, and constructs an alphabetized list of bibliographic citations.
>
> I'd like to be able to sort the entire data base chronologically, so that I can exclude, if I wish, out-of-date or early works on a subject.
>
> The citations should be written in the bibliographic format accepted in my academic discipline, and they should be stored so they can be easily and quickly printed in that format.
>
> There should be room for a short abstract.
>
> There should be a field that lets me state the source of the abstract. Some of the abstracts will have been copied from, for instance, published indexes (or downloaded from online sources). To protect myself against inadvertent plagiarism, I'd like to be able to indicate whether the abstract is mine or quoted.
>
> The key words or descriptors field should be just underneath the abstract field, so I can refer to the abstract as I'm writing the list of key words.
>
> If the work I'm cataloguing is a library book, I'd like to indicate which library has it and what its call number is.
>
> I'd like a field to indicate which works this author has cited.
>
> I'd like a special field in which I can indicate which works I'd like to obtain next time I'm at the library or bookstore.
>
> There should be a special field in which I can indicate whether I've read the work or not, and if not, whether I should (or must).
>
> I'd like to be able to indicate to which of the several projects I'm involved in the work seems relevant.

My ideal bibliography, then, would let me answer the following questions (among others):

Which works in this data base, published after 1982, are pertinent to writing productivity among college faculty and researchers?

Which books, available in the Main Library, have I promised myself that I'd read for the word processing and English composition project?

What's the title of the book on computer signal processing I read for the data communications project?

Which campus library has that copy of Shelly Turkle's *The Second Self* that I read?

Who has cited Anderson 1981?

What works on local area networks must I read for the data communications project?

Just what you'd like your bibliographic data base to do is entirely up to you; my wish list is offered merely to illustrate the potential range of applications. You may want to try my approach with a test data base so you can develop a feel for what bibliographic data base management is all about. New ideas will certainly occur to you as you do.

CREATING THE DATA BASE

Most file management programs include a special "create" mode, which helps you to define the data fields and design their arrangement on the screen. Using the create mode creates a distinct, named data base. (You can use the create mode to create as many separate data bases as you wish. Each distinct data base must, however, have its own disk.)

You can create several different bibliographic data bases (for example, "English composition bibliography" and "word processing bibliography"), but doing so isn't a good idea unless your interests are completely unrelated to each other ("electrical engineering bibliography" and "Chaucer studies bibliography" would seem to be appropriately separated). That's unlikely. Most scholars have two or three irons in the fire, to be sure, but there are some important—and often particularly fertile—areas of overlap among them. You shouldn't structure your electronic bibliographic system so that those interrelations and overlaps are programmed out. Putting all your citations in one data base, moreover, will save you some work. Works pertaining to both English composition and word processing, for instance, need be entered only once (you'd have to type the same citation twice if you had two separate data bases).

Like most file management programs, Notebook's create mode is selected automatically when the program finds, after you've started it, that no data base has yet been created. You're given the opportunity to name headings for the data

```
KEY:              |
DATE:             |
CITATION:         |
ABSTRACT:         |
SOURCE OF ABSTRACT: |
DESCRIPTORS:      |
WORKS CITED:      |
HOLDINGS:         |
CALL NUMBER:      |
GET?              |
READ YET?         |
PROJECT:          |
```

FIGURE 11-1. Blank Notebook Data Record

fields, and those headings will be displayed whenever you work with this data base.

Figure 11-1 shows a blank Notebook data record using 12 data field headings. This arrangement of data field headings is designed to do all the things on my bibliographic wish list. The DATE data field, for instance, in which the date of publication of each work will be entered, makes it possible to sort the data base chronologically.

The data fields don't look very big in the figure, but that's because Notebook keeps the size of the fields to a minimum so that the data base will remain compact. As you enter text, the fields expand so that you can enter up to 32,000 characters in each one.

DEFINING APPROPRIATE RESPONSES

Before filling in the data records with bibliographic information, it's necessary to decide what constitutes an appropriate response to the data field heading. Inconsistent responses can make the information stored in the data base all but useless. If, for instance, you answer the heading "read yet?" with "sort of," but use "yes" or "no" on all the other readings, that data record will disappear from view when you're searching the data base.

Here's a sample list of appropriate responses, which would be kept by the computer for reference while entering bibliographic data:

Key Author's last name and date of publication (e.g., Newsome 1985). This data field contains an abbreviated reference to a work that's exactly the same as ones placed in a manuscript file for processing by Notebook's sister program, Bibliography.

Date Year of publication.

Citation *University of Chicago Manual of Style* format; indent second and all subsequent lines.

Abstract   Keep it short!

Source of abstract   Options: Mine (if not taken from an index); if quoted, state the title of the source and, if available, the record number (e.g., Educational Resources Information Center Data Base EJ237982 AA532600)

Descriptors   Use this field only for general subject and concept descriptors (see Chapter 10). Since the full text of the abstract can be searched, it will serve as a list of identifiers (see Chapter 10)

Works cited   Key names (Anderson 1981, Calloway 1975) of works of interest that are cited by this work.

Holdings   These options only: Main Library, Education Library, Smallburg Public Library, University of the Midwest Library, personal collection, department collection.

Call number   Library of Congress call number, expressed on one line with period separating the fields (e.g., HQ971.S48). No spaces!

Get   These options only: yes—order; yes—library; no—not needed; have.

Read yet?   These options only: No—probably not useful; no—should read; no—must read; yes.

Project   These options only: English composition and word processing, personal computer signal processing, expert systems/artificial intelligence

Decide on your own list of appropriate responses to the data field headings and keep it right by the computer while you're working. It will help you get the most out of this bibliographic data base management system. If you were to respond "home library" instead of "personal collection" when you were filling out the field "holdings," for example, that record would be lost when you searched for works in your personal collection on a particular subject.

Note, too, that some file management programs are sensitive to upper- and lower-case characters. More than one program, for example, would consider "Word Processing and English Composition" and "Word processing and English composition" to be completely distinct entries, and a search for "Word Processing and English composition" would not find any records entered in either of the first two ways. Notebook isn't sensitive to capitalization, and that's preferable: a good file management program doesn't discard records from a search for spurious reasons such as inconsistent capitalization.

ENTERING DATA

Once you've established a data record format and made decisions about what constitutes an appropriate response in the data fields, you're ready to start entering bibliographic data. There are two ways you can add bibliographic data into your data base: by entering it physically at the keyboard or by *downloading* it from other computers or online data base services.

Entering Data with the Keyboard

Each blank data record always presents you with exactly the same headings, reminding you which information you're supposed to fill in. It's important to remember, though, that the responses must be consistent. Always keep your list of appropriate responses handy while you're working.

Figure 11–2 shows a filled-in Notebook data record.

Downloading Data

Another way to get bibliographic information into your data base is download it from other computers. To download means, in essence, to move

```
KEY:                  |Morgan and Schwartz 1984
                      |
CITATION:             |Morgan, Bradford A., and James M.
                      |  Schwartz, "The Future of Word
                      |  Processing in Academic Writing
                      |  Programs," Research in Word
                      |  Processing Newsletter 2:4 (April
                      |  1984), pp. 1-4.
                      |
ABSTRACT:             |Discusses the implications of software
                      |for computer-assisted instruction in
                      |English composition, including programs
                      |to assist students in: the heuristic
                      |stage of writing, outlining, analyzing
                      |style, and avoiding deadwood phrases.
                      |
                      |This software, by automating many
                      |traditional teaching tasks, will change
                      |the way writing teachers work: there
                      |will be less "correcting" and other
                      |drudgery and more guiding,
                      |supervising, and motivating.
                      |
SOURCE OF ABSTRACT:   |mine
                      |
DESCRIPTORS:          |computer-assisted instruction,
                      |software, English, composition,
                      |teaching, higher education. patterns of
                      |change
                      |
WORKS CITED:          |none
HOLDINGS:             |personal collection
CALL NUMBER:          |
GET?                  |have
READ YET?             |yes
PROJECT:              |English composition and word processing
```

FIGURE 11-2. Filled-in Notebook Data Record

information from one kind of computing device to another.

The most common sources of downloaded information are online data base services, which are described more fully in Part Four. When you've finished receiving data from these services with the help of communications software, you'll have a disk file, written in standard ASCII format, which probably contains several citations and abstracts that are of interest to you.

You can incorporate these citations and abstracts into your data base without having to retype them if your file management program will read data from an ASCII text file.

It will almost certainly be necessary to clean up the text file before your file management program can read it. Along with the citations and abstracts you want will have been recorded spurious information such as search questions, online messages from the service, and other unwanted material. You'll have to edit all the spurious information out before you can use the citations and abstracts. A word processing program's editing functions (described in Part Two) will make short work of the job.

Your file management program still can't read the text file, however, because it doesn't know which fields to put the information into. Using your word processing program, you'll have to code the information in the text file so that it will be inserted in the proper fields. With Notebook, for instance, material that's destined for the CITATION field would be prefaced with a percent sign, the word CITATION, and a colon (%CITATION:).

THE TEST RUN

Before you spend hours entering a large number of citations and abstracts in your data base, be sure that the data record format you've chosen is satisfactory. Most file management programs do not permit you to change the arrangement of headings once the data record format has been defined; to make any save the most minor changes, you'll have to start all over and create an entirely new data base.

It's a good idea, therefore, to test your data record format decisions on a small data base of ten or 20 citations before spending hours (more likely, days) entering the rest of them. Problems in the arrangement of data fields (or gaps in the data headings) will quickly present themselves. You can make the necessary changes in a newly created version of the data base and then enter the rest of your bibliographic citations.

SEARCHING THE DATA BASE

Like free-format information retrieval programs, file management programs let you perform simple searches as well as more complex ones using logical operators (such as AND, OR, and NOT). But they also let you:

Search using *numerical operators,* such as "less than" or "greater than."
Search using search questions that refer to more than one data field.
Create (and print) views (or subsets) of the data base.

Simple Searches

Most file management programs provide a straightforward utility for finding a particular record in the data base. Notebook, for instance, includes a "find" utility that lets you search forward or backward in the data base for the record in which a field you specify (such as "citation") starts with a word or phrase you specify (such as "Smith, Robert N.").

Searching with Logical Operators

Searching a bibliographic data base with a file management program isn't significantly different from searching a text data base with a free-format program (Chapter 10), save that you must specify the field you'd like to search on. A search question framed with, for instance, the file management program Notebook would read: "Find all the records in which the field 'descriptors' contains 'English composition' AND 'software' but NOT 'word processing software'."

Searching with Numerical Operators

Not generally found in free-format programs are numerical operators, such as "less than" or "more than," which are also useful for searching.

Here's an example of Notebook's numerical operators in action. Suppose you're starting with a simple search term, the year 1967, and you're searching on the field "date." The "less than" operator finds all the records in which the field "date" contains a year that's less than 1967, while the "greater than or equal to" finds those records in which the field date contains a year that's greater than or equal to 1967.

You may also use numerical operators for searching non-numerical fields. Here are two examples:

Find all the records in which the field "call number" contains a call number that's greater than or equal to A but less than DT.501. This command finds all the works in the bibliography with call numbers between A and DT.501.

Find all the records in which the field "project" is not equal to "personal computer signal processing." This command excludes any records in which the "project" field begins with the "personal computer signal processing" descriptor.

Searching on Multiple Fields

The addition of numerical operators makes a file management program's search tools more flexible, but what really distinguishes these programs from their free-format counterparts is the ability to search on more than one field. You may combine logical operators and numerical operators with multiple word searches to frame some particularly detailed and productive search questions.

Here are some examples of multiple-field searches:

Find all the records in which the field "date" is greater than or equal to 1982 and the field "descriptors" contains "personal computer signal processing." This strategy finds recent works on the subject.

Find all the records in which the field "holdings" is equal to "Main Library" and the field "get" contains "yes."

Find all the records in which the field "descriptors" contains "word processing" or "English composition" and the field "read yet?" contains "no—must read."

CREATING A VIEW

One particularly attractive feature of many file management programs is the ability to create a view of the data base. A view is a group of data records formed by using a search question, and it can be saved and printed. In the example we've been discussing, it would be useful to create a view with the search question: find all the records in which the field "project" contains "English composition and word processing." The result would be a specialized bibliography drawn from a larger data base that contains many more citations. A view, therefore, is a specialized way of looking at the information the data base contains.

SORTING THE DATA BASE

File management programs usually include sorting utilities that permit you to sort the data base in alphabetical or numerical order on one or more fields.

Sorting on One Field

The simplest sorts are those that involve one field only. The data base we've been discussing, for instance, could be sorted in ascending alphabetical order (that is, from A to Z) on the field "key."

Sorting on More than One Field

You may also sort your data base on more than one field, a feature that's useful when you're doing bibliographic work.

Multiple sorts are much easier to understand if you focus on their hierarchical nature. The primary sorting order—for example, alphabetical sorting by author's last name—is the main one for organizing the data base. In a large bibliographic data base, there would almost certainly be records of several works by the same author. The secondary sorting order—for example, chronological sorting by date of publication—takes care of sorting those records. The result is a data base in which all the records are alphabetized by author; where there are several citations by a single author, they're in chronological order.

Multiple sorts with Notebook are accomplished in a straightforward way by using multiple passes of the sort function. The basic principle is that, when it groups a number of records together that can't be distinguished (for example, seven records by the author "Adams" when you're sorting alphabetically using the field "citation," Notebook simply leaves them in the order it found them in. To sort the data base in the way just described (alphabetically by author, and chronologically where there are several citations by one author), you'd begin by sorting the entire data base chronologically using the field "date." Then you'd sort the entire data base alphabetically by citation (the first word of which is the author's last name).

PRINTING THE DATA BASE

File management programs generally give you several options for printing your bibliography. You may print the entire data base, if you wish, or just a portion of it—a view, in other words. And you may print just a few of the data fields or, if you prefer (and it's recommended for backup purposes), every field in the data record. Finally, you can choose to send the output to the printer or write it to a standard disk file for further modification with a word processing program.

These printing options are selected by the printer control section of the program, which is sometimes called the report generator. The term "report" is a sign of these programs' business origins; many of them were originally designed to produce standard business reports and analyses on such matters as inventory levels. If you encounter the term "report" in your program's manual, just substitute the word "printout."

Designing the Print Format

Because you've so many printing options before you, you'll have to make some decisions about what you want printed before you can use your program's printer control feature. When you've made your decisions, you'll use a special part of the program to create a printing template.

Just what you want printed depends on your purposes at the moment. For backup purposes, it's a good idea to print out the entire bibliography periodically (after sorting it alphabetically), including all the information in every data field. Normally, however, you'll be printing only a view and, what's more, you'll print only some of the data fields.

Suppose, for example, I'm planning a trip to the Main Library. I use Notebook's search features to make a view of all the records in which the field

[CALL NUMBER]

[CITATION] | |

FIGURE 11-3. Notebook Printing Template

"descriptors" contains "composition" AND "software" but NOT "word process-ing programs" AND the field "read yet?" contains "No—must read." Then I sort the view alphabetically by call number. Finally, I create a special printing template that prints only the fields I need for the trip to the library, the call number and citation.

Using the Printing Template

The printing template is best thought of as a kind of sieve that determines which of the data fields is going to pass through it and get to the printer.

Figure 11-3 shows a simplified Notebook printing template. Only two of the 12 fields actually contained in the data records are placed in it, and those are the only two fields that will be printed. And they'll be printed, what's more, precisely the way they're arranged on the template. The contents of the field "call number" will be printed first, followed by a blank line. Then the field "citation" will be printed. The two special symbols (||) tell the program to skip two lines after each listing.

If you prefer, you can insert text in the template, and the program will print that text every time it prints a data record (Figure 11-4).

BIBLIOGRAPHIC HORIZONS

How well an FMS-based bibliography management program functions depends on the size of the data base. A scholar who tried to create a data base containing all known references (good or bad, useful or useless) on a given subject would probably press an FMS to its limits. But there's no reason to do so. Online data base services maintain massive bibliographic data bases with millions of

Call Number: [CALL NUMBER]

Citation: [CITATION] | |

FIGURE 11-4. Notebook Printing Template with Two Headings

citations and abstracts on every conceivable subject. A comprehensive bibliographic data base, therefore, already exists; you can search its contents from your personal computer and see the results right on your display screen. With that resource in mind, you can keep your personal bibliography short and compact, restricting the material in it to just those good sources that figure in your work.

Online data base research is thus part of the overall approach to bibliographic data base management recommended in this book. And you'll want, therefore, to give it a try. Once you do, it's just possible that you'll decide online searching (see Chapters 12 and 13) may well be the most useful thing you can do with your personal computer, surpassing even word processing.

RESOURCES

On bibliographic data base management for personal computers, see Bradford A. Morgan and James M. Schwartz, "Database Management for Teachers and Researchers, Part 1," *Research in Word Processing Newsletter* 2:7 (Oct. 1984), pp. 1–3, and "Database Management for Teachers and Researchers, Part 2," *Research in Word Processing Newsletter* 2:8 (Nov. 1984), p. 4. For a review of software for bibliographic work, see Modern Language Association, "Bibliography Programs for Humanities Scholars," *MLA Newsletter* 15:3 (Fall 1983), p. 6. A bibliographic system using a business-oriented data base management program is described in Jeannette Sullivan, "Using dBase II for Bibliographic Files," *Online* 9:1 (Jan. 1985), pp. 46–51.

PART
FOUR

COMMUNICATING

SOFTWARE FOR TELE- COMMUNICATIONS

A desktop computer is a complete computer in itself, but it would be a mistake to see it as hermetically sealed and separate from the rest of the world. Computers are about communication as much as they are about processing. For a computer to do something interesting, for instance, programs and data must be communicated to it. And after the processing's done, the computer communicates the results to you by way of video display, the printer, or even a voice synthesis system.

There's a world of things that scholars can do with *telecommunications*, or links between computers that make use of the telephone system. These applications are so useful and so easy to achieve, in fact, that no scholarly computer should be without communications capabilities:

Online data base research Perhaps the most useful telecommunications application for scholars is online data base research, or the searching of the massive bibliographic (and nonbibliographic) data bases maintained by several companies on huge mainframe computers. For a fee, a personal computer user can access these services and search electronic versions of standard reference works (such as *Sociological Abstracts* or *Zoological Record*).

Computer bulletin boards A computer *bulletin board* is a personal computer devoted to receiving, one at a time, incoming calls that themselves originate from computers. When the call is answered, the bulletin board computer sends a message (which appears on the caller's display screen) explaining the bulletin board's purpose and options, which may include such facilities as *electronic mail*, downloading of programs and data files, computer conferences on particular topics, and news bulletins. Bulletin boards can be set up quite inexpensively and have several promising academic applications.

Point-to-point electronic mail Point-to-point electronic mail involves the sending, over telephone lines, of a disk file from one computer directly to another. Suppose, for instance, you're working on a manuscript with a colleague. Instead of mailing each other versions of the manuscript, which would delay the process, you can exchange drafts of the manuscript using point-to-point electronic mail.

Point-storage-point electronic mail Another electronic mail technique is to send the material to be mailed to an intermediary, such as MCI Mail, who stores it in a large computer. When the person for whom the material is intended calls the intermediary, the computer displays a message that mail is waiting and provides an opportunity to read it or download it (capture it on a disk file).

The avenue to this world of telecommunications lies along some specialized electrical circuitry with which your computer may or may not come equipped. You'll need an *asynchronous communications* board and an RS-232 serial port, included with many (but not all!) computers, and a *modem*, almost always a $100–$200 optional accessory. Appendix I discusses the necessary hardware in detail and explains how it works. But you don't need to worry about all that while you're telecommunicating; like the other components of your computer, the asynchronous board, serial port, and modem are invisible to you while you're at work. The key, as usual, is software that "knows" how to operate these devices without your worrying about them. Once everything is connected, all you need to do is turn on your modem, load your telecommunications program, and you're ready to go.

This chapter introduces telecommunications software. Chapter 13, "The Online Reference Library," explores the world of online bibliographic data base services. Chapter 14, "Networking," introduces scholarly applications of electronic mail, computer conferencing, local area networks, and computer bulletin boards.

A TYPOLOGY OF TELECOMMUNICATION SOFTWARE

Telecommunication software, happily, is reasonably priced. Some of the best programs available are free: they're in the public domain. Even better, it isn't difficult to choose a telecommunication program that will suit your needs nicely.

Telecommunication programs, by the way, are often called *terminal emulation programs* because they transform your computer into a device that, electrically speaking, is indistinguishable from the telecommunications-based remote work-stations (or terminals) you've probably seen working with mainframe computer systems. The two major kinds of telecommunication programs are distinguished by how much control they give you over your computer once the communication is made. *Dumb* telecommunication programs (aptly named) ignore your computer's power and storage capabilities; *smart* ones let you make use of such capabilities as capturing the incoming data on disk. You want a smart program.

DUMB TELECOMMUNICATION PROGRAMS

Many computers come with a free dumb telecommunications program, which permits your computer to emulate a dumb terminal, that is, the kind of terminal you'd be likely to find in an older mainframe system: one with no processing or storage capabilities of its own. When the program's loaded, your computer becomes a standard "vanilla" terminal, so that anything typed at the keyboard will be displayed on the screen and sent out through the RS-232 port (for an explanation of these terms, see Appendix I). The messages received from the distant computer will be shown to you on the display screen.

Dumb terminal programs will permit you to use a modem and contact distant computers, including those operated by online data base services, but they're of very limited use. Dumb terminals achieve only the most basic kind of electrical connection with other computers, namely, the kind of simple connection that permits you to receive messages sent by a distant computer and to reply to them. Dumb terminals can't, however, store the received information on disk or perform any other manipulations that would involve computing power. You only have one chance to see the incoming information, then, during its rapid passage before your eyes on the screen.

SMART TELECOMMUNICATION PROGRAMS

A smart terminal is one that has its own processing and storage capabilities. Smart telecommunications programs are highly desirable because they permit you to store or capture on disk or print the information that's coming in through the serial port. They also include *communication protocols*, or conventions for information exchange, which let you do fancier things than just send and receive messages. When both linked computers are running software that uses the same communications protocol, they can exchange complex files (and even programs) with each other.

The XMODEM Protocol

The most commonly used communications protocol in the world of personal computers is Ward Christiansen's XMODEM protocol, and—like Christiansen's telecommunication program Modem7—it's in the public domain. Almost all personal computer telecommunications programs are based on the XMODEM protocol. That means, therefore, that any two personal computers running virtually any telecommunications programs can exchange files and programs with each other by telecommunications links.

Mainframes and minicomputers, unfortunately, use different communications protocols and usually can't even use the XMODEM protocol. That's why until recently it was very difficult to connect personal computers with larger ones.

The KERMIT Protocol

A new communications protocol called KERMIT, also in the public domain, was developed precisely to provide the same kind of easy links between personal computers and mainframe computers that have thus far obtained between personal computers. Versions of KERMIT are available for DEC and IBM mainframes as well as for the IBM Personal Computer and for the Apple Macintosh. When both the mainframe and the personal computer are running KERMIT, they can exchange complex files (for instance, fully formatted bibliographies or compiled programs) with each other without difficulty.

If you're affiliated with an academic institution, you might wish to check with the computer center's staff to find out whether the mainframe is running KERMIT and, if so, what sort of resources would be available to you were you to equip your personal computer with a KERMIT-based telecommunication program. KERMIT indeed provides the foundation for what can become an excellent way to share resources in an academic community, and there's every reason to suspect that it will gain widespread acceptance. Scholars can, for instance, post bibliographies, course syllabi, and other resources on the mainframe, making them available through the KERMIT protocol to their colleagues for downloading to their own personal computers.

PUBLIC DOMAIN VERSUS COMMERCIAL SOFTWARE

You needn't spend much money on a smart telecommunications program, since some of the best programs available at any price are in the public domain (for instance, MacTep for the Apple Macintosh or Modem7 for CP/M computers) or available on approval (for instance, PC-Talk and 1-Ringydingy for the IBM PC). The public domain programs, such as Modem 7, may be freely copied and distributed. PC-Talk and 1-Ringydingy are freely copiable; the authors of the programs ask only that if you approve the program and wish to use it that you send them a modest donation.

Two copies of a program such as 1-Ringydingy, Modem 7, or PC-Talk are all you need for point-to-point electronic mail applications, since point-to-point electronic mail requires only two computers equipped with communications programs that use the same communication protocol.

To take just one example, 1-Ringydingy (Buttonware, P.O. Box 5786, Bellevue, WA 98006, for the IBM Personal Computer) surpasses the capabilities of some expensive commercial programs. 1-Ringydingy uses the XMODEM protocol for file transfers and provides several alternatives for communication with a variety of computers, including those that use XON-XOFF characters to control signal transmission and reception. You may capture incoming data to a disk file. It is fully suitable for such purposes as electronic mail and online data base searching.

Commercial communication programs do everything that public domain programs do, such as facilitating telecommunication connections between personal computers (almost all of which use the XMODEM protocol) and permitting you to capture on disk the information you capture while online. In addition, the better of these programs include the ability to emulate specific kinds of sophisticated terminals, or remote workstations of mainframe computers, such as the DEC VT100 or IBM 3101. These terminals have more control keys and options than the simple terminal that is emulated by a dumb telecommunications program.

Just because these programs can emulate these fancy terminals doesn't mean that you can exchange files with the mainframe. There's still the protocol problem. But having those extra control keys and options means more convenient control over the mainframe's operation.

Nevertheless, it's an arguable point that it's better to use one of the mainframe's terminals if one is available to you and if you're not interested in downloading anything. A personal computer set up with a telecommunications program can communicate with the mainframe at rates set by the modem (300 or 1200 baud). (See Appendix I for an explanation of modem transmission/reception speeds.) Today's mainframe terminals, however, are directly connected to the mainframe by coaxial cables and other links, and offer much faster data transfer rates (9600 and 12,000 baud are common figures).

One example of a commercial program is MacTerminal (Apple Computer, 20525 Mariani Ave., Cupertino, CA 95014, available for the Apple Macintosh). MacTerminal is an asynchronous telecommunications program for the Apple Macintosh that uses the XMODEM protocol. In that sense it's virtually identical to most public domain programs, save that it takes full advantage of the Mac's graphics display to present the user with an exceptionally easy-to-use command system. What distinguishes MacTerminal from the public domain programs, however, is its availability to emulate the DEC VT100 and IBM 3278 terminals. In its 3278 telecommunications mode, for instance, the program displays on the screen a diagram of the 3278 terminal's 36 special function keys, which can be activated as if they were keys on the keyboard.

RESOURCES

A readable introduction to telecommunications is Alfred Glossbrenner, *The Complete Handbook of Personal Computer Communications: Everything You Need to Go Online with the World* (New York: St. Martin's, 1983). On the technical aspects of asynchronous communications, see Joe Campbell, *The RS-232 Solution* (Berkeley: Sybex, 1984).

On personal computer/mainframe communications, see Bill Catchings, "Can We Talk? The Micro to Mainframe Connection," *PC: The Independent Guide to IBM Personal Computers* (Jan. 22, 1985), pp. 108–113, and in the same issue, Charles Daney, "A Micro-Mainframe Primer," pp. 115–130. KERMIT is extensively described in two articles by Frank da Cruz and Bill Catchings: "Kermit: A File-Transfer Protocol for Universities, Part 1: Design Considerations and Specifications," *Byte* (June 1984), pp. 255–278, and "Kermit: A File-Transfer Protocol for Universities, Part 2: States and Transitions, Heuristic Rules, and Examples," *Byte* (July 1984), pp. 143–145, 400–403. On public domain software, see Robert A. Froehlick, *The Free Software Catalog and Directory* (New York: Crown Publishers, 1984), Alfred Glossbrenner, *How to Get Free Software* (New York: St. Martin's, 1984), and John Markoff and Ezra Shapiro, "Public Domain Games," *Byte* (March 1985), pp. 207–218.

THE ONLINE
REFERENCE LIBRARY

Computer technology, as was foreseen as early as 1945, offers the potential of automating the storage and retrieval of scientific and scholarly literature. By 1961 the first successful experiment in large-scale bibliographic computing—the Medical Literature Analysis and Retrieval System (MEDLARS)—had been attempted. By the late 1960s, technological breakthroughs had made feasible the online, or direct and interactive, searching of the bibliographic data bases. Subscribers to the information vendor could use remote terminals to gain access to the vendor's central computer via the medium of telephone lines.

But several vexing issues arose. Who would pay for these services? How could they be made accessible to the scholars and scientists who would use them? Should the federal government assume responsibility for the massive expenditures that these services would require? During the 1970s it became clear that although the government would play a major role in funding the creation of data bases, their distribution would be left to the private sector. Several companies were formed to distribute information to subscribers.

The companies involved—BRS Information Technologies, DIALOG Information Services, Inc., and ORBIT Information Retrieval System—made massive investments in equipment, and to recoup their investment were obliged to charge premium prices for their services. Online charges of $100 per hour or more are common, effectively putting these services beyond the reach of the researchers and scientists for whose benefit their creation was originally envisioned. College and university libraries could afford to subscribe to these services, but they were then faced with a troubling issue: owing to the high cost of online searching, they were forced to restrict use to a minimum or, in direct contravention of the strong value they place on free access, they were forced to charge fees. Because these online resources were so expensive and accessible only through the mediation of librarians, they had—until 1982—relatively little impact on the actual patterns of scholarly and scientific library research.

So long as the user base remained small, there was little hope that this pattern would change. But the rise of the personal computer, beginning in the late 1970s and well established by 1982, introduced a promising new trend: the wide distribution of a tool that (when equipped with communications software and a modem) could do precisely what a remote terminal does—better, in fact, because a personal computer permits the user to store the retrieved information on disk.

A fundamental economic fact made the personal and home computer market extremely appealing to online data base vendors: corporate and institutional users work only during the 8:00 to 5:00 business day. Although it would cost comparatively little to keep the computers running for, say, 22 hours of the day, they were sitting idle two-thirds of the time. The obvious response wasn't long in coming. The two biggest online data base services, BRS Information Technologies and DIALOG Information Services, embarked on an experiment: they made a budget version of their services available to personal and home computer users during the evenings, nights, and weekends. Thus were born BRS/After Dark and DIALOG's Knowledge Index.

The evening services, to be sure, aren't the same as their daytime counterparts, and that's both good and bad. What's good is that both services are much easier to use than their full-scale professional counterparts, and they're available at a fraction of the daytime services' cost. What's bad is that neither contain the full roster of the daytime services' data bases. (DIALOG, for instance, offers over 200 data bases on every conceivable subject, but its nighttime version, Knowledge Index, offers only about a tenth of them.) But both budget services offer the more popular data bases, and what's more, new data bases are being added as time goes on.

Should you attempt using these services yourself? By all means. The budget services are available for very reasonable prices. If you can afford to spend between $10 and $25 per month on research, there's no reason you can't make use of these services, and the results will pay off handsomely. You'll find that your research horizons will broaden, your research productivity will improve, and your grasp of the literature will become sharper. There's reason to suggest, in fact, that you'll actually achieve better results searching these data bases yourself rather than letting a professional librarian do it for you, but this point will require some explanation and I'll return to it below. Nor will you find searching these data bases difficult. If you've put into practice the information management techniques suggested in Part Three, you already know the lion's share of what's required to use online data base services fruitfully.

It should be stressed from the start that, gushing predictions of the library's demise notwithstanding, online data base research is at best only a supplement to traditional library research techniques. Subscribing to an online data base service will not and cannot liberate you entirely from the very special kinds of research experiences a good library can provide. But it can let you do certain kinds of research tasks at high speeds.

This chapter introduces online data base services in general and the budget nighttime services in particular. Assumed in the pages to follow is a basic knowledge of certain terms and concepts, such as *data field, data record,* and *logical operator.* If you have yet to read Part Three, especially Chapter 9 and Chapter 10, you may wish to do so now since it covers these and other key concepts used in this chapter.

Note, too, that the online data base services discussed in this chapter should be distinguished from "information utilities" (such as The Source or Compu-Serve) or videotex services. Information services provide such features as electronic mail, electronic banking, online swap shops, airline reservations, up-to-the-minute stock quotes, and the like. They do not seek to provide the kind of scientific and scholarly information with which this chapter is concerned and they are not, therefore, covered.

This chapter provides an overview of bibliographic data base searching. Sections include:

"Introducing Online Data Base Services"   This section explains what kind of information you can find online, introduces bibliographic data bases, describes their structure, and introduces the basic commands used in online searching.

"Searching a Bibliographic Data Base"   This section presents a widely recommended search strategy that will prove productive for most scholarly and scientific research purposes.

"Ordering Hardcopy"   This section explains how one service permits you to order photographic reproductions of documents while online.

Not treated in this chapter are the complex issues of choosing a data base vendor and identifying which of the hundreds of data bases best suits your needs. You'll find help, however, in Appendix II ("Choosing a Bibliographic Data Base Service") and Appendix III ("A Scholar's Guide to Online Data Bases").

INTRODUCING ONLINE DATA BASE SERVICES

Online data base services suitable for scientific and scholarly research purposes are provided by two kinds of for-profit companies: *data base producers,* which create the data bases, and *online vendors,* which market the data bases and make them available to libraries, institutions, and end users.

Think of the data base producers as if they were wholesalers, and online vendors as if they were retailers. Just as two supermarket chains will carry almost the same lines of wholesalers' products, online vendors tend to carry similar lines of data bases. But there are some exceptions; some data bases are available only from one vendor.

THE THREE TYPES OF ONLINE INFORMATION

The information online vendors offer is of three types:

Bibliographic data bases are based, generally speaking, on the standard reference works you can find in any research library's references section, and they are produced by the same companies or organizations that print these reference works. A single data base, which may contain several million data records, usually covers only a single discipline or area of human knowledge (examples are *Sociological Abstracts, The Zoological Record, Language and Language Behavior Abstracts, The MLA Bibliography,* and *The Economic Literature Index.*

Nonbibliographic data bases provide direct computer access to massive amounts of quantitative data, such as time series, statistical data, and price indexes. An example is Predicasts Terminal System Time Series, which offers computer-readable time series of population characteristics, labor force statistics, and the like.

Full-text data bases make available online the full text of certain publications, such as *Harvard Business Review, Academic American Encyclopedia,* and *The Wall Street Journal.*

Our concern here centers on bibliographic data bases, but the merits and uses of the other two kinds should not be ignored. Most academic users are on strict budgets and will prefer to consult the print versions of full-text data bases for casual reading, but it must be remembered that these full-text data bases can be searched with all the speed and accuracy a computer can provide; they may, therefore, serve your research purposes more than occasionally. Nonbibliographic data bases provide data that can be downloaded to your computer and analyzed with a spreadsheet program.

DESCRIPTION OF A BIBLIOGRAPHIC DATA BASE

Bibliographic data bases differ somewhat in their structure, but the most common elements are the data record, the basic index, and supplementary indexes.

The Data Record

The basic unit of information storage in the data base, the data record, contains several data fields or locations for specific kinds of information, which are usually about a dozen in number. Among the fields generally included are ones for the accession number, the author's name, the author's affiliation, the title, the source, the year of publication, identifiers (words that describe the specific content of the document), descriptors (words that describe the general subject categories under which the record has been placed), a note on the work's language and country of publication, and an abstract. Some data bases offer additional data fields that provide more tools for information retrieval.

Figure 13-1 shows part of a data record from the *Biosis Previews* data base, a massive reference work for the biological sciences. Like most online bibliographic data bases, it includes fields for the work's title, author's name, and the like. What's special about *Biosis Previews* is the well-conceived indexing system. Apart

---

AU	SINGARAJAH-K-V
TI	OBSERVATIONS ON THE OCCURRENCE AND BEHAVIOR OF MINKE WHALES BALAENOPTERA-ACUTOROSTRATA OFF THE COAST OF BRAZIL
SO	SCI REP WHALES RES INST TOKYO O (35). 1984. 17–38.
YR	1984
KW	MATING ELECTRIC SHOCK SWIMMING SEX RATION MORPHOLOGY PHYSIOLOGY HYDROGRAPHY TOPOGRAPHY TEMPERATURE DAY LENGTH CURRENT
MJ	CHORDATE TAXONOMY: MAMMALIA (MJ07003). BEHAVIOR BIOLOGY: ANIMAL BEHAVIOR (MJ07003). ECOLOGY: ANIMAL (MJ07508) ECOLOGY: OCEANOGRAPHY (MJ07512) ANATOMY/HISTOLOGY: GROSS (M11102) PHYSIOLOGY: GENERAL STUDIES (MJ12002)
BC	BALAENOPTERIDAE (BC85810)
LG	ENGLISH (EN)
IN	LAB. MARINE BIOL. COMPARATIVE PHYSIOL., DEP. SYSTEMATICS ECOL., CCEN, FEDERAL UNIV. PARAIBA, JOAO PESSOA-58000 BRAZIL.
AB	Field observations on minke whale morphology and physiology, the hydrography and topography of the Brazilian whaling ground and catch statistics from 1963-1982 are presented. In the past 20 yr, 12,494 minke whales have been taken off Brazil; only 3 were taken prior to 1963. Of those animals thought to be mature, females predominate in the catch (2 females; 1 male). The population appears to remain at an exploitable level, although other species in the area have been considerably reduced. The most important environmental conditions associated with the arrival of the minke whale in these tropical breeding grounds appear to be an optimum temperature of 26-27 degree c, day length, reduced turbulence and an amiable surface content.

FIGURE 13-1. Part of a <u>Biosis</u> <u>Previews</u> Data Record

from the usual identifier (KW for key words) field, records are categorized by major concept codes (MJ) and biological classification (BC). The organization of these concept codes and classifications is highly appropriate for a data base in the biological sciences.

Because each data base tends to have its own special organization of data fields, an organization that is shaped by the nature of its subject matter, it makes excellent sense to do some background reading on how the data base is organized. At a minimum, take a look at the description of the data base that is included in the manual supplied when you subscribe. To be sure, you can search online data bases without doing this kind of reading, but you'll find that doing so will markedly improve your search technique. You'll find a directory of data bases most likely to interest scholars and scientists in Appendix III. Listed among other pertinent facts are readings that can help you master a data base's particulars.

The Basic Index

The online vendors' massive computers do not actually search the data records themselves. They search, instead, a basic index. The basic index is a massive file that contains all the words and terms (except for articles and prepositions) contained in the title, identifier, descriptor, and abstract fields of every data record in the data base. All these terms are stored together with information indicating to the computer the locations of the pertinent data record or records.

Understanding this point is the key to using online bibliographic data bases successfully. If you specify as a search term a word which is not in the basic index, you will be told that the computer has no records on the subject—even though there may actually be a great many of them. Consider, for example, the fact that most data bases do not index author's names in the basic index. Were you to try searching for K. V. Singarajah's article by searching for "Singarajah, K.V.," you'd think that *Biosis Previews* didn't have a record of his article on Minke whales. It does—but you used a term that isn't in the basic index.

How do you know which terms are in the index and which ones aren't? You have three options:

Printed thesaurus Most online bibliographic data base producers sell print-based thesauruses, and the more popular ones—such as ERIC's—tend to be shelved in library reference sections.

Trial and error If you've tried a search term with no results, try using a synonym.

Online thesaurus By far the best of these three options is the online thesaurus, or a thesaurus you can see right on your computer screen. To see the thesaurus, you use a command such as EXPAND (Knowledge Index) together with the search term you're thinking about using (such as "China"); you're shown the dozen nearest terms. Right away you can determine not only whether the term is listed in the basic index, but also how many records are stored that pertain to it (Figure 13-2). Over a thousand records would be retrieved by a search for "China or PRC," but nary a one would by a search for "People's Republic!" Note that this appealing and useful feature is included with Knowledge Index but not, sadly, with BRS/After Dark (at this writing).

Constructing searches with terms in the basic index is, as will be seen below, the best of the several available options, but it invariably produces irrelevant material. Indeed, you're not doing badly at all if fully half the records you retrieve are completely irrelevant. (That's why professional librarians call searches using basic index terms *dirty searches*.) The reasons are two:

Multiple meanings Many—perhaps most!—words in the basic index have more than one meaning. "Commune," for example, refers not only to an intentional utopian community, but also to a common and not at all utopian administrative unit in many European societies. Any search for material on communes, therefore, is bound to produce many records which pertain not to such matters as Shakers and the Amana Colonies but rather to the history and sociology of local political organizations in countries such as France and Belgium.

Terms mentioned in abstracts Often a data record will contain a passing reference to a topic that really has very little to do with the work's content. For instance, a work on a Midwestern factory town might include, in its abstract, the sentence "There's nothing *utopian* about the organization of work roles in Mudburg . . ."; the computer—literal as always—will dutifully index this record under "utopian."

Dirty searches can be vexing and, worse, expensive, but they're sometimes preferable for reasons to be explored below. Just remember that even the best searchers wind up with irrelevant data records.

Additional Indexes

Most data bases also have separate indexes for author's name, language, place of publication, year of publication, and other material that is not indexed in the basic index. In *Biosis Previews*, for example, there's a separate index for biological classifications (the BC field), and you can search it by specifying a field identifier (for example, BC = Balaenopteridae) in the search question. Doing so forces the computer, in essence, to search only on the specified field.

On the surface, that seems like a quick and accurate way to get to the heart of the matter. If you wanted to find all the records pertinent to the Balaenopteridae, for example, you could—or so it seems on first glance—finish the job quickly and cleanly by searching only on the biological classification field. But that is not recommended as an initial search strategy.

```
EXPAND CHINA
Ref Items  Index-term
E1     1   CHIMU
E2     6   CHIN
E3  1303  *CHINA
E4     1   CHINACH
E5     1   CHINANTEC
E6     2   CHINANTECO
E7     1   CHINANTLA
E8     3   CHINAS
E9    29   CHINATOWN
E10   15   CHINATOWNS
E11    1   CHINBOTSU
E12   34   CHINE

EXPAND PEOPLE'S REPUBLIC OF CHINA
Ref Items  Index-term
E1     3   PEOPLEHOOD
E2   753   PEOPLES
E3   108  *PEOPLES REPUBLIC OF CHINA
E4     5   PEOPLING
E5    10   PEORIA
E6     1   PEOTRY
E7     8   PEP
E8     2   PEPER
E9     1   PEPITONE
E10    1   PEPLICATION
E11   10   PEPPER
E12    2   PEPPERED

EXPAND PRC
Ref Items  Index-term
E1     1   PRBLEMATIC
E2     2   PRBLEMS
E3    13  *PRC
E4     1   PRCF
E5     1   PRD
E6     1   PRDRUCJU
E7  1345   PRE
E8     2   PREABORTION
E9     1   PREACADEMIC
E10    1   PREACCEPTORS
E11   14   PREACH
E12   30   PREACHED
```

FIGURE 13-2. Online Thesaurus

Searching only for those records which contain Balaenopteridae in the BC field will quickly and accurately show you records that are 100% pertinent (that's why library professionals call such searches *clean searches,* as opposed to the dirty searches just mentioned). That's all well and good. The problem is that all other records will be thrown out. Among them, to be sure, will be many records which refer to the Balaenopteridae only peripherally, and good riddance to them. But excluded as well will be many more records that are germane, but have been thrown out because they are classified under other rubrics.

You're now ready to grasp why it's a good idea to search bibliographic data bases yourself. Online research is expensive, and libraries have budgets. For this reason, professional searches tend to prefer clean to dirty searches. They look good: they produce high rates of accuracy. The problem, however, is that they do not include all the material which is pertinent to the overall topic the patron wants to research.

USING COMMANDS

Online bibliographic data bases are searched by using just a few basic commands, and all vendors tend to use the same ones (although they may use different names for them). To be sure, some vendors require the commands to be typed in at the keyboard (the command-driven approach), while others let you select commands from menus (the menu-driven approach). Even so, the commands boil down to the same basic categories:

BEGIN or DATABASE followed by a four-letter code representing the data base you'd like to search.

SELECT or FIND followed by the search term or terms you're interested in. You may use the logical operators AND, OR, and NOT (see Chapter 9). The results of the search aren't displayed on the screen; rather, you're told how many documents the search strategy has retrieved.

DISPLAY or PRINT (followed by instructions about which data records you would like displayed on the screen) lets you display the results of a search.

LOGOFF ends the search session and terminates your connection to the service.

SEARCHING A BIBLIOGRAPHIC DATA BASE

The pages that follow illustrate an eight-step search strategy you may find helpful. The steps are:

Choose the right data base.
Develop a search strategy.

Log on.
Enter the search terms.
Display the data records.
Revise the search strategy (if necessary).
Log off.
Download the records.
Save the retrieved records to disk

CHOOSING THE RIGHT DATA BASE

Online data base vendors offer between several dozen and several hundred separate data bases, and at any one time you're only searching one of them. The quality of the results you obtain depends on whether you've chosen the correct data base for your search. If you're doing research on bilingual education, for example, you'll be better off in *Bilingual Education Bibliographic Abstracts* (BRS/After Dark) than you would be in *Psycinfo.* For more information on choosing data bases for particular subjects, see the Resources section at the end of this chapter.

Often it's necessary to search more than one data base to build a good list of relevant citations. Bilingual education is a case in point. Relevant citations will be found not only in *Bilingual Education Bibliographic Abstracts* but also in *Education Resources Information Center* (ERIC) and *Language and Language Behavior Abstracts.*

One of the chief benefits of the expensive daytime search services is the availability of a master subject index to the dozens of data bases the services carry. You search this index just like an ordinary data base, except that its results tell you how many records are available on the subject in each of the several data base likely to cover it. Subject indexes, unfortunately, are not available on the budget nighttime services, but then again there's less overlap in the subject coverage of the few available data bases.

DEVELOPING A SEARCH STRATEGY ON PAPER

The time to work out your search strategy is before you go online and start paying for every second of connect time.

In general, the search strategy I recommend begins with a search for the most important or most pertinent subject or concept. In almost all cases this strategy will produce more records than you could conveniently or economically view on screen, so you then narrow down the number of items retrieved by using procedures that are least likely to exclude relevant records. The strategy boils down to three principles:

Begin with a search for the most important or most significant concept, the broadest one you can conceive of that's at the heart of your interests. Almost certainly, you'll retrieve more records than you can conveniently view. If so, narrow down the search with progressively more detailed concepts.

Think of as many synonyms as you can for your search terms. Get help from the data base's thesaurus, which may be available online (if not, you might find a copy in a nearby university library). Use multi-character wild card symbols freely (see Chapter 9).

As you phrase your search questions, link only two terms and concepts at once. If your search involves three or more concepts (for instance, inflation and political change and France), do it in two or more stages.

Example: The Economic Organization of Chinese Collectives

Suppose, for example, you're interested in China, and more specifically, in the economic organization of Chinese collectives, and you'd like to see what *Sociological Abstracts* has to offer in that subject. Here's how these three basic principles work out in practice.

To begin crafting your strategy, draw a line down the center of a blank sheet of paper. On the left side, write at the top "Set 1" followed by the main or most significant concept (here, China); then write "Set 2" at the top of the other side followed by the next most significant subtopic (collectives). (We'll leave "economic organization" aside for a moment.) Now think of as many synonyms for these terms as you can, and list them under the main terms (Figure 13–3). If your search involves only two sets of concepts (such as bilingual education and education testing or Balaenopteridae and social behavior), you needn't do any more planning at this point. But the search we're planning here has a third set of concepts (those that come under "Economic organization") and they have to be included too.

Now take out a second piece of paper and draw a line down its middle. Label the two columns Set 1 and Set 2 as before. Place under Set 1 the phrase "China AND collectives" and, under Set 2, "economic organization" and synonyms (Figure 13–4).

Search Strategy--Stage 1

Set 1	Set 2
China	Collective
People's Republic of China	Collectives
Chinese	Commune
PRC	Communes

FIGURE 13-3. First Stage of Search Strategy

Search Strategy--Stage 2

Set 1

China and Collectives

Set 2

Economic Organization
Work
Labor

FIGURE 13-4. Second Stage of Search Strategy

Note that the results of Stage 1 become Set 1 for Stage 2. If you planned to work with still another term, say "Canton province," the results of Stage 2 would become Set 1 for Stage 3 (China AND collectives AND economic organization AND Canton), and so on.

Using Wild Cards (Truncation)

Remember that it's easy to cripple a search by using an overly specific search term. "Communal societies," for example, may seem like a good search term, but a search for that term in *Sociological Abstracts* turns up only three old references.

The reason for this search strategy's failure is that the term "communal societies" is too restrictive. It excludes, for example, anything indexed under commune, communes, communal, communalism, and communality, all of which are pertinent to the subject.

Using a "wild card" or truncation symbol can vastly increase the number of records found. In BRS/After Dark, the wild card symbol is a dollar sign ($); in Knowledge Index, it's a question mark (?). These symbols work exactly the same. When added to a truncated version of a word, the search term returns all the records containing the truncated root and all possible stems that come after it. COMMUNE$, for instance, finds records with COMMUNE and COMMUNES— and, it turns out, there are 483 of them: an enormous increase over the three records found with COMMUNAL SOCIETIES.

Be careful, however, not to truncate the search word too much. COMMUN$ might seem like an attractive way to catch *communal* and even *communal societies,* but it also snares *communism, communistic,* and more. It returns, in fact, 11,164 records.

LOGGING ON

When you subscribe to BRS/After Dark or Knowledge Index, you'll sign an authorization slip permitting the service to charge your credit card for the subscription fee and online usage. You'll receive in the mail a copy of the service's user guide, your account number, and your security password.

To log on, you need a telecommunications program (Chapter 12) and the necessary hardware, including a modem (Appendix I). After the communications program is loaded, you're presented with a menu that permits you to choose the terminal emulation mode, in which everything you type at the keyboard is sent through the computer's serial port. With an autodial modem, you enter the code that tells the modem to dial, followed by the telephone number of the nearest telecommunication network:

AT D 321-3456

and press the return key. The modem dials the network's number; after the network's computer answers the phone, you'll hear (through the modem's speaker) a loud signal (it sounds something like a bosun's pipe) that tells you you're successfully connected. You then press the return key and type in a message telling the telecommunication network which of its customers you'd like to be connected with. Just how this is done depends on the network you're using. With Tymnet, it's as simple as, for instance, typing in KI (for Knowledge Index).

You're then speedily connected with the online data base service, and the service sends its greeting (through your modem and serial port). When you've successfully entered your account number and password, you're connected—and connect time charges have started (Figure 13-5).

The question mark at the bottom of the screen is a prompt telling you that the system's waiting for you to enter a command, and it hints at one of the major differences between Knowledge Index and BRS/After Dark: Knowledge Index isn't menu-driven, and BRS/After Dark is. (In a menu-driven system, procedures are controlled by choosing options from a menu.)

In a non-menu-driven system, you have to memorize the commands (or keep a reminder sheet near your computer). The command you'll enter at this point in your Knowledge Index search is BEGIN followed by a four letter code naming the data base you wish to search.

BRS/After Dark's menu-drive procedures accomplish exactly the same thing: they take you to the point where you enter a four-letter code that identifies the data base you want to search. The differences are that you don't have to memorize the code and the process takes longer.

Figure 13-6 shows, for example, BRS's main data base selection menu. To begin a search, you choose the data base category in which you're interested by

---

```
DIALOG INFORMATION SERVICES
ENTER ACCOUNT NUMBER:
ENTER PASSWORD:
LOGON AT 18:36:44 EST
WELCOME TO KNOWLEDGE INDEX

?
```

FIGURE 13-5. Log on Message

YOU ARE NOW CONNECTED TO THE BRS AFTER DARK SEARCH SERVICE.
THE FOLLOWING CATEGORIES OF DATABASES ARE AVAILABLE FOR
SEARCHING:

CATEGORY   DESCRIPTION

1   SCIENCE AND MEDICINE DATABASES
2   BUSINESS AND FINANCIAL DATABASES
3   REFERENCE DATABASES
4   EDUCATION DATABASES
5   SOCIAL SCIENCES AND HUMANITIES DATABASES

TYPE IN CATEGORY NUMBER THEN HIT ENTER KEY FOR
CATEGORY OF DATABASES DESIRED:

FIGURE 13-6. BRS/After Dark's Main Data Base Selection Menu

typing the number corresponding to the category you want and then pressing the
return key.

Let's suppose you choose option 5, social sciences and humanities data
bases. The system then presents you with the menu shown in Figure 13–7.

To choose *Sociological Abstracts,* for example, you'd enter SOCA and press the
return key.

Although BRS/After Dark is menu-driven and Knowledge Index isn't,
there's really very little difference between the two systems, both in the way they
operate and in the demands they place on users. Knowledge Index does lack
menus, but you need to learn only three commands (BEGIN, to start a data base;

SOCIAL SCIENCE AND HUMANITIES DATABASES
****

DATABASE NAME   LABEL

ABLEDATA   ABLE
FAMILY RESOURCES   NCFR
MENTAL MEASUREMENTS YEARBOOK   MMYD
NATIONAL REHABILITATION INFORMATION
    CENTER   NRIC
PUBLIC AFFAIRS INFORMATION SERVICE   PAIS
PRE-PSYC   PREP
PSYCINFO   PSCY
RELIGION INDEX   RELI
SOCIOLOGICAL ABSTRACTS   SOCA

TYPE IN LABEL FOR DATABASE DESIRED:

FIGURE 13-7. BRS/After Dark's Social Sciences and Humanities Menu

```
S1----->PEOPLE'S REPUBLIC OF CHINA OR PRC OR CHIN$
A1      1388 DOCUMENTS FOUND

S2----->COLLECTIVE$ OR COMMUNE$
A2      536 DOCUMENTS FOUND

S3----->S1 AND S2
A3      191 DOCUMENTS FOUND
```

FIGURE 13-8. Entering Search Terms in Stages.

FIND, to start a search; and DISPLAY, to show the results of a search) to use most of the system's features.

ENTERING THE SEARCH TERMS

We'll continue with the example introduced above to illustrate a typical search.

The first step in the search is to enter the search terms for Stage 1, that is, PEOPLE'S REPUBLIC OF CHINA OR PRC OR CHIN$ AND COLLECTIV$ OR COMMUNE$. If these terms could all fit on the one line, the whole expression could be entered at once using parentheses, as in the following example:

(APPLES OR ORANGES) AND (WHOLESALE OR RETAIL)

but there isn't room. Each set can be entered in stages (see Figure 13-8).

S1, the first search question, nets almost 1400 documents; S2, the second search question, nets 536. S3, which combines them using AND logic, produces 191—still too many to look at. That's normally the case for the first stage of a search, and it's a good sign: it means that you haven't narrowed your search down to the point that you're excluding potentially relevant material.

Now it's time to bring the Stage 2 set into play (see Figure 13-9).

Finally we're down to a manageable number. Forty-five documents, to be sure, is quite a few, and if you wanted to display them all with a 300-baud modem you'd be in for about 20 minutes of online time. Still, it might be worth it. An important point to remember here, however, is that the documents displayed first are the ones most recently added to the data base, and the 45 documents will be displayed in chronological order (roughly, not exactly). To look at the first ten or 15 documents in this list will give you an excellent overview of the most recent literature on this topic, minus a few irrelevant documents.

```
S4----->S3 AND (WORK OR LABOR OR ECONOM$)
A4      45 DOCUMENTS FOUND
```

FIGURE 13-9. Entering the Stage 2 Search Terms.

DISPLAYING THE DATA RECORDS

Once you've pared the number of documents retrieved down to a manageable number, take a look at the first data record to make sure you're on the right track. The command PRINT (BRS/After Dark) or DISPLAY (Knowledge Index) lets you see the documents *in a set*, such as S3 or S4, and gives you several options for viewing them:

Short Enough information to indicate the document's usefulness. What's displayed varies from data base to data base, but always included is the document's title; sometimes included are additional bibliographic details.

Medium Full bibliographic details but no abstract.

Long Full data record including abstract.

You may also specify a range of documents to be displayed on the screen (for example, 1 to 5 or 1 to 20). For our purposes here, let's have a look at the short display of the first five records (see Figure 13-10).

```
       1
AU   Goodman, David S.G.
TI   The "De-Maoization"   of  the People's Republic of
     China:  Processes and Problems
SO   Europa Archiv 1981, 36,16,25 Aug, 477-484


       2
AU   Perry, Elizabeth J.
TI   Collective Violence in China, 1880-1980
SO   Theory and Society   1984, 13, 3, May, 427-454.


       3
AU   Walder, Andrew G.
TI   Participative Management and Worker Control in China
SO   Sociology of Work and Occupations   1981, 8, 2,  May,
     224-251.


       4
AU   Gonzalez, Nancie L.
TI   The Organization of Work in China's Communes
SO   Science   1982. 217, 4563, 3 Sept, 898-903.


       5
AU   Lee, Rance P. L.
TI   Chinese and Western Medical Care in China's Rural
     Commune: A Case Study
SO   Social Science and Medicine   1981, 15A, 2, Mar, 137-
     148.
```

FIGURE 13-10. *Five Retrieved Records (Short Format).*

This list provides an excellent example of the "dirty" search strategy's virtues (and liabilities). Although only two of the documents retrieved are obviously relevant to the topic, on closer inspection all five seem to contain something of interest. Consider, for example, the abstract of Elizabeth Perry's article "Collective Violence in China":

> Collective violence in China is typically interpreted as the response of the peasantry to its own decline. This conceptual scheme appears inappropriate to the actual situation. While **China** has experienced a process of state-building over the past century, it has also experienced a process of the strengthening of local **collectivities.** An alternative model is outlined on the basis of historical data from the later Qing period, the republican period, the communist revolution, and the People's Republic. A variety of theories that might aid in understanding the Chinese case are examined, including concepts of socialist corporatism, ultrastable systems, small-peasant **economy,** and agricultural socialism.

This document would not have been retrieved by a "clean" search, or one that required the descriptor or identifier field to contain the key words (these fields contain only China, Chinese; violence, violent; collective violence, China, 1880–1980). The record was retrieved, instead, because the three necessary search terms were present in the abstract (boldfaced in the above example).

The price of the "dirty" search strategy, however, is the retrieval of documents which may turn out to be irrelevant or unwanted. Here's the abstract of David S. G. Goodman's "The 'De-Maoization' of the People's Republic of China":

> Changes in the administration of the **People's Republic of China** following the Communist Party's 1980 resolution to reevaluate Mao Zedong's role are examined. Following Deng Xiaoping's decisive speech at the Party congress, changes were made in **economics** and law, and toward a **collectively** controlled leadership; Mao was criticized as a person, whereas the theory known as "Maoism" remained untouched. The trials of the "Gang of Four" are discussed in relationship to Mao's role, and the dismissal of Hua Guofeng as a way of dealing with divisions within the Party is elaborated on.

This document does not appear to be pertinent to the search topic; it was, nevertheless, retrieved owing to the presence in the abstract of the three boldfaced search terms.

REFINING THE SEARCH STRATEGY

The search just discussed appears successful and, after viewing the short form of the documents, it would make good sense to use the display command to print out ten, 20, or more of the records in medium (full citation) or long (citation and abstract) form, capturing the data on disk. Just how many you display and capture depends on how far back in the literature you wish to go—remember, the documents are displayed in rough chronological order (actually, in the order in which they were added to the data base, which is approximately chronological). For this list, displaying 20 records takes you back to 1976. That's probably sufficient; the significant sources which appeared before that date would doubtless be cited in these papers.

It often happens, however, that at this stage you still have too many citations—or too few. Here are some suggestions.

Too Many Citations

If the search retrieves too many citations to work with conveniently (say, 100 or more), you may use several techniques to narrow down the number of documents found. (*Note:* consult the BRS/After Dark or Knowledge Index manuals for the specifics on how to carry out these limitation techniques; I'm concerned here with pointing out their existence rather than supplying all the necessary details.)

Restrict the output to English-language citations If you're not interested in foreign language works, you may limit the output to English-language works only.

Use a NOT operator Some searches tend to produce a high number of unwanted documents that all belong to a particular category. For instance, a student of U.S. communal studies searching for COMMUNE will invariably retrieve works on the European administrative unit of the same name; to exclude them, search for COMMUNE NOT (FRANCE OR BELGIUM OR GERMANY).

Restrict the output to a specified range of publication dates If you're only interested in the most recent documents, you may restrict the search to those documents published within, say, the past two years.

Reduce truncation If a search for ECONOM? produces too many documents, try reducing the amount of truncation. ECONOM? retrieves a very wide variety of terms. If, however, you're really only interested in ECONOMIC ORGANIZATION and a few related terms, try ECONOMIC ORGANIZ$ instead.

Use the SAME or WITH operators BRS/After Dark gives you, besides the usual AND, OR, and NOT operators, two additional operators that can be used for framing more precise search questions. The SAME operator searcher is used instead of AND (ECONOM? SAME CHINA); it searches for records that contain those two terms within the same field or text paragraph. The WITH operator searches for records that contain the two terms within the same sentence. Avoid using these operators for Stage 1 of the search; they may exclude pertinent material. Use them only to narrow down a search that retrieves too many documents.

Use an additional AND operator An additional way to cut down the number of documents retrieved is to add another AND expression (for instance, ECONOMIC ORGANIZATION AND CHINA AND COLLECTIVES AND CANTON PROVINCE).

Limit by code number A glance at a complete data record will reveal that in most instances, concept codes, desciptors, and identifiers are numbered (e.g., violence, violent [480600]). If you wish, you can add to the search question an AND operator followed by the code number, limiting the search to just those documents that positively contain it.

Restrict the search to one field The least desirable way to limit the number of documents retrieved is to restrict the search to one field (e.g., substitute a clean search). This technique will result in high accuracy—no unwanted documents will be retrieved—but many relevant documents will be omitted. For example, a search for BALAENOPTERIDAE AND SOCIAL BEHAVIOR in a life sciences data base produces over 100 documents using the dirty technique; the clean technique nets only 44.

Too Few Citations

Retrieving too few (or no) citations is actually more serious than retrieving too many, since it gives the impression—which is more often incorrect than correct—that the data base contains no pertinent material. Try these strategies to broaden a search:

Check spelling An incorrectly spelled search term will retrieve no citations.

Increase truncation Increasing the amount of truncation widens the scope of the search (for example, ECON$ nets far more documents than ECONOMIC ORGANIZATION).

Think of additional synonyms In the above example, a search that did not include WORK and LABOR along with ECONOMIC ORGANIZATION and related terms would have netted far fewer "hits." Use OR logic to include the synonyms (UTOPIA$ OR COMMUNE$ OR INTENTIONAL COMMUNIT$). In the massive ERIC data base, FRESHMAN WRITING PROBLEM$, for example, returns only one record. But (FRESHMAN OR FRESHMEN OR FIRST YEAR) AND WRITING PROBLEM$ nets 23.

Split up two-word search terms with the OR operator If a search for INTENTIONAL COMMUNITY does not retrieve enough documents, try INTENTIONAL OR COMMUNITY.

Reduce the number of AND terms in the search question GEOLOGY AND HIGH SCHOOL AND PROGRAM DEVELOPMENT, for example, returns no records in the ERIC data base. Knocking off the last AND (leaving GEOLOGY AND HIGH SCHOOL) returns 58, some of which turn out to be pertinent.

Try another data base Sometimes you'll find that you're better off searching another data base. If you try locating records relevant to BILINGUAL EDUCATION AND BROWNSVILLE (Texas) in ERIC, for instance, you won't find a thing. But the *Bilingual Education Bibliographic Abstracts* (BEBA) has two records netted by those terms.

LOGGING OFF

Once you've finished the search, use the logging off command as quickly as possible to get off the system. You'll be presented with a message informing you how much you'll be charged for the search.

SAVING THE RETRIEVED RECORDS TO DISK

A good terminal emulation program lets you capture what you're receiving on disk. If the data base management program you're using can read a standard ASCII text file, you can transfer the bibliographic citations and abstracts you've captured to your bibliographic data base or print them with your printer.

Downloading to a bibliographic data base isn't quite as easy as it sounds. There's a good deal of extraneous information in the disk file, such as search questions and the system's prompts, that has to be edited out. What's more, you'll probably have to code the information so your data base management program can tell where one record or field begins and ends. Figure 13–11 shows the coding necessary for Notebook II (Chapter 11) to read the downloaded data.

Researchers who often download citations and abstracts from online data bases will wish to look more than casually at the automatic downloading software offered by Personal Bibliographic Software, Inc. (P.O. Box 4250, Ann Arbor, MI 48106, available for the IBM PC and PC-compatibles and intended to work with Professional Bibliographic System, PBS's dedicated bibliographic FMS (see Chapter 11). Documents captured online can be automatically transferred to bibliographic data records in your bibliographic data base.[1]

---

[1] An MBASIC program for automatic editing of downloaded files is listed in Clyde W. Grotophorst, "Another Method for Editing Downloaded Files," *Online* 8(5) (Sept. 1984), pp. 85–93.

%Start:
%Key:Singarajah 1984
%Citation: Singarajah, K.V., "Observations on the
            Occurrence and Behavior of Minke
            Whales (Balaenoptera acutorostrata)
            Off the Coast of Brazil," Sci. Rep.
            Whales (Res. Inst., Tokyo) 0 (35)
            (1984), pp. 17-38.
%Abstract: Field observations on minke whale morphology and
    physiology, the hydrography and topography of the
    Brazilian whaling ground and catch statistics from
    1963-1982 are presented. In the past 20 yr,
    12.494 minke whales have been taken off Brazil; only
    3 were taken prior to 1963. Of those animals thought
    to be mature, females predominate in the catch (2
    females; 1 male). The population appears to remain
    at an exploitable level, although other species in the
    area have been considerably reduced. The most
    important environmental conditions associated with
    the arrival of the minke whale in these tropical
    breeding grounds appear to be an optimum temperature
    of 26-27 degree c, day length, reduced turbulence
    and an amiable surface content [. . .]
%Source of Abstract: BIOSIS PREVIEWS (BRS/After Dark)
%Biological Classification:BALAENOPTERIDAE
%End:

FIGURE 13-11. Edited Data Record

ORDERING HARDCOPY

You may find that the abstract alone will give you all the information you need, but more often it's necessary to take a first-hand look at the citation you've found. But that doesn't necessarily mean a trip to the library. From Knowledge Index, you can order hardcopy versions of citations you've found while you're online, and you'll receive them within a week or two.

The service, to be sure, isn't cheap. At this, writing, Knowledge Index charged $6.25 per item plus $0.20 per photographed page. A 20-page article, then, would cost $10.25, and five of them would cost $51.25. It's important, however, to keep these costs in perspective. Five articles found with the online data base service's search techniques may very well represent the heart of the literature for your subject, and being able to have them delivered to your door, after spending only 20 minutes to find them online, may seem like a luxury even at these prices. Remember: what's your time worth?

DATA BASE AVAILABILITY

BRS/After Dark and Knowledge Index are excellent and attractive resources for scholars provided they've made available the data bases you need for research in your field (see Appendix II for lists of data bases available at this writing). You'll probably find, for example, that scholars in sociology, education, and biology are well situated for online research, but historians and philosophers will find these nighttime services less attractive. Table 13–1 shows some of the data bases that the budget services cannot provide.

The problem isn't that data bases don't exist for these fields—as you'll see in a moment, they do—it's just that they're available only on the midpriced services such as BRKTRHU (see Appendix II) or on the expensive, daytime services such as BRS or DIALOG. BRKTHRU, a new BRS venture, makes the full roster of BRS data bases available with a BRS/After Dark-type menu-driven interface, making it quite easy to use. More expensive than BRS/After Dark, BRKTHRU's charges are still lower than the main BRS service.

Searching the big systems, BRS and DIALOG, will appeal to only a few readers of this book. Although anyone who has learned how to search BRS/After Dark or Knowledge Index successfully can readily learn how to search BRS or DIALOG, it can't be denied that searching these systems is challenging; they're complex and they offer advanced features (such as the ability to save search strategies) that this chapter does not discuss. Moreover, they're expensive. Searching DIALOG, for example, will cost $1.00 to $1.50 per minute. Unless you're independently wealthy or have a very generous research budget, you'll probably want to leave the searching of these data bases to library professionals (who can do them for you at rates subsidized by the library).

IS ONLINE SEARCHING WORTH THE COST?

Since most bibliographic data bases are founded on print-based reference works that you can find in any research library's reference section, it is reasonable to ask why one should pay for their use when the print source can be freely consulted at no expense. The truth is that online bibliographic searching has both advantages and disadvantages; the question is whether using them makes sense for you.

THE ADVANTAGES OF BIBLIOGRAPHIC DATA BASES

In general, bibliographic data bases offer the following advantages over their print-based counterparts:

TABLE 13-1
SELECTED DATA BASES OF INTEREST TO SCHOLARS NOT AVAILABLE ON NIGHTTIME SERVICES

Data Base Name	Subject
America: History and Life	American history and culture
ArtBibliographies Modern	Art history and criticism
Economic Literature Index	Economics
Historical Abstracts	Non-American history
MLA Bibliography	Literature and linguistics
Philosopher's Index	Philosophy
Population Bibliography	Demography

Speed The larger online data bases permit several million data records to be searched in a matter of seconds.

Comprehensiveness In contrast to print-based reference media, which are usually bound by year, all save the largest online data bases contain a decade or more of citations and abstracts in a single file. Using print-based media, for example, one would have to consult ten volumes to find all the references on a single topic published between 1975 and 1985. The same search can be conducted in seconds using the reference work's online counterpart by typing in a single command. Moreover, because online data bases index hundreds or even thousands of journals on a subject, users are less likely to remain dependent on a few core journals in a field. Studies have shown that about half the relevant literature for a research question is likely to be found outside those core journals.

Multiple-criterion searches If you're looking for the 1983 references to "metallurgy" in *Chemical Abstracts,* you might as well use the print-based version. Suppose, however, you're looking for all the references you can find (say, from 1972 to 1985) that pertain to metallurgy, photochemical processes, and technological advances. If you're using the print-based version of the work, get ready for a long and tedious ordeal. You'll probably have to go through hundreds—maybe thousands—of citations by hand and cope with 13 volumes. The same search can be conducted in seconds online. Much of the online data bases' appeal and utility is described by pointing out their ability to perform searches using multiple criteria and logical operators (AND, OR, and NOT; see Chapter 9 if you're not familiar with these operators).

Local access If a research library is right next door, you're in luck. But most scholars and scientists find that just traveling to the library and back again consumes too much time. Online data base research effectively puts the reference section of a library where you are most likely to work: in your office and at home (if you have a computer there).

Currency The information in most bibliographic data bases is updated at least every 2 months; some data bases are updated weekly. Print-based reference works are often 6 to 18 months old. To find the latest sources, use their online counterparts.

THE DISADVANTAGES OF BIBLIOGRAPHIC DATA BASES

Online bibliographic data bases represent a major and extremely valuable research resource, but by no means should you believe the oft-repeated cliche that they'll replace their print-based counterparts or books. They have several disadvantages which ensure that scholars and scientists will continue to use libraries:

Absence of the "serendipity factor" Anyone who has ever done library research knows the value of the "serendipity factor," or the high probability of discovering, while browsing, valuable works whose existence could not have been predicted before visiting the library. Many of these works contain bibliographies that are themselves important sources of discovery. Online research is less serendipitous than browsing in a library. It's still so expensive that browsing of any kind is ruled out completely. And the online data records, although they include citations and abstracts, do not list the works cited (with the exception of a few specialized data bases such as the online version of the *Social Science Citation Index*).

Few records prior to 1970 Most data base producers have made no attempt to include works published before they began operating. The earliest producers got going around 1967, and many more followed during the 1970s. It's rare indeed, therefore, to encounter a work in online sources that was published before 1970. As time goes on, however, this problem decreases in magnitude, owing in large measure to the frenetic rate at which new works are being produced. In chemistry, for instance, the literature from 1967 on constitutes more than 60 percent of the total literature in that subject; by the end of the decade it will very likely constitute 75 percent.

Variability of results To extract good results from online research, you must know what you're doing. A novice user isn't likely to retrieve much useful information; indeed, he or she is likely to come away from the experience believing that the online data base is close to useless. Knowing what you're doing contributes materially to the retrieval of useful information.

Retrieval of irrelevant information   Even the best search techniques will produce records that are completely irrelevant to the search topics.

Gaps in data base coverage   Private-sector data base producers and online vendors have responded to the market, which demands information on science and technology more frequently than it demands information on the social sciences, the humanities, and the arts. There are, to be sure, data bases in the latter subjects, including religion, philosophy, and art, but coverage tends to be more spotty, and some subjects, such as world ethnology, are completely unrepresented.

RESOURCES

A readable general introduction to online data base services is Alfred Glossbrenner, "Dialog, BRS, and ORBIT: The Encyclopedic Databases," in his *The Complete Handbook of Personal Computer Communications: Everything You Need to Go Online with the World* (New York: St. Martins, 1983). In the same vein, see Steven Levy, "Who's Got the Data," *Popular Computing* (April 1983), pp. 68–74, and his "Cutting Online Costs," *Popular Computing* (Oct. 1983), pp. 71–78. Recent popular works are Barbara Newlin, *Answers Online: Your Guide to Informational Databases* (Berkeley: Osborne–McGraw Hill, 1985). More technical works are the dated but important Manfred Kochen, ed., *The Growth of Knowledge: Readings on the Organization and Retrieval of Information* (New York: John Wiley, 1967); F. W. Lancaster, *Toward Paperless Information Systems* (New York: Academic Press, 1978); and Brenda Gerrie, *Online Information Systems: Use and Operating Characteristics, Limitations, and Design Alternatives* (Arlington, VA: Information Research Press, 1983). Nonbibliographic data bases are covered in Ching-Chih Chen and Peter Hernon, *Numeric Databases* (Norwood, NJ: Ablex Publication Corporation, 1984).

Online search strategies are discussed in Carol H. Fenichel and Thomas H. Hogan, *Online Searching: A Primer* (Marlton, NJ: Learned Information, 1981); Douglas R. Knox and Marjorie M. K. Hlava, "Effective Search Strategies," *Online Review* 3:2 (June 1979), pp. 148–152; Arthur L. Adams, "Planning Search Strategies for Maximum Retrieval from Bibliographic Databases," *Online Review* 3:4 (Dec. 1979), pp. 373–379; H. H. Teitelbaum and Donald T. Hawkins, "Database Subject Index," *Online* 2:2 (April 1978), pp. 16–21; Charles L. Gilreath, *Computerized Literature Searching: Research Strategies and Databases* (Boulder, CO: Westview Press, 1984).

On online data base searching by scholars, see Stephen K. Stone, "Computer Searching: A Guide for the Uninformed Scholar," *Academe* (Nov./Dec. 1982), pp. 10–15; Julie M. Neway, "The Role of the Information Specialist in Academic Research," *Online Review* 6:6 (Dec. 1982), pp. 527–538; Warren J. Haas, "Computing in Documentation and Scholarly Research," *Science* 215 (12 Feb. 1982), pp. 857–860; Stuart J. Kolner, "The IBM PC as an Online Search Machine—Part I: Anatomy for Searchers," *Online* 9:1 (Jan. 1985), pp. 37–45; "The IBM PC as an Online Search Machine—Part II: Physiology for Searchers," *Online* 9:2 (Feb. 1985), pp. 39–46; Gerald Jahoda, "Effects of Online Bibliographic Searching on Scientists' Information Style," *Online Review* 5:4 (1981), pp. 323–333.

On selecting the right data base for a search, see Henry H. Teitelbaum and Donald T. Hawkins, "Database Subject Index," *Online* 2:2 (April 1978), pp. 16–21; Charles L. Gilreath, *Computerized Literature Searching: Research Strategies and Databases* (Boulder, CO: Westview Press, 1984), which provides an excellent overview by subject area (e.g., social sciences, humanities, etc.); Judith Wagner, "Multiple Data Base Use: The Challenge of the Data Base Selection Process," *Online* 1:4 (Oct. 1977), pp. 35–41; J. J. Angier and B. A. Epstein, "Multidatabase Searching in the Behavioral Sciences," *Database* 3:3 (Sept. 1980), pp. 9–15, and 3:4 (Dec. 1980), pp. 34–40; R. Donati, "Spanning the Social Sciences and Humanities through DIALOG," *Online* 1:4 (Oct. 1977), pp. 48–54; Henry Mendelson, "Social Work Online," *Database* 7:3 (Aug. 1984), pp. 36–55; Fern Brody and Maureen Lambert, "Alternative Databases for Anthropology Searching," *Database* 7:1 (Feb. 1984), pp. 28–34; Robert G. Skinner, "Searching the History of the Social Sciences Online," *Database* 8:1 (Feb. 1985), pp. 28–33; J. D. Falk, "In Search of History: Bibliographic Databases," *History Teacher* 15:4 (Aug. 1982), pp. 523–544; and A. W. Goudy, "Music Coverage in Online Databases," *Database* 5:4 (1982), pp. 39–57.

NETWORKING

14

Scholarship and science are formally organized into recognized academic disciplines, each with its own departmental boundaries within the academy and its own professional organization or organizations on the regional, national, and international levels. The disciplines serve a variety of professional, political, and pedagogical functions, but most studies strongly indicate that the real centers of intellectual life in academia are not well described by disciplinary boundaries. On the contrary, they are likely to be found within small interdisciplinary networks of no more than 200 active members. These networks are of two kinds:

Learning communities Within a college or university, the centers of intellectual life and creativity are likely to be found in learning communities, or small, interdisciplinary networks of faculty and students who share common interests.

Research networks Within research subjects, intellectual vitality is likely to be found in similarly small and interdisciplinary networks of linked researchers at many institutions who stimulate each other by sharing methodologies, research experience, informal descriptions of research results, prepublication drafts, bibliographies, and other resources. These networks are often called invisible colleges, a term that is not fully satisfactory because of its derogatory connotation of secrecy and elitism. In fact, most of these research networks are open, but the nature of existing, traditional communication networks is such that many would-be participants—especially those at isolated institutions—are unable to participate in them.

The evidence suggests that intellectual vitality in an institution or a research subject is closely related to the existence of these communication

227

networks. Within the university, learning communities foster dialog, overcome faculty isolation, encourage the sharing of pedagogical approaches, stimulate curricular integration, create a sense of belonging, and sharpen awareness of fundamental scholarly, scientific, and pedagogical values. Within a research subject, research networks contribute significantly to the quality of research by defining appropriate research questions, establishing canons of evaluation, fostering the sharing of appropriate methodologies, and creating a sense of common purpose. Just as significantly, the evidence indicates that the lack of such networks is intellectually stifling: it leads to theoretical and pedagogical poverty, an unawareness of links with others' work, and a lack of replication and progress.

Given the significance of these networks, it is hardly surprising that efforts are now under way to foster them by using computer technology. Computers provide new channels for communication that are of great promise for scholarly networking:

Electronic mail Scholars who have personal computers can exchange computer-based material (proposals, manuscripts, bibliographies, etc.) using electronic mail links.

Computer conferencing Some electronic mail services offer computer conferencing, an online communication technique that permits many personal computer users to take part in a computer-based discussion. Most computer-based conferences are open to the public, but you may elect to restrict access to the conference to only those who share a password.

Local area networks (LAN) Local area networks link personal computers—anywhere from two or three to 30,000—together with direct high-speed cable connections. At one end of the LAN spectrum are simple networks that connect a few personal computers and permit them to share an expensive printer or hard disk. At the other end are the massive, highly complex systems now being set up at many universities, systems that will permit thousands of students and faculty to communicate and share resources.

Personal computer-based bulletin boards Bulletin board software for personal computers, available in the public domain, permits a personal computer owner to set up a miniature version of an online data base service (Chapter 13). Bulletin boards, a favorite pastime of computer hobbyists, have much promise for small scholarly networks.

ELECTRONIC MAIL

Electronic mail, broadly defined, refers to the sending (*uploading*) and receiving (downloading) of documents over computer channels. Those channels might consist of telephone links achieved with telecommunication software and modems (see Chapter 12 and Appendix I), or they might make use of the faster connections available in local area networks (see below). What's of interest here is electronic mail by telecommuncation links; local area network applications are discussed later on.

Electronic mail links achieved through the telephone lines are of two kinds: point-to-point and point-storage-point.

POINT-TO-POINT ELECTRONIC MAIL

Point-to-point electronic mail refers to the direct connection, over the telephone system, of two personal computers. Any two scholars who both have personal computers, telecommunication software, and modems can give point-to-point electronic mail a try.

Here's an illustration of point-to-point electronic mail in action. Carol and Walter, who are working on a book together, are separated by the 150 miles that divides their two universities. They're nearing the book's completion, and with a deadline facing them, they're looking for a faster way to exchange chapter drafts than the pokey U.S. mail system.

Carol and Walter both have personal computers, although they're different brands, and the machines are equipped with telecommunication software and Hayes Smartmodems, which include a feature that automatically answers incoming calls. They decide to give point-to-point electronic mail a try.

To begin the process, Carol gives Walter a call to tell him that she's ready to send a chapter (a disk file written in straight ASCII text). After hanging up, Walter plugs his modem into the phone jack, turns it on, turns on his computer, and loads his communication program. He chooses the command option that downloads to a disk file the data received from an incoming call. Now he can do anything he likes; the rest of the operation is automatic.

Carol, in the meantime, turns on her modem and computer and loads her communication program. She selects the option that lets her send a disk file. At the agreed-on time, she uses the command that dials Walter's number, and once Walter's modem has answered the telephone, she uses the command that sends the disk file. When the transmission is complete, she uses a command that tells the modem to sever the connection.

Checking his computer a little later, Walter finds that the transmission has occurred. He uses the command that saves the captured material to disk. Then he exits the telecommunications program, loads his word processing program, and takes a look at Carol's chapter. He'll do some editing, add some new material, and by tomorrow the revisions will be back in Carol's hands.

POINT-STORAGE-POINT ELECTRONIC MAIL

The major disadvantage of point-to-point electronic mail is that the timing of the transmission has to be carefully coordinated. An auto-answer modem, to be sure, simplifies the process, but the receiver still has to know roughly when the transmission is coming so that the computer and modem will be ready.

Point-storage-point electronic mail avoids this problem. Instead of uploading the material directly to the receiver, you send it instead to an electronic mail service that stores it in its computer's auxiliary memory. The receiver's computer then contacts the electronic mail service (at the receiver's convenience) and when the receiver logs on, the service displays a message: "Mail waiting." A few keystrokes send the document on its way through the telephone lines, and the transmission is completed.

The disadvantage of point-storage-point electronic mail is its cost. MCI Mail (2000 M St. NW, Washington, DC 20036), for instance, charges an annual mailbox fee of $18.00. Sending a 500-character message costs $1.45; 501 to 7500 characters cost an additional dollar, as does each succeeding block of 7500 characters. All messages are cleared every 24 hours unless you pay an additional $10.00 per month, in which case your message will be stored for 24 hours.

Readers interested in nighttime data base services (Chapter 13) will be pleased to know that point-storage-point electronic mail services are available with both BRS/After Dark and Knowledge Index. BRS/After Dark provides direct access to MCI/Mail, a major electronic mail utility. Knowledge Index provides its own electronic mail system, DialMail. For more details on point-storage-point electronic mail vendors, see the Resources section at the end of this chapter.

COMPUTER CONFERENCING

Computer-based conferencing has been around for about 15 years, but only recently has it become cheap enough for widespread potential use in scholarship. Previous computer conferencing systems required participants to pay steep subscription and usage fees.

COMPUTER CONFERENCING DEFINED

Computer conferencing is, in essence, a group discussion of a topic using the computer as a medium. The conference itself consists of a linked collection of electronic mail messages, resembling memos or letters, which all pertain to a particular topic. The computer keeps a record of all the messages you've already read, so you won't see messages twice (unless you want to).

EXAMPLE: DIALMAIL

Here's an example to illustrate how computer-based conferencing works. Tom Brown is an economist with strong interests in economic development, particularly in Latin America. He's the organizer of an informal Latin American Studies group in his scholarly organization, and the participants decide to carry on an online conference on Latin American development issues. Tom logs on to Knowledge Index and chooses DIALMAIL; in a moment he's scanning the new messages available in the conference (Figure 14–1).

Tom decides to look at all three new contributions, and gives a command that sends the messages scrolling past his screen. He has the option of sending private answers to the people who placed these entries in the conference or, if he wishes, he can create his own public entry (which will appear as a new item on every other participants' screen as they log into the conference).

LOCAL AREA NETWORKS

Local area networks are networks of personal computers directly connected by high-speed cable links. Local area networks require special hardware apart from the cable connectors (see Appendix I); each computer in the network needs a special communication circuit board that gives it access to the special, high-speed communication system the network provides.

The term "local area" is right on target: most LANs permit cable lengths of no more than several hundred feet or, at the extreme, a half-mile. Within that range, networks of as many as several hundred personal computers have been achieved. Most, however, are small, linking five to 20 computers.

LANs VERSUS TIME-SHARING SYSTEMS

LANs should be distinguished from *time-sharing* systems available with most minicomputers and mainframes. Time-sharing systems permit many users—several hundred or more—to gain access to a big computer using a remote terminal. The terminal itself has no processing capabilities; it's just a way of communicating with the big computer, which may be positioned some distance away. Even though many people might be using the big computer at the same time, each user has the illusion of private access to the system and complete control over it. LANs, in contrast, are linkages among full-fledged computers. Each station in the network has its own processing capabilities.

---

3 new messages found in Latin American Development

No.	Posted	Lines	From	Subject
1	4/05/85	108	A. BALLANTINE	Econ. Dev. & Population
2	4/17/85	48	R. JACOBS	Guatemala
3	4/19/85	205	M. SCOLA	Dev. Policy in Mexico

FIGURE 14–1. Directory of Messages in Computer-Based Conference

RATIONALES FOR LAN INSTALLATIONS

If every computer in a local area network has its own processing capabilities, what, then, is the point of the network? Three major rationales underlie the installation of most local area networks at this writing:

Sharing expensive accessories Many personal computer accessories, such as laser printers and high-capacity hard disks, are extremely expensive, and it's prohibitive to equip each computer in the network with all the desired accessories. A network permits several personal computer users to share a printer or disk drive.

Creating local electronic mail linkages A local version of electronic mail becomes available for the network's participants. If the participants are members of a work group, installing a local area network can speed and streamline the communication process among them considerably.

Sharing software Another common rationale for installing LANs is the appealing prospect of sharing software; presumably, a "master" computer could be set up with one copy of an expensive program, which all participants could use and share. It should be clearly noted, however, that most personal computer software is not designed to be used by more than one network participant at once. The only software that can be completely trusted in this situation is software that's specifically designed for it. For example, ZyLab Corporation, the makers of ZyIndex (the free-format information storage and retrieval program discussed in Chapter 10), makes a special version of the program (ZyIndex Plus) that's designed to work in a local area network setting. At this writing, only a small proportion of personal computer programs were suitable for network applications.

LANs AND SCHOLARLY NETWORKS

Local area networks can play a fruitful role in linking the members of an academic department, providing each member with access to expensive peripherals and giving everyone a sophisticated channel for communication. Not surprisingly, many LAN installations in colleges and universities are occurring at the departmental level, since the department is such a basic unit of funding and communication. That's fine, but there's one drawback to this department-centered approach: some of the most fruitful and interesting communication networks in the academic setting, especially the inherently interdisciplinary learning community, cross departmental boundaries.

An expensive and complex solution to this problem is to build a network whose scope embraces the entire campus, an approach now under way at several of the United State's most prestigious (and wealthy) universities. The ultra-sophisticated LANs now under construction will eventually link thousands of computers in a single massive network. The goal is a "paperless university" in which memos, typed student papers, and other paper-based media will become relics of the past. In most cases, these projects probably could not have been undertaken were it not for corporate gifts amounting to millions of dollars' worth of equipment, cash, and technical support. Because companies prefer to bestow such gifts on prestigious universities, scholars at state colleges, private liberal arts colleges, and community colleges aren't likely to benefit.

BULLETIN BOARDS

Personal computer bulletin board systems, which are junior, personal computer–based versions of online data base systems (see Chapter 13), have for years been the darling of computer hobbyists. They have two possible applications in scholarship: first, to provide the faculty at institutions lacking campus-wide LANs with an inexpensive option for networking, and second, to provide a communications medium for invisible colleges, the nationwide (and often international) informal networks of scholars who share a subject interest.

THE HOBBYIST'S BBS

All you need to get started with a bulletin board system (BBS) is some public domain software, a computer with two disk drives, a telephone line, and word of mouth to spread the news that your system is up and running. And many personal computer hobbyists do just that, opening up their computer to all and sundry just to see what happens.

What happens, often, is lots of fun. The BBS ethos is decidedly nonprofit and communalistic; if you take something from a BBS (for instance, downloading a program), you're expected to contribute something in return, even if it's just a poem or recipe. A favorite pastime of personal computer hobbyists, much to the satisfaction of AT&T, is to discover some new (and perhaps distant) BBS telephone number, call it up, and explore what it has to offer. Some bulletin boards specialize in messages and conferences about a particular brand of computer; others make available public-domain software for direct downloading over the telephone lines; and still others specialize in some subject unrelated to computers, such as sex, drag racing, or cooking. Not surprisingly, BBS systems are evanescent: they rarely last longer than six months.

THE SCHOLAR'S BBS

Most public bulletin boards are of little interest to scholars, save for those interested in downloading public domain software (and students of American folk culture). But BBS software is of excellent quality (hobbyists would demand no less!) and, what's more, many fine BBS programs are in the public domain. A group of scholars could get together and, for a relatively small expenditure, set up a private communication network using BBS software and a host computer. Such a network could greatly enhance their internal communication.

Personal computer bulletin board systems are, to be sure, markedly less sophisticated and powerful than systems such as ARPANET or EIES; they can handle only one caller at a time, and communication takes place at the slow pace imposed by telephone connections (300 to 1200 baud). Nevertheless BBSs should prove quite adequate for their intended use. Learning communities and research networks seldom attract more than 200 participants at once; indeed, there is considerable evidence that the average size of these networks is much smaller. Many of them have only a dozen or two active participants at any one time. A modest personal computer bulletin board system operating during nights and weekends would handle the needs of a network of one or two dozen scholars quite well.

The sections to follow describe in detail the creation of a computer bulletin board system designed to enhance communication links in a learning community or research network. The discussion covers:

Creating a computer bulletin board, including selecting hardware and software.

Using a computer bulletin board and its features such as electronic mail and document downloading.

CREATING A COMPUTER BULLETIN BOARD

A computer bulletin board system requires the following equipment:

Computer   A functioning bulletin board system can be set up with a surprisingly modest computer system; indeed, given the slow speed of telecommunications, there is little advantage to equipping the system with the latest and fastest equipment. An Apple IIe, a Kaypro II, and other inexpensive or modest systems will suffice. The system should, however, have two disk drives; the ability to add a hard disk if needed later is an attractive feature.

Modem   Many bulletin board programs assume that you're using the Hayes 300/1200 baud Smartmodem, an autoanswer/autodial modem superbly suited to bulletin board work. Other autoanswer modems will work with most programs, but equipping your system with the Hayes Smartmodem will eliminate most incompatibility problems.

Bulletin board software   Several excellent bulletin board programs are in the public domain, and improved versions of them are available from several sources at reasonable prices. For academic purposes, the software should provide participants with general electronic mail (mail readable by all callers), personal electronic mail (mail readably only by the person to whom it is addressed), and downloading (or capturing on the caller's disks) of documents. The software should be capable of installation in a short time and should require no programming skills of the system operator.

Word processing program   A simple word processing program is generally required for installing the bulletin board software and customizing the material that will be shown callers on the screen.

Separate telephone line   The system requires its own telephone line, which cannot be used for other purposes while the system is in operation.

If you're employed by a college or university, you might attempt to persuade your institution to donate the necessary equipment. Another option, especially if you're working with a network of about 100 participants or more, is to ask for $10 or $20 contributions, a request that seems quite reasonable given the potential benefit.

The *system operator* (*sysop* in personal computer jargon) is responsible for setting up the system and maintaining it, an undemanding task. Remember that the system operator is not solely responsible for providing rich materials for users. What will make the system appealing, for the most part, are the contributions made by the users themselves: electronic mail messages, bulletin board messages addressed to everyone in the network, and the like. The system operator's responsibilities should ideally be limited to making sure that the system is up and running when it's supposed to be, providing materials (such as bibliographies and manuscripts) for downloading, occasionally running a compacting program to delete material that the participants have marked for deletion, scanning the user-contributed material occasionally for the work of pranksters, and handling malfunctions.

The bulletin board system operates in the following way. Once the bulletin board software has been installed, a simple procedure with most programs, the computer and modem (which is directly connected to the telephone outlet) are turned on and the system waits for a call. When a call arrives, the autoanswer modem answers the call and the program goes to work, presenting the caller with an initial display screen and a set of command options. The caller may then choose to make use of the system's resources, such as electronic mail or document downloading.

Only one caller at a time may use the system, so computer conferencing—an online dialog among two or more users—is unfortunately impossible. (The system operator, however, may converse with the caller.) Nevertheless, general mail entries can take on the appearance of a dialog as they accumulate. Callers should be encouraged to comment on the entries they have read.

Getting people involved in the system requires some planning. There's a potentially vicious circle of nonparticipation: the value of the system will depend almost completely on the extent of user participation (and the quality of the material available online). If few people participate, or if the participants are marginal to centers of activity in the network, the system may never get off the ground. A good strategy would be to secure the participation of the network's central figures and have available from the first day of operation a large amount of attractive material, such as a major research bibliography, reports on recent research, comments on recent controversies in the literature, and so on.

Efforts should be made, moreover, to include people in the network who have not traditionally been able to participate in learning communities or research networks. It's not necessary to expend much money to get the word out. Notices in scholarly newsletters and magazines can, for example, often be inserted without charge.

EXAMPLE: THE PILGRIM BBS

To illustrate the academic potential of a computer bulletin board system, the pages that follow explore a hypothetical computer-based bulletin board system called PILGRIM.

PILGRIM is an imaginary bulletin board that is addressed to a nationwide informal network of scholars from a wide variety of disciplines (anthropology, geography, history, history of religions, and religious studies) who share an interest in religious pilgrimage. It illustrates the potential of an excellent commercial BBS program called PC BBS, which is available for the IBM Personal Computer and compatibles (available from George Peck, 211 Yacht Club Way #326, Redondo Beach, CA 90277).

When a call is received, PC BBS displays a welcoming message on the screen (Figure 14-2). The caller is asked to enter his or her name and institutional affiliation. The system then checks to see whether any electronic mail messages have been addressed to the caller.

```
Welcome to PILGRIM
Please enter your FIRST name CHELVA
Please enter your LAST name SUBRAMANIYAM
With what institution are you affiliated?  NORTH CENTRAL STATE UNIVERSITY
CHELVA SUBRAMANIYAM FROM NORTH CENTRAL STATE UNIVERSITY
Is this correct? YES
Is this your first time on PILGRIM? NO


Checking CHELVA SUBRAMANIYAM'S MAILBOX...
Sorry, you have no Personal Mail waiting.

Command (D,E,F,L,M,N,O,S,T,'?' or 'H' for help): ?
```

FIGURE 14-2. First Message Displayed

The system is controlled by the caller, using alphabetical commands mnemonically related to their function (e.g., <D> ESCRIPTION, <F>ILE). These commands are entered when the prompt "Command (D,E,F,L,M.N,O,S,T, '?' or 'H' for help):" appears on the screen. In Figure 14-3, the caller has entered a question mark to see a menu of command options. The menu, which appears on the screen after the ? or H command is given, is shown in Figure 14-3.

The <D>ESCRIPTION option displays on the screen a description of the bulletin board's nature and purpose (Figure 14-4).

Choosing the <M>AILBOX option brings to the screen another set of options (Figure 14-5) that permit the user to:

> View an index of general mail (mail addressed to all users of the system).
> Scroll through the general mail entries and view the full text of any that are of interest.
> Leave messages for a particular person (Personal Messages) or messages for all users of the system.
> Delete messages left previously.

The general mail entries themselves potentially constitute a dialog of immense value on several ongoing threads of thought and research. Viewing the

---

```
At Command Prompt enter:
     <?> for a short command summary.
     <D>ESCRIPTION describes PILGRIM.
     <E>CHO toggles between character echoing and no echoing by
the host.  Use   this  command if two characters are printing on
your terminal when  you type a character.
     <F>ILE invokes the file transfer program.
     <H>ELP to print this message.
     <L>INEFEED  toggles line feed transmission by  host.
Normally,  PILGRIM  sends  LFs  after Carriage Returns.  This
may  cause  double  spacing in your text.  If so, enter "L" at
the command prompt  to stop LFs.  Entering the "L" again will
restart them.
     <M>AILBOX invokes the electronic mail program.   It features
mail for all  users,  as  well  as  personal mail to  allow
users  to  leave   individual messages for one another.
     <N>EWS for PILGRIM system news.
     <O>FF to log off the system.
     <S>TATUS gives  log-on time,  connect time,  and status of
the ECHO  and  LINE-FEED options.
     <T>ALKBACK allows you to leave comments to the system
operator.

     -- END OF HELP --

Command (D,E,F,L,M,N,O,S,T,'?' or 'H' for help): ?
```

FIGURE 14-3. Help Menu

PILGRIM is a bulletin board system operating on an IBM PC
equipped with a Hayes 300/1200 baud Smartmodem and a 10Mb hard
disk. It is intended for the use of students, scholars, and
researchers interested in religious pilgrimage and allied
subjects such as the history of religions, tourism, and theology.

Access to this system is open to anyone. If you find the material
available here to be of use to you, please respect the
contributions which your colleagues have made to this system by
crediting them—and by making your own contributions!

A donation of $20 ($10 for students or retired) is requested and
brings you a bimonthly newsletter. PILGRIM NEWS. Please send
your contribution to Laura Stephens, Department of Religion,
Greeneville State University, College Town, CA 99999.

THE BIBLIOGRAPHY OF RELIGIOUS PILGRIMAGE is available for
downloading using the <F>ile option. Citations and abstracts are
entered in a format which is automatically readable using
Notebook (Pro/Tem Software, Stanford, CA). If you do not have
Notebook, use your word processor's search and replace functions
to remove the % symbols. The bibliography is split into several
files for user convenience. PILGRIM.BIB is the basic
bibliography. Updates are numbered UPDATE1.BIB, UPDATE2.BIB,
etc. Please suggest references using the <M>ailbox option.

FIGURE 14-4. <D>ESCRIPTION Option

index (Figure 14–6) provides a quick overview of the themes that preoccupy the
participants' thoughts.

To view the full text of an entry, the caller scrolls through the entries one by
one (beginning from the most recent or the earliest contributions) and uses the
<R>EAD command to reveal text of a desired entry (Figure 14–7).

The <F>ILE option makes available materials for downloading (or capturing on the caller's disk). The hypothetical system discussed here makes available
two kinds of documents for downloading—bibliographic files and working papers
(Figures 14–8 and 14–9).

<S-> Scan Reverse, <S+> Scan Forward, <I-> Index Reverse, <I+>
Index Forward

<R> Read Message, <L> Leave Message, <D> Delete Message,
<P>ersonal Messages

<H> for help, <E> to end

Enter your choice

FIGURE 14-5. <M>AILBOX Option

Msg#	Date	From	Subject
120	09-29-1984	AMY SCHWARTZ	AZTEC VS. MAYAN PILGRIMAGE
121	10-05-1984	ED PLANTZ	MAYAN PILGRIMAGE
122	10-06-1984	GUILLERMO ORTEGA	AZTEC PILGRIMAGE
123	10-06-1984	LAKSMI AIYER	PILGRIMAGE IN SINGAPORE
124	10-08-1984	ED PLANTZ	MORE MAYAN PILGRIMAGE
125	10-09-1984	ROSA CALVINO	REPORT FROM AAA MTGS
126	10-11-1984	GUILLERMO ORTEGA	COMMENT ON JENKINS.MS1
127	10-12-1984	AMY SCHWARTZ	MAYAN VS. AZTEC PILG
128	10-14-1984	RICHARD JENKINS	COMMENT ON CHEUNG.MS1
129	10-15-1984	ROSA CALVINO	PILGRIMAGE IN PORTUGAL
130	10-15-1984	CHEN CHEUNG	TOURISM VS. PILGRIMAGE
131	10-16-1984	ERIC BAKER	TOURISM OR PILGRIMAGE?
132	10-18-1984	LAKSMI AIYER	INVITATION TO AIP MTGS
133	10-19-1984	CHEN CHEUNG	TOURISTS AT GRAND CANYON
134	10-19-1984	SARA MICHAELS	MORE ON LOURDES
135	10-19-1984	DAVE GREENE	TOURISM AT IRISH SITES

FIGURE 14-6. General Mail Index

As this hypothetical example illustrates, a computer bulletin board system can provide an excellent and highly democratic environment for research networking and communication within a learning community, but the quality of the system depends heavily on the quality of participation. That quality will probably remain high as long as participants are made aware of the fundamental ethic of bulletin board usage, as it has arisen in the personal computer world: if you take something from the bulletin board, you are obliged to contribute something of equal or greater value.

EFFECTS OF COMPUTERIZED NETWORKS

Computer-based electronic mail and bulletin board systems have been around a while now—long enough for their effects to be evaluated. The results of these studies argue strongly for the applicability of such systems to informal intellectual networks.

Communications routed through computers tend to be much less formal than written communications. Participants seem to show little concern for typographical or other writing errors and do not object to such errors in others' work, assuming the system as a whole to have more in common with an informal telephone call than a formal written communication. When formal communications are called for, in fact, people tend to write letters instead of using existing electronic mail channels.

Participants find the computer communication channel to be strongly egalitarian. No one can be "shouted down" and in the computer's impersonal

Msg # 116 From: SARA MICHAELS   Date sent: 09-05-1984
Subject: LOURDES IN 1983

<R>ead, <N>ext, or <E>nd: N

Msg # 117 From: ERIC BAKER   Date sent: 09-05-1984
Subject: HARRISON'S THEORY

<R>ead, <N>ext, or <E>nd: N

Msg # 118 From: DAVE GREENE   Date sent: 09-05-1984
Subject: PILGRIMAGES IN IRELAND

<R>ead, <N>ext, or <E>nd: N

Msg # 119 From: PAOLO REYNARD   Date sent: 09-09-1984
Subject: PILGRIMAGES IN PORTUGAL

Msg # 120 From: AMY SCHWARTZ   Date sent: 9-29-1984
Subject: AZTEC VS. MAYAN PILGRIMAGE

<R>ead, <N>ext, or <E>nd: R

I've been working on the differences between Aztec and Mayan
pilgrimages during the period immediately prior to Conquest and
immediately afterward, and I'd love to hear from anyone else
working in this area. Here's an interesting citation:

>   Alba, Agustin Martinez, "Change and Continuity in
>   Indigenous Pilgrimage Traditions: Michoacan and
>   Yucatan," Journal of Religious Pilgrimage and Religious
>   Festivals 12. (1984), pp. 119-140.

What's apparent so far is that the collapse of Mayan political
systems prior to the conquest seems to be a major factor in
distinguishing the two traditions—Aztec pilgrimage seems to have
a fairly pronounced political/symbolic function that's closely
connected with the imperial ambitions of Tenochtitlan.

FIGURE 14-7. General Mail Entries

The following files are available for download...

PILGRIM.BIB   UPDATE1.BIB   UPDATE2.BIB
UPDATE3.BIB   JENKINS.MS1   CHEUNG.MS1
CHEUNG.MS2   CALVINO.MS1

FIGURE 14-8. <F>ILE Option

FILES FOR DOWNLOADING

THE BIBLIOGRAPHY OF RELIGIOUS PILGRIMAGE
****
The bibliography of religious pilgrimage consists of a basic
bibliography (PILGRIM.BIB) and monthly updates. The
bibliographic citations and abstracts are formatted for automatic
downloading for users of Pro/Tem's Notebook data base management
program; users of other bibliographic programs should delete the
% symbols using the search and replace features of a word
processor.

PILGRIM.BIB - (126 citations and abstracts, 30K) to 8-1-84

UPDATE1.BIB - (21 citations and abstracts, 8K) to 9-1-84

UPDATE2.BIB - (9 citations and abstracts, 3K) to 10-1-84

UPDATE3.BIB - (38 citations and abstracts, 12K) to 11-1-84

WORKING MANUSCRIPTS AND RESEARCH REPORTS
****
These materials have been provided for prepublication
distribution and comment. Please do not quote from them or
otherwise utilize their contents without the author's permission.

JENKINS.MS1 - Richard Jenkins, "Priests, Pilgrims, and
Merchants: Pilgrimage and the Economic Integration of Central
Asia, ca. 940-1150 AD" (42K)

CHEUNG.MS1 - Chen Cheung, "Nature Pilgrimage and the Vision of
Wilderness in the American West" (21K)

CHEUNG.MS2 - Chen Cheung, "Research Notes on Accounts of
Wilderness in 19th Century Travel and Description Literature"
(16K)

CALVINO.MS1 - "Pilgrimage Catchment Areas in Portugal: A
Religious Geography" (31K)

FIGURE 14-9. Directory of Downloadable Documents

environment, everyone's contribution is presented as potentially equal in
validity. One does not, moreover, have to master subtle metalinguistic and
kinesic skills—the kind of skills which can make or break a contribution made at a
physical meeting—to communicate effectively. The result is a communication
channel which (in spite of its informality) strikes participants as markedly
cerebral; it is judged to be highly appropriate for intellectual discussions, but
highly inappropriate for discussions of persons and emotions. Communicating
via computer, participants tend to agree, is a good way to exchange information,

ask questions, exchange opinions, stay in touch, and generate ideas; it is not a suitable medium for decision making, resolving disagreements, getting to know each other, or bargaining.

These new communication channels do have one major drawback. The lack of face-to-face feedback removes communication inhibitions and makes it difficult to tell when you've offended someone. The result, all too often, is *flaming:* an outburst of aggressive and often profane language that is likely to be regretted later. When you're using these channels of communication, therefore, bear in mind that there are real people—people with feelings—on the other end of the line, and not just a computer.

RESOURCES

On the social organization of scientific networks, see Derek de Solla Price, *Little Science, Big Science* (New York: Columbia University Press, 1963); M. J. Mulkay, "Sociology of the Scientific Research Community," in *Science, Technology, and Society: A Cross-Disciplinary Perspective* (London: Sage Publications, 1977); and Jonathan R. Cole and Stephen Cole, *Social Stratification in Science* (Chicago: University of Chicago Press, 1973).

Firms that provide point-storage-point electronic mail are The Source, Source Telecomputing Corporation, 1616 Anderson Rd., McLean, VA 22102; CompuServe Information Service, 50000 Arlington Centre Blvd., Columbus, OH 43220; MCI Mail, 2000 M. St. NW, Washington, DC 20036; Easylink, Western Union, 1 Lake St., Upper Saddle River, NJ 07459; DialMail (Knowledge Index), DIALOG Information Services, 3640 Hillview Avenue, Palo Alto, CA 94304.

On point-source-point electronic mail, see Henry Fersko-Weiss, "Electronic Mail: The Emerging Connection," *Personal Computing* (Jan. 1985), pp. 71–79, and Audrey Mandela, "Electronic Express," *Popular Computing* (March 1985), pp. 82–88.

On local area networks, see the special issue of *PC: The Independent Guide to IBM Personal Computers* (Feb. 5, 1985); Henry Saal, "Local Area Networks: An Update on Micro-computers in the Office," *Byte* (May 1983), pp. 60–79; E. G. Bronner, *The Local Area Network Book* (Indianapolis: Howard W. Sams, 1984); or George R. Davis, ed., *The Local Network Handbook* (New York: McGraw-Hill, 1982).

Private computer conferencing facilities are made available by EIES, Computerized Conferencing and Communications Center, 323 High Street, Newark, NJ 07102, and DialMail (Knowledge Index), DIALOG Information Services, 3460 Hillview Ave., Palo Alto, CA 94304. Communitree Group (1150 Bryant St., San Francisco, CA 94103) markets a program (called Committee First Edition, for the Apple II) that makes computer conferencing possible with a personal computer system.

On computer-based conferencing, see Louis Jaffe, "Convenient Conferences," *Popular Computing* (March 1985), pp. 88–94; Starr Roxanne Hiltz and Murray Turoff, *The Network Nation: Human Communications via Computer* (Reading, MA: Addison-Wesley, 1978); Allen Newell and Robert F. Sproull, "Computer Networks: Prospects for Scientists," *Science* 215 (12 Feb. 1982), pp. 843–852; and Ronald E. Rice and Donald Case, "Electronic Message Systems in the University: A Description of Use and Utility," *Journal of Communication* 33:1 (Winter 1983), pp. 131–152.

On bulletin boards, see Alfred Glossbrenner, "Computer Bulletin Board Systems," in his *The Complete Handbook of Personal Computer Business Communications: Everything You Need to Go Online with the World* (New York: St. Martin's, 1978); Tom Beeston and Tom Tucker, *Hooking In: The Underground Computer Bulletin Board and Guide* (Westlake Village, CA: Computerfood Press, 1984); and Mike Cane, *The Computer Phone Book* (New York: New American Library, 1984).

Public domain BBS software is widely available from computer users groups. See Robert A. Froehlick, *The Free Software Catalog and Directory* (New York: Crown Publishers, 1984) and Alfred Glossbrenner, *How to Get Free Software* (New York: St. Martin's, 1984). A public domain BBS for the IBM PC is RBBS-PC, a new version of which will include full conferencing capabilities.

George Peck, 211 Yacht Club Way #326, Redondo Beach, CA 90277 sells an outstanding BBS program for the IBM Personal Computer and compatibles. A Macintosh BBS is sold by Connick and Associates Inc., 2329 Old Trail Drive, Reston, VA 22901

PART
FIVE

CRUNCHING NUMBERS

SOFTWARE FOR NUMBER-CRUNCHING

In the summer of 1957, the scientist J. C. R. Licklider decided to study just how he spent his time while working. Licklider found, to his dismay, that "about 85 percent of my 'thinking' time was spent getting into a position to think, to make a decision, to learn something I needed to know." Licklider spent hours, for example, plotting graphs. "When the graphs were finished, the relations were obvious at once, but the plotting had to be done to make them so." The sobering truth was that Licklider spent most of his time on "essentially clerical or mechanical" work, and he had to admit that sometimes what he did stemmed from considerations of clerical feasibility rather than scientific merit.[1]

Not a little of Licklider's effort was devoted to information management—keeping records—and he would have doubtless found the techniques in Part Three, "Managing Information," of great value. But Licklider was doing some number-crunching, too. Now the number-crunching Licklider was doing wasn't anything fancy; it was just tedious. He was studying experimental determinations of a function relating intelligibility to the noise component in spoken communication. The problem was that every experimenter used a slightly different measure of the noise ratio, and all the data had to be recalculated using a common formula so they would be comparable. "When they were in comparable form," Licklider wrote, "it took only a few seconds to determine what I needed to know." But the drudgery required to get there made the project almost intolerably difficult and encouraged indefensible compromises.

Licklider's experiences sound all too familiar to any scholar who juggles numbers, and that means everyone who has ever, for instance, included even a

---

[1] "Man-Computer Symbiosis," originally published in *ETC.: A Review of General Semantics* 24:1 (1967), reprinted in *Perspectives on the Computer Revolution,* Zenon Pylyshyn, ed. (Englewood Cliffs, NJ: Prentice-Hall, 1970), p. 309.

simple table of numbers (such as a population table) in a scholarly paper. Computer assistance is obviously welcome. That's no news these days, of course, to veteran and expert number crunchers, who are likely to be familiar with mainframe statistical packages such as SPSS and SAS.[2] Yet these sophisticated statistical packages are unsuitable for prosaic calculation tasks that, like Licklider's data on speech to noise ratios, involve simple but monstrously repetitive arithmetic operations.

In 1978, Dan Bricklin, then a student at Harvard Business School, had suffered through the Licklider dilemma so frequently that he decided to do something about it. Bricklin spent hours every evening on financial case analyses, which required repetitive (but arithmetically simple) calculations on large tables of numbers. If just one calculation was changed, all the other numbers had to be recalculated by tedious hand methods. He persuaded a friend who knew how to program, Robert Frankston, to help him develop a program for microcomputers that could handle these kinds of simple, repetitive calculations. One year later, VisiCalc—the first *spreadsheet* program—was on the market. The term "spreadsheet" had its origins in the large worksheets accountants use.

The name VisiCalc (short for *visible calculator*) is an excellent description of the program's major achievement: it provides a visual representation of precisely the kind of calculating process that people are likely to do on paper. You can see the numbers, all neatly lined up in columns. But unlike a piece of paper, you can embed arithmetic formulas into the spreadsheet that tell the computer which numbers to consider and what to do with them. And like a word processing program, you can almost instantly copy or replicate these formulas all the way down a column or across a row. Using a spreadsheet program like VisiCalc, for instance, Licklider could have typed in his data, added a conversion formula, copied it down the column, and watched the program do in seconds the conversions that took him hours to complete.

Spreadsheet programs have grown in complexity and power since Bricklin's first effort, and a most agreeable addition to them has arisen: graphics programs that can take data from specified rows and columns in a spreadsheet and automatically transform them into charts and graphs.

Spreadsheet programs have descended like balm from the heavens on scholars who, like Licklider and Bricklin, once labored long over repetitive but simple arithmetic calculations and chart plotting. There are few scholars indeed who won't have uses for these tools once it's understood that they're designed for simple, repetitive number-crunching tasks that scholars from all over the academy—including the humanities—are likely to find themselves saddled with.

This chapter introduces spreadsheet software and graphics packages, presenting a brief overview of these programs' capabilities. The next chapter, "Crunching Grades," presents a single, in-depth example of exactly the kind of number-crunching that spreadsheets were born to do: managing student grades.

---

[2] A version of SPSS, incidentally, is now available for the IBM PC XT. See the Resources section at the end of this chapter for more information.

INTRODUCING SPREADSHEET SOFTWARE

All spreadsheet programs are surprisingly similar; what follows could apply equally to just about any spreadsheet package on the market, from the earliest version of VisiCalc to the latest one of Lotus 1-2-3. There are, to be sure, some differences, but we'll put them aside for now. At the heart of the spreadsheet is the *cell matrix*, the ease with which you can embed formulas into the cell matrix, and the ease with which you can copy formulas from one cell to another.

THE CELL MATRIX

All spreadsheet programs display a matrix of rows and columns, called a spreadsheet or worksheet, that is similar to a bookkeeper's ruled paper. Each intersection of a row and column is called a *cell*. The more basic programs, such as VisiCalc and SuperCalc, offer roughly 250 rows by 60 columns, while the more advanced ones, such as the integrated programs, offer from 256 columns and 2048 rows (Lotus 1-2-3) to 256 columns by 8192 rows (Symphony). Only a small portion of the actual worksheet is shown at any one time. It's useful, therefore, to think of the video display as if it were a picture frame or window being held over a much larger piece of paper.

You can enter data on the worksheet just the way you'd enter data on paper. You can even add headings and lines to clarify the worksheet's meaning (Figure 15–1).

```
    | A                     ||  B  ||  C  ||  D  |
  1 |
  2 |
  3 |                    Table 21.
  4 |
  5 |            Occupations by Household
  6 |                  McLehner County
  7 |
  8 |========================================================
  9 |                      Year of Survey
 10 |                      ------------------------------
 11 |Occupation            1900    1910    1920
 12 |========================================================
 13 |
 14 |Agricultural Labor     485     390     151
 15 |Artisan/Trade          211     145      97
 16 |Farming               1924    1430     980
 17 |Industrial Labor       590     874    1429
 18 |Small Business         210     270     380
 19 |
 20 |
```

FIGURE 15-1. Data and Headings Entered on Worksheet

Each cell has a name. The intersection of column B and row 20, for example, is called B20. You'll use the names to tell the program what to do. For instance, when you want it to multiply something, you tell it, "Multiply the number in cell____" using a cell name. You can also refer to cell ranges. The expression B8..B19 means "the cells from B8 through B19, inclusive."

FORMULAS

Formulas tell the program how to calculate data you've referred to using *cell references*. In Figure 15-1, you can find the sum of the figures in Column B—the survey results for 1900—by inserting a formula in cell B20 (actually, the formula could be placed anywhere on the spreadsheet, but it always makes good sense to keep the spreadsheet as visually sensible as possible).

The formula begins with a special symbol (here, @) that tells the computer that what follows is a formula (and not a heading or a number). Right after the special symbol is the formula's name, in this case, SUM, and enclosed within parentheses is the *range* of cells you want acted on. Here's what the formula looks like:

$$@SUM(B14..B18)$$

What this formula means, in essence, is "Take the numbers in cells B14 through B18 and add them together. Show the sum in this cell."

You don't see the formula in the cell; it's hidden (but you can see what it is by moving the cursor to the cell and looking at a special formula display area). What's visible is the formula's result (see cell B20 in Figure 15-2).

COPYING OR REPLICATION

If what you've just seen was all spreadsheets could do, that alone would justify their widespread acceptance and use. But the best is yet to come.

Every spreadsheet program comes equipped with a replication or copy command, which permits you to copy the values or the formulas from one cell or one range of cells to another.

That sounds familiar enough; one can do copying operations with a word processing program. But copying with a spreadsheet program is a far more powerful and useful operation. To understand why, it's necessary to grasp how the program understands cell references.

The formula @SUM(B14..B18) inserted in Cell B20 doesn't actually look that way to the computer. What it looks like is more like this: "Take the figures in the same column, starting with the sixth row up and running down to the fourth row up, and add them."

```
  | A                        || B    || C    || D    |
 1|
 2|
 3|                        Table 21.
 4|
 5|              Occupations by Household
 6|                    McLehner County
 7|
 8|================================================================
 9|                         Year of Survey
10|                   ---------------------------------
11|Occupation             1900     1910     1920
12|================================================================
13|
14|Agricultural Labor      485      390      151
15|Artisan/Trade           211      145       97
16|Farming                1924     1430      980
17|Industrial Labor        590 .    874     1429
18|Small Business          210      270      380
19|
20|          TOTAL:       3420
```

FIGURE 15-2. Result of Formula Inserted in Cell B20

Let's suppose you copy the formula in B20 to the next cell right, C20. You're not actually copying verbatim the formula @SUM(B14 .. B18). On the contrary, you're copying the expression "Take the figures in the same column, starting with the sixth row up and running down to the fourth row up, and add them." Now you can predict what happens. Instead of adding the figures in Column B, the copied formula adds the figures in Column C. Just to make you think the program is smart and to keep everything crystal-clear, the copied formula appears (if you examine it by looking in the formula display area) this way:

@SUM(C14..C18)

Figure 15-3 shows its result.

Replication, obviously, is a major reason for the spreadsheet's appeal; yet its true power still hasn't been revealed. You can copy a formula, not just to another single cell, but to a whole range of them. Imagine, now, that this spreadsheet has data for 50 years, spread laterally across the top of the spreadsheet and running far beyond the visible right margin. To replicate the Cell B20 formula across the whole spreadsheet, all you'd have to do is specify the range (for instance, C20 .. Z20), and the formula is replicated instantly. As you stare into the green or amber depths of the display screen, the results of the calculations cascade across the screen as if by magic.

	A	|| B	|| C	|| D	
1								
2								
3		Table 21.						
4								
5		Occupations by Household						
6		McLehner County						
7								
8	==
9			Year of Survey					
10								
11	Occupation		1900		1910		1920	
12	==
13								
14	Agricultural Labor		485		390		151	
15	Artisan/Trade		211		145		97	
16	Farming		1924		1430		980	
17	Industrial Labor		590		874		1429	
18	Small Business		210		270		380	
19								
20		TOTAL:	3420		3109			

FIGURE 15-3. Results of Copying Formula to Cell C20

RESOURCES FOR FORMULA WRITING

Once you've grasped these basic points about spreadsheet programs, you have a good idea of what they can do and why they're so popular. There remains only to round out the picture by describing the tools these programs give you for crafting formulas.

Operators

Operators, or symbols that represent arithmetic or relational operations, provide you with a way of telling the program how to perform calculations. Operators may be used with values (100 + 120) or cell references (B8 + C10). Table 15-1 lists the operators commonly provided with spreadsheet programs.

Translating arithmetic operations into their spreadsheet equivalents requires caution in all but the simplest expressions. VisiCalc, for example, evaluates expressions from left to right unless parentheses are supplied, so the expressions 1 + .05 * B1 and 1 + (.05 * B1) would produce different results. Most other programs use precedence rules (for an example, see Table 15-2), which can also be overriden by parentheses. In general, use parentheses liberally to avoid errors.

Parentheses may be nested to indicate further precisely how the expression should be evaluated. In the following example,

TABLE 15-1
SPREADSHEET OPERATORS

Arithmetic Operators	Relational Operators
+ addition	= equal to
* multiplication	< > not equal to
− subtraction	< less than
/ division	> greater than
∧ to the power of	<= less than or equal to
% percent	=> greater than or equal to

$$((A1 \; / \; A2) \; + \; (B1 \; / \; B2)) \; * \; 10$$

the division operations would take place before the addition; the last operation to be performed would be the multiplication.

Functions

You can insert quite a complex mathematical expression into a cell using the techniques and operators just described, but for some operations it's quicker and easier to use a *built-in function,* such as @SUM Table 15–3 lists the built-in functions provided with advanced spreadsheets; even the earliest spreadsheets have a high proportion of them.

Built-in functions are usually prefixed with a special symbol (such as @), which tells the computer that what follows is not text but rather a reference to a built-in function; they are usually followed with an *argument* that tells the program what to act on. For example, the expression

$$@ROUND(B10)$$

rounds off the value in cell B10.

TABLE 15-2
PRECEDENCE OF ARITHMETIC OPERATIONS: SYMPHONY

Precedence	Operator	Operation
1	+	addition
	−	subtraction
2	*	multiplication
	/	division
3	−	negative numbers
4	∧	exponentiation

TABLE 15-3
SPREADSHEET FUNCTIONS

Mathematical Functions	Statistical Functions	Logical and Other Functions
Absolute value of number	Average of series of values	Choose a value from a list
Arc cosine of number	Maximum of series of values	If/then/else expressions
Arc sine of number	Minimum of series of values	Look up a value on a list
Arc tangent of number	Number of values in series	
Cosine of number	Standard deviation of series of values	
Integer of number	Sum of series of values	
Log (base e) of number	Variance of series of values	
Modulus when a number is divided by x		
Pi		
Power of number		
Random number		
Round number off		
Sine of number		
Square root of number		
Tangent of number		

Range Expressions

You may refer to more than a single cell so long as the cells are contiguous in some way, or to put it another way, they constitute a range of cells. The range A1 through B4 (expressed A1..B4 in one program's conventions) includes the cells A1, A2, A3, A4, B1, B2, B3, and B4. A range can also comprise a row (or part of a row) of cells (A1..Z1) or a column (or part of a column) of cells (A1..A256). It cannot, however, include cells that are not contiguous in some way.

A useful and intuitively sensible feature provided with the more recent programs is *range naming*, which lets you give a name to a range of cells. Suppose, for example, Column B contains the scores for Quiz 1 in cells B9..B58. If you're using a spreadsheet that has range naming, you can use the Name Range command to name these cells "Quiz1." Whenever you refer to the range in expressions, you can simply use the name "Quiz1" instead of retyping the range B9..B58. The following two expressions are all that one program needs, for instance, to find the mean and standard deviation of a set of scores once they have been named:

@AVG(QUIZ1)
@STDDEV(QUIZ1)

COMMANDS

Every spreadsheet program provides commands that let you perform basic operations. We've already discussed the replication command. Also included in all programs are commands for moving around in the spreadsheet; editing; formatting; printing; and file operations.

Moving Around in the Spreadsheet

In a large spreadsheet, moving to portions of the spreadsheet not visible on the screen can be very slow if you try scrolling the screen one column or row at a time. The computer must refresh the entire screen for each movement of one column or row, and the result, save in the fastest systems, is tedium. The best spreadsheet programs therefore provide a "go to" command that lets you jump immediately to a specified cell.

Editing

Most spreadsheets provide the following editing tools:

Edit   The contents of the cell cannot be directly edited once they have been entered by pressing the return key. Most programs, however, permit you to edit a selected cell's contents by using the edit command. The edit command brings the cell's contents back to the cell entry area for revision.

Delete   The delete command permits you to erase the contents of a single cell, a range of cells, or the entire spreadsheet.

Formatting

Formatting commands let you define the appearance of numbers and text in specified ranges or throughout the entire worksheet. Among the more common formatting commands are:

Number formatting   A cell, a range, or the entire worksheet can be formatted so that numbers are displayed and printed in general format, with all significant figures shown after decimal point and scientific notation used for figures too large to fit in the cell; dollar-and-cents format, with two decimal places and dollar signs; scientific notation; or with a fixed number of decimal places.

Text formatting   Headings can be formatted flush left, centered, or flush right.

Printing

Spreadsheet programs can either print a range of cells or the entire spreadsheet. If the spreadsheet is larger than a single 8½-by-11 inch page, they automatically distribute it over as many pages as necessary to print all the active areas. Advanced functions include a label printing utility, which inserts headings on each and every printed page, and formula printing, which prints the normally hidden formulas as well as the visible cell contents.

File Operations

Like other personal computer programs, spreadsheets provide facilities for basic file operations, such as writing and retrieving disk files. Very desirable additional features are:

Copying from one spreadsheet file to another The best spreadsheet programs permit you to copy a range of cells (including formulas) from another spreadsheet file to the one you're working on. This feature is of enormous value because it lets you create relatively small, easily managed spreadsheets for particular functions. Chapter 16, for example, shows how to manage student grades by creating a spreadsheet for raw scores, another one for calculating standard scores, and a third for recording grades.

File linkage A few spreadsheet programs let you establish permanent links between different spreadsheet files so that updating one automatically updates the others.

Writing standard text files The ability to print to a disk file in standard ASCII format will prove of genuine value for most scholarly writers who will often work with spreadsheets like the one illustrated in this chapter (the table of occupations by household). Once all the calculations have been completed, this spreadsheet can be printed to a disk file which (unlike the nonstandard spreadsheet file format) can be directly read by your word processing program, saving you the trouble of retyping it.

Command Macros

An advanced but enormously appealing and valuable feature, found in the more recent spreadsheet programs, is the ability to create macros. In essence, a macro is nothing more than a stored collection of keystrokes which, when activated by a special macro command, are entered just as if you had typed every one of them. Suppose, for example, you have created a spreadsheet that you update regularly, recalculate, and print. To do the updating virtually automatically, you could create a macro that contains all the necessary keystrokes to set in motion all the required operations.

A TYPOLOGY OF SPREADSHEET PROGRAMS

Spreadsheet programs are surprisingly similar, and there's a great deal of similarity and obvious kinship between the earliest version of VisiCalc and the snazziest, latest version of Symphony. Indeed, if you know how to use VisiCalc, you won't have any trouble with Symphony's spreadsheet.

That said, it's common to summarize the differences among spreadsheets using the following terms:

First-generation programs (Examples: early versions of VisiCalc, Super-Calc, public domain spreadsheet programs.) Lacked such features as built-in logic functions, the ability to print an ASCII disk file, interfaces with graphics software, or statistical functions. They were marked by relatively simple formatting and printing functions.

Second-generation programs (Examples: SuperCalc^3, Multiplan/Microsoft Chart for Macintosh, Lotus 1-2-3.) Include such features as built-in logic functions, ASCII file printing, range naming, well-conceived interfaces to data base management and graphics programs, statistical functions such as variance and standard deviation, and sophisticated formatting and printing capabilities. SuperCalc^3 and Lotus 1-2-3 include data base management and graphics capabilities.

Spreadsheets in integrated programs The two big integrated packages of 1984, Framework and Symphony, include ultrasophisticated spreadsheets with ready interfaces to word processing, graphics, telecommunication, and data base management programs, together with macro facilities that constitute true programming languages.

SPREADSHEET HORIZONS

Spreadsheet programs can work with graphics software and word processing programs, and the results make them even more attractive.

THE GRAPHICS CONNECTION

Graphics programs are designed to work by themselves or, in some cases, with spreadsheet programs, and the latter are preferable.

Graphics programs with spreadsheet interfaces permit you to specify a range of values on the spreadsheet and have them transformed, automatically and rapidly, into pie, chart, line, scatter, or column charts. These charts have obvious uses for many of the tasks that scholars do, such as preparing illustrations for publications or classroom use.

THE WORD PROCESSOR CONNECTION

Most spreadsheet programs can write to a disk file using the standard ASCII characters, producing a neatly formatted table bereft of row and column numbers and other extraneous symbols. You can, in other words, create all the tables for a scholarly article (for instance), letting the spreadsheet program take care of the calculations. When you're finished, you can print the tables to disk files. Having loaded your word processing program, you can use the file merging command (see Chapter 3) to incorporate the tables into your document.

SPREADSHEET APPLICATIONS

To suggest how a scholar might use spreadsheet software, here's a brief hypothetical illustration. A religious studies researcher, Stewart Adams, has just completed a survey of participation by five African ethnic groups in a regional pilgrimage in West Africa.

Having consulted reservation records kept in a government-sponsored guesthouse at the pilgrimage site, Stewart has obtained some interesting statistics on ethnic group participation levels during the past ten years. To analyze the data, he sets up a spreadsheet, listing the years for which he has data (1975 through 1984) across the top of the spreadsheet and the five ethnic groups (1 through 5) in the first column on the left side of the spreadsheet. He then uses his graphics program to plot the data, and quickly discovers a pattern: participation of four of the tribes has held more or less constant, but participation by ethnic group tribe 3—a group composed mostly of farmers—has risen dramatically. Stewart finds that this pattern helps to explain a trend of change that he and others have noticed in the site, a trend toward a religious concern with the fertility of the earth.

Stewart decides to play around with the figures, trying out a famous spreadsheet technique called *what-if analysis*. What-if analysis involves changing some of the values on the spreadsheet to see what happens to the overall pattern. It turns out that, even though participation levels by group 3 grew significantly over the ten years for which he has data, from 1979 through 1981 group 3's participation increased only slowly owing to a major civil conflict in the group's province. Stewart decides to see what the trend would have looked like if there had been no conflict and group 3's participation had continued growing at the pace set by the 1975–1978 data. He plugs in the necessary figures from 1979 through 1981 and gives the command that generates a new chart from the revised data. As Stewart expected, the rise in participation is even more marked, and—one might surmise—the impact of group 3 on the site would have been even greater.

Stewart decides to try another spreadsheet technique, forecasting, to see what might happen in the future if this trend continues. Using a technique called linear regression, Stewart applies a formula to the historical values—the ones for which he has data—and projects the trend they embody into the next ten years, 1985 through 1995. By 1988, group 3 alone would outnumber all other ethnic groups in pilgrimage participation, if present trends continue. The pilgrimage,

Stewart concludes, seems on its way to becoming closely identified with group 3 and its particular religious concerns.

These techniques—simple calculation and graphing, what-if analysis, and forecasting—can handle many number-crunching jobs that scholars do. As you've just seen, they can also do something more: they can provide a supple tool for thought, exploration, and discovery.

RESOURCES

On VisiCalc and spreadsheet software generally, see Stanley R. Trost and Charles Pomernacki, *VisiCalc for Science and Engineering* (Berkeley: Sybex Computer Books, 1983), and Thomas B. Henderson, Douglass Cobb, and Gena B. Cobb, *Spreadsheet Software: From VisiCalc to 1-2-3* (Indianapolis: Que Books, 1984).

On software for more advanced mathematics and statistics, see Peter Callamaras, "Statistical Software: a Buyer's Guide to Seven Major Types of Statistics Packages," *Popular Computing* (Oct. 1983), pp. 206–220; James Carpenter, Dennis Deloria, and David Morganstein, "Statistical Software for Microcomputers: A Comparative Analysis of 24 Packages," *Byte* (April 1984), pp. 234–264; Alan J. Fridlund, "Taking the Numbers Bull By the Horn: Four Statistics Packages Provide a Range of Power and Features," *InfoWorld* (Feb. 11, 1985), pp. 42–49 (includes review, *inter alia,* of SPSS-PC); P. A., Lachenbruch, "Statistical Programs for Microcomputers," *Byte* (Nov. 1983), pp. 560–570; Milos Konopasek and Sundaresan Jayaraman, "Expert Systems for Personal Computers: The TK!Solver Approach," *Byte* (May 1984), pp. 137–154, and their *The TK!Solver Book: A Guide to Problem-Solving in Science, Engineering, Business, and Education* (Berkeley: Osborne-McGraw-Hill, 1984); Mark Zachmann, "The Versatile Variables of TK!Solver," *PC: The Independent Magazine for IBM Personal Computers* (Sept. 1983), pp. 489–498.

On spreadsheet technique, note well: Henry Fersko-Weiss, "Avoiding Spreadsheet Disaster," *Personal Computing* (March 1985), pp. 112–117, and Doran Howitt, "Avoiding Bottom-Line Disaster," *InfoWorld* (Feb. 11, 1985), pp. 26–30.

CRUNCHING GRADES

Generations of teachers have been exhorted to pay some attention to the process by which grades are calculated, but with little success. To be sure, most conscientious teachers attempt, at least initially, to examine the distribution of test scores, to make rational decisions about assigning grades, and perhaps even to calculate standard scores, whose merits are well known. But the tedium involved in doing these calculations by hand (even with the aid of a calculator) soon defeats all but the most zealous. In other words, grades are a classic target for the spreadsheet solution.

The pages to follow present a spreadsheet approach to grading with standardized test scores. The discussion is intended to illustrate one of many possible scholarly and teaching applications of spreadsheets, particularly how two or more spreadsheets can be linked together to build up a particularly powerful approach to number-crunching. You may or may not find the approach to grading useful. Even if you don't, however, the example will suggest other spreadsheet applications.

This grade-crunching approach uses three separate (but related) spreadsheets:

Raw scores worksheet This worksheet contains no formulas or functions. It's used for recording raw student scores.

***T*-Score master worksheet** This worksheet takes a set of scores for a test and automatically transforms them into standardized *T* scores, which express the raw scores as a normal distribution with a mean of 50 and a standard deviation of 10.

Grade weighting worksheet This worksheet stores the grades computed by the *T*-score master worksheet and assigns weights to them. When all the scores have been finished, the student's final grade is computed and displayed.

THE RAW SCORES WORKSHEET

The first of the three spreadsheets involved in this grade calculation system is intended solely for recording raw scores, that is, the unmanipulated test results. It contains no formulas, no cell references, and no built-in functions. It's a good record book; in keeping with its function, the raw scores are protected (using the "protect" command) so that they can't be inadvertently altered.

Figure 16-1 shows the beginning of what will eventually be a fairly large raw scores worksheet. Thus far the results of only two (of ten) quizzes are shown. Also to be added later are the scores for the midterm and the final examinations.

```
|       A            |   B   |   C   |
 1|Political Science 121
 2|Spring Term
 3|
 4|Raw Scores Worksheet
 5|==================================================
 6|Name                Quiz 1   Quiz 2   Quiz 3  Quiz 4
 7|--------------------------------------------------
 8|Abrams, Tony          31       78
 9|Callahan, Ron         35       81
10|Carey, Julia          36       85
11|Doland, Joy           33       71
12|Epstein, Edward       45      100
13|Fallows, Arnold       27       71
14|Graveller, Henry      31       78
15|Howard, Robert        28       69
16|Jenkins, Barbara      49       98
17|Karril, Monica        36       88
18|Lee, Steve            31       71
19|Neuman, Jennifer      35       83
20|Oswald, Tom           42       94
21|Patterson, Mike       18       72
22|Patterson, Tim        39       87
23|Rowland, Joshua       34       81
24|Rozier, Dawn          41       92
25|Sanders, Laura        48       95
26|Sandman, Sarah        31       85
27|Walters, Paul         36       78
```

FIGURE 16-1. Raw Scores Worksheet

THE T-SCORE MASTER WORKSHEET

The scores shown in Figure 16–1 confront us with a classic problem: how can you compare them meaningfully? One quiz had 50 possible points; the other had 100. An apparent solution to the problem would be to double the scores for quiz 1 (or halve the scores for quiz 2), but there are some solid statistical arguments against doing so.

Imagine two quizzes like these, one with 50 and the other with 100 possible points, and imagine too that the results of the first quiz have been doubled. Both, therefore, have a scale of 100 and, on examination of the scores, it turns out that the average score of both of them is 70. A 75 on one quiz means the same thing as a 75 on the other, right? Not necessarily. Suppose, on the first quiz, that the class performed with surprising unanimity: most of the scores were within the range 65 to 75, with only a very few scoring as low as 62 or as high as 78. And suppose, too, on the second quiz, that the scores were highly variable: although the average was 70, some students received scores as high as 98 and others got scores as low as 20. Clearly, a 78 on the first quiz is a pretty extraordinary performance, while a 78 on the second one isn't nearly so impressive.

Making meaningful judgments about any two sets of scores, even if they both have 100 points possible to begin with, requires an assessment of the scores' variability. Knowing precisely how variable the first set of scores is, for instance, gives you some solid ground for saying a 78 is an extraordinary performance on the first test and not so extraordinary on the second.

A very handy way to approach this problem is to translate these scores so that, in place of the relatively meaningless 0 to 50 or 0 to 100 scale, they're expressed in terms of a score's standing relative to the other scores for the quiz. One way to achieve this kind of translation would be to rank the students' scores, giving the highest score a 1, the next highest a 2, and so on. But this approach still doesn't indicate how extraordinary (or ordinary) a score is; if, for example, one exceptionally well-prepared student received a 98 on a test for which the next highest score was a 71, her rank of 1 would not be distinguished from the student who ranked 1 with a score only one point above the second in rank. It's for that reason that statisticians recommend z scores, which express a score in terms of how many standard deviations it stands from the average. A particular score, for instance, might be said to stand $+1.5$ standard deviations from the mean, or -0.5 standard deviations from the mean.

What does it mean to say that a score stands $+1.5$ or -0.5 standard deviations from the mean? In a normally distributed set of scores, a set of scores whose overall shape, when graphed according to frequency, approximates the familiar bell curve, approximately 68 percent of the scores will fall within one standard deviation of the mean. A score that's more than one standard deviation away from the mean, therefore, can be said to stand in fairly rarefied territory: only 32% of the scores—16% of them very good, and 16% of them very bad—

stand on the extremes. A score that's two standard deviations away from the mean is truly exceptional: only about 5% of the scores will fall above or below two standard deviations from the mean. To say to a student, then, "your score was truly exceptional: you scored two standard deviations above the mean," is to say something with a definite meaning: you know from your computations that the student stands in the very highest of ranks in the class.

The only problem with z scores is that some people don't like looking at negative signs; further, before the computer, the negatives made computations difficult. So z scores are usually translated into more familiar terms by multiplying them by 10 and adding 50, producing T scores.

THE SPREADSHEET DESIGN

The T-score master worksheet whose creation is here described automatically calculates the T scores from the raw student score data. We'll discuss setting it up in a moment, but first here's an overview of its design and function.

To create the spreadsheet, you begin by using a command (such as "file combine" in Symphony) that reads the students' names and data from a specified range of cells (for instance, A8 through B27) in the raw scores worksheet. Then you add built-in functions and formulas to section 2 that compute the mean, the minimum and maximum scores, and the number of test scores reported. Next you insert, in column C, a formula that calculates how far each score stands away from the mean (in other words, its deviation from the mean); in column D is added a formula that squares the deviations. Column E calculates the z score by dividing the deviation by the standard deviation. Multiplying the z scores by 10 and adding 50 gives the T-scores in column F. Figure 16-2 shows the spreadsheet's design.

If your spreadsheet has built-in functions for finding the standard deviation of a range of scores, you can omit column C. Add a row in section 2 for the standard deviation and refer to that cell, instead of D35, for the standard deviation.

CREATING THE SPREADSHEET

Reading the Data from the Raw Scores Worksheet

The first step in creating this spreadsheet is to transfer the student names and the quiz 1 scores from the raw scores worksheet. To be sure, you could set up the spreadsheet without any data, and that's the ultimate goal: you'll eventually transform this spreadsheet into a master spreadsheet that can be used with any data set. When you're creating a spreadsheet master, however, it's always a good idea to have some data around—that way if you enter a formula that's incorrect,

```
  |     A      |  B   |   C   |    D    | E  | F
 1|
 2|          North Central State University
 3|          Political Science Department
 4|
 5|            T SCORE COMPUTATION MASTER
 6|
 7|
 8|1.  Computation of T Scores
 9|=====================================================================
10|Name               Scores  Devs.    Devs.^2     Z       T
11|=====================================================================
12|
13|
14|
15|
16|
17|
18|
19|
20|
21|
22|
23|
24|
25|
26|
27|
28|
29|
30|
31|
32|-------------------------------------------------------------------
33|                    Sum of sq.
34|                    Variance
35|                    Std. Dev.          Avg.
36|                    CHECK              Std. Dev.
37|
38|2.  Score Statistics (Calculation Area)
39|=========================================
40|Count
41|Average
42|Maximum
43|Minimum
44|-------------------------------------------------
45|
```

FIGURE 16-2. Design of Spreadsheet for Computing T Scores

the error will at least be potentially obvious. That's why the previous chapter suggested that you create a master using data and strip the data from the master after you've tested it.

Most spreadsheet programs give you a command that reads a specified range of cells from another spreadsheet file, so long as it's on the same disk. In Symphony, for instance, the file combine command does the job. You simply position the cursor where you want the data to appear and use the command; it permits you to specify the range of cells you want read (here, A8 through B27, the names and quiz 1 scores from Figure 16–1). After pressing the return key to initiate the command, the names and scores fall into place (Figure 16–3).

Adding the Formulas to Section 2

The next step involves inserting the necessary formulas into section 2. Here's what the expressions look like (in Lotus 1-2-3 and Symphony format; slight modifications will be necessary for other programs):

```
Cell B40:   @COUNT(B12..B31)
Cell B41    @AVG(B12..B31)
Cell B42    @MAX(B12..B31)
Cell B43    @MIN(B12..B31)
```

```
 8|1.  Computation of T Scores
 9|=============================================================
10|Name              Scores  Devs.   Devs.^2   z      T
11|=============================================================
12|Abrams, Tony        31
13|Callahan, Ron       35
14|Carey, Julia        36
15|Doland, Joy         33
16|Epstein, Edward     45
17|Fallows, Arnold     27
18|Graveller, Henry    31
19|Howard, Robert      28
20|Jenkins, Barbara    49
21|Karril, Monica      36
22|Lee, Steve          31
23|Neuman, Jennifer    35
24|Oswald, Tom         42
25|Patterson, Mike     18
26|Patterson, Tim      39
27|Rowland, Joshua     34
28|Rozier, Dawn        41
29|Sanders, Laura      48
30|Sandman, Sarah      31
31|Walters, Paul       36
32|-------------------------------------------------------------
```

FIGURE 16–3. Student Names and Raw Scores

Adding the Formulas to Section 1

Finding the T scores requires finding the scores' deviations from the mean, the square of these deviations, the sum of the squared deviations, the variance, and the standard deviation. Were you to calculate these scores by hand, you'd probably set up a worksheet that looks exactly like the one that's shown in Figure 16-1, with columns for each step of the calculations. That's why the spreadsheet is set up this way: whenever possible, your spreadsheet should look as familiar as possible. It's much easier that way to detect design or entry errors.

There's quite a good deal of calculation to be done, but calculating is the spreadsheet's forte. You need insert only seven formulas.

To begin, insert the formula for calculating the scores' deviations from the mean (note the absolute reference to the cell that contains the mean):

```
Cell C12    B12-$B$41
```

and replicate the formula down the column. Now insert the formula to square the deviations:

```
Cell D12:    C12∧2
```

and replicate the formula down the column.

To find the sum of the squared deviations, the variance, and the standard deviation, use these formulas:

```
Cell D33:    @SUM(D12..D31)
Cell D34:    @AVG(D12..D31)
Cell D35:    @SQRT(D34)
```

Cell D36 provides an automatic check of whether you've entered these formulas correctly. It solves for the standard deviation by another route:

```
Cell D36:    @SQRT(D33/B40)
```

Cells D35 and D36 should show the same result. If they differ, you've probably used the wrong cell reference somewhere in one of your formulas.

Next, insert the formula to calculate the z scores (note the absolute cell reference to the cell that reports the standard deviation):

```
Cell E12:    C9/$D$35
```

and replicate the formula down the column. To find the T scores, use this formula:

```
Cell F12:    E12*10+50
```

and replicate it down the column.

Once you've finished inserting the formulas, the T scores appear (Figure 16-4). To make sure they've been calculated correctly, insert two additional checking formulas:

```
 8|1.   Computation of T Scores
 9|=========================================================
10|Name              Scores  Devs.    Devs.^2    z      T
11|=========================================================
12|Abrams, Tony         31   -4.30     18.49   -0.60   44.03
13|Callahan, Ron        35   -0.30      0.09   -0.04   49.58
14|Carey, Julia         36    0.70      0.49    0.10   50.97
15|Doland, Joy          33   -2.30      5.29   -0.32   46.81
16|Epstein, Edward      45    9.70     94.09    1.35   63.46
17|Fallows, Arnold      27   -8.30     68.89   -1.15   38.48
18|Graveller, Henry     31   -4.30     18.49   -0.60   44.03
19|Howard, Robert       28   -7.30     53.29   -1.01   39.87
20|Jenkins, Barbara     49   13.70    187.69    1.90   69.01
21|Karril, Monica       36    0.70      0.49    0.10   50.97
22|Lee, Steve           31   -4.30     18.49   -0.60   44.03
23|Neuman, Jennifer     35   -0.30      0.09   -0.04   49.58
24|Oswald, Tom          42    6.70     44.89    0.93   59.30
25|Patterson, Mike      18  -17.30    299.29   -2.40   25.99
26|Patterson, Tim       39    3.70     13.69    0.51   55.14
27|Rowland, Joshua      34   -1.30      1.69   -0.18   48.20
28|Rozier, Dawn         41    5.70     32.49    0.79   57.91
29|Sanders, Laura       48   12.70    161.29    1.76   67.63
30|Sandman, Sarah       31   -4.30     18.49   -0.60   44.03
31|Walters, Paul        36    0.70      0.49    0.10   50.97
32|---------------------------------------------------------
33|              Sum of sq.   1038.2                .
34|              Variance       51.91
35|              Std. dev.       7.21    Avg   50.00
36|              CHECK           7.21    StDev 10
37|
38|2.   Score Statistics (Calculation Area)
39|=========================================================
40|Count            20
41|Average          35.3
42|Maximum          49
43|Minimum          18
44|---------------------------------------------------------
```

FIGURE 16-4. Calculation of T Scores

```
Cell F35:    @AVG(F12..F31)
Cell F36:    @STD(F12..F31)
```

The formula in cell F36 requires a built-in standard deviation function. The formulas in these two cells should return, respectively, an average of exactly 50 and a standard deviation of exactly 10. If they don't, there's an error somewhere.

CREATING THE T-SCORE MASTER

Now that the *T*-score worksheet has been successfully tested with data, it may be saved to disk with a file name indicating its present contents (such as

QUIZ1TS, short for "quiz 1 T scores"). To create the master spreadsheet, strip the names and the scores by using the program's erase or clear command and save the spreadsheet to disk using a different file name (such as TSMASTER, short for "T-score master"). *Note:* because you've removed the scores, error messages (such as "ERR") will appear in many or most of the cells. Ignore these messages for now.

Once the *T*-score master worksheet has been successfully created, you can use it to compute the *T* scores for additional quizzes or tests. To compute the scores for quiz 2, for instance, you'd use the spreadsheet command that reads data from a specified range of cells in another spreadsheet file (the raw scores worksheet). The scores file down the screen and in moments, all the error messages disappear, the calculations are done, and the results appear (Figure 16–5).

Scores	Deviations	Devs.^2	Z Scores	T Scores
78	-4.85	23.5225	-0.52	44.80
81	-1.85	3.4225	-0.20	48.02
85	2.15	4.6225	0.23	52.30
71	-11.85	140.4225	-1.27	37.30
100	17.15	294.1225	1.84	68.38
71	-11.85	140.4225	-1.27	37.30
78	-4.85	23.5225	-0.52	44.80
69	-13.85	191.8225	-1.48	35.15
98	15.15	229.5225	1.62	66.24
88	5.15	26.5225	0.55	55.52
71	-11.85	140.4225	-1.27	37.30
83	0.15	0.0225	0.02	50.16
94	11.15	124.3225	1.20	61.95
72	-10.85	117.7225	-1.16	38.37
87	4.15	17.2225	0.44	54.45
81	-1.85	3.4225	-0.20	48.02
92	9.15	83.7225	0.98	59.81
95	12.15	147.6225	1.30	63.02
85	2.15	4.6225	0.23	52.30
78	-4.85	23.5225	-0.52	44.80

Sum of sq.	1740.55	
Variance	87.0275	87.0275
Std. Dev.	9.328853	9.328853

2. Score Statistics (Calculation Area)

Count	20
Average	82.85
Maximum	100
Minimum	69

FIGURE 16-5. T Scores for Quiz 2

Analysis of the quiz 2 results shows that, in sharp contrast to quiz 1, the scores are not nearly as varied. Although quiz 2 had 100 possible points, the standard deviation—a fundamental measurement of variation in the scores—is just over two points higher than the standard deviation of the quiz 1 scores (which had only half as many possible points). The average score, moreover, is high. A score of 70% would have been acceptable on quiz 1—indeed, that was approximately the average score—but on quiz 2 it's more than a standard deviation below the mean.

Once you have results from more than one test in a class, you may wish to create a spreadsheet that contains nothing but the student's names and the T-score results. Doing so permits you to get a quick picture of where a student is going in relation to the rest of the class. Figure 16–6 shows the T-score results from both quiz 1 and 2.

Although the results of only two quizzes are available, there's reason to suspect that Joy Doland, Robert Howard, and Steve Lee are headed for trouble in the course. They're headed down and they clearly need help. Mike Patterson is doing poorly and needs help too, but at least he's on the upswing and deserves

```
|        A          |    B   |   C   |
 1|Political Science 121
 2|Spring Term
 3|
 4|T Scores
 5|===================================
 6|Name              Quiz 1   Quiz 2
 7|-----------------------------------
 8|Abrams, Tony       44.03    44.80
 9|Callahan, Ron      49.58    48.02
10|Carey, Julia       50.97    52.30
11|Doland, Joy        46.81    37.30
12|Epstein, Edward    63.46    68.38
13|Fallows, Arnold    38.48    37.30
14|Graveller, Henry   44.03    44.80
15|Howard, Robert     39.87    35.15
16|Jenkins, Barbara   69.01    66.24
17|Karril, Monica     50.97    55.52
18|Lee, Steve         44.03    37.30
19|Neuman, Jennifer   49.58    50.16
20|Oswald, Tom        59.30    61.95
21|Patterson, Mike    25.99    38.37
22|Patterson, Tim     55.14    54.45
23|Rowland, Joshua    48.20    48.02
24|Rozier, Dawn       57.91    59.81
25|Sanders, Laura     67.63    63.02
26|Sandman, Sarah     44.03    52.30
27|Walters, Paul      50.97    44.80
```

FIGURE 16-6. T-Score Results from Quiz 1 and Quiz 2

encouragement. Monica Karril and Sarah Sandman are improving and merit a pat on the back.

FROM T SCORE TO LETTER GRADE

What is the relationship between T scores and letter grades? Ultimately, that's up to you. But T scores, because they're normally distributed, provide you with information about where a particular score stands in relation to the rest of the class. Table 16-1, for instance, shows the proportion of the class whose score falls below a particular T score.

To translate these scores into letter grades, suppose that at your institution a typical introductory class achieves the grade distribution shown in Table 16-2. These levels of performance can be readily converted into their T-score counterparts (Table 16-3).

These equivalents can be used to construct an automatic letter grade equivalent for the T scores. The trick is to use a built-in function called lookup, which locates a table of score ranges, finds a particular value, and then looks up the corresponding grade. This procedure, to be sure, has its limitations, and should be used only with caution. For one thing, the T scores, with their fine distinctions, give the impression of great accuracy. But with small classes, the razor-fine distinctions the T scores make aren't as meaningful as they are with larger classes. And who's to say a particular class is typical? You may wish to adjust the grade distribution for "bright" or advanced classes.

With those caveats in mind, here's how the lookup feature works. You'll need to make some additions to your T score master worksheet:

Add a column (column G) in part 1 and title it "Grades."

Add, at the bottom of your spreadsheet, a new work area (No. 3) as shown in Figure 16-7. With most programs, the values must be listed in ascending order.

In cell G12, insert the following formula:

```
@LOOKUP(F12,A50..A59,1)
```

which says, in English, take the value in cell F12 and locate it in the range of values from cells A50 to A59. When a value greater than the lookup value (the one in cell F12) is found, the lookup function stops searching and moves back to the previous value. Alternatively, when a value equal to the lookup value is found, the lookup function stops searching. Then it moves one column to the right and reports the value found there to the cell.

Copy the formula down column G.

Add, at the bottom of column G, a @SUM function to determine the class's average score.

TABLE 16-1
T SCORES AND CLASS STANDING

T Score	Proportion of Class Below the Point	T Score	Proportion of Class Below the Point
82.9	.9995	48.7	.45
80.9	.9990	47.5	.4
78.7	.9980	46.1	.35
78.1	.9975	44.8	.3
76.5	.996	43.3	.25
75.8	.995	42.3	.22
74.6	.993	41.6	.2
73.3	.99	40.8	.18
71.7	.985	40.1	.16
70.5	.98	39.2	.14
69.6	.975	38.3	.12
68.8	.970	37.2	.1
68.1	.965	36.6	.09
67.5	.96	35.9	.08
66.4	.95	35.2	.07
65.5	.94	34.5	.06
64.8	.93	33.6	.05
63.4	.91	32.5	.04
62.8	.9	31.9	.035
61.7	.88	31.2	.03
60.8	.86	30.4	.025
59.9	.84	29.5	.02
59.2	.82	28.3	.015
58.4	.8	26.7	.01
57.7	.78	24.2	.005
55.2	.7	21.9	.0025
53.9	.65	20.3	.0015
52.5	.6	19.1	.0010
51.3	.55	17.1	.0005
50.0	.5		

Source: J. P. Guilford, *Fundamental Statistics in Psychology and Education*, 4th ed. (New York: McGraw-Hill, 1965), p. 520.

The lookup feature isn't easy to grasp at first, but three examples should clarify how it works:

Tony Abrams' *T* score on quiz 1 was 44.03, and that's the value in F12. Lookup takes this value and goes hunting in the range from A50 through A59. It passes 42.3 (cell A53), but then bumps up against 50 (cell A54), which is too high, so it "falls back" to cell A53. Then it looks one column over (to cell B53) and reports the value (2) in cell G12.

TABLE 16-2
AVERAGE PERFORMANCE IN FRESHMAN CLASS

Grade	Percent
A	9
A−	3
B+	5
B	16
B−	7
C+	10
C	28
C−	11
D	8
F	3

TABLE 16-3
T-SCORE EQUIVALENTS

Grade	Percent	Percent Below	T Score
A	10	90	62.8
A−	2	88	61.7
B+	4	84	59.9
B	14	70	55.2
B−	5	65	53.9
C+	15	50	50.0
C	28	22	42.3
C−	12	10	37.2
D	8	2	29.5
F	2	0	

Suppose someone scored 59.9. Lookup would go down to cell A57 and stop dead right there, reporting 3.33.

If the score were 59.8, however, it would "fall back" to Cell A56, and report 3.

It's up to you, of course, how to configure the cutoff points in column A of the lookup table. This distribution would probably be considered low for most colleges and universities today, the "gentleman's C" having become the "gentleman's B."

Figure 16-8 shows the additions to the spreadsheet master and the grades as calculated.

```
46|3.  Grade Conversion Table (Data Entry Area)
47|=================================================
48|T Score       Grade
49|-------------------------------------------------
50|  Ø             Ø
51|  29.5          1
52|  37.2          1.67
53|  42.3          2
54|  50            2.33
55|  53.9          2.67
56|  55.2          3
57|  59.9          3.33
58|  61.7          3.67
59|  62.8          4
60|-------------------------------------------------
61|
```

FIGURE 16-7. Lookup Table

THE GRADE WEIGHTING WORKSHEET

The final step in this spreadsheet approach to grade computation is the construction of the grade weighting worksheet, which lists the letter grades (that is, their numerical equivalents) for each test or quiz and determines the final grade on the basis of a formula that ascribes weights to each test or quiz. A lookup table transforms the numerical version of the final grade to its letter counterpart.

The letter grades for each test or quiz can—and indeed, should—be read into the spreadsheet from column G of the *T*-score master worksheet. Reading in the scores (rather than retyping them) minimizes the chance of typing errors.

The spreadsheet's design (Figure 16-9) emphasizes the common-sense principles recommended in Chapter 13. It begins with a table of the weights (expressed in percentages) to be assigned to each quiz or test (section 1); to make sure the weights add up to 100 percent, a SUM function is added to cell B15.

The numerical course grade is calculated by a rather lengthy formula that refers to the values inserted in section 1 (that way you can play around with them to determine the impact of varying weighting schemes). Here's what the formula in cell G23 looks like (in Lotus 1-2-3 or Symphony format):

```
((B23**$B$9)+(C23*$B$10)+(D23*$B$11)+(E23*$B$12)+(F23*$B$13))/100
```

Note the absolute cell references (prefaced with $ signs) that "nail down" the references to section 1. Copying the formulas down column G yields the results immediately.

The final column, column H, includes the following formula in cell H23:

```
@LOOKUP(G23, $A$49..$A$59),1)
```

which, translated into English, reads: "Take the value in cell G23 (the numerical final grade) and go down the list of values listed from A49 to A59. When a value is

```
 8|1.   Computation of T Scores
 9|============================================================
10|Name                Scores  Devs.   Devs.^2   Z     T      Grade
11|============================================================
12|Abrams, Tony          31   -4.30    18.49   -0.60  44.03  2
13|Callahan, Ron         35   -0.30     0.09   -0.04  49.58  2
14|Carey, Julia          36    0.70     0.49    0.10  50.97  2.5
15|Doland, Joy           33   -2.30     5.29   -0.32  46.81  2
16|Epstein, Edward       45    9.70    94.09    1.35  63.46  4
17|Fallows, Arnold       27   -8.30    68.89   -1.15  38.48  1.75
18|Graveller, Henry      31   -4.30    18.49   -0.60  44.03  2
19|Howard, Robert        28   -7.30    53.29   -1.01  39.87  1.75
20|Jenkins, Barbara      49   13.70   187.69    1.90  69.01  4
21|Karril, Monica        36    0.70     0.49    0.10  50.97  2.5
22|Lee, Steve            31   -4.30    18.49   -0.60  44.03  2
23|Neuman, Jennifer      35   -0.30     0.09   -0.04  49.58  2
24|Oswald, Tom           42    6.70    44.89    0.93  59.30  3
25|Patterson, Mike       18  -17.30   299.29   -2.40  25.99  0
26|Patterson, Tim        39    3.70    13.69    0.51  55.14  2.75
27|Rowland, Joshua       34   -1.30     1.69   -0.18  48.20  2
28|Rozier, Dawn          41    5.70    32.49    0.79  57.91  3
29|Sanders, Laura        48   12.70   161.29    1.76  67.63  4
30|Sandman, Sarah        31   -4.30    18.49   -0.60  44.03  2
31|Walters, Paul         36    0.70     0.49    0.10  50.97  2.5
32|------------------------------------------------------------
33|               Sum of sq.   1038.2    Class grade = 2.3875
34|               Variance       51.91
35|               Std. dev.       7.21   Avg    50.00
36|               CHECK           7.21   StDev  10
```

[. . .]

```
46|3.   Grade Conversion Table (Data Entry Area)
47|============================================================
48|T Score        Grade
49|------------------------------------------------------------
50|  0              0
51|  29.5           1
52|  37.2           1.67
53|  42.3           2
54|  50             2.33
55|  53.9           2.67
56|  55.2           3
57|  59.9           3.33
58|  61.7           3.67
59|  62.8           4
60|------------------------------------------------------------
```

FIGURE 16-8. Computation of Grades (Column G)

found that is greater than the value in Cell G23, fall back one row to the lesser value and move one column right. Then report in cell H23 the value that appears there."

A final touch to this spreadsheet is the function AVERAGE, which states the class' average grade.

THE MACRO CONNECTION

Third-generation spreadsheet programs such as Lotus 1-2-3 and integrated programs such as Symphony or Framework offer powerful macro commands. These commands can, for instance, include instructions that copy a range of cells from one spreadsheet to another, cause the spreadsheet to recalculated, or print a range of cells to the printer—all with a single keystroke.

Without going into the complexities of how you'd go about creating a macro for this grade-crunching system, here's an illustration of how nicely one could serve it. To begin, you'd give a command that sets a special grade-crunching macro called ADD into motion. It would begin by displaying a menu asking to which class's grade sheet you'd like to add scores. After you respond, it shows you a blank grade sheet with the students' names listed. After you write in the raw scores, pressing another command sets off a complex series of commands that moves the raw scores to the T score worksheet, determines the grades, and posts them to the grade weighting worksheet, which serves as the master gradebook for the class. Finally, it prints out a list of the completed grades with the students' names listed in alphabetical order.

Writing good macros isn't as easy as most of the other personal computer techniques discussed in this book, and that's because it's genuinely within the realm of programming. Even so, it's worth attempting if you often work with spreadsheets and think you could benefit from the kind of automation it makes possible.

SOME CAUTIONS

Like all statistical tools, this grade-crunching system is both powerful and potentially misleading. It should be used only with a clear awareness of its limits:

Spurious distinctions The T-score scale from 0 to 100 gives the impression of razor-sharp, finely honed distinctions, but that appearance is illusory with small classes. A student who receives a 61.69 T score (i.e., B+), for example, will be distinguished by a full letter grade (not considering plusses and minuses) from a student who scores a 61.70 (A−), but the distinction is probably absurd under most circumstances. Be sure to pay close attention to borderline cases when computing the scores.

1 | North Central State University
2 | Department of Political Science
3 |
4 | FINAL GRADE COMPUTATION MASTER
5 |
6 |
7 | 1. Weights to Assign to Tests and Quizzes
8 |

9	Quiz 1	7.5%
10	Quiz 2	12.5%
11	Midterm	25%
12	Quiz 3	17.5%
13	Final	37.5%
14		
15	TOTAL	100%

16 |
17 |
18 |
19 | 2. Data Entry Area for Test and Quiz Grades
20 |

	Name	Quiz 1	Quiz2	Midterm	Quiz3	Final	Course Grade	
21								
22								
23	Abrams, Tony	2	2	2.75	2.5	4	3.03	B
24	Callahan, Ron	2	2	2.5	2.5	2.75	2.49	C+
25	Carey, Julia	2.5	2.5	3.5	4	2.75	3.11	B
26	Doland, Joy	2	1.75	2.5	2.75	2.5	2.41	C+
27	Epstein, Edward	4	4	1	2	2	2.15	C
28	Fallows, Arnold	1.75	1.75	1.75	2	2	1.89	C
29	Graveller, Henr	2	2	2	2	2	2.00	C
30	Howard, Robert	1.75	1	1.75	1	1	1.24	D
31	Jenkins, Barbar	4	4	2.5	2.5	2.75	2.89	B
32	Karril, Monica	2.5	3	2.75	2.75	1.75	2.39	C+
33	Lee, Steve	2	1.75	2	2.5	2	2.06	C
34	Neuman, Jennife	2	2.5	2.75	3	2.5	2.61	B-
35	Oswald, Tom	3	3.75	4	3	3.5	3.53	A-
36	Patterson, Mike	0	1.75	2	2	2	1.82	C
37	Patterson, Tim	2.75	2.75	2.5	1.75	3	2.61	B-

38	Rowland, Joshua	2	2	1	1	1	1.20	D
39	Rozier, Dawn	3	3	3	2.75	3.5	3.14	B
40	Sanders, Laura	4	4	4	4	4	4.00	A
41	Sandman, Sarah	2	2.5	3	3	2	2.49	C+
42	Walters, Paul	2.5	2	1	0	1	1.06	D
43								
44				Class Average			2.4059	C+
45								
46								
47	3. Final Grade Lookup Area							
48								
49	0	F						
50	0.75	D						
51	1.375	D+						
52	1.5	C-						
53	1.75	C						
54	2.375	C+						
55	2.5	B-						
56	2.75	B						
57	3.375	B+						
58	3.5	A-						
59	3.75	A						
60								
61								

FIGURE 16–9. Final Weighted Average Spreadsheet

Changed grades and make-ups A serious drawback to this grading system emerges when you wish to change a grade because of a scoring error or record a student's make-up test. Bear in mind that T scores are a measure of a student's performance relative to the rest of the class. Changing even one of the grades alters the computations for all of them. (You can see this for yourself by trying a "what-if" analysis on one of the T-score worksheets.) Probably the best way to deal with this problem is to hand the quizzes or tests back without letter grades and give the students a specified time (say, 48 hours) to see you about grading errors or make-ups; after that time, you can "freeze" the results, calculate the grades for the test, and hand them out.

The best argument to be made for this computer-based grading system is that by doing the tedious calculations for you, it lets you put more thought into the difficult grading matters that require judgment and case-by-case consideration. But be sure to exercise that judgment and consideration, because this approach in itself does not, and cannot, tell the whole story of a student's performance.

RESOURCES

Quite a few dedicated grade-crunching programs are available (an example is Gradisk, Wiley Educational Software, 605 Third Ave., New York, NY 10158), but—as I hope this chapter has convinced you—the general-purpose and flexible number-crunching tools provided by spreadsheet software are far superior tools for grading. Moreover, a spreadsheet program can be put to many other uses, but a dedicated grading program can't.

For more information on z and T scores, consult any good educational statistics textbook, such as Edward W. Minium, *Statistical Reasoning in Psychology and Education* (New York: John Wiley, 1978), pp. 123–160.

APPENDICES

SYSTEM EXPANSION

Expanding a personal computer system can greatly enhance its capabilities and increase its suitability for specialized applications. Discussed in the pages to follow are expanding memory (both main and auxiliary), adding input and output devices (such as optical character readers and voice synthesizers), adding hardware for communications (such as a serial port and a modem), adding hardware for local area networks, and equipping your printer with accessories (such as buffers and silencers).

EXPANDING MEMORY

With many personal computers, you can expand both the main or random access memory (RAM) and the auxiliary memory (disk drives).

EXPANDING THE MAIN MEMORY

Not all computers' memory boards are expandable. The Kaypro II, for instance, comes with 64K, and there's nary a socket for another byte. The Apple Macintosh, too, comes with a limited set of memory chip sockets. You can expand the Mac's standard 128K memory to 512K by using higher capacity 256K memory chips in place of the standard 64K ones, but it's a tough job: the chips are soldered in place.

Far more congenial is expanding the memory in the IBM Personal Computer. In its standard configuration, the PC comes with its main circuit board (often called the *motherboard*) filled up with memory chips (or fully populated, in computer jargon). That being the case, you'll have to purchase an additional, slip-in circuit board to hold the additional memory. Most of these memory boards are sold by third-party suppliers such as AST Research (2121 Alton Ave., Irvine, CA 92714); their products include some additional accessories IBM "forgot" to put in the standard configuration, such as printer and modem ports. If you're planning to buy a PC, buy one of these multipurpose boards (such as the AST Six Pack Plus) rather than one of IBM's single-purpose boards (such as the asynchronous adapter for telecommunications; see below). These boards usually come with 64K of memory. Adding more is easy. You simply buy the chips—nine of them per 64K—and press them onto the board.

When the IBM PC was introduced, its 640K memory limit seemed virtually inexhaustible. But those days are gone. Many programs now require 256K or even 384K of memory, leaving comparatively little space for all the rest of the information that has to reside in the memory, such as the operating system and the data. But a new development in the PC arena, bank switching, has lifted the PC's memory limit to a full 4 megabytes, more than many mainframe computers have.

Bank switching is one of those clever hardware integration techniques like disk-based virtual memory (see Chapter 2), that makes the machine seem more powerful than it really is. Even though the PC's microprocessor can address only 640K at once, it can switch among 640K banks rapidly (so long as it has the proper electronic guidance and the necessary hardware attached). The necessary hardware comes in the form of Intel Corporation's Above Board memory expansion board, which includes the required software.

With such massive memory reserves, RAM "disks" are sure to become more popular. A RAM disk is a way of making the computer think that a certain block of main memory isn't main memory at all, but rather a superfast disk drive. If you have a floppy disk drive defined as Drive A and a hard disk defined as Drive C, you could set up a RAM "disk" as Drive D; so far as the computer would be concerned the allocated memory would be treated exactly like a disk drive. You could, therefore, copy a program and data to it, and operate them just as if they were based on a disk. That means faster operation—faster, indeed, than a hard disk, which for all its speed is still a mechanical device.

RAM "disks," however, have a big built-in drawback. Main memory, whether allocated to a RAM disk or not, is volatile: if there's an interruption in the power supply, it loses its contents and they are not recoverable under any circumstances. That's a danger while you're working, of course, but the peril is even greater. RAM "disks" emulate disks so well that it's easy to forget that you're working in the main, rather than the auxiliary, memory. "Saving" your work to "disk" at the end of a session accomplishes nothing. You haven't truly saved your work to disk until you've copied the RAM "disk" contents to the safe haven of a real, genuine magnetic medium. And if, after "saving" your work, you forget to do that, it's bye-bye to hours of work.

EXPANDING THE AUXILIARY MEMORY

Floppy disk drives are slow and have limited capacities. Sooner or later, you'll begin to desire a hard disk. Hard disks spin at ten times the floppy's speed, and in place of 200K or 360K of storage, you've got 10 or 20 megabytes.

Buying a hard disk used to be as economically trying as buying a computer, but mass production has brought about dramatic price declines. Indeed, the price of hard disks for the IBM PC dropped $1000—from $1500 to $500—while this book was being written! Not all hard disks are that cheap, however. If you've been stuck with a nonexpandable system such as a Kaypro or an Apple Macintosh, you'll have to pay more than that, chiefly because the disk requires its own case and power supply.

If buying a hard disk is within your budget, however, it's strongly recommended. Hard disks will improve your computer's performance significantly. Almost all programs use virtual memory techniques, storing little-used parts of the program or the data on disk for retrieval as needed. The swapping operations that bring this information into and out of memory are speeded considerably with a hard disk installed. Indeed, they become all but transparent.

Personal computers equipped with hard disks still need at least one floppy disk drive, since all personal computer software comes to you supplied on floppy disks. Many systems can support four drives or more, meaning that you could set up a personal computer with two floppies and two hard disks if you wish (and if your computer's power supply is up to the job).

An additional attraction of the hard disk is a massive increase in disk storage capacity, but this feature has its liabilities. If you create a file that's larger than your floppy disk's capacity (say, 360K), you can't back it up by copying it to a disk in the floppy drive. And that means you're in trouble. What will you do if, having spent a year creating a massive 2-megabyte disk file containing all your research notes, the hard disk crashes and takes all your data with it? Such things happen.

If you're planning on creating files larger than your floppy drive's capacity, you'll have to think about buying some kind of device for backup purposes. Often used are streaming tape drives, which can back up the contents of an entire 10-megabyte hard disk in several minutes. Because hard disks have become so inexpensive, however, another option is simply to purchase a second hard disk. If you have one hard disk installed internally, you can add a second one that's set up for external use (with its own power supply), and use it routinely to back up the internal hard disk at the end of a day's session.

A new star on the auxiliary memory horizon is the optical disk, a spinoff of the digital disk technology that's overturning the staid complacency of the vinyl 33⅓ rpm long playing record industry. At this writing, however, optical disk drives—the cheap ones, anyway—only offered read-only storage; to put it another way, they could play back, but not record. Even so, many potential uses spring to mind. Optical disks have mind-boggling storage capacities, which go far beyond even the theoretical limits of magnetically encoded media. Already achieved are information densities of a gigabit (one billion bits) per square centimeter.

To consider the potential of this technology, imagine that on a shelf next to your computer, you have five or six optical disks that take up less room than two or three paperback books. The disks are designed to work in a compact disk drive connected to your computer. On them, you have the full text of the *Encyclopedia Britannica*, the *Oxford English Dictionary*, *Roget's Thesaurus*, and *Webster's Unabridged Dictionary*, with every page searchable using lightning-fast versions of the data management programs introduced in Chapter 9. Such wonders are not yet available, but they're feasible.

EXPANDING INPUT AND OUTPUT OPTIONS

Computers take in information (input), do things to it (processing), and display the results (output). Normally, information comes in from the disk drives and keyboard, and results go out on the video display and printer. But those aren't the only options. A computer can accept visual images, read typed manuscripts, and even talk back to you.

INPUT

As with everything else in the personal computer world, the price of input devices has dropped so dramatically that adding, say, an optical character reader (once laughably expensive) is now within the reach of every personal computer owner. Here's a brief sampler.

Optical Character Recognition

Optical character recognition (OCR) devices contain sensing devices that scan typewritten text, convert it into ASCII code, and feed the results into your computer through its serial port (see "Hardware for Communications," below). The obvious benefit of optical character readers is getting text into the computer without retyping it.

The more reasonably priced optical character readers are at their best when reading standard typewriter script, such as that produced by the IBM Selectric. They're less adept at reading printed text, but some of them can indeed handle that job too.

Consider the benefits of automatically reading printed material into your computer. Chapter 10 discusses the personal computer–based management of massive textual data bases and introduces automatic indexing software that automatically creates an index of the stored text. A researcher could use an optical character reader to create a massive textual data base of key readings in a field, every word of which could be located in seconds by computer searching techniques (see Chapter 9).

Digitizers

Digitizers use a camera to capture an optical image. They then convert that image into a digital representation, which can be displayed on the screen of any computer with a bit-mapped video display (see Chapter 2). The AT&T True Vision Image Capture Board (for the IBM Personal Computer and PC-compatibles), for instance, lets you use a video camera or video disk player to produce images that it then digitizes and displays on the PC's display screen. Thunderware's ThunderScan (21 Orinda Way, Orinda CA 94563) for the Apple Macintosh and Apple Imagewriter, available for an incredible $249, gives you a complete digitizing system of cunning design. The scanning module snaps into the Imagewriter printer in place of the ribbon cartridge and digitizes an image that it automatically rolls up using the Imagewriter's platen. Although slow—it takes about 20 minutes to digitize an 8-by-10 inch photograph—ThunderScan gives you sophisticated digitizing technology for a very low price (no camera is necessary).

What in the world would you use a digitizer for? Consider this: just about every academic has (or should have) some kind of collection of images, whether they're pictures of archaeological artifacts, drawings of the behavior of sub-atomic particles, or photographs of social interaction patterns. Generally speaking, they're in a big pile somewhere that you're going to organize just as soon as you can, right? Well, a digitizer—together with a graphics-oriented file management program—can do all that organization for you. Microsoft File, a superb file management program for the Apple Macintosh, for instance, permits you to set up a data base in which one of the data fields is a picture field. The picture can be a MacPaint illustration or a digitized photograph. In the other fields you can insert text describing the picture.

Suppose, for instance, you're about to give a lecture on the archaeology of ancient Mexico, in particular the sites Santa Isabel Iztapan and Texquixquiac. You search for the relevant images by typing the search term (artifact AND photograph) AND (Santa Isabel Iztapan OR Texquixquiac). In seconds the computer puts together a subset of the images. With another command the Apple Imagewriter starts cranking out superb renditions of the illustrations. A quick stop at the photocopying machine reproduces them, and in the space of about 15 minutes you've created several sheaves of handouts for your class to inspect at close range.

Voice Input Systems

Computers, as the computer textbook author Donald Sanders says, already share one attribute in common with people: they talk better than they listen. As you'll see in a moment, voice synthesis output systems are highly developed, but voice recognition systems—that is, voice input systems—aren't. At best, a computer can recognize only a few hundred words, and even then, it has to go through a training period to grow accustomed to your voice.

A few programs permit you to don a microphone and order them around vocally, so long as you stick to one-word utterances. You can say, "Save!" and the operation gets going (probably).

OUTPUT

Output devices are as numerous and, increasingly, as inexpensive as some of the input devices just discussed. As you'll see, there are more ways besides the standard video monitor and the printer to find out what the computer's done to your data.

Speech Synthesizers

Speech synthesizers can "read" the contents of an ASCII-based text file with a surprising degree of intelligibility, although it sounds as if you're listening to a Czechoslovakian robot. Speech synthesizers hold much promise for writers; after all, a large part of writing quality depends on developing an ear for how your writing sounds. One could write for a while, then sit back and have the synthesizer read it to you. Gaps in logic and awkward phrases, the sorts of thing you might miss while proofreading on paper, would leap out at you.

Slide-Making Systems

An accessory bound to interest teachers is a slide-making system, an output device that creates 35-millimeter color slides that capture images from the video display. These systems are popular in the business world for creating slides of business charts, but they have many potential applications in education, too. The ThunderScan/Microsoft File image processing system just described for the Macintosh, for example, could generate the images—say, a series of archaeological artifacts or architectural floor plans—and the slide-making device could capture them on film for classroom projection.

Projection Systems

A more direct version of the output technique just mentioned is to take the computer to the classroom and hook it up with a projection system, a device that reproduces the computer's video display screen on a scale big enough for a whole class to see.

HARDWARE FOR TELECOMMUNICATIONS

The telephone system is a reliable and extensive network of connections that computers can use, but that system wasn't designed for computers. Special equipment—an asynchronous communications board, an RS-232 serial port, and a communications program—is needed to enable computers to communicate over the telephone lines.

THE ASYNCHRONOUS COMMUNICATIONS BOARD

Communications within the computer's confines occur at very high speeds because there's a wire for each of the 8 bits in a byte. An entire byte can, therefore, be communicated simultaneously, with each one travelling in synchrony along with the parallel circuits. And that's exactly why you can't hook your computer up to the telephone system without some extra equipment. Phone lines don't have eight wires. They can't send and receive eight bits simultaneously. In fact, they can only send and receive one bit at a time in a series.

The asynchronous communications board, a special circuit board within your computer, is intended to convert the parallel data stream within your computer to a bit-after-bit serial transmission that the telephone system can handle. At its heart is a tiny chip called the universal asynchronous receiver/ transmitter (UART). Its main job, as its name indicates, is to receive serial transmissions and convert them so that the computer's parallel circuits can handle them and to transmit serial data that have been converted from their parallel counterparts.

The term "asynchronous" in the UART's name gives you a good clue to another of its functions. In a parallel data transmission circuit, all 8 bits in a byte arrive simultaneously, so there's no need for any special signal that tells the receiving device, "that's a byte." What's more, the arrival and departure of data are synchronized by the heartbeat pulse of the computer's clock, which pulses a million or more times per second. When data are transmitted serially, one after another, there's a problem: how does the receiving device know where one byte stops and the next begins? Worse, serial transmission rates occur at much slower (and inherently uneven) speeds: they're inherently asynchronous. The UART copes with this problem by inserting special bits in the transmission, called start and stop bits, which tell the receiving computer "here's where a byte starts," and "here's where a byte stops."

Many computers come with an asynchronous communications board already included in the stock configuration, and they should. Sadly, however, the trend is to make this necessary piece of circuitry an option. When you're shopping for a system, be sure to ask whether or not the asynchronous communications board is included in the purchase price and take this board into account in making cost comparisons. Here's a tip: if a computer has an RS-232 serial port, you can bet good money that it has the board.

THE RS-232 SERIAL PORT

The RS-232 serial port is a standardized input/output connector designed to facilitate connections between a wide variety of computers and modems. The standard is controlled by the Electronic Industries Association (EIA), and it grew out of a collaboration in the late 1960s between EIA, Bell Laboratories, and manufacturers of telecommunications equipment. It's one of the few things about your computer that's reasonably standardized.

You needn't concern yourself with the details of RS-232 ports, cables, and connectors if you buy a standard, popular modem such as the Hayes Smartmodem, since they include their own properly configured RS-232 cables. You should be forewarned, however, that connecting devices other than modems to this port can prove to be a frustrating experience. Printers, for instance, are available in both serial and parallel versions; the parallel version is usually much simpler to connect successfully.

The Modem

Just because data have been converted from a parallel transmission format to an asynchronous serial one doesn't mean the telephone lines are compatible. The signals coming out of the RS-232 port are still digital signals: they're all-or-nothing pulses that have little in common with the kind of information that normally flows over telephone wires.

The telephone system isn't very good at transmitting unmodified digital information accurately. The phone system is designed for the human voice, which produces a remarkably complex configuration of sound frequencies that oscillate between 300 and 4000 cycles per second. The telephone system is designed to encode, transmit, and decode an electrical representation of the human voice, with its particular frequency range and complex patterning. To transmit digital information accurately, then, you need an additional device that transforms the digital signals coming out of the computer into a form that the phone system was designed to handle.

That's exactly what a modem (modulator-demodulator) is for. The modem takes the digital signals coming out of the computer and converts (or modulates) them into the electrical equivalent of warbles that oscillate between 1050 and 2250 cycles per second, right in the center of the human vocal range.

Like the asynchronous communications board, the modem is also a device not only for transmitting but also for receiving. When it receives properly modulated signals coming over a telephone line, it demodulates them or transforms them back into their digital equivalent.

Full- and Half-Duplex Modems

Not all modems, however, can transmit and receive simultaneously. A *half-duplex modem,* like a citizen's band radio, can only do one thing at a time. *Full-duplex modems* can receive and transmit data at the same time. Half-duplex modems are not recommended for any of the applications discussed in this book.

300- and 1200-Baud Modems

Modems vary, too, in the speed with which they can transmit and receive data. Modem transmission speeds are measured in *bauds,* a measurement that's a survival from the age of the telegraph. The term refers to the number of signals (or in digital terms, bits) occurring each second.

A 300-baud modem transmits information at speeds up to about 350 to 400 words per minute, which is quite slow. It could take a 300 baud modem an hour to transmit (or receive) a scholarly manuscript of appreciable length. Offsetting the slow speed, however, is the low price. The 300-baud modems are sometimes termed "Bell system 103–compatible," referring to the communication standard that governs their transmission characteristics.

A 1200-baud modem transmits information at speeds up to about 2000 words per minute. A 1200-baud modem is highly desirable when you're working with long-distance telecommunications or online data base services, but the initial cost is higher. The 1200-baud modems are sometimes termed "Bell system 212A–compatible," referring to a second communication standard. Avoid 1200-baud modems that are Bell system 202–compatible. These modems are half-duplex modems (they cannot transmit and receive simultaneously.)

Using a Modem

Modems have no controls besides an on-off switch because you control them directly from the computer's keyboard. Once you've loaded a communications program that permits your computer to emulate a terminal (more on communications software below), everything you type on the keyboard will be sent out the RS-232 port when you press the return key. You can communicate with your modem by prefacing these messages with a special code. One popular modem, for example, uses the code AT. To get the modem to do something, such as dial the telephone number of a communications service, you type in the code AT followed by the "dial" code (D) and the telephone number.

HARDWARE FOR LOCAL NETWORKS

The personal computer world is dreadfully flawed by a lack of standards, and nowhere is this trait more pronounced than in the world of local area network hardware. A welter of competing network systems, each using mutually incompatible approaches to data transmission, vie for a position in the marketplace.

To illustrate what's involved in setting up a local area netowrk, let's look at just one of these systems, the 3Com EtherSeries for IBM Personal Computers (3Com Corporation, 1365 Shore Bird Way, Mountain View, CA 94043). EtherSeries is designed to be used with a hard-disk PC, an IBM PC XT, as the central computing resource station or *server*. That computer's resources, which could include (for instance) a 32-megabyte hard disk and a laser printer, are available to several dozen or more participants in the network.

Each participant's computer, which must also be an IBM PC, needs an EtherLink board that plugs into one of the PC's expansion slots. You'll also need a starter kit, coaxial cable, and other hardware for a four-work station cost of over $7,000. The more work stations you add, however, the less the cost per work station. Additional work stations can be added for the cost of the cable plus about $650 for the EtherLink board.

PRINTER ACCESSORIES

Two all but indispensable accessories for printers are buffers and silencers.

BUFFERS

Printers, even dot matrix printers, are slow enough to tie up your system while they churn through a lengthy manuscript. If you're working with a slow letter-quality printer, the tie-up could well last all day.

Printer buffers solve this problem by creating a temporary storehouse for your computer's printer output. Essentially a bank of random access memory that uses the same memory chips as your computer's main memory, buffers are inserted between the computer and the printer. When a buffer is hooked up, the computer thinks it's working with a super fast printer and sends out the printer output just as fast as it can. So far as the computer is concerned, therefore, the whole printing operation is over in short order, and it returns control to you. You can use the computer for whatever you wish—indeed, you can turn it off.

Of course the material hasn't actually been sent to the printer. It has been stored in the buffer's memory, and it's the buffer that takes over the slow, tedious task of doling the material out to the printer, line by line, at whatever slow speed it requires.

Printer buffers, as you've doubtless concluded, make a very welcome addition to a personal computer system, especially when you're working with long manuscripts.

SILENCERS

Personal computer printers that use direct-impact technology, such as letter-quality or daisywheel printers, are noisy—so much so, in fact, that they might even damage your hearing. Printer silencers address this problem by enclosing the printer in a soundproofed box.

Printer silencers are especially attractive options when you've equipped your system with a printer buffer. A printer buffer lets you keep on working with your computer even as a lengthy document is being printed. But the printer's racket may stop you from concentrating. The silencer mutes the sound enough so that you can write even as the printer is clattering away.

CHOOSING A BIBLIOGRAPHIC DATA BASE SERVICE

APPENDIX II

Dozens of online data base vendors now make their services available to personal computer users, but most specialize in business or technical information. Scholars who wish to try online searching will probably choose among the four vendors that specialize in scholarly and scientific information:

> **BRS/After Dark** A menu-driven, nighttime/weekend service, a subsidiary of BRS Information Technologies. BRS/After Dark offers a major subset of the BRS system's data bases at low cost. Designed for home computer users, BRS/After Dark is exceptionally easy to use.
>
> **BRKTHRU** A menu-driven service that offers the full roster of Bibliographic Retrieval Service's data bases at moderate prices during the daytime (less during evenings and weekends).
>
> **Knowledge Index** A command-driven (but approachable) evening/weekend service offering a small subset of DIALOG Information Service's data bases at low cost.
>
> **DIALOG** A full-service, professional system offering more than 200 data bases, some of which, although costly, will prove of great interest to some scholars.

This appendix surveys these four data base vendors from the scholar's point of view. Appendix III, "Online Data Bases," discusses in detail the data bases likely to prove of greatest interest to scholars.

Your choice among the options discussed here should be guided, above all, by the availability of data bases pertinent to the subject you're researching. If one of the budget nighttime data base services such as Knowledge Index or BRS/After Dark has the data base you want, then you're in luck. If not, you may wish to consider one of the midpriced services like BRKTRHU or perhaps a higher-priced service such as DIALOG. Before concluding that a particular data base will suit your needs, however, you'll want to consider very carefully just what it has to offer. Some guidelines for evaluating data bases will be found at the end of this appendix.

BRS/AFTER DARK

BRS/After Dark, a budget nighttime and weekend service offered by BRS Information Technologies, is designed expressly for home users of personal computers. Completely menu-driven, the system makes it easy for inexperienced users to perform productive searches. Users familiar with more advanced systems such as DIALOG, however, will miss features such as saved search procedures, online document ordering, and online thesauruses. The system is quite slow when the full text of menus is presented, but once the basics have been mastered the menus can be suppressed.

BRS/After Dark's comprehensive data base list (Table II-1) has much to offer the research scholar. Included are such excellent sources as AGRICOLA, ARTS AND HUMANITIES SEARCH, BIOSIS PREVIEWS, CA/SEARCH, DISSERTATION ABSTRACTS, ERIC, INSPEC, LANGUAGE AND LANGUAGE BEHAVIOR ABSTRACTS, MATHFILE, PSYCINFO, THE RELIGION INDEX, SOCIAL SCISEARCH, and SOCIOLOGICAL ABSTRACTS. (For in-depth descriptions of these and other data bases of interest to scholars, see Appendix III.) Covered well are education, the social sciences, and the natural sciences, with some coverage of the arts and humanities. BRS/After Dark also offers several full-text data bases, including ACADEMIC AMERICAN ENCYCLOPEDIA, AMERICAN CHEMICAL SOCIETY JOURNALS ONLINE, and INTERNAL REVENUE SERVICE PUBLICATIONS.

BRS/After Dark's charges are (at this writing) the lowest of the four online vendors discussed here. An initially stiff subscription fee of $75.00 is compensated by low connect time/royalty charges, which vary from $6.00 to $25.00 depending on the royalties assessed for the data base you're using. The connect time fees includes telecommunications charges.

BRS/After Dark could be recommended without hesitation to this book's readers were it not for an objectionable feature: a $12.00 monthly minimum charge, assessed against your credit card whether or not you use the system. As it stands, BRS/After Dark can be recommended with enthusiasm only to those who are certain to make fairly heavy use of the system. Remember that a typical literature search online takes about 10 to 20 minutes, so BRS is assuming that you'll do about eight such searches per month—an unrealistically high figure for most scholars, save during peak periods of productivity. It's very likely, therefore, that sooner or later BRS/After Dark will charge you for time you didn't use.

TABLE II-I
BRS/AFTER DATA BASES

ABI/INFORM (business)
ABLEDATA (resources for the disabled)
ABSTRAX 400 (popular periodicals)
ABSTRACTS OF WORKING PAPERS IN ECONOMICS
ACADEMIC AMERICAN ENCYCLOPEDIA (full text)
AGRICOLA (agriculture)
AMERICAN CHEMICAL SOCIETY PRIMARY JOURNALS DATABASE
(full text of chemistry journals)
ARTS AND HUMANITIES SEARCH
ASSOCIATION PUBLICATIONS IN PRINT
BILINGUAL EDUCATION BIBLIOGRAPHIC ABSTRACTS
BIOSIS PREVIEWS (biology)
BOOKS IN PRINT
CA/SEARCH (chemistry)
CATALYST: RESOURCES FOR WOMEN
DISC (microcomputers)
DISSERTATION ABSTRACTS
EDUCATIONAL RESOURCES INFORMATION CENTER
EDUCATIONAL TESTING SERVICE TEST COLLECTION
EXCEPTIONAL CHILD EDUCATION RESOURCES
FAMILY RESOURCES
HBR/ONLINE (full text of Harvard Business Review)
HEALTH PLANNING AND ADMINISTRATION
ICRS MEDICAL SCIENCES DATA BASE (full text of medical journals)
INSPEC (physics and computer science)
INSTITUTE OF ELECTRICAL ENGINEERS DATA BASE
INTERNAL REVENUE SERVICE PUBLICATIONS (full text)
INTERNATIONAL PHARMACEUTICAL ABSTRACTS

KIRK-OTHMER ENCYCLOPEDIA OF CHEMICAL TECHNOLOGY (full text)
LANGUAGE AND LANGUAGE BEHAVIOR ABSTRACTS
MANAGEMENT CONTENTS (business)
MATHFILE (mathematics)
MEDLARS (clinical medicine)
MENTAL MEASUREMENTS YEARBOOK
NATIONAL COLLEGE DATABANK
NATIONAL INFORMATION SOURCES ON THE HANDICAPPED
NATIONAL REHABILITATION INFORMATION CENTER
NATIONAL TECHNICAL INFORMATION SERVICE
ONLINE MICRO-SOFTWARE DIRECTORY
ONTARIO EDUCATION RESOURCES INFORMATION SYSTEM
PATDATA (patents)
PRE-MED (current publications in clinical medicine)
PRE-PSYC (current publications in clinical psychology)
PSYCINFO (online version of Psychological Abstracts)
RESOURCE ORGANIZATIONS AND MEETINGS FOR EDUCATORS
RESOURCES IN COMPUTER EDUCATION
RESOURCES IN VOCATIONAL EDUCATION
ROBOTICS INFORMATION
PUBLIC AFFAIRS INFORMATION SERVICE
RELIGION INDEX
SCHOOL PRACTICES INFORMATION FILE
SOCIAL SCISEARCH (Social Science Citation Index)
SOCIOLOGICAL ABSTRACTS
TEXAS EDUCATION COMPUTER COOPERATIVE
VOCATIONAL EDUCATION CURRICULAR MATERIALS

Note: Data bases listed in boldface type are described in Appendix III.

BRKTHRU

Provided by BRS Information Technologies, the same company that offers BRS/After Dark, BRKTHRU is aimed at a growing market: companies and institutions that wish to provide their professional employees with access to online search services without putting them through the extensive training they would need to use the main BRS system. BRKTHRU, accordingly, is menu-driven; it's quite similar to BRS/After Dark, and inexperienced users will find the system easy to master. Unlike BRS/After Dark, however, BRKTHRU offers BRS's full line of 70 data bases (Table II-2) and is available days, nights, and weekends. BRS plans to add advanced search features, such as online document ordering, in the future.

BRKTHRU costs more than BRS/After Dark, but significantly less than the professional system for library researchers (BRS). To be sure, the initial subscription fee is lower ($50.00, which brings you $25.00 of free system usage and the system manual). But there is a $35.00-per-hour fee for connect time and telecommunications that does not include data base royalties. The royalty charges can add up to $60.00 an hour or more to the basic $35.00 fee. An expensive data base such as SOCIAL SCISEARCH (the online version of the *Social Science Citation Index*) costs $105.00 an hour. However, there is no monthly minimum.

Charges are reduced considerably for evening and weekend use. The connect time charge drops to $17.50 an hour, and royalty fees are similarly reduced. An hour of search time in SOCSCISEARCH, for example, costs $60.00, including connect time and royalties; an hour in PSYCINFO (the online version of *Psychological Abstracts*) costs $28.50. Even with the evening or weekend price reductions, BRKTHRU is still more expensive than BRS/After Dark. Most scholars will probably prefer BRS/After Dark rather than BRKTHRU, unless:

> Your institution is willing to pay for the search time (BRKTHRU is set up for institutional billing, but BRS/After Dark isn't).
> You prefer to search during the day.
> You plan to search infrequently, and hope to avoid BRS/After Dark's $12.00-per-month minimum.
> You're interested in a BRKTHRU data base that BRS/After Dark lacks.

The latter condition is not likely: Most of the BRS data bases of interest to scholars are already available on BRS/After Dark.

KNOWLEDGE INDEX

Knowledge Index, like BRS/After Dark, is an evening and weekend subset of a larger and much more expensive service (DIALOG Information Services).

TABLE II–2
BRKTHRU DATA BASES (SELECTED LIST)

All the data bases available on BRS/After Dark plus:

AMERICAN MEN AND WOMEN OF SCIENCES (biography)
BOOKSINFO (directory of books in print)
COMPENDEX (engineering)
CALIFORNIA UNION LIST OF PERIODICALS
DRUGINFO (drug and alcohol abuse)
ENERGYLINE (energy-related literature)
ENVIRONLINE (environmental literature)
EPILEPSYLINE (epilepsy)
FEDERAL ENERGY DATA INDEX
FINANCIAL TIMES COMPANY INFORMATION (business)
GPO MONTHLY CATALOG (U.S. government publications)
HARFAX INDUSTRY DATA SOURCES (business)
HEALTH AUDIOVISUAL ONLINE CATALOG
INDEX TO FROST & SULLIVAN MARKET RESEARCH REPORTS (business)
INDUSTRY AND INTERNATIONAL STANDARDS (technical)
INSTRUCTIONAL RESOURCES INFORMATION SYSTEM
MEDOC (U.S. government documents on health)
MENTAL HEALTH ABSTRACTS
MILITARY AND FEDERAL SPECS AND STANDARDS
NATIONAL INFORMATION CENTER FOR EDUCATIONAL MEDIA
PTS INTERNATIONAL FORECASTS
PTS INTERNATIONAL TIME SERIES
PTS PROMPT (business)
PTS US FORECASTS
PTS US TIME SERIES
ULRICH'S INTERNATIONAL PERIODICALS DIRECTORY
UNIVERSAL SERIALS AND BOOK EXCHANGE

Note: Data bases listed in boldface type are described in Appendix III.

Unlike BRS/After Dark, however, it's command-driven rather than menu-driven, making it more challenging to first-time users (but more convenient for experienced ones). However, English-language error messages, an online help feature, and the system's simplicity make Knowledge Index friendlier than its professional counterpart, DIALOG.

Knowledge Index currently offers significantly fewer data bases than BRS/After Dark. From the scholar's point of view, the list's major attractions—and they are few in number (Table II–3)—are the current-affairs data bases, LEGAL RESOURCES INDEX, MAGAZINE INDEX, NATIONAL NEWSPAPER INDEX, and NEWSEARCH. A sophisticated electronic mail service, DialMail (described in Chapter 14) offsets the skimpy data base list to some degree, as does the availability of online document ordering.

For users who plan more than casual or occasional searching, Knowledge Index is more expensive than BRS/After Dark. It's cheaper, to be sure, to sign up: a $35.00 subscription fee brings you the excellent Knowledge Index manual and two hours of free search time. It's the connect time/royalty fees that are significantly higher: there's a flat, $24.00-per-hour fee (including telecommunication charges) no matter which data base you're using.

One point in Knowledge Index's favor is the lack of a monthly minimum charge. Unlike BRS/After Dark, which assesses a $12.00 monthly minimum whether you use the system or not, you pay only for the searching you actually do.

TABLE II-3
KNOWLEDGE INDEX DATA BASES

ABI/INFORM (business)
ACADEMIC AMERICAN ENCYCLOPEDIA
AGRICOLA (agriculture)
BIOSIS PREVIEWS (biology)
BOOKS IN PRINT
COMPUTER DATA BASE (computer science)
DRUG INFORMATION FULLTEXT
EDUCATIONAL RESOURCES INFORMATION CENTER
ENGINEERING LITERATURE INDEX
GOVERNMENT PUBLICATIONS REFERENCE FILE
ICC BRITISH COMPANY DIRECTORY (business)
INSPEC (physics)
INTERNATIONAL PHARMACEUTICAL ABSTRACTS
INTERNATIONAL SOFTWARE DATA BASE
LEGAL RESOURCE INDEX (legal literature)
MAGAZINE INDEX (435 popular serials)
MATHFILE (mathematics)
MEDLINE (clinical medicine)
MENTAL HEALTH ABSTRACTS
NATIONAL NEWSPAPER INDEX (Christian Science Monitor, Los Angeles Times, New York Times, Wall Street Journal, Washington Post—current)
NATIONAL TECHNICAL INFORMATION SERVICE
NEWSEARCH (Christian Science Monitor, Los Angeles Times, New York Times, Wall Street Journal, Washington Post—over 30 days old)
OCCUPATIONAL SAFETY AND HEALTH
PETERSON'S COLLEGE DATA BASE
PSYCINFO (psychology)
STANDARD AND POOR'S NEWS (business)
TRADE AND INDUSTRY INDEX (business)

Note: Data bases listed in boldface type are described in Appendix III.

DIALOG

DIALOG is a full-service, command-driven professional search system that has been described as a "supermarket" of information, and it's an apt description indeed. DIALOG offers more than 200 data bases.

Under DIALOG's Standard Service Plan, you pay nothing to subscribe, although DIALOG recommends the purchase of the DIALOG manual at $50.00 and a DIALOG training seminar at $145. If you've had some experience with online searching, however, and particularly with Knowledge Index, you could probably skip the training seminar. The big expenses come when you log on. Telecommunication charges run $10.00 per hour for Tymnet or Telenet and $6.00 per hour for Dialnet, DIALOG's own packet-switching network. Data base royalty/connect time charges vary from about $25.00 to $35.00 per hour for government-supplied data bases such as ERIC to $150.00 per hr. or more for privately supplied data bases. DIALOG marketing people say that a typical DIALOG search costs from $1.00 to $1.50 a minute.

Considering the enormous appeal of some of the data bases in DIALOG's list (Table II–4), these charges may not be prohibitively high. Available on DIALOG, for instance, are AMERICA: HISTORY AND LIFE, ARTBIBLIO-GRAPHIES MODERN, FOUNDATION INDEX, HISTORICAL ABSTRACTS, THE PHILOSOPHER'S INDEX, RILM ABSTRACTS, and more. (Note, however, that some of DIALOG's attractions, such as FAMILY RESOURCES or LANGUAGE AND LANGUAGE BEHAVIOR ABSTRACTS, are available on BRS/After Dark at a fraction of DIALOG's price.) If these data bases lie in the center of your research interests, searching DIALOG occasionally may make good sense. A typical 10- to 20-minute search will cost between $12.50 and $25.00—not much more than it would cost to drive to a downtown library, park the car, spend the day in the library, and buy a hamburger for lunch.

When searching DIALOG, however, it pays to be mindful of the major variations in data base connect time/royalty charges. Most—but not all—of the data bases scholars will find of interest are reasonably priced. Searching ERIC on DIALOG, for example, costs little more than searching a typical data base on BRKTHRU. Some of the business and technical data bases, however, charge $150 or more per hour. DIALOG isn't for browsing unless you're independently wealthy.

COMPARING COSTS

Considering only the charges you incur after you've subscribed to an online data base vendor's services, BRS/After Dark is clearly the cheapest (and DIALOG is clearly the most expensive; see Table II–5).

Users who anticipate light usage, however, should remember the costs of the subscription fee. If you're only planning to do two hour's worth of searching,

TABLE II–4
DIALOG DATA BASES (SELECTED LIST)

All the data bases shown in Table II–3 plus:

AIM/ARM (instructional materials)
AMERICA: HISTORY AND LIFE (American & Canadian history)
AMERICAN MEN AND WOMEN OF SCIENCE
AMERICAN STATISTICS INDEX (U.S. statistical reports)
APTIC (air pollution)
AQUACULTURE (water research)
AQUATIC SCIENCES AND FISHERIES ABSTRACTS
ARTBIBLIOGRAPHIES MODERN
AV ONLINE (audio-visual materials)
BIOGRAPHY MASTER INDEX
BOOK REVIEW INDEX
BUSINESS/PROFESSIONAL SOFTWARE DATABASE
CAB ABSTRACTS (agriculture)
CANADIAN BUSINESS AND CURRENT AFFAIRS (news)
CAREER PLACEMENT REGISTRY (employment)
CHEMICAL REGULATIONS AND GUIDELINES
CHEMLAW
CHILD ABUSE AND NEGLECT
COMPENDEX (engineering)
CONFERENCE PAPERS INDEX (science, engineering)
CONGRESSIONAL RECORD ABSTRACTS
CLAIMS™ (sophisticated patent index system)
CRIS/USDA (agriculture)
DERWENT WORLD PATENT INDEX
DISSERTATION ABSTRACTS
DOE Energy (energy research)
ECONOMIC ABSTRACTS INTERNATIONAL
ECONOMIC LITERATURE INDEX
EI ENGINEERING MEETINGS (conference papers)
ELECTRIC POWER DATABASE
EMBASE (Excerpta Medica)

ENCYCLOPEDIA OF ASSOCIATIONS
ENERGYLINE (energy)
ENERGYNET (directory of energy-related persons and firms)
ENVIROLINE (environmental studies)
ENVIRONMENTAL BIBLIOGRAPHY
EXCEPTIONAL CHILD EDUCATION RESOURCES
FACTS ON FILE (news summary)
FAMILY RESOURCES
FEDERAL INDEX (index of federal activity)
FEDERAL REGISTER ABSTRACTS
FEDERAL RESEARCH IN PROGRESS
FLUIDEX (fluid engineering)
FOOD SCIENCE AND TECHNOLOGY ABSTRACTS
FOUNDATION DIRECTORY
FOUNDATION GRANTS INDEX
GEOARCHIVE (geology)
GEOREF (geology)
GPO MONTHLY CATALOG (U.S. government publications)
GRANTS (government and private)
HEALTH PLANNING AND ADMINISTRATION
HISTORICAL ABSTRACTS (world history)
IRIS (water quality)
ISMEC (mechanical engineering)
LABORLAW
LANGUAGE AND LANGUAGE BEHAVIOR ABSTRACTS
LIFE SCIENCES COLLECTION
LIBRARY AND INFORMATION SCIENCE ABSTRACTS (LISA)
MAGAZINE ASAP™ (full text of 50 popular serials)
MARC (Library of Congress accessions since 1968)
MARQUIS PRO-FILES (professional Who's Who)
MARQUIS WHO'S WHO

TABLE 11–4 (continued)
DIALOG DATA BASES (SELECTED LIST)

METADEX (metallurgy)
METEOROLOGICAL AND GEOASTROPHYSICAL ABSTRACTS
MIDDLE EAST: ABSTRACTS AND INDEX
MIDEAST FILE
MLA BIBLIOGRAPHY (modern languages)
NATIONAL CRIMINAL JUSTICE REFERENCE SERVICE
NATIONAL FOUNDATIONS
NICSEM/NIMIS (handicapped children)
NONFERROUS METALS ABSTRACTS
NURSING AND ALLIED HEALTH
OCEANIC ABSTRACTS
PAPERCHEM (pulp and paper manufacturing)
PATLAW (patent law)
PHILOSOPHER'S INDEX
POPULATION BIBLIOGRAPHY
PSYCALERT (latest publications in psychology)
PUBLIC AFFAIRS INFORMATION SERVICE
RELIGION INDEX
REMARC (Library of Congress accessions before 1968)
RILM ABSTRACTS (musicology)
SCISEARCH (Science Citation Index)
SOCIAL SCISEARCH (Social Science Citation Index)
SOCIOLOGICAL ABSTRACTS
SPIN (physics, astronomy, geophysics)
STANDARDS AND SPECIFICATIONS
TELEGEN (genetic engineering and biotechnology)
TEXTILE TECHNOLOGY DIGEST
TRADEMARKSCAN^{TM} (trademarks)

TSCA INITIAL INVENTORY (Environmental Protection Agency's list of chemical substances)
ULRICH'S INTERNATIONAL PERIODICALS DIRECTORY
UNITED STATES POLITICAL SCIENCE DOCUMENTS
UPI NEWS
WASHINGTON POST NEWS
WATER RESOURCES ABSTRACTS
WATERNET (water utilities)
WELDASEARCH (welding)
WILEY CATALOG/ONLINE (book publisher's catalog)
WORLD AFFAIRS REPORT (Soviet press)
WORLD ALUMINUM ABSTRACTS
WORLD TEXTILES
ZOOLOGICAL RECORD

Note: Data bases listed in boldface type are described in Appendix III.

TABLE II-5

COST OF "TYPICAL" 15-MINUTE SEARCH

Vendor	Cost per Minute, $	15 Minutes, $
BRS/After Dark*	0.22	3.30
Knowledge Index	0.40	6.00
BRKTHRU (evenings/weekends)	0.54	8.12
BRKTHRU (day)	1.08	16.25
DIALOG	1.25	18.75

Note: Computed using the median data base connect time/royalty charge (for example, $30 per hour for BRKTHRU and $75 per hour for DIALOG).
    *$12.00 monthly minimum

for instance, Knowledge Index emerges as the cheapest vendor (Table II-6). (Remember, too, that BRS/After Dark charges you $12.00 per month minimum, making the service a bad deal for light users.) With heavier usage, however, the effect of the subscription fee disappears (Table II-7).

TABLE II-6

COST OF TWO HOURS OF SEARCHING

Vendor	Cost per Minute, $	2 Hours, $
BRS/After Dark*	0.22	101.40
Knowledge Index	0.40	83.00
BRKTHRU (evenings/weekends)	0.54	114.80
BRKTHRU (day)	1.08	179.60
DIALOG	1.25	150.00

Note: Computed using mandatory subscription fees and the median data base connect time/royalty charge (for example, $30 per hour for BRKTHRU and $75 per hour for DIALOG).
    *$12.00 monthly minimum.

TABLE II-7

COST OF TEN HOURS OF SEARCHING

Vendor	Cost per Minute, $	10 Hours, $
BRS/After Dark*	0.22	207.00
Knowledge Index	0.40	275.00
BRKTHRU (evenings/weekends)	0.54	374.00
BRKTHRU (day)	1.08	690.00
DIALOG	1.25	750.00

Note: Computed using mandatory subscription fees and the median data base connect time/royalty charge (for example, $30 per hour for BRKTHRU and $75 per hour for DIALOG).
    *$12.00 monthly minimum.

RESOURCES

Addresses of Vendors

BRS/After Dark
BRS Information Technologies
1200 Rt. 7
Latham, NY 12110
800/345-4277

Knowledge Index
Dialog Information Services
3640 Hillview Ave.
Palo Alto, CA 94304
800/227-5510

BRKTHRU
BRS Information Technologies
1200 Rt. 7
Latham, NY 12110
800/345-4277

DIALOG
DIALOG Information Services
3640 Hillview Ave.
Palo Alto, CA 94304
800/227-1927

Publications

Three excellent journals, available in most libraries, will keep you up to date on the latest in online data base research: *Database, Online,* and *Online Review.* Aimed primarily at professional librarians who do online searching, the journals often include articles of interest to end users—in particular, college faculty who do online searching with their own personal computers. Be forewarned, however; you may search the stacks in vain for these journals because they're often shelved in the library's online searching office.

On BRS/After Dark and Knowledge Index, see Angela Jackson, "BRS/After Dark: The Birth of an Online Service," *Online* 7(5) (Sept. 1983), pp. 12–29; Marydee Ojala, "Knowledge Index: A Review," *Online* 7(5) (Sept. 1983), pp. 31–34; and Carol Tenopir, "DIALOG's Knowledge Index and BRS/After Dark: Database Searching on Personal Computers," *Library Journal* 108(5) (March 1, 1985), pp. 471–474.

ONLINE
DATA BASES

APPENDIX III

Of the thousands of online data bases available, a high proportion—about 90 percent—pertain to business or technical subjects. Only a few suit research in the traditional disciplines, the ones typically represented in a university's college of letters and science.

This appendix surveys the highlights of this small but growing segment of online resources. It does not pretend to be exhaustive. Besides business and technical data bases, excluded are data bases whose focuses are primarily clinical or vocational, such as MEDLINE (the clinical medicine data base) and THE SCHOOL PRACTICES INFORMATION FILE (a data base of teaching strategies and resources).

To exclude these business, technical, clinical, and vocational data bases isn't to claim that they're insignificant in any sense or that scholars have no use for them. On the contrary, they're gold mines for anyone doing research in the subjects they cover. But they're well covered already by several published works (see Resources at the end of this appendix). Rather, the aim here is to present (in the limited space available) a survey of the bibliographic and research data bases scholars are most likely to consult. These data bases have received comparatively little coverage elsewhere.

EVALUATING A DATA BASE

Before concluding that a particular data base will meet your research needs, you'll want to consider the data base's subject, the sources from which it's derived, the data base's size, the date records begin, and the type of records contained.

DATA BASE SUBJECT

Each entry attempts to epitomize each data base's subject, but it's well to remember not to take the subject too literally. SOCIOLOGICAL ABSTRACTS (subject: sociology), for example, indexes most of the significant journals in anthropology, and AGRICOLA (subject: agriculture) is an excellent source for rural sociology.

Knowing which data base to search is, in fact, something of an experienced searcher's trick. The big, professional systems, such as DIALOG, offer massive, unified subject search files that tell you (for a given search term) where you're most likely to hit pay dirt. But this appealing and useful feature is not available to searchers of the budget nighttime/weekend services. You'll want to pay close attention, therefore, to the "other subjects" entries in the description of each data base in this Appendix below so that you can form a good picture of what's in a particular data base. Often, you'll need to search more than one data base to achieve good coverage of your topic.[1]

SOURCES

Some data bases (for instance, LANGUAGE AND LANGUAGE BE-HAVIOR ABSTRACTS) are little more than electronic versions of print-based reference works—works that you can find in a good library's reference section. If that's so, why use them? Why not simply use the print-based media?

Besides the obvious point that online reference works can be searched far more quickly (and accurately) than manual volumes, they're preferable for another reason: they combine several years' worth of print-based indexes. That alone can deliver you from much tedious thumbing through volume after volume in the library when, for example, you're trying to locate five years' worth of references pertinent to a topic. More useful still are data bases like NATIONAL NEWSPAPER INDEX that combine the listings of two or more print-based reference works. They make it possible to do simultaneous multiyear, multi-reference searches, providing an obvious advantage over print-based reference works. And some online bases (example: POPULATION BIBLIOGRAPHY) have no print-based counterparts at all.

Some data bases (example: ERIC) are partially based on print-based reference works, but include much other material (position papers, conference papers, unpublished manuscripts, research reports, and so on) collected by the clearinghouse that compiles the data base. These data bases tend to offer much

---

[1]On choosing a data base in the social sciences and humanities, see Robert Donati, "Social Sciences and the Humanities through DIALOG: Part I of Two Parts," *Online* 1:4 (Oct. 1977), pp. 48–54; Part II, *Online* 2:1 (Jan. 1978), pp. 41–52; and Donna R. Dolan, "Social and Behavioral Sciences," in *Online Search Strategies*, Ryan E. Hoover, ed. (White Plains, NY: Knowledge Industry Publications, 1982), pp. 137–172.

information that is unavailable anywhere else, and that's good; but the drawback is that much of the material is of poor quality. The computer has no way of distinguishing the good material from the bad, so a search in one of the data bases that contains information of this type is likely to produce a high proportion of unusable references.

DATA BASE SIZE

The data bases listed in this Appendix range from small ones that contain only ten of thousands of records to gigantic ones with five million or more. Because they're updated frequently—most are updated monthly or even biweekly—the appendix lists their sizes in relative terms:

Small Fewer than 100,000 citations.
Medium 100,000 to 500,000 citations.
Large 500,000 to 1,000,000 citations.
Very large More than 1,000,000 citations.

Big isn't necessarily better: small files aren't necessarily bad if their coverage is sharply focused. Very large data bases, moreover, are divided into separate files of one to two million records each, and that means inconveniences while searching. Typically, each file covers two to five years of the literature—for instance, File A (1969–1974), File B (1975–1979), File C (1980–1984), and File D (since 1985). Since these files are completely separate, searching in File D will net no records from File C. You'll have to duplicate your search in File C if you're interested in records from the years it covers.

DATE RECORDS BEGIN

Very few data bases include records before 1965; indeed, most begin coverage of the literature from 1972 or even later. In most cases, it's impracticable to index material published before the data base's origin, so pertinent material appearing before the date records begin will not be retrieved by a search.

On the surface, the shallow time depth data bases offer would seem to limit their usefulness. Yet so rapid has been the growth of literature in most fields that more than half of all the scholarly and scientific literature ever published has appeared in the past 15 years. The rate of growth is highest in the scientific and technical areas; some 6000 to 7000 scientific articles are written every day, and their number doubles every 5.5 years.[2]

[2]Daniel Bell, "Techne and Themis," in his *The Winding Passage* (New York: Abt Books, 1980), p. 54.

Even though it's likely that a given data base will contain at least 50 percent of the literature on a topic, it's well to remember that a thorough search will make use of print-based media for works that appeared before the data base's origin.

TYPE OF RECORD

Data bases vary in the type of information they present on the screen:

Citations only   The record contains the bibliographic citation, descriptors, identifiers and other data fields.

Citations and abstracts   The record contains the bibliographic citation, descriptors, identifiers, other data fields, and an informative abstract.

Full text   The data record includes the full text of the original document, excluding illustrations.

Most of the data bases listed in "Online Data Bases" offer abstracts as well as citations, and the abstract's text is included in the search. Since an abstract can tell you whether or not a citation is likely to prove pertinent, data bases that do not include them (example: MLA BIBLIOGRAPHY) tend to be less useful. A few data bases include the full text of the article. Full text data bases are fun, interesting—and expensive. It takes time to scroll all that text past you on the screen, and the vendor's meter is ticking away.

LISTING OF DATA BASES

ABSTRAX 400

Main Subject: All subjects

Abstrax 400 provides coverage of 400 popular periodicals such as *Newsweek* and *National Geographic*. Comparable to MAGAZINE INDEX, it may prove useful to researchers concerned with current events or the popular literature.

Sources: 400 popular periodicals
Size of data base: medium
Records begin: 1980
Type of records: citations and abstracts
Online vendors: BRS, BRS/After Dark, BRS/BRKTHRU

Produced by:
Information Sources, Ltd.

Distributed by:
J.A. Micropublishing, Inc.
271 Main St.
P.O. Box 218
Eastchester, NY 10707

ACADEMIC AMERICAN ENCYCLOPEDIA

Main subject: all subjects

A full-text data base, the *Academic American Encyclopedia*'s online version has two important advantages over its print-based counterpart: it's updated twice per year, and its entire text is searched every time you key in a search term. You'll be shown, therefore, every passage in the entire encyclopedia that's pertinent to the subject you're searching. Included are more than 29,000 articles, including the full text of the last printed edition (1980) plus many updates since then.

Sources: *Academic American Encyclopedia*, 1980 version plus updates
Size of data base: medium
Records begin: 1980
Type of records: full text
Online vendors: BRS, BRS/After Dark, BRS/BRKTHRU, DIALOG, Knowledge Index

Produced by:
Grolier Electronic Publishing, Inc.
95 Madison Ave.
New York, New York 10016

References:
Peter R. Cook, "Electronic Encyclopedias," *Byte* (July 1984), pp. 151–170.

AGRICOLA

Main subject: agriculture
Other subjects: excellent coverage of related aspects of other disciplines as they pertain to agriculture, such as agricultural economics, agricultural ecology, botany, chemistry, entomology, ethnology, forestry, rural sociology, and women's studies

Produced by the National Agricultural Library, this data base provides comprehensive coverage of all aspects of agriculture. Indexed are more than 600 journals as well as a very wide variety of books, monographs, pamphlets, government documents, research reports, publications of national and international organizations specializing in agriculture, and other sources. Since the data base constitutes the catalog of the National Agricultural Library, unusually good coverage of books distinguishes this data base from most others.

Sources: The National Agricultural Library acts as a clearinghouse for agricultural information and solicits a wide variety of materials for its collection (and this data base). Print-based versions of the data base are the *Bibliography of Agriculture, The National Agricultural Library Catalog,* and other reference works.

Size of data base: large
Records begin: 1970
Type of records: citations and abstracts
Online vendors: BRS, BRS/After Dark, BRS/BRKTHRU, DIALOG, Knowledge Index

Produced by:
U.S. Department of Agriculture
Science and Education Administration
Technical Information Systems
National Agricultural Library Building
Beltsville, MD 20705
301/344-3829

References:
"A Comparison of the Coverage of Agricultural and Forestry Literature on AGRICOLA, BIOSIS, CAB, and SciSearch," K. M. Brook, *Database* 3 (March 1980), pp. 38–49.
"AGRICOLA," Jeffrey Peters, *Database* 4:1 (March 1981), pp. 13–27.
Agricultural/Biological Vocabulary (U.S.D.A. Science and Education Administration), free pamphlet.
Agricultural Journal Titles and Abbreviations (Oryx Press, 2214 North Central at Encanto, Suite 103, Phoenix, AZ 85004).
Agricultural Terms (Oryx Press)
FNIC Controlled Vocabulary (U.S.D.A. Science and Education Administration), free pamphlet on the food and nutrition section of AGRICOLA.
List of Journals Indexed (U.S.D.A. Science and Education Administration), free brochure.

AMERICA: HISTORY AND LIFE

Main subject: U.S. and Canadian history
Other subjects: related topics such as economic history, ethnic studies, folklore, oral history, prehistory, Native Americans, popular culture, women's studies, etc.

This data base broadly covers the history, culture, and current affairs of the United States and Canada. Over 2000 journals are indexed, including many local and special-interest journals, as well as books and book reviews.

Sources: *America: History and Life, Part A: Article Abstracts and Citations, Part B: Index to Book Reviews,* and *Part C: American History Bibliography*
Size of data base: small
Records begin: 1964
Type of records: citations and abstracts
Online vendors: DIALOG

Produced by:
ABC/Clio Information Services
P.O. Box 4397
Santa Barbara, CA 93103
805/963-4221

References:
America: History and Life, Part D: Annual Index (ABC/Clio Information Services); includes thesaurus and list of the periodicals covered.
"In Search of History: Bibliographic Databases," by J. D. Falk, *History Teacher* 15:4 (Aug. 1982), pp. 523–544.
Online (ABC/Clio Information Services), free brochure.
Online User Manual (ABC-Clio Information Services).

AMERICAN CHEMICAL SOCIETY PRIMARY JOURNALS DATABASE

Main subject: chemistry
Other subjects: related topics in other disciplines, such as biochemistry, electrochemistry, geophysics, etc.

This full text data base covers more than 51,000 articles appearing in 18 primary journals published by the American Chemical Society. Records are searchable by author, title, source journal, and abstract; when retrieved, the full text of the article, including footnotes, references, and captions, can be displayed.

Sources: journals published by the American Chemical Society—*Journal of the American Chemical Society, Biochemistry, Journal of Organic Chemistry,* and others
Size of data base: medium
Records begin: 1980
Type of records: citations, abstracts, and full text
Online vendors: BRS, BRS/After Dark, BRS/BRKTHRU

Produced by:
American Chemical Society
1155 16th Street NW
Washington, DC 20036
800/424-6747

References:
Basic User's Guide to Full Text Chemical Data Bases (American Chemical Society, 1155 16th Street NW, Washington, DC 20036), free brochure.

ARTBIBLIOGRAPHIES MODERN

Main subject: art history (19th and 20th centuries)
Other subjects: collectors and collecting, art education, exhibitions, folk art, furniture, photography, sculpture, etc.

A comprehensive data base covering 19th and 20th century architecture, art, art history, artists' biographies, crafts, design, galleries, and museums.

Sources: *ARTbibliographies Modern*
Size of data base: small
Records begin: 1974
Type of records: citations and abstracts
Online vendors: DIALOG

Produced by:
ABC/Clio Information Services
P.O. Box 4397
Santa Barbara, CA 93103
805/963-4221

References:
ARTbibliographies Modern (ABC/Clio Information Services), free brochure.
Online (ABC/Clio Information Services), free brochure.
"Searching the Visual Arts: An Analysis of Online Information Access," D. Brady and W. Serban, *Online* 5 (Oct. 1981), pp. 12–32.

ARTS AND HUMANITIES SEARCH

Main subject: arts and humanities, including archaeology, architecture, art, classics, dance, film, TV and radio, folklore, history, language, literature, music, philosophy, theater, theology, and religious studies

Other subjects: humanistic studies in the social sciences

ARTS AND HUMANITIES SEARCH is the online version of the *Arts and Humanities Citation Index*. It has three noteworthy features. Like SCISEARCH and SOCSCISEARCH, an ARTS AND HUMANITIES SEARCH data record contains no abstract. Instead, it lists the works cited in the indexed article's bibliography. Second, you can use this bibliographic cross-referencing to discover relationships among works in the literature. The broad, interdisciplinary coverage, moreover, shows those relationships even if they stray into other subjects. ARTS AND HUMANITIES SEARCH provides, therefore, an outstanding foundation for literature review in any arts or humanities discipline. Its availability on BRS/AFTER DARK will probably make that online vendor irresistably attractive for many readers of this book. Third, the online version—unlike the print version—makes all this useful information available since 1980 in a single data base, vastly simplifying and speeding the search process (which formerly involved juggling several years' worth of big, clumsy volumes) when more than one years' citations are desired. Indexed every other week are 1300 of the world's leading arts and humanities journals, and coverage includes articles, letters, editorials, notes, meeting abstracts, discussions, and even errata; note, however, that books are not indexed (*Books in Print* provides good coverage here). Also included are published reviews of musical performances, films, records, and art exhibits. Although ARTS AND HUMANITIES SEARCH is a major resource for scholarly work, note that it's new: records go back only to 1980.

Sources: *Arts and Humanities Citation Index*
Size of data base: Medium
Records begin: 1980
Type of records: citations and reference list
Online vendors: BRS, BRS/After Dark, BRS/BRKTHRU

Produced by:
Institute for Scientific Information
University City Science Center
3501 Market St.
Philadelphia, PA 19104
800/523-1850

BILINGUAL EDUCATION BIBLIOGRAPHIC ABSTRACTS

Main subject: bilingual education
Other subjects: related aspects of social science disciplines, such as anthropology, education, psychology, sociology, social welfare, and others

Produced by the National Clearinghouse for Bilingual Education, this data base contains a wide variety of material on bilingual education, second language instruction, ethnic/linguistic minorities, and related subjects. Included are journal articles and books, as well as conference papers, position papers, review essays, program descriptions, nonprint media, classroom materials, and other material.

Sources: This data base is produced by the National Clearinghouse for Bilingual Education, which solicits a wide variety of materials for inclusion in this data base. There is no printed equivalent, and much material in this data base is not available anywhere else.

Size of data base: small
Records begin: 1977
Type of records: citations and abstracts
Online vendors: BRS, BRS/After Dark, BRS/BRKTHRU

Produced by:
National Clearinghouse for Bilingual Education
1555 Wilson Boulevard Suite 605
Arlington, VA 22209
800/336-4560

BIOSIS PREVIEWS

Main subject: biology
Other subjects: agriculture, anatomy, biological aspects of the behavioral sciences, biochemistry, botany, experimental medicine, genetics, immunology, nutrition, parasitology, public health, veterinary science, zoology.

BIOSIS previews, one of the largest online databases, is a huge repository of life science literature. Included are citations and abstracts from over 9000 journals and monograph series, as well as conference papers, book reviews, books, research reports, research notes, research communications, and other sources.

Sources: *Biological Abstracts, Bioresearch Index,* and *Biological Abstracts/Reports, Reviews, Meetings*
Size of data base: large
Records begin: 1969
Type of records: citations and abstracts
Online vendors: BRS, BRS/After Dark, BRS/BRKTHRU, DIALOG, Knowledge Index

Produced by:
BioSciences Information Service
2100 Arch St.
Philadelphia, PA 19103
800/523-4806

References:
BIOSIS BioScene (BioSciences Information Service), free bimonthly newsletter.
BIOSIS BioSearch (BioSciences Information Service), free quarterly newsletter.
The BIOSIS Information System: A Self-Teaching Outline (Biosciences Information Service), free 20-page guide to BIOSIS information retrieval.
BIOSIS Search Guide/BIOSIS Previews Ed. (BioSciences Information Service), 600-page search manual.

BOOKS IN PRINT

Main subject: all subjects

Produced by the R. R. Bowker Company, Books in Print is an online version of the familiar bookstore reference work, but with two important advantages: it's much more comprehensive, and it's updated monthly. Included in the single data base are all of Bowker's several reference works, making this data base far more comprehensive than the print-based work of the same name.

Sources: *Books in Print, Subject Guide to Books in Print, Forthcoming Books, Subject Guide to Forthcoming Books, Books in Print Supplement, Scientific and Technical Books in Print, Medical Books in Print, Business and Economics Books in Print, Paperbound Books in Print,* and others.
Size of data base: medium
Records begin: current year
Type of records: citations only
Online vendors: DIALOG, BRS, BRS/After Dark, BRS/BRKTHRU, Knowledge Index

Produced by:
R. R. Bowker Co.
205 East 42nd St.
New York, NY 10017
212/916-1600

References:
Subject Thesaurus for Bowker Online Databases (R. R. Bowker Co., P.O. Box 1807, Ann Arbor, MI 48106).

CA SEARCH

Main subject: chemistry
Other subjects: related subjects in other disciplines, such as biochemistry, electrochemistry, geophysics, etc.

An online version of *Chemical Abstracts,* CA Search is a major literature research resource for chemistry and allied subjects. It does not, however, include abstracts, owing to the huge size of the literature in chemistry and chemical engineering. Indexed are journal articles from about 12,000 journals, as well as patents, government reports, and conference papers. Special search procedures take advantage of chemistry's unique nomenclature and, for searchers versed in chemistry, speed search times considerably.

Source: *Chemical Abstracts*
Size of data base: very large
Records begin: varies with vendor
Type of records: citations only
Online vendors: DIALOG, BRS, BRS/After Dark, BRS/BRKTHRU

Produced by:
Chemical Abstracts Service, Inc.
P.O. Box 3012
Columbus, OH 43210
800/848-6533

References:
CASSI KWOC (Key Word Out of Context) Index (Chemical Abstracts Service).
Headings List (Chemical Abstracts Service).
A Natural Language Term List (Chemical Abstracts Service).
"Online Use of *Chemical Abstracts:* A Primer for Beginning Chemical Searchers," *Database* 2:4 (Dec. 1979), pp. 11–21.
"The Role of Subject Expertise in Searching the Chemical Literature, and Pitfalls that Await the Inexperienced Searcher," Dana Lincoln Roth, *Database* 8:1 (Feb. 1985), pp. 43–48.

CHILD ABUSE AND NEGLECT

Main subject: child abuse and neglect
Other subjects: related aspects of behavioral science disciplines, including education, psychology, sociology, and social welfare

Produced by the U.S. Department of Health and Human Service's National Center on Child Abuse and Neglect, this data base contains a wide variety of information on child abuse, including research reports, journal articles, court decisions, legislative documents, summaries of pertinent audiovisual materials, descriptions of service programs in child abuse and neglect, and statistics from case reports.

Sources: *Child Abuse and Neglect Research; Projects and Publications; Child Abuse and Neglect Programs; and Child Abuse and Neglect Audiovisual Materials*
Size of data base: small
Records begin: 1965
Type of records: citations and abstracts
Online vendors: DIALOG

Produced by:
U.S. Department of Health and Human Services
National Center on Child Abuse and Neglect
P.O. Box 1182
Washington, DC 20013
202/755-0590

References:
Child Abuse and Neglect Thesaurus (Clearinghouse on Child Abuse and Neglect Information, P.O. Box 1182, Washington DC 20013).

CONGRESSIONAL RECORD ABSTRACTS

Main subject: political science
Other subjects: legislative aspects of all subjects

This data base provides concise summaries of all significant material—bills and resolutions, amendments to bills and resolutions, committee and subcommittee reports, speeches, comments in debates, and more—from the *Congressional Record.*

Sources: *Congressional Record*
Size of data base: medium
Records begin: 1981
Type of records: citations and miniabstracts
Online vendors: DIALOG

Produced by:
Capitol Services, Inc.
415 Second Street NE
Suite 200
Washington, DC 20002
202/546-5600

References:
Congressional Record Abstracts User Aid (Capitol Services, Inc.) free for online users.
CSI Online Review (Capitol Services, Inc.) newsletter for database users.

DISSERTATION ABSTRACTS ONLINE

Main subject: U.S. doctoral dissertations in all fields (professional degrees such as M.D., LL.D. not included)

The online version of *Dissertation Abstracts* offers coverage (citations only) of approximately 99 percent of the dissertations presented to accredited American universities since 1861. Coverage of master's degrees is selective and dates to 1962. Records added since July 1980 include abstracts.

Sources: *Dissertation Abstracts International*
Size of data base: large
Records begin: 1861 (citations), 1980 (abstracts)
Type of records: citations (1861–1980), citations and abstracts (since 1980)
Online vendors: DIALOG, BRS, BRS/After Dark, BRS/BRKTHRU

Produced by:
University Microfilms International
Dissertation Publishing
300 North Zeeb Rd.
Ann Arbor, MI 48106
800/521-0600

ECONOMIC LITERATURE INDEX

Main subject: economics
Other subjects: related aspects of other disciplines, such as economic development, international economics, economic anthropology, etc.

This data base provides thorough coverage of mainstream economics. Indexed are over 200 economic journals. Its usefulness is limited by the lack of abstracts.

Sources: *Index of Economic Articles* and *Journal of Economic Literature*
Size of data base: medium
Records begin: 1969
Type of records: citations only
Online vendor: DIALOG

Produced by:
Journal of Economic Literature
P.O. Box 7320
Oakland Station
Pittsburgh, PA 15213
412/578-3869

ECONOMICS ABSTRACTS INTERNATIONAL

Main subject: international economics
Other subjects: related aspects of other disciplines, such as international relations, area studies, economic anthropology, etc.

This data base, produced by the Dutch Ministry of Foreign Affairs, covers market trends, economic development, economic climate, and other aspects of the economy worldwide. Emphasis is placed on Europe, with substantial coverage of Asia and other areas. About half the citations are in English. Covered are journals, books, government publications, research reports, and reference works.

Source: *Economic Titles and Abstracts*
Size of data base: small
Records begin: 1974
Type of records: citations and abstracts
Online vendor: DIALOG

Produced by:
Netherlands Foreign Trade Agency
Bezuidenhoutseweg 151
2594 AG
The Hague
Netherlands

ERIC

Main subject: education
Other subjects: counseling, personnel services, special needs children, gifted children, languages and linguistics, reading, testing and evaluation

ERIC is a comprehensive data base covering all aspects of education. Produced by the Department of Education's Educational Resources Information Center, ERIC has two sections, one covering instructional materials and the other instructional research. Included are records on research reports, theses, conference papers, journal articles from more than 700 education journals, pamphlets, evaluation studies, and other materials. Hardcopy may be ordered from ERIC's Document Reproduction Service (EDRS) at low cost. Another source of hardcopy is ERIC's regional distribution centers, more than 650 in number, which collect ERIC documents on microfiche. *Note:* Searches for material on exceptional children (both gifted and retarded) should begin with a companion data base, Exceptional Child Education Resources.

Sources: ERIC is a federally funded clearinghouse for educational materials of all kinds, including many otherwise unavailable items such as lesson plans, position papers, curriculum guides, and bibliographies. Print equivalents for the indexed articles and research reports are the *Current Index to Journals in Education* and *Resources in Education.*

Size of data base: medium
Records begin: 1966
Type of records: citations and abstracts
Online vendors: BRS, BRS/After Dark, BRS/BRKTHRU, DIALOG, Knowledge Index

Produced by:
U.S. Department of Education
ERIC Processing and Reference Facility
4833 Rugby Ave Suite 301
Bethesda, MD 20814

References:
All about ERIC (ERIC Processing and Reference Facility), free pamphlet.
A Bibliography of Publications about the Educational Resources Information Center (ERIC Processing and Reference Facility), free pamphlet.
"Comparison of Overlap: ERIC and Psychological Abstracts," by J. Caldwell and C. Ellingson, *Database* 2 (June, 1979), pp. 62–67.
Directory of ERIC Microfiche Collections (ERIC Processing and Reference Facility) free pamphlet.
How to Prepare for a Computer Search of ERIC: A Nontechnical Approach, Judith Yarborough (ERIC Document Reproduction Service, P.O. Box 190, Arlington, VA 22210).
Interchange Newsletter (ERIC Processing and Reference Facility) free semiannual newsletter.
"Searching ERIC on DIALOG: The Times They Are A-Changin'," by K. Clay, *Database* 2 (Sept. 1979), pp. 46–66.
Thesaurus of ERIC Descriptors, 10th ed., 1984 (Oryx Press, 2214 North Central Ave., Suite 103, Phoenix, AZ 85004).

EXCEPTIONAL CHILD EDUCATION RESOURCES

Main subject: gifted and retarded children
Other subjects: hearing-impaired children, visually impaired children, physically or emotionally handicapped children, autistic children, culturally separated children

A comprehensive data base covering exceptional children, both retarded and gifted, Exceptional Child Education Resources indexes a wide variety of sources (including doctoral dissertations, position papers, research reports, conference papers, curriculum guides, books, monographs, legislative documents, administrative policy manuals, nonprint media, etc.). Its subject overlaps with ERIC, but it's much more focused: only about half the material indexed in Exceptional Child Education Resources also appears in the ERIC data base. Searches for material on any of the covered subjects should begin with this data base rather than ERIC. Designed to supplement ERIC, this data base uses ERIC's system of descriptors and identifiers.

Sources: produced by the Council for Exceptional Children, which solicits and indexes a wide variety of material
Size of data base: small
Records begin: 1966
Type of records: citations and abstracts
Online vendors: DIALOG, BRS, BRS/After Dark, BRS/BRKTHRU

Produced by:
The Council for Exceptional Children
1920 Association Drive
Reston, VA 22091
800/336-3728

References:
Discovering Special Education Resources: A Workshop on ERIC and ECER, by Lynn Smarte (Council for Exceptional Children, 1920 Association Drive, Reston, VA 22091), free pamphlet
"ECER on BRS," by Laura G. Harper, *Database* 2 (June, 1979), pp. 37–55.
Thesaurus of ERIC Descriptors, 10th ed., 1984 (The Oryx Press, 2214 North Central Ave. at Encanto, Suite 103, Phoenix, AZ 85004).

FAMILY RESOURCES

Main subject: marriage and the family
Other subjects: related aspects in other disciplines, such as anthropology, psychology, sociology, and social welfare

Family Resources covers the psychological and sociological literature on family studies. Produced jointly by the National Council on Family Relations and the *Inventory of Marriage and Family Literature* (University of Minnesota), it includes materials from 1200 journals, government documents, research reports, newsletters, instructional materials, and other sources. Special features are a work-in-progress file, a professional services directory, and a directory of family service agencies.

Sources: *Inventory of Marriage and Family Literature* (journal articles). The National Council on Family Relations acts as a clearinghouse for marriage and family materials, which it actively solicits; the data base therefore contains much material not available elsewhere.

Size of data base: small
Records begin: 1970 (nonjournal items); 1973 (journal articles)
Type of records: citations and abstracts
Online vendors: DIALOG, BRS, BRS/After Dark, BRS/BRKTHRU

Produced by:
National Council on Family Relations
Fairview Community School Center
1910 West County Road B, Suite 147
St. Paul, MN 55113
612/633-6933

FOUNDATION GRANTS INDEX

Main subject: all subjects

This data base provides information on grants, fellowships, and awards available from more than 400 philanthropic organizations in the United States. The information is obtained directly from the foundations and from other sources. Sophisticated search aids enable searching by amount of award, subject of award, and other criteria.

Sources: 400 foundations
Size of data base: medium
Records begin: 1973
Type of records: citations and abstracts
Online vendor: DIALOG

Produced by:
The Foundation Center
79 Fifth Ave at 16th St.
New York, NY 10003
212/620-4230

GEOREF

Main subject: geology
Other subjects: related aspects of other disciplines, such as economics, geochemistry, geophysics, mathematics, mining, paleontology, etc.

Produced by the American Geological Institute, this data base covers the geological literature. It includes journal articles from over 4500 journals; also covered are books, conference proceedings, dissertations, maps, government documents, research reports, and other sources.

Sources: *Bibliography and Index of North American Geology, Bibliography of Theses in Geology, Geophysical Abstracts, Bibliography and Index of Geology Exclusive of North America,* and *Bibliography and Index of Geology*
Size of data base: large
Records begin: 1961 (North America); 1967 (worldwide)
Type of records: citations and abstracts
Online vendors: DIALOG

Produced by:
American Geological Institute
4220 King St.
Alexandria, VA 22302
800/336-4764

References:
GeoRef Newsletter (American Geological Institute), free newsletter.
GeoRef Online Workshop Training Manual, Ghassan Rassam and Sharon Tahirkheli, eds., 2nd ed. (American Geological Institute).
GeoRef Thesaurus and Guide to Indexing (American Geological Institute).

GRANTS

Main subject: all subjects

Produced by Oryx Press, this data base provides information on more than 2000 currently available grants, fellowships, and awards offered by a wide variety of organizations (including federal, state, and local governments as well as private foundations).

Sources: *Grants Information System*
Size of data base: small
Records begin: current records only
Type of records: citations and abstracts
Online vendors: DIALOG

Produced by:
Oryx Press
2214 North Central at Encanto
Phoenix, AZ 85004
602/254-6156

HISTORICAL ABSTRACTS

Main subject: world history
Other subjects: related areas in other disciplines, such as anthropology, area

studies, diplomatic history, economic history, history of science, international relations, philosophy of history, rural sociology, social history, sociology, Third World studies, etc.

Historical Abstracts, a companion to America: History and Life, covers world history from 1450 to the present (excluding U.S. and Canada). About 2000 journals are indexed, as well as conference papers, festschriften, books, and dissertations.

Sources: *Historical Abstracts, Part A: Modern History Abstracts (1450–1914), and Part B: Twentieth Century Abstracts (1914 to present).*
Size of data base: small
Records begin: 1973
Type of records: citations and abstracts
Online vendors: DIALOG

Produced by:
ABC/Clio Information Services
P.O. Box 4397
Santa Barbara, CA 93103
805/963-4221

References:
"Controlled and Free-Vocabulary Indexing of the ABC-Clio Databases in History," by Joyce D. Falk, in *Databases in the Social Sciences and Humanities*, Joseph Raben and Gregory Marks (eds.). Amsterdam: North Holland, 1980, pp. 309–313.
Historical Abstracts, Part A: Modern History Abstracts, Vol. 4, Annual Index, and Part B: Twentieth Century Abstracts, Vol. 4, Annual Index (ABC/Clio Information Services, P.O. Box 4397, Santa Barbara, CA 93103), includes thesaurus and list of journals covered.
"In Search of History: Bibliographic Databases," by J. D. Falk, *History Teacher* 15:4 (Aug. 1982), pp. 523–544.
Online (ABC/Clio Information Services), free brochure.
Online User Manual (ABC/Clio Information Services).

INSPEC

Main subject: physics and computer science
Other subjects: Related subjects in other disciplines, such as biophysics, biomedical engineering, geophysics, information retrieval, material science, etc.

INSPEC (Information Services in Physics, Electrotechnology, Computers, and Control) is an online equivalent of three major indexes in electrical engineering, computer science, and physics. It's a primary literature research resource for physics, computer science, and allied subjects. 2300 journals are indexed, as are conference proceedings, technical reports, books, patents, and doctoral dissertations.

Sources: *Electrical and Electronics Abstracts, Computer and Control Abstracts,* and *Physics Abstracts*
Size of data base: large
Records begin: 1969
Type of records: citations and abstracts
Online vendors: BRS, BRS/After Dark, BRS/BRKTHRU, DIALOG, Knowledge Index

Produced by:
INSPEC
IEEE Service Center
445 Hoes Lane
Piscataway, NJ 08554
201/981-0060, ext. 380

References:
Alphabetical Subject Guide to the INSPEC Classification (IEEE), free pamphlet.
"Computer-Aided Searching in the INSPEC Database: Analysis of Subject Indexing by INSPEC and the Resulting Cost and Efficiency as Related to Various Search Strategies," M. W. De Jong-Hofman, *Online Review,* 2 (June 1978), pp. 175–198.
INSPEC List of Journals and Other Serial Sources (IEEE).
"Inspec on DIALOG," D. T. Hawkins, *Database* 5:4 (1982), pp. 12–25.
INSPEC Thesaurus (IEEE).
INSPEC User's Guide (IEEE).
"Online Data Bases in Physics," Mary Ellen Sievert and Alison F. Verbeck, *Database* 7:4 (Dec. 1984), pp. 54–63.

LANGUAGE AND LANGUAGE BEHAVIOR ABSTRACTS

Main subject: linguistics
Other subjects: related areas in other disciplines, such as anthropological linguistics, hearing pathology, interpersonal communication, learning disabilities, mental retardation, nonverbal communication, philosophy of language, poetics, sociolinguistics, stylistics, semantics, semiotics, etc.

Language and Language Behavior Abstracts is the online version of the printed reference work of the same name. It covers language, linguistics, and language behavior generally, covering about 1200 journals.

Sources: *Language and Language Behavior Abstracts*
Size of data base: small
Records begin: 1973

Type of records: citations and abstracts
Online vendors: DIALOG, BRS, BRS/After Dark, BRS/BRKTHRU

Produced by:
Sociological Abstracts, Inc.
P.O. Box 22206
San Diego, CA 92122
619/565-6603

References:
Language and Language Behavior Abstracts User's Manual, 1984 (Sociological Abstracts, Inc., P.O. Box 22206, San Diego, CA 92122).

LEGAL RESOURCE INDEX

Main subject: law
Other subjects: related subjects

The Legal Resource Index provides a comprehensive index to all significant material (including such items as obituaries and editorials) from 660 law journals, academic journals, and five major law newspapers. The data base also includes law-related citations from the Magazine Index, the National Newspaper Index, and the Library of Congress MARC book catalog.

Sources: *Current Law Index*
Size of data base: small
Records begin: 1980
Type of records: citations only
Online vendors: DIALOG, Knowledge Index

Produced by:
Online Services
Information Access Company
11 Davis Drive
Belmont, CA 94002
800/227-8431

References:
Journal Abbreviations and Publishers' Addresses in Legal Resource Index (Information Access Company), free pamphlet.
Subject Guide to IAC Databases (Information Access Company).

LIFE SCIENCES COLLECTION

Main subject: biology
Other subjects: related aspects of other disciplines, such as ecology, biochemistry, etc.

Produced by Cambridge Scientific Abstracts, the Life Sciences Collection combines the reference resources of 15 major reference works in the life sciences.

Sources: *Animal Behavior Abstracts, Biochemistry Abstracts, Calcified Tissue Abstracts, Chemoreception Abstracts, Ecology Abstracts, Entomology Abstracts, Feeding, Weight, and Obesity Abstracts; Genetics Abstracts, Immunology Abstracts, Microbiology Abstracts, Oncology Abstracts, Toxicology Abstracts, Virology Abstracts*

Size of data base: medium
Records begin: 1978
Type of records: citations and abstracts
Online vendor: DIALOG

Produced by:
Cambridge Scientific Abstracts
5161 River Road
Bethesda, MD 20816
800/638-8076

References:
Life Sciences Collection User's Manual (Cambridge Scientific Abstracts).
Periodicals Scanned and Abstracted: Life Sciences Collection (Cambridge Scientific Abstracts).
Thesaurus: Life Sciences Collection (Cambridge Scientific Abstracts).

MAGAZINE INDEX

Main subject: All subjects

Like ABSTRAX 400, Magazine Index indexes popular periodicals—435 of them—and constitutes an online version of the *Reader's Guide to Periodical Literature*, whose periodical list it duplicates. Because it includes abstracts, however, it's superior to that print-based medium.

Sources: 435 U.S. and Canadian popular periodicals
Size of data base: large
Records begin: 1973
Type of records: citations and abstracts
Online vendors: DIALOG, Knowledge Index

Produced by:
Online Services
Information Access Company
11 Davis Drive
Belmont; CA 94002
800/227-8431

References:
Access to Access: An Online User's Guide to IAC Databases (Information Access Company).
Journals Indexed in Magazine Index (Information Access Company), free pamphlet.
"Sources of Popular Literature Online: The New York Times Information Bank and The Magazine Index," by R. Slade and A. M. Kelly, *Database* 2 (March, 1979), pp. 70–83.
Subject Guide to IAC Databases (Information Access Company).

MARC

Main subject: all subjects

Produced by the Library of Congress, MARC (Machine-Readable Catalog) contains English language accessions to the Library of Congress since 1968. Library of Congress subject headings and classification codes provide the search nomenclature.

Sources: Library of Congress accessions since 1968
Size of data base: large
Records begin: 1968
Type of records: citations only
Online vendor: DIALOG

Produced by:
Library of Congress
Washington, DC 20541
800/227-1960

References:
Library of Congress Subject Headings (Cataloging Distribution, Library of Congress).
Outline of the Library of Congress Classification (Cataloging Distribution, Library of Congress).

MATHFILE

Main subject: mathematics
Other subjects: related topics in other disciplines including the history of

mathematics, computer science and automata, systems theory, physics, engineering, geophysics, etc.

Produced by the American Mathematical Society, MATHFILE indexes about 1600 journals in pure and applied mathematics. The reviews are in themselves of interest; they're written (and signed) by experts in the field other than the paper's authors.

Source: *Mathematical Reviews*
Size of data base: medium
Records begin: 1973 (abstracts, 1979)
Type of records: citations and abstracts
Online vendors: BRS, BRS/After Dark, BRS/BRKTHRU, DIALOG

Produced by:
American Mathematical Society
P.O. Box 6248
Providence, RI 02940
401/272-9500

References:
Mathfile User's Guide (American Mathematical Society).
MATHFILE: Mathematical Reviews Online (American Mathematical Society), free
  brochure.
Notes from MATHFILE (American Mathematical Society).

MENTAL HEALTH ABSTRACTS

Main subject: psychology
Other subjects: related areas in other fields, including gerontology, child development, criminology, education, sociology and social welfare, etc.

Mental Health Abstracts covers all aspects of mental health and mental illness, indexing over 1000 periodicals. Included are books, research reports, program descriptions, technical reports, monographs, dissertations, conference proceedings, grant reports, nonprint media, and other sources. This data base was formerly produced by the National Clearinghouse for Mental Health Information, but Reagan administration budget cuts ended the program. Additions to the data base have been taken over by a private company.

Sources: Formerly produced by the National Clearinghouse for Mental Health
  Information, which solicited a wide variety of materials for inclusion in this
  data base.
Size of data base: medium
Records begin: 1969

Type of records: citations and abstracts
Online vendors: DIALOG, Knowledge Index, BRS/BRKTHRU

Produced by:
IFI/Plenum Data Company
3202 Kirkwood Highway
Wilmington, DE 19808
302/998-0478

References:
Mental Health Abstracts User's Guide (IFI/Plenum Data Co., 301 Swann Avenue, Alexandria, VA 22301).

METEOROLOGICAL AND GEOASTROPHYSICAL ABSTRACTS

Main subject: meteorology, astrophysics
Other subjects: related aspects of other disciplines, such as geophysics, glaciology, environmental science, etc.

Produced by the American Meteorological Society, this data base corresponds to the print-based reference work of the same name. Indexed are 200 journals.

Sources: *Meteorological and Geoastrophysical Abstracts*
Size of data base: small
Records begin: 1972
Type of records: citations and abstracts
Online vendor: DIALOG

Produced by:
American Meteorological Society
45 Beacon St.
Boston, MA 02108
617/227-2425

MIDDLE EAST: ABSTRACTS AND INDEX

Main subject: Middle East area studies
Other subjects: related aspects of other disciplines, such as anthropology, archaeology, art, economics, education, history, languages and literatures, music, political science, religion, sociology

Produced by Northumberland Press, The Middle East: Abstracts and Index covers journal articles and doctoral dissertations related to the Arab world and the Middle East generally (Bahrain, Egypt, Iran, Iraq, Israel, Jordan, Kuwait,

Lebanon, Libya, Oman, Qatar, Saudi Arabia, Syria, Sudan, Turkey, United Arab Emirates, Yemen Arab Republic, and People's Democratic Republic of Yemen). 1500 journals and other periodicals are indexed.

Source: *The Middle East: Abstracts and Index*
Size of data base: small
Records begin: 1980
Type of records: citations and abstracts
Online vendor: DIALOG

Produced by:
Northumberland Press
1717 Boulevard of the Allies
Pittsburgh, PA 15219
412/281-6179

References:
Journal Scanning List for the Middle East: Abstracts and Index (Northumberland Press), free brochure.
Thesaurus of Indexing Terms for the Middle East: Abstracts and Index (Northumberland Press).

MIDEAST FILE

Main subject: Middle Eastern area studies
Other subjects: Related aspects of other disciplines, such as anthropology, economics, history, Islamic studies, etc.

An online version of the print-based reference work of the same name, Mideast File provides comprehensive coverage of current affairs in Libya, Egypt, Sudan, Turkey, Syria, Lebanon, Israel, Jordon, Iraq, Iran, Saudi Arabia, Yemen, and the United Arab Emirates. Indexed are 340 journals, as well as government publications, interviews, television and radio broadcasts, monographs, books, book reviews, conference papers, dissertations, official publications, and research reports.

Sources: Mideast File
Size of data base: small
Records begin: 1979
Type of records: citations and abstracts
Online vendors: DIALOG

Produced by:
Learned Information, Inc.
143 Old Marlton Pike

Medford, NJ 08055
609/654-6266

References:
Mideast File: List of Journals Scanned (Learned Information, Inc., Besselsleigh Road, Abingdon, Oxford OX13 6LG, U.K.), free brochure.

MLA BIBLIOGRAPHY

Main subject: modern languages and literatures
Other subjects: related areas in other fields, including folklore and linguistics.

The MLA Bibliography covers modern languages and literatures and indexes about 3000 journals. Also covered are books, published conference proceedings, dissertations, and book reviews. Its usefulness is sharply limited by the lack of abstracts.

Sources: *MLA International Bibliography of Books and Articles on the Modern Languages and Literatures*
Size of data base: medium
Records begin: 1976
Type of records: citations only
Online vendor: DIALOG

Produced by:
MLA International Bibliography
Modern Language Association
62 Fifth Ave
New York, NY 10011
212/741-7863

References:
MLA Directory of Periodicals: A Guide to Journals and Series in Languages and Literatures (MLA, 62 Fifth Ave., New York, NY 10011).
"MLA Bibliography Online Provides Access to Language, Literature, Folklore," by Rich Huleatt, *Database* 2:4 (Dec. 1979), pp. 11–21.
"Online with the MLA," *MLA Newsletter* 16:2 (Summer, 1984).

NATIONAL NEWSPAPER INDEX

Main subject: current events

The National Newspaper Index provides full indexing of all significant material appearing in the *Christian Science Monitor, Los Angeles Times, New York Times, Wall Street*

Journal, and *Washington Post.* "All significant material" means all articles, news reports, and editorials, as well as poetry, columns, and even letters to the editor.

Sources: *Christian Science Monitor* (western edition), *Los Angeles Times, New York Times* (city edition), *Wall Street Journal* (western edition), and *Washington Post*

Size of data base: medium

Records begin: Jan. 1, 1979 *(Christian Science Monitor, New York Times, Wall Street Journal),* Sept. 22, 1982 *(Washington Post),* November 1, 1982 *(Los Angeles Times).*

Type of records: citations only

Online vendors: DIALOG, Knowledge Index

Produced by:
Online Services
Information Access Company
11 Davis Drive
Belmont, CA 94002
800/227-8431

References:
Access to Access: An Online User's Guide to IAC Databases (Information Access Company).
Geographic Codes for IAC Databases (Information Access Company).
Subject Guide to IAC Databases (Information Access Company).

NEWSEARCH

Main subject: all subjects

NEWSEARCH is an ultracurrent data base containing up-to-date coverage of newspapers, magazines, and the legal literature. The data base is updated daily. Once per month, the older records are removed from the data base and parceled out among Legal Resources Index, Magazine Index, and National Newspaper Index.

Sources: See Legal Resources Index, Magazine Index, and National Newspaper Index

Size of data base: varies

Records begin: current month only

Type of records: citations only

Online vendors: DIALOG, Knowledge Index

Produced by:
Online Services
Information Access Company
11 Davis Drive

Belmont, CA 94002
800/227-8431

References:
Access to Access: An Online User's Guide to IAC Databases (Information Access
  Company).
Journals Indexed in NewSearch (Information Access Company).
Subject Guide to IAC Databases (Information Access Company).

PHILOSOPHER'S INDEX

Main subject: philosophy
Other subjects: aesthetics, epistomology, logic, philosophical anthropology,
history of philosophy

Produced by the Philosophy Documentation Center at Bowling Green State
University in Ohio, this data base indexes over 270 journals. Also included are
notes on works in progress and book reviews.

Sources: *Philosopher's Index, Philosophy Research Archives*
Size of data base: small
Records begin: 1940 (U.S. journals), 1967 (others)
Type of records: citations and abstracts
Online vendors: DIALOG

Produced by:
Philosophy Documentation Center
Bowling Green State University
Bowling Green, OH 43403
419/372-2419

References:
The Philosopher's Index Thesaurus (Philosophy Documentation Center).
"The Philosopher's Index," Mary Ellen Sievert, *Database* 3:1 (March 1980),
  pp. 50–62.

POPULATION BIBLIOGRAPHY

Main subject: demography
Other subjects: related subjects such as abortion, family studies, migration,
economic development, population education, family planning, fertility, population policy, population law, statistics, research methodology, etc.

This data base provides a major research resource for workers in demography.
Indexed are journal articles from about 550 journals, as well as books,

monographs, research reports, government documents, conference papers, chapters from selected books, materials distributed by population agencies, etc.

Sources: This data base is produced by the Carolina Population Center, which solicits material for inclusion in this data base; it has no print-based counterpart.
Size of data base: small
Records begin: 1966
Type of records: citations and abstracts
Online vendors: DIALOG

Produced by:
Carolina Population Center
University Square East 300A
Univ. of North Carolina, Chapel Hill
Chapel Hill, NC 27514
919/962-3006

References:
Population/Family Planning Thesaurus (Carolina Population Center).

PSYCINFO

Main subject: psychology
Other subjects: related subjects in the behavioral sciences, including psychological anthropology, educational psychology, statistics, child development, neurology, language, social psychology, etc.

PsycINFO is a major research source for psychology. Published by the American Psychological Association, PsycINFO corresponds to *Psychological Abstracts,* but it also includes relevant material from dissertations, research monographs, technical reports, conference papers, panel discussions, and case studies.

Sources: *Psychological Abstracts, Dissertation Abstracts International,* and other sources
Size of data base: medium
Records begin: 1967
Type of records: citations and abstracts
Online vendors: BRS, BRS/After Dark, BRS/BRKTHRU, DIALOG, Knowledge Index

Produced by:
PsycINFO
User Services Department
American Psychological Association
1200 Seventeenth Street, NW
Washington, DC 20036
800/336-4980

References:

"A Comparison of Overlap: ERIC and Psychological Abstracts," by Jane Caldwell and Celia Ellingson, *Database* 2 (June 1979), pp. 62–67.

"Psychological Abstracts/BRS," by Donna Dolan, *Database* 1 (Sept. 1978), pp. 9–25.

Psychological Abstracts Information Services Users Reference Manual (American Psychological Association).

Thesaurus of Psychological Index Terms, 4th ed. (American Psychological Association).

PUBLIC AFFAIRS INFORMATION SERVICE

Main subject: public policy
Other subjects: related aspects of other disciplines, such as international relations, economics, demography, sociology, and social welfare.

The Public Affairs Information Service (PAIS) data base emphasizes public policy issues with worldwide coverage. Indexed are 1200 journals, 8000 books and monographs (annually), government documents, publications of public policy agencies, yearbooks, directories, and other resources.

Sources: *Public Affairs Information Service Bulletin* and *Public Affairs Information Service Foreign Language Index*
Size of data base: medium
Records begin: 1972 (foreign language sources); 1976 (English sources)
Type of records: citations and abstracts
Online vendors: BRS, BRS/After Dark, BRS/BRKTHRU, DIALOG

Produced by:
Public Affairs Information Service, Inc.
11 West 40th St.
New York, NY 10018
212/736-6629

References:

"PAIS International," Dominic Provenzano, *Online* 5 (Jan. 1981), pp. 11–25.

PAIS Selection Policy and Periodicals List (Public Affairs Information Service).

PAIS Subject Headings List (Public Affairs Information Service).

RELIGION INDEX

Main subject: religion
Other subjects: related aspects of other disciplines, such as anthropology, history, and sociology

Produced by the American Theological Library Association, this data base covers scholarly writing in all fields on religion and theology. More than 330 journals are indexed, as are doctoral dissertations, books and book reviews. Not all journal citations, however, include abstracts.

Sources: *Religion Index One: Periodicals (From 1975 to Date), Two: Multi-Author Works (from 1970 to Date), and Three: Festschriften (1960–1969),* and other sources
Size of data base: medium
Records begin: 1949
Type of records: citations and abstracts
Online vendors: BRS, BRS/After Dark, BRS/BRKTHRU, DIALOG

Produced by:
American Theological Library Association
5600 South Woodlawn Ave
Chicago, IL 60637
312/947-8850

References:
"Religion Online—Or Is It?" R. J. Duckett, *Bulletin of the Association of British Theological and Philosophical Libraries* 2 (June, 1981), pp. 6–10.

REMARC

Main subject: all subjects

The Library of Congress has embarked on a project to put all new accessions on line (see MARC), but English language sources prior to 1968 (and foreign language sources prior to 1978) are not included. REMARC (Retrospective Machine-Readable Catalog) fills the void by providing an online data base of Library of Congress accessions from 1897 to 1978. Like MARC, the main Library of Congress data base, REMARC is searched using Library of Congress subject and classification codes.

Sources: Library of Congress shelf list, 1897–1978
Size of data base: very large
Records begin: 1897
Type of records: citations only
Online vendors: DIALOG

Produced by:
Carrollton Press, Inc.
1911 North Fort Myer Drive
Arlington, VA 22209
800/368-3008

References:
Library of Congress Subject Headings (Cataloging Distribution, Library of Congress, Washington, DC 20541).
Outline of the Library of Congress Classification (Cataloging Distribution, Library of Congress, Washington, DC 20541).

RILM ABSTRACTS

Main subject: musicology
Other subjects: related aspects of other fields, including ethnomusicology, music education, etc.

Produced by the Repertoire International de Littérature Musicale (RILM), RILM Abstracts provides coverage of music and music-related literature from books, journal articles, essays, reviews, dissertations, conferences, commentaries, and other sources.

Sources: *Rilm Abstracts of Musical Literature*
Size of data base: small
Records begin: 1972
Type of records: citations and abstracts
Online vendors: DIALOG

Produced by:
International RILM Center
City University of New York
33 West 42nd St.
New York, NY 10036
212/790-4214

References:
Bibliographic System Reference Manual, by Philip J. Drummond, 4 vols. (International RILM Center).
"Music Coverage in Online Databases," A. W. Goudy, *Database* 5:4 (1982), pp. 39–57.
RILM English-Language Thesaurus: Subject Headings for RILM Index (International RILM Center).

SCISEARCH

Main subject: sciences, including astronomy, astrophysics, biology, biomedical sciences, chemistry, computer science, earth sciences, environmental sciences, genetics, mathematics, meteorology, microbiology, physics, psychology, psychiatry, and zoology
Other subjects: scientific studies in the behavioral sciences

SCISEARCH, produced by the Institute for Scientific Information, is an online version of *Science Citations Index*. It has two noteworthy features. First, a SCISEARCH data record contains no abstracts. Instead, it lists the works cited in the indexed article's bibliography or reference list. Second, you can use this bibliographic cross-referencing tool to discover relationships among works in the literature. The broad, interdisciplinary coverage, moreover, shows those relationships even if they stray into other subjects. SCISEARCH provides an excellent foundation for literature review in any science discipline. Unlike SOCIAL SCISEARCH, its social sciences counterpart, however, SCISEARCH is so large that it has been divided into four distinct files, each with nearly two million records (1974–1977, 1978–1980, 1981–1983, 1984–present). Using the online version of this citation index is still more convenient than using the print-based version, which is issued annually and covers only one year's citation activity. Indexed are 4100 of the most important scientific journals, and significant works are drawn from an additional 800 journals and 1400 books (annually).

Sources: *Science Citation Index*
Size of data base: very large
Records begin: 1974
Type of records: citations and reference list
Online vendors: DIALOG, BRS, BRS/After Dark, BRS/BRKTHRU

Produced by:
Institute for Scientific Information
University City Science Center
3501 Market St.
Philadelphia, PA 19104
800/523-1850

References:
"SCISEARCH on DIALOG," Gretchen Savage, *Database* 1:1 (Sept. 1978), pp. 50–69.
User's Guide to Online Searching of SCISEARCH and SOCIAL SCISEARCH (Online Customer Service, Institute for Scientific Information), free brochure.

SOCIAL SCISEARCH

Main subject: social sciences, including anthropology, archeology, area studies, criminology, demography, economics, education, geography, international relations, political science, sociology, and urban planning
Other subjects: related aspects of other disciplines such as history, philosophy, and psychology

SOCIAL SCISEARCH is the online version of the *Social Science Citation Index*, a valuable research resource produced by the Institute for Scientific Information. It has three noteworthy features. First, like SCISEARCH, a SOCIAL SCISEARCH data record contains no abstracts. Instead, it lists the works cited in the indexed article's bibliography or reference list. Second, you can use this bibliographic cross-referencing tool to discover relationships among works in the literature. The broad, interdisciplinary coverage, moreover, shows those relationships even if they stray into other subjects. SOCIAL SCISEARCH provides an excellent foundation for literature review in any social science discipline. Third, the online version—unlike the print-based version—makes all the records since 1972 available in a single data base, vastly simplifying the search process when more than one year's citations are desired. Indexed regularly are 1500 of the most important social science journals, as well as significant articles selected from an additional 2400 journals in related areas.

Sources: *Social Science Citation Index*
Size of data base: large
Records begin: 1972
Type of records: citations and reference list
Online vendors: BRS, BRS/After Dark, BRS/BRKTHRU, DIALOG
Produced by:
Institute for Scientific Information
3501 Market St.
University City Science Center
Philadelphia, PA 19104
800/523-1850

References:
"ISI (Institute for Scientific Information) Services for the Social Sciences and the Arts and Humanities," by Eugene Garfeld and Susan Deutsch, in *Databases in the Humanities and Social Sciences,* Joseph Raben and Gregory Marks (eds.). Amsterdam: North Holland, 1980, pp. 315-319.
"Searching the *Social Sciences Citation Index* on BRS," Richard Janke, *Database* 1 (June 1980), pp. 19-45.
"Searching the Social Sciences Literature Online: Social Scisearch," Claude Bonnelly and Gaeten Drolet, *Database* 1 (Dec. 1978), pp. 10-25.
User's Guide to Online Searching of SCISEARCH and SOCIAL SCISEARCH (Online Customer Service, Institute for Scientific Information), free brochure.

SOCIOLOGICAL ABSTRACTS

Main subject: sociology and social welfare
Other subjects: related aspects of other disciplines, including anthropology, economics, education, psychology, etc.

Sociological abstracts is the online version of the print-based reference work of the same name. Indexed are 1500 journals, as well as book reviews, monographic publications, conference papers, and case studies

Source: *Sociological Abstracts*
Size of data base: medium
Records begin: 1963
Type of records: citations and abstracts
Online vendors: BRS, BRS/After Dark, BRS/BRKTHRU, DIALOG

Produced by:
Sociological Abstracts, Inc.
P.O. Box 22206
San Diego, CA 92122
619/565-6603

References:
"Searching Sociological Abstracts," Sandra Kerbol, *Database* 4 (June 1981), pp. 30–44.
Sociological Abstract User's Manual (Sociological Abstracts, Inc.).

SPIN

Main subject: physics and astronomy
Other subjects: related aspects of other disciplines, such as physical chemistry, biophysics, geophysics, and astrophysics

SPIN (short for Searchable Physics Information Notices) provides comprehensive coverage of U.S. and Soviet physics and astronomy. Indexed are all journal articles from journals published by the American Institute of Physics and conference papers from AIP-sponsored meetings.

Sources: journals published by the American Institute of Physics; conferences sponsored by the American Institute of Physics
Size of data base: medium
Records begin: 1975
Type of records: citations and abstracts
Online vendors: DIALOG

Produced by:
American Institute of Physics
335 East 45th St.
New York, NY 10017
212/661-9404

References:
List of Titles and CODENS (American Institute of Physics), free brochure.
Physics and Astronomy Classification Scheme (American Institute of Physics).
"SPIN," R. G. Lerner, *Online* 3:4 (1975), pp. 23-26.

UNITED STATES POLITICAL SCIENCE DOCUMENTS

Main subject: political science
Other subjects: related aspects of other disciplines, such as political anthropology, area studies, sociology, etc.

This data base indexes about 150 U.S. political science journals and corresponds to the print-based reference work of the same name.

Sources: *United States Political Science Documents*
Size of data base: very small
Records begin: 1975
Type of records: citations and abstracts
Online vendors: DIALOG

Produced by:
University Center for Industrial Studies
c/o NASA Industrial Applications Center
Univ. of Pittsburgh
710 LIS Building
Pittsburgh, PA 15260
412/624-5214

References:
Political Science Thesaurus (Univ. Center for International Studies).
"USPSD," David M. Pilachowski, *Database* 2:4 (Dec. 1979), pp. 68-77.

ZOOLOGICAL RECORD

Main subject: zoology
Other subjects: related aspects of other disciplines, such as biology, biochemistry, ecology, evolutionary biology, genetics, immunology, paleontology, physiology, etc.

An online equivalent of the print-based *Zoological Record*, this data base indexes 6000 serial publications, as well as dissertations, conference proceedings, books, monographs, and research reports. A unique taxonomical classification field permits sophisticated searches; the data base's usefulness, however, is limited by the lack of abstracts.

Source: *Zoological Record*
Size of data base: small
Records begin: 1978
Type of records: citations only
Online vendor: DIALOG

Produced by:
BioSciences Information Service
2100 Arch St.
Philadelphia, PA 19103
800/523-4806

References:
BIOSIS BioSearch (BioSciences Information Service), free quarterly newsletter.
How to Search Zoological Record Online (BioSciences Information Service), free
    brochure.
The Zoological Record Search Guide (BioSciences Information Service).

RESOURCES

Guides to online data bases are James L. Hall and Marjorie J. Brown, *Online Bibliographic Databases: A Directory and Sourcebook* (London: ASLIB, 1983); Owens Davies and Mike Edelhart, *Omni Online Database Directory, 1985* (New York: Collier, 1985); Charles L. Gilreath, *Computerized Literature Searching: Research Strategies and Databases* (Boulder, CO: Westview Press, 1984); Matthew Lesko, *The Computer Data and Database Sourcebook* (New York: Avon, 1984).

GLOSSARY

Address bus An electronic circuit that sends internal computer commands to the main memory. The more parallel circuits the address bus has, the more memory the computer can work with.

Advanced online formatter A word processing program that offers many of the benefits of batch formatting programs but simulates the appearance of the text when printed. *See* **batch formatting programs, text editor.**

Argument A variable included with commands that determine how the command will take effect; for example, with one word processing program using the command .BW with the argument 65 (as in *.BW 65*) establishes a body width or line length of 65 characters.

Arrow keys Keys with arrows printed on them that control movements of the cursor on the screen. *See* **cursor.**

ASCII American Standard Code for Information Interchange. A standard character set for computer communications which includes the numbers 0 through 9, the letters A through Z (upper and lower case), and common symbols.

ASCII collating sequence A standard computer sorting order determined by the order in which ASCII characters occur in a standard list. *See* **ASCII.**

Asynchronous communications A telecommunications format in which the transmission of data is not synchronized by a regular pulse but rather by the inclusion of start and stop bits which signal the beginning and end of a coded character.

Autoanswer modem A modem that, when connected to a phone jack using a modular plug, can automatically answer incoming calls. *See* **modem.**

Automatic indexing The construction of a key word index for a data base without human intervention.

Automatic reformatting A highly desirable feature of most word processing programs that automatically adjusts the text after an insertion or deletion.

Auxiliary memory system A memory system for nonvolatile mass storage. The auxiliary memory system is distinguished from the computer's main or random access memory, which is volatile

343

and useful only during the work session. The auxiliary memory systems of personal computers almost invariably consist of floppy and hard disk drives. *See* **floppy disk drive, hard disk, volatile, main memory.**

Background printing   A feature of some programs that permits you to print while you continue working with the computer.

Bank switching   A memory allocation technique that gets around the memory limitations of micro-processors; a microprocessor that can address only 64K, for example, can address several *banks* of 64K memory, thus enabling it to work with 128K of memory or more.

Batch formatting programs   Word processing programs that use embedded commands to determine formatting and operate in a batch processing mode. *See* **batch processing, embedded formatting command, format.**

Batch processing   Computer processing that occurs in a rigid and inconvenient input-storage-processing-output sequence. *See* **interactive processing.**

Baud   A measurement of the number of bits transmitted per second.

BBS   *See* **bulletin board.**

Bit   A single unit of computer-readable information; specifically, a binary digit expressed in binary numbers as a 0 or 1.

Bit-mapped graphics display   A computer display in which every pixel on the screen is under the computer's direct control and can be switched on or off as required. Bit-mapped graphics displays can show charts, graphics, illustrations, foreign language characters, and other images.

Boilerplate   Text that is used repeatedly.

Boolean operators   *See* **logical operator.**

Buffer   A portion of the main memory set aside for a specific storage function, such as storing the working text of a manuscript.

Built-in functions   A spreadsheet formula that is built into the program and activated merely by typing its name.

Bulletin board   A computer-based communication medium in which a single personal computer, running bulletin board software and equipped with an autoanswer modem, serves as means for computer users to post messages, participate in computer conferences, and download files. *See* **autoanswer modem.**

Byte   A group of eight binary digits or bits which represents a single alphanumeric character. *See* **bit.**

Cell   A rectangle formed by the intersection of a row and a column in a spreadsheet program.

Cell entry area   A place on the screen (usually above or below the speadsheet window) for inserting text, formulas, or values into a spreadsheet cell.

Cell matrix   A matrix of numbered rows and columns in a spreadsheet program such that each intersection of a row and a column, or *cell,* has a distinct identifying name.

Cell reference   A reference to a cell in a spreadsheet formula; returns the value which is in the referenced cell.

Centronics interface.   *See* **parallel interface.**

Clean search   A search that is restricted to the field containing a data base's descriptors. *See* **dirty search, descriptor.**

Command-driven A program that requires you to operate it by typing commands at the keyboard; often, you must memorize the commands to use them effectively. *See* **menu-driven.**

Command menu A list of command options presented on the video display screen.

Communication protocols Standards for the exchange of information among computers.

Controlled vocabulary An information storage and retrieval technique that assigns specific key words to data records, especially those key words that describe what the data records are about. *See* **data record, key word.**

Cursor A blinking rectangle or underline character displayed on the screen to indicate the point at which text will be inserted.

Data base A collection of related information.

Data base management Organizing a data base for efficient storage and retrieval of the information in it.

Data base management software Software designed to store, retrieve, sort, and print information stored in a computer data base. *See* **data base.**

Data base producers The organizations that produce the data bases used by online vendors. *See* **online vendor.**

Data bus An electronic circuit along which information travels within the computer. The more parallel circuits contained within the data bus, the faster the computer can handle information.

Data field A space for entering a particular kind of information in a data record.

Data record A single unit of related information in the data base.

Data record format The overall design of data fields which is repeated in every data record.

DBMS *See* **data base management software**

Dedicated word processor A computer built so that it functions only for word processing purposes.

Deletion buffer A temporary storage area for deleted text. Text deleted from the manuscript may be recovered from the deletion buffer, so long as no additional deletion has been made (the buffer holds only one deletion at a time).

Descriptor A key word which puts a data record into a broad general category. *See* **identifier.**

Dirty search A search that is not restricted to a data base's descriptors. *See* **clean search.**

Disk drives Magnetic storage media that are part of the computer's auxiliary memory system. The functions of the disk drive are to spin a magnetic disk, to write information to it, and to read information from it. The two chief types are floppy and hard disk drives. *See* **auxiliary memory system, floppy disk drive, hard disk, read, write.**

Disk operating system 1. A system program that integrates the computer's components (in particular, the disk drives) so that they work together properly. The disk operating system must be present in the computer's memory before applications programs may be used. 2. More generally, a package of programs that includes the disk operating system program proper and several related utilities. *See* **disk drives, utility program.**

Document Text created with a word processing program and stored on disk.

DOS *See* **disk operating system.**

Download In telecommunications, to capture incoming data in a disk file. *See* **telecommunications.**

Dumb   As used here, refers to telecommunication software that can only send messages to (and receive messages from) a mainframe computer; it cannot perform any processing operations itself or capture incoming data on disk. *See* **smart.**

Electronic mail   Letters, memos, or other documents communicated through computer channels. *See* **point-to-point electronic mail, point-source-point electronic mail, local area network.**

Embedded formatting command   Formatting commands, prefaced with a special marking character (such as @ or.), that are inserted into the text to control printing operations. Batch formatting programs read the marked file and, following the command's dictates, an output file for printing. *See* **batch formatting programs.**

Error message   A message displayed on the screen by a program informing you that the program has been unable to carry out a command you have given or has encountered some other problem.

Extension   In the CP/M and MS-DOS operating systems, the three-letter part of a file name that comes after the period (CHAP1.MSS). *See* **file name.**

File management software   A data base management program that works with only one file, or set of associated data records, at a time. *See* **data base management software, data record.**

File name   A name given to a recorded unit of information, such as a manuscript or a set of course grades, stored on disk.

File storage format   The format a word processing program uses to store text on disk. Many programs use the standard ASCII format, which includes nothing but the standard ASCII characters; recent and advanced word processing programs, however, tend to use formats that are incompatible with the ASCII standard. *See* **ASCII.**

FFISR   *See* **free-format information storage and retrieval system.**

Firmware   Software built into the computer. *See* **read-only memory.**

Floppy disk drive   A disk drive that uses floppy disks. Floppy disks, which are magnetically coated disks made of flexible plastic (hence "floppy"), are removable and provide an inexpensive approach to program and data storage when the computer is switched off.

FMS   *See* **file management software.**

Forced page break   A page break deliberately inserted at a particular location in a document; overrides a word processing program's automatic assignment of page break locations.

Format   1. To prepare a blank disk for use by imposing on it a pattern of magnetic tracks and sectors. The formatting is done by a special utility program that is usually provided with a computer's disk operating system. 2. To prepare a document for printing by giving commands pertaining to the arrangement of text on the printed page. *See* **disk operating system, document, utility program.**

Free-format information storage and retrieval system   A data base management program that permits you to store massive amounts of text with no restrictions on the format of data records. *See* **data record.**

Full-duplex modem   A modem that can both send and receive information via telephone lines at the same time. *See* **half-duplex modem.**

Full-text search   A search that tries to match a search question by considering the full text of a field or several fields in a data record. *See* **search question, data record.**

Glossary   A file that contains boilerplate text.

Gutter Extra white space inserted on the left side of odd-numbered pages and the right side of even-numbered pages to facilitate binding.

Half-duplex modem A modem that can send information via telephone lines or receive it, but not both at once. *See* **full-duplex modem.**

Hard disk An auxiliary storage medium that uses fixed or rigid magnetic platters; these platters spin rapidly within a dust-free, sealed environment, permitting information storage and retrieval operations that are 10 to 20 times faster than floppy disk drives. *See* **floppy disk drive.**

Header Text placed at the top of a page to identify its contents.

Higher-order character set The extended character set of the IBM Personal Computer; contains foreign language, scientific, technical, and graphics characters.

Icon A symbol that contains a graphic representation of that to which it refers.

Idea processing program A program that permits you to create and restructure an outline.

Identifier A key word that pinpoints the contents of a data record with specific terms.

Insertion point *See* **cursor.**

Integrated circuit A tiny chip of silicon containing a complex electronic circuit that integrates thousands of formerly discrete electronic components.

Interactive formatting A formatting process in which formatting commands, entered via menu or keyboard commands, are directly reflected in the appearance of the text on the video display. *See* **format, menu-driven, command-driven.**

Interactive processing A technique of using computers in which input, storage, processing, and output operations can be selected and controlled while a program is loaded and in the computer's memory; this technique vastly increases the computer's convenience.

Instructional management Managing the day-to-day administrative tasks of teaching, such as calculating grades.

Justification A form of paragraph formatting in which text is aligned along the right margin.

Key word A word that identifies the content of the data record. *See* **data record.**

Kilobyte (K) Approximately 1,000 bytes ($2^{10} = 1,024$ bytes)

Load To read a program from a magnetic disk into the computer's main memory.

Local area network Direct linkage (for instance, with coaxial cables) of a few to several dozen personal computers for the sharing of data and peripheral resources.

Logical operator A connector (AND, OR, or NOT) which, when used in a search question, determines the relationship between the search question's elements (searching for "food AND drink," for example, returns only those records that meet both criteria, but searching for "food OR drink" returns all the records that meet either criterion).

Macro A stored series of commands which, when activated by pressing a single key, performs a complex series of operations.

Main memory The computer's random access memory, in which programs and data are stored for processing.

Mainframe A large and powerful computer designed to meet the information needs of an entire organization, such as a government bureau or corporation.

Megabyte (MB) Approximately one million bytes.

Menu A list of options displayed on the screen from which the user can choose.

Menu-driven A program that permits you to control its operation by selecting items from a menu, or list of options. *See* **command-driven.**

Microcomputer A small computer designed for use by an individual. *See* **personal computer.**

Microjustification A printing technique in which small spaces are automatically inserted within words to even out unsightly gaps sometimes produced by right margin justification. *See* **proportional spacing.**

Microprocessor An integrated circuit containing the computer components that perform processing operations. *See* **integrated circuit.**

Minicomputer An intermediate-sized computer powerful enough to meet all the computing needs of a small- to medium-sized organization. *See* **mainframe, microcomputer.**

Modem A device that translates the computer's digital signals into signals that are suited for transmission via telephone lines (from *modulator/demo*dulator).

Motherboard The computer's main circuit board.

Mouse A control device, designed to move about on the table top so that its movements are reflected by movements of a pointer on the screen; used for giving commands and editing text.

Online Used in various senses to mean "directly connected to a computer." A printer that's ready to print is said to be *online*. When your personal computer has achieved a connection with a data base service through telecommunications, it is *online*. Increasingly, the term connotes telecommunications and is sometimes used exclusively in that sense.

Online data base services Private, for-profit companies that offer remote computer access to bibliographic, numeric, and reference information.

Online vendor A company which provides online access to online bibliographic data bases, online nonbibliographic data bases, and online full-text data bases, which are supplied by data base producers.

Operators In a spreadsheet, symbols that represent arithmetic or relational functions.

Optical character recognition (OCR) A computer input technique that uses cameras to detect typewritten or printed text and automatically translates it into computer-readable form.

Page-oriented program A word processing program that attempts to present a document on the screen more or less the way it will appear when printed on paper.

Parallel interface A method of connecting computers and printers that makes use of parallel wires; often called **Centronics interface** after the company whose printers established the standard. Parallel interfaces are usually easier to connect than **serial interfaces** *(see).*

Personal computer A microcomputer designed for ease of use by people who lack training in computer science. *See* **microcomputer.**

Pixel A *pic*ture *el*ement, or a small point of light on a computer display screen. The more distinct points of light on the screen, the greater the screen's capability of resolving detailed images.

Point-source-point electronic mail Transmission of electronic mail using the intermediary role of an electronic mail service, which stores the mail until the receiver logs onto the service's system.

Point-to-point electronic mail Transmission of electronic mail directly from one computer to another using telecommunication links.

Print merging A printing technique in which information from a data base (such as a mailing list) is automatically inserted into multiple copies of a document (such as a form letter).

Printer buffer A hardware accessory which, when connected between a computer and a printer, permits the user to continue working with the computer while a lengthy document is being printed.

Printer driver A special data file that tells a program how to operate a particular printer.

Proportional spacing A printing technique in which each character is assigned a width proportional to its size; "i" is given less horizontal space, for example, than "g." Produces the appearance of set type.

Query *See* **search.**

Queued printing *See* **background printing.**

Random access A locating technique in which it is possible to go directly to the item you want (rather than going through a sequence of items to get to it).

Random access memory *See* **main memory.**

Range In a spreadsheet, a contiguous block of cells.

Range naming In a spreadsheet, the process by which a name is assigned to a **range** *(see)*.

Read To play back information stored on a magnetic disk. *See* **load.**

Read-only memory (ROM) A permanently encoded memory bank that contains programs needed by the computer for basic operations.

Relative cell reference A cell reference that is automatically adjusted if the formula in which it is embedded is replicated. *See* **cell reference, replication.**

Replication In a spreadsheet program, the process by which cells are copied so that relative cell references are automatically adjusted. *See* **relative cell reference.**

Report Printout of a data base's contents.

RS-232 The standard that governs the asynchronous communications port used by most personal computers.

Running head *See* **header.**

Search A utility provided with data base management and word processing programs that permits the user to search a file for specified information. Data base management search utilities usually permit searching with a **logical operator** *(see)*.

Search question A search term or set of search terms, often linked by logical operators, which forms the basis for a computer-based search of a data base. *See* **data base, logical operator.**

Select *See* **search.**

Sequential access A locating technique that requires you to go through a series of items to get to the one you want.

Serial interface A method of connecting computers and printers that forces the information to travel in a series, one bit after the next; also called RS-232 or RS-232C interface after the professional standard that regulates it. Serial interfaces are usually more difficult to connect than **parallel interfaces** *(see)*.

Shell A program designed to make another program easier to use. Frequently applied to software written to make disk operating systems such as CP/M or MS-DOS more approachable for beginners. *See* **disk operating system.**

Smart   Used here to describe telecommunication software that permits you to use your computer's processing capabilities. *See* **dumb.**

Sorting   A data base management utility that permits the user to order data records in ascending or descending numerical or alphabetical order.

Spreadsheet   A computer-based worksheet for numerical work.

Status information   Information displayed on the screen about the mode in which a program is operating.

String   A series of alphabetical characters.

Style sheet   Stored information about document formatting.

Success rate   For a test item, the percentage of the class who got a test question correct.

Supported printer   A printer for which a program has a **printer driver** *(see).*

Swapping   An automatic virtual memory operation (intrusive in systems equipped with floppy disk drives) in which material is paged into and out of the main memory as needed. *See* **floppy disk drive, main memory, virtual memory.**

Telecommunications   Links between computers that make use of the telephone system.

Terminal emulation program   A program that configures a personal computer so that it can emulate a terminal or remote work station connected to a mainframe computer.

Text editor   A word processing program that includes only the features necessary for writing and editing. *See* **batch formatting programs.**

Timesharing   A property of mainframe and minicomputer systems such that each of many users appears to have full and complete control over the computer without interruption from others' use.

Utility program   A program that helps you perform essential computer operations, such as formatting or copying disks.

View   A portion of a data base that contains only the records retrieved by a search question.

Virtual memory   A memory utilization technique that makes the main memory appear much larger than it actually is. Instead of limiting document size to the available space within the memory, programs with virtual memory features store part of the document in a temporary file on disk, paging it into (and out of) the memory as needed. The advantage of virtual memory techniques is that they make it possible to work with large documents even when memory space is restricted. The disadvantage is that the auxiliary memory system is much slower than the main memory, and the paging or swapping operations can result in noticeable and intrusive delays.

Volatile   A characteristic of semiconductor main memories in which the stored information is susceptible to loss if the power is interrupted.

What-if analysis   A form of sensitivity testing in which key variables are altered to see what their impact is on a spreadsheet's results.

Wild card   A search term that ends with a special symbol, such as an asterisk or question mark, that can stand for any alphanumeric character or characters.

Window   The screen display interpreted as a frame or window through which you can see a portion of a document. Some programs allow more than one window to be open on a document at a time.

Word processing   A three-part process comprising creating a document by writing and editing, formatting the document, and printing the document. *See* **document, format.**

Word wrapping   A feature of word processing software that "wraps" words that would go over the right margin down to the next line.

Worksheet   *See* **spreadsheet.**

Write   To record information on a magnetic disk.

WYSIWYG   Acronym for "what you see is what you get," an attribute of **page-oriented** and **advanced online formatting** word processing programs *(see).*

INDEX